BATTLING BIDA IN AMERICA

GREGORY HEARY

This book is essentially a sequel and follow-up to my auto-biography: "*Catholic Seminarian turned Christian Rapper turned Muslim Fundamentalist*" and a companion to what in my opinion is my most important book: "*Beware of Ahl-Bida*". Within these pages I have accurately documented my experience battling bida (innovations in the Islamic religion) in America, specifically my locality of Western New York near and around Buffalo, New York from the Gregorian years 2012 to 2017 and slightly beyond. It is hoped the reader will benefit with a clear perspective of the dangers involved and how the people of Bida operate and the ways to successfully defeat Bida in America if such is possible at all.

This is a stand-alone book which can be read without having read the prior books mentioned. As background information about myself, for those who haven't read my biography, I was born in 1992 and raised as a Catholic Christian. I desired and trained to become a Catholic Priest from 2006 to 2011 with personal goals of becoming the Pope whereby I planned to instigate bloody Crusades against the Muslims so the Christian Faith could conquer the world. In 2009, I became a Christian Rapper and published 4 evangelical rap albums. In 2011, I surprisingly embraced Islam and became a Muslim. One problem or blessing when I became Muslim was that I didn't know any other Muslims, I had merely studied the Quran and the prophet Muhammad's biography and then researched how to become a Muslim and pray the five daily prayers. For that reason, I didn't immediately know the importance of praying in the masjid for men, including the obligatory Friday Jumuah prayer. When I found out the value of praying in the masjid or mosque in mid-2012 I hastened to comply.

By this time the FBI had already begun to harass me and my non-Muslim parents. In fact, the way my parents found out I was Muslim was because the FBI told them due to concern that I was influenced by bad friends since I became a Muslim. At the time the FBI reported this concern to my parents, while phishing for information, I had zero human friends whether Muslim or non-Muslim. My parents were the only ones I communicated with. I didn't even have virtual friends online because since I was heavily criticized on my former Christian Rapper Facebook page for becoming a Muslim and quitting music then I ended up deleting my Facebook account on December 24th, 2011 and abruptly ending my friendships with bad non-Muslim influences. At that time, I wasn't' even watching Islamic lectures on the internet because I didn't know they existed in English or what or who to watch. So the whole notion the FBI had of me being influenced by bad friends was farcical. I was merely changing my life for the better and improving my identity still in the beginning stages of research regarding my new religion. Yet prior to even informing my parents about the change, I was on the FBI list of potential threats despite not being on that list while a Christian rapper advocating genocide of Muslims and eradication of Islam while promoting Christianity through music.

Anyways since I was naturally paranoid and additionally persecuted personally by the US government so soon after becoming a Muslim then I was concerned about reports of US soldiers burning tens of thousands of Qurans in Afghanistan in 2012 and the reports that the NYPD was performing undercover surveillance in mosques in NY state. Thus when I eventually found out Muslim men have to pray in mosques especially for the Friday prayer, which cannot be missed three weeks in a row without a shariah excuse, then I was cautious of rushing to an American local mosque because I had never been before and the indicators I was exposed to led me to be afraid of what would happen to me if I went. To comply with my religious duty I decided I would just go on Fridays to a mosque in Canada across the nearby border since they seemed more friendly to Muslims there, or at least less hostile so it seemed safer. Especially since the FBI was already building a case on me for just saying the shahada (Islamic testimony of faith) via facebook when publicly announcing my surprise conversion on December 11th, 2011.

I will not repeat the story of my experiences at mosques in Canada to excess as it was told already in my biography. Suffice it to say that in Canada, despite being an American revert, I made Muslim friends when going to free Aqeedah (Creed) classes and hanging around in the masjid in between prayers. I would take notes on what we were taught in my notebook which eventually was almost confiscated by the Canadian border police during one of many interrogations. However they merely scanned my notes on Islamic creed from the classes with their scanner and finding nothing objectionable let me go on my way, hopefully learning beneficial knowledge as I had. One question I asked the teacher during class was if the creed we as Muslims are supposed to follow is the majority creed amongst people today or if it were just the majority creed in the past. Thus I phrased my question as to whether we follow the creed of the majority of the living or the majority of the dead. To which the teacher in Canada publicly replied our correct creed is still the majority in most of the world today but true Islam is not the same as "American Islam". At the time I didn't understand how true I would find this statement to be. Another thing I learned from a friend called Ahmed, who was a student in the aqeedah classes, was a detailed reasoning on why suicide bombing is sinfully unislamic despite what extremists mistakenly claim. It was very useful and I even cited some of his reasons in my later book "Proper Jihad". One day while in the Canadian mosque waiting for the Aqeedah class on the deviant sect known as the Khawarij to start, a clean-shaven Muslim asked me to eat dinner at his house. I objected because the class was about to start in a few hours and I wanted to attend and as a foreigner didn't want to go anywhere I didn't have directions to, plus as a picky eater who brought my own food already I didn't want to eat unknown food in a strange place either. However this stranger insisted that it was obligatory to accept a Muslim's invitation to eat due to a hadith from the Prophet so I reluctantly complied insisting we return to the mosque for prayers and that I want to attend the aqeedah class, I also took another known friend along with me too since this was a stranger. We then all went shopping for food and returned to the masjid for the sunset prayer, however since the class was after the nighttime prayer and we hadn't cooked the food we then went to the host's residence to eat with me expecting to be back for the nighttime prayer and class. As it turned out the meal wasn't cooked by the time for nighttime prayer as promised, and we ended up praying together at their place and missing prayer at the mosque and the class and I was stuck at their house not knowing directions on how to leave to get to the mosque where my vehicle was parked. During the meal the host then proceeded to backbite the class teacher and other students in the class accusing them of being Wahabis and extremists warning me I shouldn't learn from them. Then he would mock the beard saying prophets had access to razors so therefore they must've shaved, like him. I was rather upset at missing class on a new topic of the Khawarij which

I was clueless about. So I asked the host why he tricked me out of the class and what are Wahhabis and how do you know they are Wahhabis and what is wrong with what they teach? Do they teach magic or do they deviantly teach blind-following of a madhhab(school of thought) or what? He just said they are extremists who make things strict and will have you end up blowing yourself up in Iraq or Afghanistan. I found these accusations very ignorant because the people at class themselves already taught me how blowing yourself up as extremists do is sinful and unislamic. And then the host proceeded to watch music videos on their house tv with barely clad women and suggesting I shave, so I knew this individual was clearly unislamic themselves. I quit the music industry because music is sinful according to Islam, started growing a beard because its obligatory for Muslim men and then go all the way to Canada to learn Islam due to fear of learning wrongly in America only to have a Algerian-Canadian guy, who's friend was wearing a American flag shirt throughout the meal, tell me that music was okay, beards are extreme and other unislamic things while accusing seemingly good teachers of being extremists who he said teach the exact opposite of what I myself had heard them teach. The next week I told my friends why I missed the class on the Khawarij and how traumatized I was. My friends told each other how astonishing it was that they as a community of Muslims are putting in so much effort to get people to come to the mosque to become Muslim and learn Islam yet have some Muslims taking people out of the mosque to stop them from practicing Islam. They laughed at the scenario but it is truly a situation worth crying about. So keep this in mind for the rest of the book that I missed an entire class devoted to the topic of the Khawarij in 2012 because of another Muslim who wanted me to shave and listen to music videos under the guise of a friendly dinner. I did end up seeing that same guy about a year later in the mosque and he had a beard then, so maybe it was guidance for him in that meal as during his rant I explained to him the error of shaving despite being a new Muslim myself. Yet despite learning about the deviancy of the Khawarij later, missing one class is something that should never be taken lightly because you never know what knowledge you are missing and in my case it was very crucial information that would've made life much easier. Knowledge is priceless and ignorance is a weighty debt that is only paid when you learn and act upon what you learn sincerely/correctly.

In November 2012 CE, 11 months after I officially became a Muslim, my mom told me I had to try out the local American Sunni masjid too to see how/if it was different. I protested and planned to just keep going to Canada to pray in the masjid on Fridays until I left America and could practice Islam safely. However my mother persuaded me, despite my claims it would endanger my life to go to a masjid in New York state because of the FBI and NYPD. Thus I went with her to the masjid, against my will, to pray the noon prayer and nobody was there. My mother asked where everyone was, since she had been to see the Canadian masjid and was used to seeing hundreds of people come for prayer and I just said I didn't know it's my first time. Just because I'm a Muslim doesn't mean I know where the Muslims are. However at that moment I realized that contrary to what I had read and heard on the news, there were no undercover government agents in the masjid because I was the only guy there and I knew I wasn't undercover. So I prayed and left, my mom met some Muslim women on the way out and I thought it wasn't as bad as I had feared. The next week I came back and Muslim guys were there and I talked to some and my previous optimism was crushed. I was still very paranoid about undercover agents. So despite dressing Islamically in public around non-Muslims, when I went to the masjid I would dress in jeans and western attire. Believe it or not I was afraid to dress like a Muslim in the masjid when praying with other Muslims even though I felt perfectly fine dressing Islamically amongst non-Muslims and in public. It might seem paradoxical but I was afraid the people at the US masjid might think I was extreme if I dressed like a Muslim and they would report me and I'd get sent to Guantanamo Bay, tortured and killed if I dressed Islamically in the US masjid amongst Muslims. If I recall correctly the first Sunni Muslim guy I met at the ISNF masjid in Getzville, New York, America was the "President of the Islamic School" at that masjid. One of the first things he told me was "Your beard is too long, you should trim it." I was immediately shocked.

Abu Huraira reported:

The Messenger of Allah (ﷺ) said: "Trim closely the moustache, and grow beard, and thus act against the fire-worshippers."

Source: Sahih Muslim 260

It was narrated that 'Aishah said:

"The Messenger of Allah said: 'Ten things are connected to the Fitrah: trimming the mustache, letting the beard grow, using the tooth stick, rinsing out the nostrils with water, clipping the nails, washing the joints, plucking the armpit hairs, shaving the pubic hairs, washing the

private parts with water.'" (One of the narrators) Zakariyya said: "Mus'ab said: 'I have forgotten the tenth thing, but it may have been rinsing out the mouth.'"

Source: Sunan Ibn Majah 293 Grade: Sahih

Islamically men are commanded by God to let their beards grow and it is considered sinful mutilation to shave them, unless there is a special medical necessity to shave their beard or it's for military espionage reasons so as to infiltrate the enemy. It's not obligatory for men to have one, because not all men can grow one but whatever does grow should stay. Some scholars say if it's longer than a fist length then they are permitted to trim the amount that's longer but it's better to let it grow as men get a reward for each hair and the longer each beard hair the more the reward. However many who do trim their beard do so sinfully and incorrectly. The evidence of those who say you can trim is based on the practice of Abdullah ibn Umar who only when <u>in Mecca after Hajj or Umra</u> interpreted the ritualistic cutting of hair to apply to the beard too, while because it is sinful to shave a beard he would trim at most so that his beard would be a fist length or longer. The vast majority of scholars of all time see this beard trimming in Mecca after a pilgrimage ritual as a mistake of Abdullah ibn Umar that we expect is forgiven to him due to his many other virtues and good deeds. But today thousands of years later people just hear "You can trim your beard up to a fist length." Whereas they neither know the evidence nor do they follow the mistaken evidence correctly. If you are going to follow the opinion that says you can trim up to a fist length of beard then that opinion only allows you to do it in one city of the world; Mecca, Arabia. And you cannot trim anytime you want, but only after Hajj (which is once a year) or Umra rituals. So if you aren't in Mecca then you generally aren't allowed to trim, and even if you are in Mecca you still can't trim unless you have just completed Hajj or Umra. And then even if you are in Mecca and just completed Hajj or Umra then you can only trim so much so that your beard is longer than a fist length. So if you are outside of Mecca, you cannot trim, if you are not finishing Hajj or Umra you cannot trim and if you are going less than a fist length of growth you cannot trim. And even if you are fulfilling all those conditions of trimming then still it's seen as a mistake of a Sahabi that is not to be imitated. The prophet Muhammad said to grow it and nearly every male Sahabi grew it without any trimming. And everyone agrees it is more virtuous to grow it and that there is no virtue in trimming it at all. So even those who agree on trimming they agree that you are basically losing reward when trimming, especially if doing so outside of the conditions mentioned. The most senior Muslim Scholar alive today Shaykh Salih Fawzan even said that if you see someone who trims their beard then don't bother learning from them because they are not a student of knowledge or a scholar. And that is trimming according to the criteria of only in Mecca after a pilgrimage ritual is completed up to a fist length. So then what of those who trim when it's not after a pilgrimage, outside of Mecca and go shorter than a fist length? This is undoubtedly sinful unless they are a fool who doesn't know any better. But those who do this often say "Its allowed to trim beards." Yet this statement they utter has no wisdom behind it. Although rather than keep this error to themselves they feel insulted when someone correctly grows a beard as long as possible. And then they will say the beard is only Sunnah, not knowing the Sunnah level is actually Wajib/Fard of obligatory and not the Sunnah level of Mustahab as they mistakenly think when they use the term "Sunnah" as something that is recommended to do. The word Sunnah is used differently in different books and those who read know this but those who only hear from the uneducated or people of desires and innovations are those who mislabel Sunnah as merely recommended thereby confusing people.

Whereas if you never shave, the beard will naturally grow very slowly and the hairs fall out themselves when they grow extra long. Anyways my "beard" at that point in 2012, which had only been attempted for less than one year was much shorter than fist length and thus Islamically it would be sinful for me to trim my beard since it wasn't long enough to trim it even if one thought trimming were permissible. So one of the first pieces of "advice" I was given by American Muslim leadership was to commit a sin, immediately upon meeting me for the first time in the masjid. In fact my beard was so short in November 2012 CE, when the American Muslim told me it was "too long" that 6 months later in April 2013 CE in Canada some of my Muslim companions were teasing me about it. They shouldn't have done that but I will mention what they said to show the difference between Canadian Muslims and American ones. In November 2012 CE the American Muslim "President of the Islamic School of ISNF"(The Islamic Society of the Niagara Frontier) told me "Your beard is too long, you should trim it.", I didn't and let it grow longer. In April 2013 CE, another Christian turned Muslim jokingly told me "*You remind me of the companion of Muhammad who only had 1 hair for his beard.*" Before I could reply another friend said, "*What do you mean 1 hair? He has like 7.*"

I laughed because they had no clue what I had been told in America 6 months earlier about my beard being "too long" and here they were debating on whether I had 1 hair or 7 hairs. My guess was I had maybe 15 to 25 hairs in total but by the American Muslim standard that was "too long", yet according to the normal Muslim standard it was almost laughable. I say almost because it is disbelief to joke or mock Islamic practices but they weren't mocking the beard itself though their joking was close to being sinful; however contextually it was just a loving remark on how it was unusual to see such a small beard. Anyways by all accounts I learned very quickly that the rumors I had heard online and in Canada about "American Islam" not really being Islam was confirmed. On my 2nd visit to the Sunni ISNF masjid in NY state I was also told to do other sinful things that were unislamic that deeply distressed me regarding celebrating Halloween and dressing up in costumes so that other non-Muslim coworkers feel comfortable. Therefore I decided to not go the American Sunni masjids because I was afraid the US Muslims would think I was extreme since they seemed extremely unislamic and seemed to think I was already extreme even when I was a brand new Muslim just practicing a few basic parts of Islam and even hiding my Islamic identity by purposely dressing unislamically only in the masjid so as not to get reported as Muslim by any potential spies. I was afraid of the government's spies learning I was a Muslim, so for the US Muslims to be making me feel extreme I figured if any government spies were around they'd be practically signing my death warrant by the way they talked to me about how I dressed even though I was in mostly unislamic fashion except for a kufi, beard and pants above my ankles(as Muhammad pbuh told Muslim men to wear their pants, since dragging the pants below the ankles is sinful arrogance that prevents male humility and modesty). Therefore I continued going to Canada to pray on Fridays and never wanted to go back to a USA masjid again, lest the government spies find out I was Muslim or even worse think I was an extremist; which I hadn't even considered as a possibility until I met the American Muslims at the local Sunni masjid. There were also other concerns I had in that I thought if I dressed Islamically in American masjids since I was a new white Muslim appearing months after reports about government spies in masjids, then the other Muslims might suspect me as a likely undercover non-Muslim FBI agent. So I didn't want to dress Islamically around USA Muslims lest they think I wasn't a Muslim but was faking it and given the initial experience I had getting told my "1 hair beard" was "too long/much" I genuinely feared that if I dressed Islamically then the Muslims in America would probably report me as a terrorist. In Canada I felt I could be Islamic, but in America I was most afraid of being Islamic around other Muslims in the masjid. I had discovered some American Muslims were a different kind of unreligious extremist that I had never expected to encounter. It's really sad because after all I had been through to become a Muslim and end up in a masjid in America, just a short 11 months after becoming a Muslim, the Muslims in America made me more afraid to practice Islam among them than I was to practice Islam among non-Muslims when I didn't know any Muslims. Meeting American Sunni Muslims was disheartening. Prior to that I thought all Muslims in the world practiced Islam the same since it was so clear on what was right, wrong, recommended and disliked and everything had so much proof to back up every individual practice down to the tiniest of details. It was sad. Many Muslims in America had no clue how beautiful and full the religion of Islam is. They didn't value or know their faith. I had vastly overestimated the religiosity of the USA Muslims and became disillusioned with the extreme ignorance I saw. As someone who was Muslim less than a year it was depressing to discover I knew more about Islam than many American Muslims I met, they were even more scared to practice Islam than I was despite being from Muslim families/countries. I was afraid of their unislamic ignorance, after having started to become Islamic and good they were telling me to be unislamic and sinful like I was before Islam. They would tell me to do the opposite of what Islam teaches and I didn't understand why they would advise that because the whole point of me becoming Muslim was to practice Islam. Thus if I followed their advice and didn't practice what Islam taught I figured there was no point in becoming a Muslim if I acted the same as I was before I embraced Islam. To me religion is something you commit to wholeheartedly, if you believe in a religion you should practice what it teaches. I believed accepting the true religion would mean changing my lifestyle accordingly but they insisted I could just keep doing the same sinful stuff as before I became Muslim just like they did and that I only had to make a few tiny tweaks regarding what I believe, praying and other obvious necessities and didn't have to be "so strict about things". I didn't think I was being too strict, I just believed if Islam teaches you should do X and that doing Y is a sin then you should do X and avoid Y but the

American Muslims said that was "strict", I thought it was called practicing Islam. Yet the worst part was they told me that was what Islam taught. So it was almost like I had come out of prison after having been amongst evil and evildoers for 20 years, only to learn the "good non-criminals" preached crime was what God taught us to do in his book, via his prophets and that by trying to be Islamic/good it was unislamic/bad/extreme. If I met American Muslims before becoming a Muslim I might have never become a Muslim because most of them compromise/dilute Islam thinking it's extreme or too strict for American tastes. While their ignorance makes them believe themselves. So I had found Islam while in America but I didn't find knowledgeable confident practicing Muslims despite meeting people in the masjid claiming to teach Islam. I felt like a minority before going to the American masjids to meet Muslims and felt like a bigger minority afterwards. I feared telling them how wrong and unislamic they were because I didn't want them to accuse me of being extreme.

Eventually I found proper American masjids where they practiced and taught Islam correctly.

In January 2013 CE at the Amherst public library I met with some family members for the first time since becoming Muslim. After the meeting it was time to pray so I was just going to pray in front of the library. Although my parents were afraid my family would videotape me on their phones, laugh at me and then post the video on the internet or something. I didn't think that would happen and didn't care if it did, it was time to pray I had to pray. I was dressed Islamically so even though the ISNF masjid in Getzville was minutes away I was afraid to go there dressed Islamically because of what the Muslims might think or what the spies might think or report if they saw me dressed Islamically when the other US Muslim guys dressed like non-Muslims. If they were dressing like Muslims in the masjid I would've felt fine but I didn't want to be the only Muslim in the masjid dressed Islamically like a Muslim. Anyways my parents begged me not to pray in front of the library lest I get made fun of and they get embarrassed. So I was stuck in a dilemma in that I had to pray but my parents wanted me to pray in another location than the one I had chosen. Since their request wasn't a violation of Islamic commandments or a sin then I figured I could pray in another location so my parents would feel better about me praying in public. In the parking lot there was a nursing home nearby but I noticed you couldn't park there unless you had business being there. I noticed the only other nearby place was the police station. There were some trees and a hill about 60 yards away from it so I figured I'd just pray there and that would a safe spot where I wouldn't get beat up by anyone who saw me pray. While praying there something very unexpected happened. Many police cars started filling the parking lot and I noticed I was being surrounded by lots of police carrying guns wearing bullet proof vests. The police came closer and closer. Near the end of my prayer an officer said "*Excuse me? Excuse me! What are you doing here sire? Can you hear me? What are you doing here?"* I wondered what I should do, should I finish my prayer and ignore them or stop praying and reply? I was very close to finishing, just a few seconds away. But then I considered that there was a real possibility they might shoot me dead on the spot if I try to finish my prayer. So I said something like "Hi. I'm praying." Then they told me that I was on private property and I wasn't allowed to pray in front of the police station without permission. So I asked for permission and they did not give me permission. I told them I thought I was on public property and that given the fear my parents had just expressed about me praying in public I thought it would be best to pray in front of a police station without anybody potentially harassing me. They asked more questions about how, why and when I became a Muslim and why I was praying there at that time. I replied I was praying there because I had met with family nearby in the same parking lot complex and it was time to pray so I was praying as Islam says to pray on time and my parents didn't want me to pray by the library and I thought this was the best spot to pray in. They took my ID, scanned my license plate, searched my car and I concluded they were terrified of me, and being dressed Islamically they probably thought I was some terrorist praying before trying to blow up the station or something. At that moment I realized it might not have been the best idea to pray in front of an American police station unannounced. Initially I thought it was a great backup to my plan of praying in front of the Library, I never thought the police would raise the alarm and surround me. Anyways regarding my police station incident, they let me go without further hindrance and I redid my prayer at home. Then it hit me. If the government didn't know I was Muslim before, they probably know now after I prayed in front of a police station and gave them all my ID and verbally told them and saw them put me in the system as a Muslim and took pictures of my car with islamic bumperstickers on it. I could no longer pretend to myself that the government didn't know I was Muslim because I unintentionally announced it by doing what I did, at my parents request. Yet I still lived despite me knowing the government knew I was a practicing Muslim, and probably thought I was a "little different" than every other Muslim they knew of. In hindsight I think the correct thing to do was probably finish the prayer and risk the bullets, but I was a fool then and I've regretted not finishing my prayer due to police. However that event certainly made me much more comfortable praying in public and now I bring a prayer mat with me whenever there is a chance of praying in public. This prayer mat is not necessary but it's just a courtesy so that if police or others are curious to know what I'm doing bowing and prostrating on the ground they might better be able to tell I'm praying if they see a prayer mat than if there wasn't one, and if they figure it out then maybe I will finish the prayer more easily without interruptions. After my realization and acceptance that the US government knew I was Muslim for real, I gradually started going to the local ISNF masjid and being Islamic there. First it would be just for 1 prayer a day, months later that became 2 or 3 a day, months later 4 a day and eventually I got to the point where I would go 5 times a day. Sadly though I think many other Muslim guys who don't come as frequently to the masjid are as foolish and/or afraid as I was. That's the only reason I can think of them having. Although I don't know if it's just me or just America, but in America it's easy to get caught in a satanic trap of thinking other Muslims are undercover while they think you are undercover and then neither of you ever talk to each other. I used to have such fears more than anyone else but all such fear is foolish and even sinful for Muslims to have regarding masjids or other Muslims. In conclusion surviving persecution and confrontation was what made me finally become comfortable being a Muslim and known as a Muslim. Had I never experienced the confrontations and persecution I had feared then I never would have been able to Islamically develop. So the persecution of Muslims helped me practice Islam. I really really didn't want it, but I'm really

really really happy that I got it a lot. Today I see past persecution as a true blessing. The enemies of Islam are only scary when you don't confront them and avoid confrontation or potential persecution. Yet as much as one might try to avoid confrontation or persecution, and I really tried hard to do just that, it makes no difference because what God wills to happen will happen. All you can do is prepare to be pleased with God's decree and unafraid of anything and everything except for God and upsetting God. As long as a Muslim is doing what is right Islamically they have nothing to fear even if Islam were to become illegal. It was none other but Satan who made me afraid of persecution. My concerns over surveillance and undercover agents were unfounded and it was simply the government trying to frighten Muslims away from the masjid so less people pray in it. They fear the power of Muslim prayers in the masjid. The ultimate goal of unislamic governments is to prevent Muslims from going to pray 5 times a day in the masjid and claiming to put undercover agents in them helps them stop Muslims from praying there and distract/disunite ignorant Muslims. So they say it and sometimes do it just to intimidate Muslims and decrease masjid attendance. Regardless every masjid already comes with special agents anyways surveilling the Muslims recording all they do, they are called angels. All people have always been under surveillance with special agents observing their speech and deeds reporting it to one who can severely punish them if they say or do something islamically wrong. Thus one must never fear going to pray in the masjid, it is Satan that instills such fears. The pagans in Mecca tried to scare the early Muslims away from the masjid too, but the success was in being patient with the abuse, surveillance and harassment on the road to paradise. Masjids are the houses of Allah for his slaves to get the best prayer reception in and protection from Satan and enjoy the company of angels and believers alike. Even if some evil kafir goons were present to spy therein, which from my experience they aren't, that is their business and Muslims are going to say and do the same stuff regardless of who is watching or listening because our thoughts, speech and deeds are determined only by our concern for the Creator who is watching and listening. Even during the life of Muhammad pbuh there were many undercover non-Muslims in the masjid in Medinah to spy on the Muslims, yet they all came to pray; despite knowing 100% there were spies there because the Quran told them there were. When one truly knows Allah is watching them they don't care about what anything else may think or do to them in anticipation or due to a reaction. Rather than fear the enemies of Islam the Muslims should be more afraid and embarrassed of what Allah thinks and will do to them for not praying in the masjids rather than what disbelievers will think and do if they prayed on time in masjids, because Allah does know and is much more important.

    A member of my immediate family knew a Shia. As a result, after learning I was Muslim many family members suggested I go to the Shia masjid to see how it is. I did not want to go because I wasn't a

Shia, wasn't going to go there regularly and definitely didn't want to go there to get misguided. By this time, 2013, I had heard the differences between Sunni and Shiite were more than just political, but I didn't know many details. Having non-Muslim family members they didn't quite understand how at best Shia could be considered a different denomination, they just thought Muslim is Muslim and everyone who claims to be one is the same. It would appear to be bigotry if I continually refused to go to visit the Shia masjid called the Jaffarya Center. One day I decided to go in order to see for myself firsthand what they are really all about. When I walked in, I saw half the building was a basketball court and the other half was a prayer area. Then I prayed some voluntary prayers, known as Sunnah prayers because the prophet prayed them even though they aren't required, before the noon prayer while waiting for prayer to start any minute. Finally a person called to prayer, but it sounded very different than what the call to prayer is supposed to be and I think they mentioned the name of Ali, which shouldn't be mentioned in that manner or at that time. Anyways I line up with the rest and we are just about to pray, when I look down to where I'm going to prostrate and notice something very strange. Everyone in the entire row has a stone in the place where the Muslim is supposed to put their forehead. I was the only one who didn't have a stone in front of him. I was worried that someone would give me a stone, thinking I had forgotten one, because I wouldn't know what to do with it since Muslims don't use stones to pray. It was appalling and scary. When prostrating I had to peek to see if they were doing what I thought they were doing. Scandalously I saw them putting their foreheads on the stone when prostrating and it freaked me out. After the prayer I remained sitting, counting the Dhikr that's done after prayer on my fingers. Zikr or Dhikr or Tasbeeh is quietly saying things like "Allahu Akbar", loosely translated as God is greater, and other phrases that glorify God or ask for forgiveness. Dhikr can be done at any time, but there are certain times one should say certain zikr for extra reward, such as after the prayer. So I'm keeping count on my fingers and I notice everyone else is using beads. When I was a brand new Muslim I researched whether Muslims use prayer beads or not, because I didn't know. Initially I'd even wear the tasbeeh beads around my neck as a necklace, however I discovered that Muhammad never used prayer beads. Instead Muhammad counted on his fingers when doing Dhikr and commanded others to do the same because the fingers will bear witness as to our deeds, whereas beads won't. Since prayer beads were easily available Muhammad could've used them if he wanted to, but he intentionally didn't. This means prayer beads are a bida, or an innovation in the religion. When it comes to religion only a prophet with direct guidance from God can introduce something when it comes to worship. Also before it was decided how to publicly call Muslims to prayer, some suggested using a horn like the Jews use, or a bell like the Christians, but the prophet explicitly forbid calling people to pray the way they do because Muslims are different with a different religion and we don't imitate those of other faiths. Thus since nearly all the faiths other than Islam use prayer beads this precedent applies to forbid the beads as well. All innovated matters concerning religion that are not taught by prophets are misguidance. Therefore all religious innovations are dangerous and detestable. The prophets were taught the religion by God, to teach the people so that people can please the Creator and live how Allah wants us to. The beads were never used by prophets, so anyone today who prays with beads is actually saying that they know better than the prophets and are better worshippers than they were, even though the prophets were taught by God how to worship. This is why the classical Muslim Scholar Imam Malik said what in Arabic means: "*Whoever introduces something new to this religion, which those who came before him did not observe, must contend that the Messenger of Allah has betrayed the faith, since Allah has said:* **(Today I have** *completed for you your religion)* (5:3). *Whatever was not part of religion on that day, is no part of it today."* Another Muslim scholar and prominent companion of prophet Muhammad, Abdullah Ibn Masood warned: ""*You will find people calling you to the Book of Allah*(the Quran), *though they themselves have rejected it completely. You must seek knowledge, beware of the innovator, the intransigent and the entrenched. Always go back to the very beginning."* Who today can say God personally taught them to use prayer beads? Who today can say X prophet used prayer beads? How much money and economic resources are wasted on prayer beads? Some Muslims may say that the prophet didn't use beads but there are narrations about his companions who used pebbles, date pits, or knots in a rope to help keep count. First of all those aren't beads and beads are distinctly something which non-Muslims use which again the prophet didn't use and forbid us to imitate non-Muslims, especially in religious matters. Secondly some of the narrations used referring to an extreme minority of companions counting on other things were classified as fabricated according to the hadith scholar Sheikh Nasir ud-Deen al-Albani. Thirdly there are narrations of the companions of Muhammad and the salaf such as Ibn Masood expressly and angrily forbidding people inside of a masjid from doing dhikr on pebbles anyways, saying it was a detestable bida and grave sin.

Amr ibn Salamah said:

"We used to sit in front of the door of Abdullah ibn Masud before the dawn prayer. Then when he came out we would walk with him to the masjid. So Abu Musa Ashari came to us and said: 'Did Abu Abdur Rahman (Ibn Masud) come out to you yet?

We said: No not yet.

So he sat with us until he came out. Then when he came out we all got up to him. Then Abu Musa said to him: 'O Abu Abdur Rahman, earlier I verily saw something in the masjid which I did not recognize, and I did not see - by the praise of Allah- anything but good.

He (Ibn Masud) said: And what is that?

So he (Abu Musa Ashari) said: If you will live, then you will see it for yourself. In the masjid I saw people sitting in a circle waiting for the prayer, and in every circle there is a man. And in their hands are pebbles. Then he (the man) says: 'Say Allahu Akbar hundred times', and they will say Allahu Akbar hundred times. Then he will say: 'Say La ilaha illa Allah hundred times', and they will say La ilaha illa Allah hundred times. And he says: 'Say Subhan-Allah hundred times' and they would say Subhan-Allah hundred times.'

He (Ibn Masood) said: And what did you say to them?

He (Abu Musa Ashari) said: I did not say anything to them, waiting for your opinion or waiting for your command.

He (Ibn Masud) said: Why did you not tell them to count their sins and assure them that none of their good deeds would be lost?

Then he left and we left with him until he reached a circle from one of these circles. So he stopped at them and said: What is this I see that you are doing?

They said: O Abu Abdur-Rahman, with these we count the takbir, tahlil and tasbih.

He (Ibn Masud) said: Then count your sins. How fast did you not become destroyed? Here the companions of your Prophet are great in numbers, here are his clothes which have not yet decayed and his bowl which has not yet broken. By the One in whose Hand my soul is in, either you are upon a religion which is better in guidance than the millah of Muhammad, or you are opening the door to misguidance.

They said: By Allah, O Abu Abdur-Rahman, we only wanted to do good.

He (Ibn Masud) said: 'And how many wants to do good but do not achieve it. Verily the Messenger of Allah narrated to us that a people will read the Quran but it will not reach beyond their throats. By Allah, I do not know but perhaps most of them will be from you.'

Then he turned away from them.

We saw most of those circles attack us on the day of An-Nahrawan along with the Khaawarij."

Source: Sunan Ad Darimi 210

However even IF the narrations about the salaf counting on other than their fingers were authentic and the narrations saying the salaf forbid counting on pebbles and such weren't, there is nothing at all to prove beads were used. Beads were widely available and could've been used but they weren't. The argument of bead users is to claim pebbles, date pits and ropes are the same as beads but they aren't because no disbelievers count dhikr on pebbles, date pits or rope knots yet most all disbelievers use beads. Plus Muhammad said to count on our fingers. So when the prophet says count on your fingers, that's what one does. Also the Quran instructs Muslims that when they differ amongst themselves to refer it to Allah(via the Quran) and the Messenger(via the Sunnah) and the Messenger said to count dhikr on our fingers. It doesn't say refer to companion so and so, it says refer to Allah and his Messenger first and foremost. Some Muslims mistakenly think that having good intentions makes something good, even if it's not a part of the Sunnah or opposing the Sunnah of

Muhammad. For example, Muslims know the Sunnah is to count dhikr on the fingers but will use the beads anyways saying their intentions are good. Imām Sa'īd bin Al-Musayyib once saw a guy with such a mentality praying after dawn more than the 2 units of the 1 voluntary Sunnah prayer which Muhammad would do before the obligatory prayer. The guy was praying a lot of extra prayers when Muhammad only used to do 1 voluntary prayer at that time of the day. So Imam Sa'id forbade the guy from praying. The guy said, "*Is Allāh going to punish me for praying?*" Sa'īd told him, "*No, but He will punish you for contradicting the Sunnah.*" Unfortunately Satan manipulates the good intentions of people and makes them think that it's ok to make things up in regards to worship. Satan loves this even more than when people sin, because a sin is easy to recognize as wrong and when a person sincerely repents they are forgiven. Although people rarely repent for practicing a religious innovation, because they don't ever consider that what they are doing is wrong. This amounts to people following their own desires and ideas instead of the divinely inspired instructions revealed to prophets. Essentially God told his creatures to worship a certain way to get rewarded, and then they say, *"well it's easier or more convenient to do it like this"*. Doing something the prophets didn't teach and opposing them for something else implies that you know better than God who taught the prophets. When it comes to worship if you cannot prove that the prophet did it or his companions, then it can't be accepted as a valid way to worship. Despite good intentions it's impossible to get closer to God doing something that God has not legislated or instructed you to do.

- Good intention + Good action = Good deed
- Bad intention + Bad action = Bad deed
- Bad intention + Good action = Bad deed
- Good intention + Bad action = Bad deed

While the prayer beads might at first seem innocent or pious they are actually very bad and should be eliminated. Even outside of the religious legal ruling, socially speaking the prayer beads are bad economically and they draw attention to the bead counter leading to arrogance or worse. Regarding prayer beads al-Ghazali commented: *"People count with self-satisfaction the number of times they have recited the name of God on their prayer beads, but they keep no beads for reckoning the number of idle words they speak."* Sadly many use prayer beads both non-Muslim and Muslim alike out of ignorance, cultural tradition and habit, but that still doesn't make it right. When going to masjids if I even see prayer beads laying around I secretly pick them up and throw them in the garbage bin so as to protect people from the evil innovation.

While counting dhikr on my fingers I heard the Shia say "What's he doing?" which made me realize the jig is up and now they know that I'm not one of them, if they hadn't already figured it out when I did the "Sunnah" prayers. So I had decided to leave immediately after finishing, before they confronted me. Suddenly everyone stood up and began to pray again. I was completely surprised since the next prayer wasn't for a few hours. Since there was a row of people behind me I couldn't just leave. I prayed again not knowing what was going on, how long they would pray for or what they were praying. After that I was wondering "How am I going to get out of here?" After the second prayer the person on the right got up shook the imam's hand, then turned around facing everyone else standing beside the imam. Then the next person in the row shook the imam's hand and the other guy's hand, then stood next to him forming a line facing the rest. This continued happening like a sports team tunnel with everyone going down the line shaking hands before getting in line themselves. I went through the line and faced the rest like everyone else. One thing I noticed was that all the people had black marks on their forehead, which I guessed was from prostrating on stones. I didn't see whether the people picked up their stones or left them on the ground. However I decided that I wasn't going to leave until I got some answers as to what the heck was going on. I asked a Shia guy what the reason was behind the stones. I learned that they use the stones so "they don't forget that they are on earth". On the face of it this reasoning is ludicrous. When in their life has a person not been on earth? How could anybody ever forget they are on earth if they always have been on earth and don't know what it's like not to be there? I asked him, "Did the prophet Muhammad peace be upon him ever use stones when he was praying?" The guy didn't respond, but I already knew the answer was no. That means it is an innovation to prostrate on stones and is not part of the religion of Islam. Later I learned they use stones from a specific place, called Karbala in Iraq, from the site of the grave of Husayn the son of Ali. Then I asked a Shia guy what they think about Ali, so I could hear what a Shia thinks with my own two ears. What I heard was inappropriate and incorrect, and is worse than what Christians say about Jesus, I'm not even going to mention it lest it spread their extremely deviant opinion. Then I asked what the second prayer was and why they didn't pray the noon prayer on time. They said because it was the weekend they combine the noon and afternoon prayers to make it more convenient. Now combining those two prayers is allowed if there is a legitimate reason, such as if you are traveling, or if there is very bad weather that would make it dangerous for people to go to the masjid repeatedly. But to combine the prayers just because it's the weekend is not a legitimate reason. A Muslim adapts their life to the religion, a Muslim doesn't adapt the religion to suit their life. Later I'd learn that Shia also do wudu/ablution incorrectly too. After that the Shia asked me to join them later that week for their holiday. It was a Shia holiday and I didn't even know it existed or that a holiday was coming up. I said "What holiday?" learning it was a holiday dedicated to a descendant of Ali. I declined their invitation because none of the companions of the prophet or the prophet celebrated it. This holiday is another innovation there is no basis for in Islam, just as is Maulid or the birthday celebrations of Muhammad which some

Sunnis and Sufis fall into not knowing the Fatimite Shia invented the bida of the Maulid celebration to compete with Christian Christmas. Then I left the Shia masjid never to return again and reprayed because it is not permissible to pray behind someone whose innovation is severe enough that it makes them a non-Muslim as the Shiite heresies do. Later I did further research on what Shias believe and how big and numerous the differences between Sunni and Shia are. Shiism is an entirely different religion than Islam despite them looking similar to Muslims, and talking similarly, they are extremely different in almost every way. Personally in my opinion of all religions in the world Shiism is probably the worst out of all. I only say probably because of Mormonism. Whereas Mormon Christians not only believe in a chain of prophets from Joseph Smith in colonial America up to the modern day but they believe each planet has a different god and that those who correctly worship the god of their planet get to become gods themselves after they die, where they then create their own planet and creatures who will worship them. Mormons will even admit they are polytheists and plan to become Gods after they die and that if you join them you can become a God too and get worshipped by your future creatures. So given those facts about Mormons it differs on my mood on whether I think Shiism or Mormonism is the worst religion in the world; so far. Sometimes it's Shiism and other days it's Mormonism. They are both so evil it's hard to tell which is worse. Mormon theology is worse but the Shiite's access to authentic prophetic data and their distortion and lies gives them less excuses to be so evil as they be.

In 2013 CE my mother and maternal grandparents also came with me on a visit to the local Sunni ISNF mosque. Since one of the women my mom met was the wife of the Imam(prayer leader) named Nizam she had been taking Arabic lessons with his wife named Sawda. I also took Arabic lessons with a Syrian refugee who had memorized the Quran, who if I recall was named Hafiz Noor, who also led Taraweeh prayers there during Ramadan. My grandfather Joseph even prayed next to me for a prayer behind Imam Nizam and got a English Quran translation to read, despite not being Muslim he said he enjoyed it a lot. I didn't think he would pray nor did I ask him to, he just did it on his own probably not wanting to be left out as odd. I didn't even teach him wudu ablution because I didn't think Joseph would attempt to pray; even though he didn't fulfill the conditions for a valid prayer it was a good sign I thought. I had hope for him as he was the most well-read non-Muslim in my family possessing hundreds, if not thousands, of non-fiction books and being pro-Palestine and anti-Israel. Previously my grandfather had also trained to be a Catholic Priest becoming disillusioned with the falsehood of Christianity and embraced atheistic philosophy. My grandfather Joseph frequently asked me questions about Islam and was interested in becoming Muslim except he feared getting circumcised as is required for Muslim men. I believe circumcision was a major issue for him because since he was in his nineties and uncircumcised he feared the surgery. When I asked a guest imam in Canada if my grandfather would need to be circumcised he said that he would eventually need it to be done if he became Muslim but that it is possible nowadays to have it done professionally painlessly. Still my grandfather didn't like that answer much. My mom's Arabic classes with Sawda soon ended though because her husband Nizam's visa did not get renewed so he would have to leave his position as Imam of the ISNF masjid in Getzville/Amherst.

In January 2014 CE, Mr. Qadri became Imam at the ISNF masjid in Getzville, NY. However I typically went to the Canadian masjid for Friday Jumuah from 2012-2014 because I was paranoid about the alleged spying by NYPD and I had a bad experience my first time at the local ISNF masjid. Another time in the pre-Qadri era I went to try going to pray the morning fajr prayer there and the masjid was locked for a long time so I had to pray the sunnah and fajr prayers outside of the masjid alone. So due to those experiences I decided to just keep going to the Canadian masjid for Friday Jumuah and I only really went to the American ISNF one whenever my non-Muslim mom had a class with Sawda. Later as my faith and knowledge grew I wanted to pray 5 times a day in a masjid and was tired of getting harassed when crossing the international border. Therefore in 2014 I started going to the local ISNF masjid increasingly more until I was going 35 times a week most of the time for each daily prayer. I did not know Imam Nizam well enough to form an opinion of him before he left. However the search for a new Imam was very short and only took a few months before the ISNF president Mr. Yasin announced at the end of 2013 they picked Mr. Qadri and would initially pay him $10,000 a year for a 1-year contract while providing free housing for him and his family at the neighboring house which ISNF owned. In comparison in Canada they were without an Imam for 7 years because the community had an uproar due to their Imam forbidding certain acts of sinful bida at a wedding. Since insincere and ignorant people didn't like hearing that they were guilty of bida at a celebration, they threatened their Imam. So the Canadian Imam said there was no need to threaten him, he will just resign; so he resigned and that mosque had no Imam for 7 years and had to invite lecturers for each Friday Jumuah while knowledgeable people would help out teaching free classes. When they finally got a new Imam in Canada, whose origin was Egyptian, they paid him $70,000 for a one-year contract. I later learned through personal conversation that the new ISNF Imam Mr. Qadri was almost the same exact age as me, which in 2014 I turned 22. Qadri also told me he had memorized the Quran at the age of 13, if I correctly recall, and then studied Islam for 6 years in a Darul-Uloom in South Africa after dropping out of middle school. Although Qadri did obtain his GED after coming back from South Africa. Yet even with the currency exchange difference, for the Canadian mosque to be paying their Imam $70k a year and the American mosque to be paying $10k a year seemed like a big discrepancy to me when they are supposed to do the same exact job. So despite claiming Qadri was selected for the role so soon out of all other candidates because of growing up close to the local Buffalo community(Qadri was born and raised in Toronto, Canada from Pakistani ethnic background) it was probably a case of ISNF leadership ordering the cheapest Hanafi Imam they could get to suite their Hanafi inclined Indo-Pak community as soon as possible.

Regarding Madhhabs(Schools of Thought), Hanafi or otherwise, the role of Muslim scholars is to derive the correct ruling on an issue by using the knowledge and massive amount of information which they've learned. Sometimes Muslim scholars make mistakes because there is absolutely no single scholar who knows everything or every proof, which is why one must follow the strongest most correct opinion with the strongest proofs regardless of whether it's from their favorite scholar or not. Limiting oneself to only one specific individual scholar or madhhab means you will be guaranteed to make the mistakes made by that single scholar or madhhab. Muslim Scholars are like doctors, they are qualified to give you sound advice but even the best sometimes make a mistake and misdiagnose or give an incorrect prescription, thus by referring to other scholars as well to see who has the strongest proof is like getting multiple opinions from doctors. Sometimes the doctors can all be right but some doctors are more right and offer a better regiment to follow that result in a more healthy spiritual relationship with God that is more rewarding. While sometimes some doctors can be wrong simply because of lack of data or miscommunication on behalf of the patient. The thing is that many factors come into making an Islamic legal ruling or fatwa, and different circumstances can cause different rulings. A doctor may give the same, different or even contradicting health advice to everyone in the world but that doesn't mean he/she isn't giving everyone the correct advice to each individual. This is because different people in different environments have different rules to follow to live a healthy lifestyle, even though they are all humans, external factors affect them differently. Unfortunately in the West some Muslims use this as an excuse and say that because they aren't in an Islamic country then they can do all kinds of sins, like buy a house with interest; which is something they can't do because they have lawful alternatives such as renting. Now if they already have a mortgage and didn't know it was forbidden, or they're a new Muslim and got the house beforehand then different legal rulings apply based on those individual situations. So Islam does have some flexibility that you should be aware of. The religion doesn't change with the times, nor does it adapt to the times, but Islam has built in principles within "Usool ul-Fiqh" which are used to apply Islam the correct way throughout all time in every circumstance for every individual. So while Islam strictly stays the same, some flexibility exists regarding some things. Allah makes Islam easy, but remember it's Allah who facilitates the ease, not the people themselves, scholars don't change the religion they just extract the correct Islamic ruling for each particular individual situation. Sometimes it even happens where two different people can ask the same exact question and receive 2 different answers/rulings because the individuals and their circumstances are different. So every legal ruling does not always apply to every person, some do some don't. A sick person won't have the same responsibilities as a healthy person because they don't have equal abilities, likewise for men and women, or new Muslims and old Muslims. The problem is some play games with this and look up fatwas from scholars on the internet or keep asking the same question to every scholar until they get the answer they want so they can exploit every loophole that can possibly exist, purposely following the minority opinions, easiest opinions, or the rare mistakes which a scholar made so they can live however they want to doing every sin they like and then they claim they are Muslims who submit as slaves to God. That is not Islam. That's like going to every doctor you can and they all tell you you're unhealthy foolishly endangering your life and must stop doing certain things or you will die, until one doctor is finally found who says it's ok to do what you're doing and then you go around telling everyone that all the stuff you're doing is perfectly fine, and even healthy because a doctor told you so. This is what happens with bead users who will find a scholar that tells them it's okay to use prayer beads and there are scholars who will say this even though it's wrong. Likewise there are some scholars who say suicide bombing in a military battlefield with the ruler's permission is permissible too, even though that's wrong, I'm not joking it's possible to find Muslim Scholars who say such things. So just because someone finds a scholar who gives them an answer doesn't mean it's the right answer. Even though the flexibility exists where extreme circumstances can allow for actions that wouldn't be allowed under ideal circumstances, sometimes the correct course of action is to practice Islam fully without utilizing the concessions or flexibility that Islam allows for. This requires sincerity and knowledge. Both are required to practice Islam correctly, having only one without the other leads to doubts, extremism, sin, hypocrisy and potentially disbelief. You also need to know how to get knowledge and be aware of what you don't know. Some people even need scholars' opinions on the opinions of other scholars to understand correctly. Whereas the lazy people tend to do Taqleed(blind following) and just stick to following one scholar or school of thought blindly without even bothering to learn the proofs/evidences or the rulings of other scholars on the matters. The only person one can legally make Taqleed of today is Prophet Muhammad, everyone else is prone to be mistaken regarding religious matters and are automatically disqualified from being blindly followed via Taqleed due to them not being prophets guaranteed to be religiously correct. However since people who make Taqleed are less knowledgeable, which in fact makes the Taqleedi ineligible from someone else making Taqleed of them according to the principles of Taqleed, then many become fanatical to the extent of partisanship.

Sound knowledge is needed to determine the correct course of action, generalizing is dangerous and emotionalism leads to sinful errors. Then we run into trouble between the difference of what something says and what something means, which is why we have to look at how did the prophet Muhammad and his companions interpret Islamic data, and to do that you need full comprehensive knowledge. Now if you don't have full comprehensive knowledge then you ask Muslim scholars to clarify the correct opinion and even if one is a scholar, the scholars are smart enough to know that they should ask other scholars as well to concur. Thus the same Islamic principles used to learn what is the correct thing to do, which some may think "goes too deep", is actually the very thing that eliminates and prevents extremism. The reason innocents get killed in the name of Islam is because some people don't follow these principles of knowledge but place their hopes in good intentions and sincerity. If you recall this is the same principle that let us know prayer beads are bad. Whereas some may think me saying prayer beads are not allowed is extreme, but in actuality the extremist methodology is the one used by the bead user. The only difference is one uses it to justify beads and the other uses it to justify suicide bombings of civilians, but they use the same exact principle. That is why these "little things" are fundamentally very important. The problem is that the Islamic doctrine is rarely presented to people completely and many just want a one-word answer when a one-word answer is not correct regardless of what it is. Before you can accept the correct answer you have to know how the correct answer can be found. Such as in math in order to do addition you not only need to know the numbers you are adding, but you need to know addition as well or else you may come up with the wrong answer even though you are using the correct information. 1+2 can equal many different things if someone doesn't correctly apply the fundamental principle of addition, even though they'd be correct when they discuss what 1 and 2 mean. Likewise 2+1 or 4-1 could be used to arrive at the same answer. But to have the correct Islamic answer one must use the correct authentic information according to the correct methodology with the correct principles and the correct intention. Basically it's Fundamental. Those who don't take a fundamentalist approach are guaranteed to be fundamentally wrong even if against all odds they happen to randomly get the correct answer somehow. The fundamentalist may not always be right since they are human, but they will be right fundamentally and that is why Muslim scholars can have different and even conflicting opinions yet both can be considered right methodologically. It does not literally mean all answers from Muslim scholars are right, it means they used the right methodology the right way with authentic information correctly and have the qualifications and apparently sincere pure intentions. Although sometimes the differences amongst Muslim scholars can all be right and one answer is just "more right or more correct" or as I'd say "they're all valid but some are healthier than others". Yet sometimes scholars are fundamentally right whilst being wrong and that is why it's dangerous to be a blind follower of just one scholar or madhhab, a blind follower is one who doesn't even look at the proofs or reasons scholars give for their answers. Likewise sometimes the majority opinion can be wrong too. Blind following is forbidden in Islam. Muslims don't follow scholars we follow the Quran and the prophet. A scholar's job is to organize the abundant amount of information available to present the correct proof to determine the best decision. Yet if one isn't a scholar themselves they may not understand scholastic principles or the level of authenticity of the proof, similar to how a patient visiting many doctors might not understand which doctor's opinion is best. So they'd ask a doctor to explain which doctor's opinion is best and why, the problem some have regarding religion is that they don't bother to learn why a certain opinion is best or most correct and thereby can fall into errors unknowingly. Prophets were sent to explain the fundamental and specific principles, give us authentic information and be living examples because there are some issues that arise where people simply don't naturally know what God wants them to do in a specific situation. The prophets told us what to follow and that is what we are to follow. Today scholars exist simply to pass along the best correct legal ruling in our present time based on the proof and evidence already relayed to us by God and his prophet(s), so that those who don't yet know the best correct thing to do and why it's best can benefit from their knowledge when the matters are unknown or confusing. Scholars aren't followed, one follows the proof the scholars present which comes from the Quran and Sunnah. One famous Muslim scholar Imam Abu Hanifa even said what means: "*it is prohibited for a Muslim to say what we say until he knows from where we took.*" Meaning a Muslim must know the "why" and the reasons why a scholar gave such a ruling and the proof from which that ruling was based on before they repeat such a ruling to someone else. This is a fundamental principle related to the addition analogy, in that you can't share the correct answer with someone unless you know the full equation that resulted in that answer. Otherwise you wouldn't know if it's correct. So in Islam there is the short answers of "*yes, no*" and "*it depends*" as well as the long answer, however all of these answers require proof and if an answer/ruling is ever given without a proof then one is to say "Godwilling that is correct" or "And God knows best" but it's safest to say that stuff anyways just in case. Another famous scholar Imam ash-Shafi'i used to say: "*if a hadith is authentic then that is my madhhab.*" A madhhab is a "school of thought", this statement of his reveals that his "school of thought" or methodology was what is called Ahl-hadith. Which means Imam Ash-Shafi'i would base his religion upon the Quran and Sunnah and the early generations of Muslims (the salaf). He didn't base his religion upon what scholars said but the authentic proof. To illustrate what this means once a man came to Imam Ash-Shafi'i and said: "*O Imam! The prophet said in a hadith such and such about such and such, so what do you say?"* In reply Imam Ash-Shafi'i got angry and said: *"What is this?! Does it look like I have come out of a Church!? You say to me that the Prophet has said such and such and then you ask me what my view is on the matter?! I have no view except that view of the Prophet!"* Thereby he revealed that the prophetic guidance is the religion of Islam. His response also reveals how he'd answer the issue of counting dhikr on prayer beads or the fingers. The rightly guided Muslim scholars didn't follow scholars, as some people do today, they followed the Quran first and foremost since that is the book of Allah. However the book without the teacher is not sufficient. The prophet Muhammad was the teacher of Allah's book. So if scholars couldn't find an answer directly in the Quran they followed the Prophet Muhammad's Sunnah. Hence Imâm Mâlik stated, *"I am but a man. I make mistakes sometimes and I am correct sometimes, so examine my opinions and accept anything that agrees with the Book(Quran) and Sunnah; and leave anything that does not agree with the Book(Quran) and Sunnah."*

Yet the prophet(teacher) is no longer alive today. So what do you do if you can't ask the teacher for the answer to your specific question directly? You ask your classmates who are taking the same class from the same teacher using the same book. Thus if scholars still didn't find a direct answer from the Quran and Sunnah they would get the answer from the statements of the companions of the prophet Muhammad. The statements of the companions regarding belief were given more importance than their statements on jurisprudence. If there were a rare instance when the companions differed on a certain matter of jurisprudence then the scholars would simply say what all the various opinions that existed were. Whatever scholars found in the Quran they used the Sunnah to judge it and anything found within the Sunnah they would judge according to the understanding of the salaf (the first 3 generations of Muslims after the prophet). This is the pure religion of Islam. Why is it just the first 3 generations of Muslims who are traditionally considered the "salaf" or pious predecessors? Because in authentic hadiths in both Sahih Bukhari and Sahih Muslim it is reported that Muhammad said what means: "*The best of my Ummah(nation) is my generation, then those who follow them, then those who follow them.*" So Muhammad himself gave his stamp of approval for the first 3 generations of practicing Muslims. The problem which occurred later is that after the early scholars died some people misunderstood their Ahl-hadith or Salafi methodology and instead just followed the scholars' opinions which the scholars got from the Quran, Sunnah, or Companions, but the later followers of the scholars followed those opinions without knowing the proofs and determined that the scholar's opinion in itself was a proof since they knew the scholar's wouldn't make an opinion if there wasn't proof for it. Yet there is a huge difference between agreeing with a scholar because of their proof vs. agreeing with a scholar because you know they wouldn't say something unless they had proof. The latter is blind following. As a result "Madhhabs" later developed that were schools of thought based upon the opinions of such scholars and/or their students and then madhhabs developed based on the students of these madhhabs so that today there are madhhabs within madhhabs. Tragically these same salafi scholars such as Imam Abu Hanifa, Imam Malik, Imam Hanbal and Imam Shafi'i who based their opinions on proofs and told people not to blindly follow scholars, or to accept a scholar's statement as a proof, ended up being blindly followed themselves. It'd almost be funny if it weren't so tragic. For example there is the Hanafi madhhab which purportedly teaches according to the methodology of Imam Abu Hanifa, then the Maliki madhhab purportedly teaching the methodology of Imam Malik, then the Shafi madhhab purportedly teaching the methodology of Imam Shafi then the Hanbali madhhab purportedly teaching the methodology of Imam Hanbal. All these schools of thought give different jurisprudential rulings. However all these Imams had the same exact Creed and methodology in reality and actually taught each other. For example

Imam Abu Hanifa's students taught Imam Malik and Imam Malik was a teacher of Imam Shafi and Imam Shafi was also a student of the same students of Imam Hanifa who taught Imam Malik. While Imam Shafi was a teacher of Imam Hanbal. What this proves is that none of these illustrious scholars believed in blindly following the opinions of their sheikhs. If Imam Hanbal believed in taqlid he'd have been a Shafi'i. If Imam Shafi believed in taqlid he'd have been a Malikki. If Imam Malik had believed in taqlid he'd have been a Hanafi. While if Imam Abu Hanifa had believed in taqlid he'd have been a Massoodi since one of his teachers' teacher was Abdullah ibn Masood. Of the 4 most popular madhhabs the Hanbali is technically the most refined and accurate because Imam Malik refined Imam Abu Hanifa's fiqh, while Imam Shafi refined both of their fiqh, while Imam Hanbal refined all their respective fiqhs but the chain of jurisprudence doesn't stop there. Scholars today still refine fiqh correcting any errors scholars in the past may have made due to lack of information or errors. The madhhabs themselves claim to refine themselves as well. Although fundamentally none of their madhhab methodologies teach taqlid, some Muslims who belong to these madhhabs mistakenly believe in taqlid and teach it. To be clear many people today who claim to belong to such madhhabs based on certain scholars' teachings aren't all blind followers of scholars, most of them research the proofs their scholars base their rulings on but then some don't bother checking the counter arguments of the other scholars who may have better proofs. While if they do check the other opinions, sadly some tend to just follow their own madhhab's opinion out of prejudice, which is incorrect to do. Yet this very practice of not checking the opinions of rival madhhabs is contrary to the alleged founders of the madhhabs. For example Imam Shafi as a student of Imam Malik agreed with some things he taught, then he moved to learn from Imam Malik's Hanafi teachers and changed his opinions on some things he previously agreed with from Imam Malik, then later in life he changed opinions again on some things based on proof he found that indicated the correct position on certain matters were different than what both his Maliki and Hanafi teachers had taught. So the Imams always followed what they believed was the strongest proof, using the Quran, Sunnah and statements/practices of the salaf as their sources for authentic information. For example once Imam Malik was told by someone how the amount of water that prophet Muhammad used for wudu was X amount and not the amount which Imam Malik was teaching people based on a certain hadith the person had heard. So Imam Malik, who lived in Medinah, told the man to wait while he got the cup which Muhammad used to use so they could see if the guy's hadith was true or not. That was the type of proof scholars would use, one guy comes and basically says "*My teacher told me Muhammad used X amount of water and you are wrong to say it was Y amount because my teacher said so!*" and Imam Malik basically replies "*Well you brought me an alleged statement of Muhammad about how much water he used and I brought you the actual cup he used. So look at the cup yourself and see if your teacher's statement is true when you fill the cup with water. It doesn't matter what your teacher told you, we have the cup to prove the truth. Which do you think is more likely to be accurate about the amount of water Muhammad used for wudu? His cup or your teacher? Can the cup make a mistake or be wrong? If the cup implies your scholarly teacher is wrong then which opinion will you believe to be correct?"* It's a funny story but sad at the same time because some people have such a devotion to blindly following their teachers that it is spiritually unhealthy and leads them to have incorrect beliefs which leads to incorrect practices based on following teachers/scholars instead of following the proofs provided by teachers/scholars. This doctrine is also commonly found in the kafir schools where they teach you "the teacher is always right" and "to pass the test you have to give the answer the teacher wants" but the test of life doesn't work that way. God gave us proof and prophets with proofs to know the right answers for the test of life and God and the prophets also told us how to find the answers to any issues that may arise after the prophets depart. Neither God nor the prophets taught to "Just follow what your scholars teach you." That's exactly how the Jews and Christians were led so far astray. Furthermore during Imam Hanbal's life the Islamic religion was almost corrupted by an oppressive Mu'tazila government who tried to get Muslim scholars to say the Quran was not the word of God but was manufactured/created. The Mu'tazilas used force and intimidation to coerce the scholars into saying what they were told. 700 Muslim scholars around Baghdad were tested by the Mu'tazila inquisitors and of the 700 only 4 resisted changing their Islamic beliefs, Imam Ahmed Hanbal was one of those 4. So in the area around Baghdad only about 0.05% of Muslim scholars resisted the inquisition and remained firm upon the correct belief. The important point about this well documented dark era in Islam is that those who blindly followed the Hanafi, Malikki, and Shafi madhhabs succumbed to the Mu'tazila error in that era entirely due to their blind following of the scholars. Imam Hanbal knew the danger of Islam itself vanishing if he too gave in to the anti-Islamic inquisition. After being whipped 1,000 times, he was told by the other Muslim scholars that it was "islamically permissible" for him to say words of disbelief and agree with the Mu'tazila in order to save his life. Imam Hanbal replied, "*If I remained silent and you remained silent, then who will teach the ignorant?*" The reason Imam Hanbal didn't remain silent and opposed the unislamic doctrine insisting the Quran was the uncreated verbatim word of God was because the proof said his position was right and that the "scholars" were wrong even though they were a majority of 99.95%. Hence not only does Imam Hanbal's stand for Islam prove how blind following is wrong but it also proves that the majority opinion can be wrong too, thus meaning democracy and voting is wrong. This raises another issue in that some mistakenly think that if the majority of people are doing something then it's part of Islam or if the majority of Muslims aren't doing something then it's not part of Islam. Regarding such a poisonous philosophy there was an incident that occurred amongst an ignorant person, a scholar and the scholar's student that reveals how foolish the "But all the other people" doctrine is. Abdullah bin Al-Hasan used to sit with the scholar Rabî'ah bin Abdul Ar-Rahman. One day they were revising and studying various practices from the Sunnah when a man in the gathering said, *"[But] this is not what is practiced [by the people]."* 'Abdullah said, *"So if the ignorant become so numerous that they become the rulers and judges, will they then be a proof over the Sunnah?"* Rabî'ah said, *"I bear witness that these are the words of the sons of the Prophets."* Meaning the prophets and their sons refuted this doctrine of "people power" because it is satanic/democratic. Yet despite Imam Hanbal's lesson in following the proofs instead of the majority or the scholars, today some Muslims incorrectly blindly follow Imam Ahmed Hanbal himself despite him teaching to only follow the proofs his entire life. Some will even say *"Oh Imam Hanbal said to do X, okay I'll do that because he said so. All I need to know is what Imam Hanbal said to do or what X madhhab says to do. I don't need to know why they say to do X, I trust that they are right because they are smart scholars and know more than me."* Hopefully you can see how foolish this type of methodology is. For such people who insist this is somehow Islamic or prophetic, Imam Hanbal himself said, *"Do not follow my opinion, neither follow the opinion of Malik or Ash-Shafi, nor Awzai, nor ath-Thari, but take from where they took (authentic hadith)."* So those who blindly follow Imam Hanbal or any scholar is explicitly disobeying these very same scholars. Despite claiming to be following them they are not because the scholars all said *"Do not follow me, follow the authentic information taught by the prophet Muhammad."* Furthermore Imam Ahmed said: *"I asked Imam ash-Shafi'i about taqleed and he said, 'It is like an animal carcass which is eaten out of desperation, it should only be done out of dire necessity.'"* Although at least the Sunni madhhabs today aren't as bad as they used to be. It used to be that in many masjids all 4 madhhabs would pray at different times because they disagreed with each other and each madhhab only wanted to follow what their scholars taught so they wouldn't pray with other Muslims. This even happened in Mecca of all places! During the era of peak Madhhabism instead of Muslims performing 5 prayers a day if a bird were to observe them they would see 20 prayers a day because the 4 main Sunni madhhabs were so stubborn upon blindly following their scholars that they refused to pray together. It wasn't until 1925 CE when the descendants of Ibn Saud and the students of the students of Muhammad ibn abdul Wahhab took over Mecca that they put a stop to this deviant practice of all 4 madhhabs praying separately in Mecca. At the time the Muslim world was outraged that the "Wahhabis" (as they were derogatorily called) told the Muslims they were all supposed to be praying together even if they had different madhhabs and demolished the various Makhtabas(places for prayer leader from each Madhhab to stand) making it so there was just one establishing prayer as it was supposed to be done. Today though nearly every Muslim in the world agrees the "Wahhabis" were right and that mere differences in maddhhab don't justify Sunnis praying separately. Yet some taqleedis, who tend not to even know the history of the deviant taqleed of madhhabism that led Muslims to pray apart as recently as 1924 CE, still resent the Muslims who correctly brought Muslims back to praying correctly and deride those Muslims with the label of "Wahhabi" trying to insinuate they make taqleed of a particular personality Muhammad ibn abdul-Wahhab rather than practicing Islam. Which is rather ironic because if you ask taqleedis they say "Wahhabis" are extremists for making taqleed of Muslims who say it's forbidden to make taqleed. The Taqleedis hypocritically contradict themselves by saying people sinfully blindly follow those who say it's sinful to blindly follow non-prophets. The Taqleedis say one should only blindly follow those who say it's not sinful to blindly follow, whereas true Muslims don't do taqleed of anyone but prophet Muhammad. Notice I said true Muslims, I did not say the majority. Needless to say taqleed is not what Islam teaches nor what Muhammad taught Muslims. And when did this concept of Taqlid creep into the Muslim nation? After Shia started saying their Imams and Scholars were infallible. <u>No Muslims did Taqlid before the Shia existed</u>. Neither will Jesus follow a Madhhab when he returns to earth either, Jesus will live life as a Salafi Muslim. To justify taqlid, hadith fabrications were invented such as the most famous one where they say "If you have no sheikh/Imam then Satan is your sheikh/Imam." This is the calling card of taqleedis but prophet Muhammad never said this, it's a purely unislamic fabricated statement of falsehood, invented to promote the falsehood of blindly following Imams. Taqlid is the core methodology of Shi'ism but to be explicitly clear not everybody who does Taqlid is a Shia. Due to this matter of Madhhabs and the blind following of Madhhabs some Muslim scholars like Sheikh

Muhammad Sultan Al-Ma'soomi Al-Khajnadee have said that following a Madhhab is a bida or forbidden innovation. Note that one can follow one of the Sunni Madhhabs if they don't have adequate knowledge, but if/when they learn that the correct opinion on something is different than that Madhhab's opinion then they must follow what is correct instead of that Madhhab's opinion on that matter. Unfortunately some Madhhab followers are blind followers who follow scholars without knowing their reasons or evidences used for saying things in matters of jurisprudence. The trouble is that some today forget that these prestigious scholars in the past taught to follow the proof and not the scholar themself and that the only human one should blindly follow is the most recent/final prophet. Fortunately, unlike in other religions, the Quran today is exactly the same as it was during the time of Muhammad, the prophetic Sunnah is preserved in the Hadith as well as is the information about the Sahabah and Salaf.

Imam Ash-Shabi (A companion of Ali, Sa'd, Abu Hurayrah and Abu Said al Khudri who died in 724 CE and was a teacher of Abu Hanifah) said:

"Had I pondered my problem in the beginning as I did towards the end of the matter, I would have only relayed what had been agreed upon by Ahl-Hadith."

Abu Hanifah said:

"Stick to the athaar (narrations) and the way of the Salaf and beware of newly invented matters, for all of it is innovation."

Source: as-Suyootee in Sawnul-Mantaq wal-Kalaam

Ar-Rabee ibn Sulaymaan said:

"One day Ash-Shaafi narrated a hadith, and a man said to him "Do you accept that O Abu Abdullah?" He said, "If I narrate a saheeh hadeeth from the Messenger of Allah and I do not accept it, then bear witness that I have lost my mind."

Source: Ibn Battah in Al Ibaanah

Imam Ahmad said:

"If you see anyone speaking ill of the Companions of the Messenger of Allah, doubt his Islam."

Source: Al-Laalikaa'ee in As-Sunnah, 2359

Imam Ahmad ibn Hanbal said:

"The basic principles of Sunnah in our view are: adherence to the way of the Companions of the Messenger of Allah, following their example and forsaking bidah, for every bidah is a going astray."

Source: Al-Laalkaa'I in Sharh Usool Ahl as-Sunnah

Imam Malik said:

"Truly I am only a mortal: I make mistakes (sometimes) and I am correct (sometimes). Therefore, look into my opinions: all that agrees with the Book and the Sunnah, accept it, and all that does not agree with the Book and the Sunnah, ignore it."

Source: Ibn Abdul Barr in Jaami Bayaan al Ilm

Imam Abu Hanifah said:

"When I say something contradicting the Book of Allah the Exalted or what is narrated from the Messenger, then ignore my saying."

Source: Al-Fulaani in Eeqaaz Al Himam 50

Imam Ash-Shaafi said:

"The Muslims are unanimously agreed that if a sunnah of the Messenger of Allah is made clear to someone, it is not permitted for him to leave it for the saying of anyone else."

Source: I'laam by Ibn Qayyim

Muhammad Sultan al Masoomi Khajnadee said:

"None of the Imams urged to anyone to follow their Madhahib, on the other hand all of the Imams advised, "Take from where we have taken."

In other words follow the Quran and Sunnah. Many of the sayings of later religious leaders, which were inaccurate, were attributed towards Imams and their sects. If they had happened to see or hear those statements which had been referred and attached to their names, they would have not only disowned the statements but also disapproved of them strongly.

All the religious scholars of olden times who were considered to be the luminaries of Islamic knowledge, always brought evidence from the Quran and Sunnah, and to take counsel from these two sources. It is a proved fact that Imam Abu Hanifa, Imam Malik, Imam Shafii, Imam Ahmad, Sufyan Thawri, Sufyan bin Uainah, Hasan Basri, Qadi Abu Yusuf, Muhammad bin Hasan Shaibani, Imam Awzaai, Abdullah bin Mubarak, Imam Bukhari, Imam Muslim, and other venerable religious scholars always warned the people against making innovations in religious matters. They always advised people to be careful and cautioned them against following anyone except the sinless Prophet, no one is sinless except him, however pious and God-fearing he may be. So anything which is in accordance with the Quran and Sunnah is acceptable and anything which is contrary to or inconsistent with the Quran and Sunnah will be rejected altogether. Imam Malik said: "The views and opinions of everybody may be accepted or rejected except he who is resting in this grave." While saying this, Imam

Malik pointed towards the grave of the Prophet. All the religious scholars and Imams warned and prevented the people from mindless and blind imitation. Allah at many places in the Quran has rebuked such blind followers. History is witness that mindless and blind following of religious leaders and ancestors leads the people to infidelity."...

"Later religious leaders and intellectuals wrote volumes over volumes and thousands of pages and the masses took those writers as Jurists, whereas their knowledge about Islam was shallow. These so-called scholars made it incumbent on people to follow one of the four Imams and prohibited them from following another at the same time. In other words they raised up the Imams to the level of the Prophets – to whom Scriptures are revealed – and made it obligatory to obey every word of the Imam. Would that these so-called scholars had understood the preaching of the Imams. Most of them only know the name of their Imam and nothing more than that. Even more strange is that a few of the later scholars contrived some issues and attributed these issues to one of the imams, and succeeding generations too took the

concocted issues as Imams' verdicts and started following them without any verification, whereas there is no relevancy between Imams' viewpoints and these innovated issues. So, Imams are free from such precepts."

Source: Hadiyyatus-Sultan ila Muslimi Biladil-Yaban

Waliullah Dahlawee said:

"For the first two centuries of the Hijra era people were not aware of any Madhhab, as fact of the matter, no Madhhab existed at all during that time. For that reason nobody knew any Madhhab and did not follow anyone except Allah's Messenger. Sahabah, Tabiun and the succeeding generation of the Tabiu followed their consensus and did not follow any individual. So anybody who ignores this consensus and opts all the sayings, verdicts and views of any one Imam and does not try to search and confirm it from the two basic sources, the Quran and Sunnah, is acting against the tenets of faith."

Source: Insaf fi Bayan Asbab al Ikhtilaf

Muhammad Sultan Masoomi Khajnadee said:

"It is our foremost duty to avoid stubbornly following one particular Imam and his Madhhab. Concerning various religious matters, if anyone follows strictly one particular Madhhab, sect or person, surely he will not act upon many Hadith, rather there is possibility of going against many of the Hadith of the Prophet. Going against Hadith is infidelity and faithlessness."...

"If we follow a specific Madhhab or a person, leaving aside a Hadith of the Prophet whose following is obligatory, who will be more misguided and unwise than us? Regarding following a Madhhab, the last thing which can be said is only illiterate and unschooled individuals may follow an Imam without fixation of anyone in particular. An individual who loves all Imams equally and benefits from all of theme in various religious matters and acts upon the view which is more near to the Quran and Sunnah, this act of his is appreciable and is in accordance with the way of the faithful. He who deviates from the right way of Tabiun and sticks to one specific Imam and is prejudiced in his favor, is similar to one who leaves aside all Companions of the Prophet and follows one only, as the Shia and Khawarij do. This is the way of

heretics and apostates. Quran, Hadith and Ijma denounces them."

Source: Hadiyyatus-Sultan ila Muslimi Biladil-Yaban

Ibn Taymiyyah said:

"If an individual follows only one from the four Imams – Imam Abu Hanifah, Imam Shafii, Imam Malik, and Imam Ahmad bin Hanbal – and in connection with certain issue he finds a more positive and stronger argument than that of his own Shaikh or Imam, and leaves the weaker argument and embraces the strong one, this act of his is estimable. All religious scholars thought that it made no difference to the faith of the follower; on the other hand, it is said that he is dearer to the Prophet and nearer to the truth than a person who follows only one Imam eagerly and blindly and pays less heed to the Sunnah of the Prophet. He who follows Imam Abu Hanifah and thinks his Imam is always correct in every religious matter and everyone should follow him, and all other Imams who differ with him are not reliable, is certainly ignorant; such thinking may lead him to

blasphemy and infidelity. We seek refuge with Allah from this evil."

Source: Fatawa Misriyah

Muhammad al-Ameen Shanqiti wrote in his Tafsir:

"As for the type of taqleed about which the later scholars differ with the companions and other from those generations whose excellence has been testified to, then it is the performing of taqleed of one particular scholar only, to the exclusion of other scholars. This type of taqleed is neither proven by the texts of the Book and the Sunnah, nor was it the view of any of the companions of Allah's Messenger, nor anyone else from the first three generations whose excellence has been testified to. Likewise, it opposes the saying of the four Imams since none of them held the view that it was binding to adhere to the saying of a single person to the exclusion of all the other scholars. Rather, the taqleed of one particular scholar is an innovation of the fourth century AH. Whoever claims contrary to this should specify to us one man from the first three generations who obligated [people to follow] the Madhhab of one specific man, and

he will not be able to bring that whatsoever because it did not happen at all."

Uthman Dan Fodio wrote in Hidayat ut Tullab:

"Neither Allah in His Book, nor the Prophet in his Sunnah made it obligatory that one particular madhhab should be followed, nor did we hear any of the early scholars enjoining a person to follow one way. If they had done that, they would have committed a sin by not allowing people to act in accordance with hadith which that particular way did not give weight to."

So the problem has nothing to do with lack of information or the authenticity of information, but is simply that some Muslims have fundamental issues regarding their methodology on how to find out or how to acquire and determine an Islamic legal ruling. It doesn't mean they aren't Muslims, it just means they aren't a fundamentalist because their methodology has some fundamental issues. Keep in mind that doesn't mean what they believe or do is automatically wrong, because as has been explained one can still get the correct answer even though they are fundamentally wrong. Many times such Muslims' beliefs and practices are correct and based on authentic correct information, so the thing that causes an occasional issue is usually just a difference in methodology. Such differences in methodology are what cause differences among Muslims, most are valid differences that are perfectly fine to have and many Muslims exist who do the same exact things I do for the same exact reasons even though we're using different methodologies. There is no hierarchy in Islam, so regardless of one's methodology every Sunni attends the same masjids for the most part. Don't misunderstand it thinking there are special masjids depending on one's methodology, there typically aren't; except for the Shia and some extremist Sufis and sects that are outside the fold of Islam but claim to be within the fold of Islam like Ahmadiyya. This causes a slight amount of chaos at masjids because not only do the multiple masjids of Sunnis pray in the same masjids but the various Sunni sects do as well and sometimes the masjid can be composed of many different "Muslims" who have very different theologies. I mean just imagine if all the different denominations of Christians prayed together in the same church with everybody claiming to be "Christian" but nobody saying which type of Christian they were. Sects believe in different theologies, creeds and doctrines while madhhabs believe in different methodologies and scholastic approaches to rulings of jurisprudence. Muslims can have different madhhabs and still believe in the same religion, but the different sects of Muslims can have theological differences which result in them believing in different religions yet they all say they believe in Islam and follow it correctly and go to the same masjids. Christians generally have separate churches for each sect/denomination, Muslims generally don't. Hence I say masjids can be slightly chaotic from a theological aspect if it is theologically diverse, which is dangerous for Muslims who don't know the prophetic theology and can be misled by those who belong to deviant sects without knowing it. However it's very important to remember the distinction between madhhabs and sects. You could be part of the same sect as someone who belongs to a different madhhab and/or you could be part of the same madhhab as someone while belonging to a different sect than them. Surface similarities may be all that exist or on the surface people could seem very different while being theologically the same, in theory. To put it in Catholic terms the Sunni Madhhabs would be like different religious orders, in that within Catholicism there are Jesuits, Franciscans, Benedictines, Dominicans and others. Now technically all people who belong to and follow those various Catholic orders are all considered Catholics even though they all pray slightly differently, however Jesus didn't belong to any of those orders and didn't teach any of those orders. Thus those various Catholic orders are not really based on the prophet Jesus or his teachings but on the teachings of specific Catholic individuals. Catholicism isn't based on Jesus' teachings either, but for the sake of argument/example we'll say the religion of Jesus predates those Catholic orders. So a follower or adherent of those various Catholic orders cannot really say they are fundamentally or fully following the religion of Jesus; even if Catholicism were theoretically taught by Jesus which it wasn't. So since all the modern madhhabs of today, arose long after the prophet Muhammad, those madhhabs while they may be within the fold of Islam are not the pure 100% fundamental methodology taught by Muhammad. There used to be many Sunni madhhabs, but over time most went extinct and today the number of famous mainstream Sunni madhhabs has been reduced to 4. Maybe there will be less in the future or more, but the Ahl-Hadith (Salafi) methodology has always existed and will until the end. Sadly those who tend to follow one of the 4 famous madhhabs tend to not know or believe there are other methodologies and they incorrectly ignorantly assume that Ahl-Hadith or Salafi is something new or innovated when it's actually the original prophetic methodology. The word Salaf is even used in the Quran and there are hadith where the Prophet used the word as well. Sometimes it is heartbreaking because of the arrogant passionate ignorance some Muslims have not knowing that the Salafi methodology is the prophetic methodology. Such aversion to the way of the salaf is theologically a type of aversion to the way of Muhammad and his companions and their students and those students' students. As a result of their confusion some of the non-salafi Muslims then treat the rightly guided Muslims like they are innovators or extremists or even non-Muslims because they mistakenly think they are wrong about a certain practice being recommended, permissible or forbidden. Case in point being the prayer beads, telling people their prayer beads are sinful to use can result in negative reactions even if you warn them with kind compassion. As an example there are many ways to "forbid the beads", I've learned some ways are better than others. Now you could give all the reasons why they are bad or you can take a different approach more suited to the individual and the situation. For instance, once I saw a stranger using the beads sitting next to me and there were only a few minutes until the prayer time. Being harsh and rude likely wouldn't work but I didn't want to just be quiet about it, I had to say something to "forbid the evil of the beads". But what? I just told him how I read the prophet Muhammad said to count dhikr with your fingers because they will testify for you on the day of Judgement. He said yes, and continued using the beads. However Islamically I did essentially forbid him and tell him to use his fingers and not the beads by telling him Muhammad said to use the fingers. Now he might mistakenly think the beads count as the fingers, but in the sight of God I did tell him and conveyed the message so maybe it will sink in some day. Then I started counting on my fingers so he could see me counting so perhaps he would subtly learn that I was telling him the beads were incorrect without explicitly saying that or maybe he will choose the fingers voluntarily. However though he may have still continued using the beads me saying what I said was better than being silent letting him continue the sin, plus he had no negative reaction to that. Although then I figured if in another situation like that I could also make an audible dua after that asking God to guide the Muslims away from the bida of prayer beads and to the Sunnah of counting dhikr on their fingers. That might have gotten a more unpleasant reaction but also may be more effective. Also I could even offer to buy the beads off him and explain I want to buy them to throw them away because using beads is bida which is so certainly bida that I'm willing to pay you to prevent you from doing such an invalid act of worship. I use this as an example for how to "kindly forbid", many unfortunately know why something is wrong but don't know how to "forbid evil" effectively. In fact with every bida, and God knows best, I think it's a good idea to audibly ask God in dua to "Guide the Muslims away from the bida of X" so that although you aren't confrontationally telling them about it being bida they may hear it is bida due to hearing your dua and reconsider, research, change and repent. In the end you have to ask God to guide them anyways since you cannot guide/correct them unless God decrees guidance for them. Yet some ignorant or arrogant people will react negatively to corrections/advice no matter how it's done. The Muslim book is the Quran, our teacher is prophet Muhammad, his students were the sahabah who were and taught the salaf. Later and modern Muslim scholars are students and tutors of Islam. Our goal is one, to pass the test of life successfully completing our journey on the road to paradise. Blind following is forbidden, however a convoy is the safest way to travel. Thus Muslims follow in the footsteps of the prophets which have also been followed by earlier generations.

Thawban narrated the Messenger of Allah said:

"I only fear for my Ummah from the misguiding A'immah." He said that the Messenger of Allah said: *"There will never cease to be a group from my Ummah manifest upon the truth, they will not be harmed by those who forsake them until Allah's Decree comes."*

Source: Jami` at-Tirmidhi 2229 Grade: Sahih

The Ummah is the Muslim nation, so the prophet taught there will be one group of Muslims who are more rightly guided than others and some A'immah (scholars) that lead people astray. It doesn't mean people who aren't of the Ahl-Hadith or Salafi methodology aren't Muslims, many of them are. In fact theologically the majority of Muslims of all time are Salafi and everyone pays lipservice to "following the way of the salaf", it's just that methodologically some Muslims incorrectly follow other ways. However there are different types of Muslims and the goal is to be the best of the best so that we get rewarded with the best in paradise as well as in this life. Ahlus Sunnah wa Jamah is another term for Salafi, although this has recently become a more generic term that encompasses and is used by most all Sunni sects even if they aren't really following Islam fully or correctly. Many misunderstand the word "Jamah" thinking it means the majority opinion of Sunni Muslims however it actually refers to the majority opinion of the rightly guided; meaning the first 3 generations of Muslims known as the Salaf and those who follow the way of the Salaf. In some places and times one person has been the Jamah even though they were the minority.

It is reported that Isḥāq bin Rāhuway said:

"If you ask the ignorant: 'Who are Al-Sawād Al-A'ẓam (Main Body of the Muslims)?' they will say, 'All the people (together).' But they do not know that The Jamā'ah (Main Body) is a scholar who follows the footsteps of the Prophet and his way. So whoever is with him and follows him is [one of] The Jamā'ah, but whoever contradicts him in it leaves The Jamā'ah."

Source: Abū Nu'aym, Ḥilyatu Al-Awliyā

Abdullah ibn Masood said:

"The Jamaah is whatever agrees with the truth even if you are alone."

Source: Reported in Taarekh Dimashq with an authentic chain of narration.

Abu Shamah said:

"The order to stick to the Jamaah means sticking to the truth and its followers; even if those who stick to the truth are few and those who oppose it are many, since the truth is that which the first Jamaah from the time of the Prophet and his Companions were upon. No attention is given to the great number of the people of futility coming after them."

Source: Al Baa'ith Alal-Bidah Wal Hawaadith

The scholar Hasan al-Basri who died in 728 CE said:

" If a man from amongst the Salaf were to be sent forth today, he would not recognize anything from Islam." He put his hand on his cheek and added, *"Except this prayer (<u>s</u>alâh)."* Then he said, *"But by Allâh, this does not apply to the person who lives in this unfamiliar time, never having seen the Righteous Predecessors, but who sees [instead] the innovator calling to his bid'ah, and the follower of worldly wealth calling to his materialism, but Allâh protects him from all this and makes his heart love and aspire to those Righteous Predecessors, asking about their way, searching and trying to follow in their footsteps, and adhering to their path. Such is a person who will be recompensed with an immense and great reward. So be you all like this, by Allâh's permission"*

The Scholar Al-Awza'i who died in 774 CE said:

"Hold fast to the narrations of the Salaf, even if people abandon you. Beware of the opinions of men, no matter how much they beautify it with their speech, for indeed the matter will become manifest whilst you will be upon the correct straight path concerning it."

The scholar Abdullah Ibn Abi Zayd al Qairawani who died in 996 CE said:

"Salvation lies in seeking protection in the Book of Allah Almighty and the Sunnah of His Prophet and following the path of the believers and that of the best of generations of the best community produced for mankind. Reliance on that is protection. Salvation lies in following the righteous Salaf."

The scholar Abu Al-Qasim Al-Lalikai who died in 1013 CE said:

"From the greatest of statements, and the clearest of proofs and reasoning, is Allah's Book, the clear truth, then the saying of the Messenger of Allah –Sallallahu Alayhi wa Sallam- and his pious companions, then what was agreed upon by the Righteous Salaf, then holding on to it until the day of judgement, and avoiding

innovations and listening to it from what was innovated by the misguided."

The scholar Al-Khateeb Al-Baghdadi who died in 1071 CE said:

Allaah has made these people – Ahl al-Hadith (salafis)– the pillars of sharee'ah, and He has destroyed through them all abhorrent innovations (bidas). They are the trustees of Allaah among His creation, the intermediaries between the Prophet (peace and blessings of Allaah be upon him) and his ummah. They are the ones who are striving hard to protect his religion; their light is shining, their virtues are well known, the signs of their sincerity are obvious, their way is prevailing, and their evidence is supreme. Every group has its own focal point which is based on whims and desires, apart from the people of hadeeth, whose reference point is the Qur'aan, whose evidence is the Sunnah and whose leader is the Messenger to whom they belong; they do not pay any attention to whims and desires, and they do not care about personal opinions. They are content with what is narrated from the Messenger, and they are the ones who are entrusted with it and they take care of it. They are the guardians and keepers of the faith, the vessels and bearers of knowledge. If there is a difference of opinion concerning a hadeeth, people refer to them, and what they rule is what is accepted and listened to. Among them are prominent faqeehs, great imams, ascetics who are well-known among their tribes, men who are known for their virtue, skilled reciters of Qur'aan and good speakers. They are the majority and their way is the right way. Every innovator pretends to be following their path, and cannot dare to claim any other way. Whoever opposes them, Allaah will destroy him, and whoever goes against them, Allaah will humiliate him. They are not harmed by those who forsake them, and those who stay away from them will not prosper. The one who cares for his religion needs their help, the one who looks down on them is a loser, and Allaah is able to support them.

The sheikh Ibn Taymiyya who died in 1328 CE said:

Hence it is clear that the people who most deserve to be called the victorious group are "Ahl al-Hadeeth wa'l-Sunnah", who have no leader to follow blindly apart from the Messenger of Allaah peace and blessings of Allah be upon him. (They only do taqlid to/of God's prophet and no one else no matter who it is.) *They are the most knowledgeable of people concerning his words and deeds, the most able to distinguish between what is sound and what is not. Their imams have deep knowledge of that, they are the ones who understand its meanings and are the most sincere in following it. They accept it and believe in it, and act upon it. They show love to those who adopt it and they show enmity to those who oppose it. They are the ones who measure any idea against that which is proven in the Qur'aan and Sunnah, so they never adopt any idea and make it one of the basic principles of their religion unless it is proven in that which the Messenger brought. Rather they make that which the Messenger brought, the Qur'aan and Sunnah, the foundation and basis of their beliefs. With regard to the issues concerning which people dispute, such as the attributes of Allaah, the divine decree, the threat of Hell, the names of Allaah and the principle of enjoining what is good and forbidding what is evil, etc., they refer that to Allaah and His Messenger. They examine the general ideas concerning which the different groups dispute, and whatever of these ideas is in accordance with the Qur'aan and Sunnah, they approve of it, and whatever goes against the Qur'aan and Sunnah, they reject it. They do not follow conjecture or whims and desires. For following conjecture is ignorance and following whims and desires without any guidance from Allaah is wrongdoing."* He also said in another statement that: *"There is no shame in declaring oneself to be a follower of the salaf, belonging to it and feeling proud of it; rather that must* *be accepted from him, according to scholarly consensus. <u>The madhhab of the salaf cannot be anything but true.</u> If a person adheres to it inwardly and outwardly, then he is like the believer who is following truth inwardly and outwardly. If he adheres to it outwardly only, and not inwardly, then he is like the hypocrite; he is to be accepted as he appears to be, and what is hidden in his heart is left to Allah."*

Thus personally I don't use the label Ahlus Sunnah wa Jamah much because everybody tends to think it means them and everyone says they are upon that methodology just like how everyone says they follow the Quran and the Sunnah too; even the Shia. Whereas the term Salafi is also a term used by people who may be trying to be or thinking they are Salafi, but they really aren't due to ignorance or for other reasons. So Ahl-Hadith is the classic term for what is popularly called Salafiyyah or Salafi. Which is pure unadulterated Islam as taught by the prophet Muhammad. In other words it is Islam in it's pure fundamental prophetic format. It's the safest and most rewarding lane on the Islamic road to paradise whereas all the other lanes have potholes which if one drives in those lanes they may or may not hit and if they do it could stop them from continuing, damage them, or cause them to veer off the road without knowing it. Following a madhhab with Taqlid or "blind following" is not the way to travel the road to paradise, just imagine putting a blindfold on and then trying to walk in a perfectly straight line for the rest of your life. It's impossible to even walk across a continent via blind following, so you are definitely not going to successfully travel the road to paradise being blindfolded. Taqlid is a spiritual blindfold, it's better than nothing because by following directions without seeing the proofs there is a tiny possibility you could walk in the right direction for a few steps, but Satan is sure to trip you up eventually; that is if you don't fall or go astray all by yourself. Although since people who practice taqlid tend to blindly follow people who practice taqlid, then those guilty of taqlid are tantamount to the blind being led by the blind being led by the blind and only God knows the length of the blind chain of taqlid. Satan doesn't even need to try to trip people who do taqlid. Such a calamity isn't guaranteed to happen if one doesn't take the Ahl- Hadith lane, but personally I'm not going to take such risks, because I don't want to take any detours to the hellfire before entering paradise. This is because when the prophet taught how all the other sects the Muslims will split into will be in the hellfire that didn't mean permanently for all of them. Some sects of so-called alleged Muslims are outside the fold of Islam and will be eternally punished in hell, others aren't and will just be temporarily punished prior to entering paradise, while for some people on those stray Islamic paths it will depend on the specific individual if Allah enters them into paradise without a detour to the hellfire. Also there is a difference between a Muslim being punished in hellfire and a non-Muslim, because for disbelievers their torment is doubled and it's eternal. Although if you are cautious like me and never want to enter hellfire then the safe path is salafi. Now does a Muslim have to identify themselves as "Salafi"? No, but they are supposed to have that methodology and believe/live accordingly. Usually I refer to myself as a Muslim or a Muslim Fundamentalist Godwilling, unless I'm having a technical scholastic conversation with someone who will understand what I mean when I say Salafi or Ahl-Hadith. Yet it is dangerous to mislabel oneself and thereby misrepresent an entire movement, hence the Scholar Salih Al-Fawzan said, "*Calling oneself Salafi, if it is true, is fine and there is nothing wrong with it. But if it is a mere claim, then it is not permissible to call oneself a Salafi when one is not following the way of the salaf.*" So because I'm smart enough to know that I'm not really following the way of the salaf 100%, as any salafi who reads this book will know, then I feel I should clarify that I'm trying to be salafi and that's the goal but officially I don't think I make the cut or rightly deserve to claim such a noble title for myself. I may forget and use the label from time to time but while I may be salafi according to the modern definition, the salaf themselves likely would not consider me to be a salafi despite my intentions, efforts and claims to be trying. This is because I give my own opinions and speculations much more authority than a salafi is supposed to. I say/write things they didn't say/write based on my own research so technically that's not quite the salafi way. Although sometimes with certain people it's better to identify oneself methodologically since one shouldn't be ashamed of trying to follow the correct pure Islamic methodology and to distinguish oneself from those upon other methodologies. So while some may dispute whether one should call themself salafi or not, there is consensus that it's the pure prophetic methodology and that even though everyone might not be one all the Muslims should strive to be one. So any can say they are trying to be one, if they actually are /intend to do so and aren't just faking it to bring ill repute upon the methodology. The label dilemma is similar to how Sunni Muslims typically don't call themselves Sunni unless it's to distinguish themselves from the Shia. You don't have to call yourself a Sunni either but sometimes circumstances dictate that you should. The trouble is we don't know what path or lane we will be on when our time on the test of life is up and we die, thus we say Godwilling. Muslims even say "I'm a Muslim, Godwilling" because many think they are Muslims but in the sight of God they aren't. Plus we recognize that the guidance comes from Allah alone, if God doesn't bless us with the guidance of Islam then we have no chance. This is because guidance is not a constant thing in that once you are guided then you will always be guided. It's similar to being healthy, being healthy once doesn't mean you will always be healthy nor does it mean that you are currently healthy. Just ask anyone who has gone to a doctor feeling fine thinking they are healthy only to learn they have a deadly disease and didn't know it. Or ask anyone who has ever gotten lost while traveling even though they had the correct instructions and were trying to follow them. So when Muslims pray we not only ask God for guidance to the straight path of those whom he's blessed(the prophets, sahabah and salaf) but also for him to help us to worship Allah alone. We actually admit we need God to help us to worship him. While we also ask God to protect us from being or becoming like those who were misguided and earned God's anger (ie. the Jews) or of those who have gone astray (ie. the Christians). This is because the Jews and Christians at one time had the truth and were on the path to paradise, but despite historically receiving Muslim prophets and books of guidance they rejected Islam, distorted it, and chose a different path than that which the prophets were sent to teach us. Thus the prophet Muhammad was sent to guide them and all mankind. In every unit of every prayer Muslims ask God for this guidance because it's so important and Allah himself instructed us to ask him for this. When God specifically says *"ask me for this frequently every day"* then you know it is definitely a vital, precious and valuable gift. Sometimes in life the long answer is necessary in order to get the correct answer, because by shortening it or blindly following then some may come to the wrong conclusions.

In Ramadan 2014 CE I noticed the first problem with the new local ISNF Imam. After Mr. Qadri publicly read hadith from Riyad as-Saliheen about not fasting or breaking fast until you sight the crescent moon a person asked Qadri what we should do since they follow calculations at the ISNF masjid instead of following the moon sighting as the prophetic hadith says to do. In reply Qadri said that as long as you follow the scholars that's fine, with him not even giving an answer to the question. Thus he promoted taqlid (blind following) but I didn't say he was wrong to permit calculations in opposition to moon sighting, I just felt that was the first sign of something disagreeable about him. Personally Qadri told me he was following the moon sighting for his fast, I don't know which local or global, but I found this odd in that he personally would practice something different than what he publicly would advocate and allow. Whereas all Sunnis agree moonsighting is the only valid way to calculate months including the month of Ramadan and only the Shia and Liberalist modernists are mistaken in permitting calculations. Yet since the contention between global and local moonsighting sadly remains a valid contentious issue, I will decline on commenting further on the matter of moonsighting.

In fall 2014 CE I brought my mom to the masjid for her to hear a special lecture from a mufti visiting the ISNF masjid from Mecca. During the mufti's Arabic talk Mr. Qadri translated what the mufti said into English on the spot including two sahih hadith:

It is narrated on the authority of Abu Huraira that the Messenger of Allah (ﷺ) observed:

By Him in Whose hand is the life of Muhammad, he who amongst the community of Jews or Christians hears about me, but does not affirm his belief in that with which I have been sent and dies in this state (of disbelief), he shall be but one of the denizens of Hell-Fire.

Source: Sahih Muslim 153

Abu Musa Al-Ash'ari reported:

Messenger of Allah said, "On the Day of Resurrection, Allah will deliver to every Muslim, a Jew or a Christian and say: 'This is your ransom from Hell-fire."'

Source: Riyad as-Salihin 432 Grade: Sahih

After the lecture my mom wanted me and her to ask the mufti from mecca if I could go to a potential funeral if my maternal non-Muslim grandparents died. My mom thought I was overreacting by telling them in advance to their death that if they die as non-Muslims I cannot go to their funeral or participate in funeral rituals as their will requests. My mom also wanted to ask whether I have to change my name of Gregory to an Islamic name as I planned to legally do so after having written and published my auto-biography under my original name. The mufti gently explained how I cannot go to my non-Muslim grandparents' funeral in the event of such a scenario due to the false religious rituals and false impression it will give regarding their final destination of hellfire if they die upon other than Islam and that it is better to change my name because it will help me to have an Islamic identity. Upon observing his answers which he gave in English directly himself, the common people at ISNF then took my mom and me aside saying the mufti is wrong and doesn't know what he is talking about because he is a foreigner and they gave incorrect incomplete reasoning as to why I should go to kafir funerals and not change my name citing local knowledge being more valuable than wisdom from the expert "mufti" from Mecca.

Many of the locals cited the incident where prophet Muhammad stood up for a Jewish funeral that was passing by, not knowing this practice was actually later abrogated and forbidden by Muhammad. Plus standing and getting out of the way is entirely different than attending the ritual itself. Whereas then some will incorrectly use hadith that apply to Muslim funerals of standing and following them to the graveyard and incorrectly equate Muslims and non-Muslims when the two are not equal at all.

Narrated Ubadah ibn as-Samit:

The Messenger of Allah (ﷺ) used to stand up for a funeral until the corpse was placed in the grave. A learned Jew (once) passed him and said: This is how we do. The Prophet (ﷺ) sat down and said: Sit down and act differently from them.

Source: Sunan Abi Dawud 3176 Grade: Hasan

It was narrated from Ibn 'Abbas and Al-Hasan bin 'Ali that:

a funeral passed by them and one of them stood and the other sat. The one who stood up said: "By Allah, I know that the Messnger of Allah stood up." The one who was sitting said: "I know that the Messenger of Allah sat."

Source: Sunan an-Nasa'I 1926 Grade: Sahih

Waqid bin `Amr bin Sa`d bin Mu`adh said:

I saw a funeral among Banu Salimah so I stood up. Nafi' bin Jubair said to me: Sit down, and I will tell you something decisive about this: Mas`ood bin al-Hakam az-Zuraqi told me that he heard 'Ali bin Abi Talib in Rahbatal-Koofah saying: The Messenger of Allah (ﷺ) told us to stand up for funerals; then later on he remained seated and told us to remain seated.

Source: Musnad Ahmad 623 Grade: Sahih

It was narrated that Abu Ma'mar said:

"We were with 'Ali and a funeral passed by him, and they stood up for it. 'Ali said: "What is this?' They said: 'The command of Abu Musa.' He said: 'Rather the Messenger of Allah stood up for a Jewish funeral but he did not do it again."'

Source: Sunan an-Nasa'i 1923 Grade: Sahih

So my mom was confused due to the ignorant locals contradicting the correct foreigner and decided to meet the new ISNF imam with me, her and him to discuss further and help me assimilate to American society as she felt I was becoming unrealistically impractical regarding my islamicity and opposition to American cultural practices, while to her the local Muslims at American masjids were more to her taste.

In subsequent meetings with Qadri, my mom and I, Qadri expressed his belief to my mom that the bible was abrogated and that was why people have to be Muslims today (which is an ambiguous statement that is only partially correct). Then privately in a follow up meeting between me and Qadri alone when we discussed our meeting with my mom, then Qadri told me that it is wrong for me to label non-Muslim Christian relatives as kafirs/disbelievers.(which is dangerously wrong to say) In 2014 though I was less knowledgeable and didn't understand the error or significance of Mr. Qadri telling me Christian cousins weren't kafirs and that not every disbeliever or non-Muslim is a kafir. As I was writing my dawah biography at the time due to suggestions from my friends in Canada and their new Imam who was translating the Quran into English at the time, I figured I would send Qadri a rough draft of my book via email to review so as not to be unknowingly preaching extremism in my book(s). Mr. Qadri also claimed to be a follower of the Hanafi Madhhab and I expressed my claim of trying to be Salafi. I did not know at that time that most people of Bida/innovation hide behind Hanafiyyah and just presumed he was still Ahlus-Sunnah wa Jamah in Aqeedah and just chose

Hanafi as a specific school of fiqh giving him the benefit of the doubt. It was only in later conversations with him that I learned he was trained to be an Imam at a Darul-Uloom school in South Africa.

Later in 2014 CE I started taking tajweed classes with Qadri to learn tajweed (rules of Arabic recitation of the Quran). During tajweed class Qadri told me prophet Muhammad knew what the letters like Alif Lam Meem and such meant but kept the meanings secret without telling anybody. I told Qadri he was wrong because that would have meant Muhammad failed to convey the message and that none but Allah knows what the mutashabiyat verses mean. I do not know if Qadri changed his errant position or not. Qadri also attributed evil to Allah in his tafsir of surah falaq whereas I believed nothing was 100% evil and that evil is not attributed to Allah but to our own sins. So little by little I was starting to see warning flags of ignorance from Qadri regarding basic matters.

In 2015 CE Mr. Qadri told me I cannot call the Roman Catholic Christian Pope a kafir/disbeliever because he doesn't know enough about Islam to be labeled a kafir. This time I recognized the severe error and I considered never going back to the ISNF masjid again because this was too big of an error to let slide. However I learned this error during my Friday morning Tajweed class and that same day my mom planned to go to the Jumuah prayer to listen to Qadri's lecture. So I was conflicted because even though I felt like running away and never interacting again my non-Muslim mom may not understand my caution and she might miss out on a beneficial lecture. At this time there was a huge mistake on my part due to the Ikhwani Muslim Brotherhood deviant principle of accepting the good and ignoring the bad for the sake of benefits. This principle is poison and the calling card on which Bida survives and thrives, yet not knowing better I decided I would address this issue with Qadri in private to correct him and continue going to the ISNF masjid since I felt it would benefit my non-Muslim mom that day more than me not going with her or going somewhere else unexpectedly.

 I later privately persuaded Qadri that the Pope is indeed a kafir because he claims infallibility, does confession(personally claiming to forgive people's sins) and communion(turning bread and wine in blood and body of Jesus/God) all of which make one defacto kafir regardless of their knowledge of Islam. Mr. Qadri finally agreed that you can call the Pope a kafir and it's okay. I didn't inquire as to what Qadri thought of other non-Muslims if they were kafirs or not because I didn't want to discover an even bigger error if I didn't have to.

I would notice other minor issues but nothing too major and I would often email Mr. Qadri polite corrections on such mistakes to help him out and to check my own understanding of Islam as correct. Additionally I would give Qadri suggestions on how to increase masjid attendance and do dawah to our neighbors, such as putting up Islamic signs/billboards outside the mosque near the time of Christmas saying "God can't have kids or parents" or "Jesus is Muslim" or reading hadith after both fajr and isha prayers instead of just after Isha. I also gave him a brochure the Imam in Canada had designed to send out to the neighborhoods of Canada via the mail informing them about Islam inviting them to visit the Canadian masjid. I made such dawah recommendations in 2015. Since it was typically only me and Qadri and a handful of others attending the masjid for daily prayers I felt we were developing a true friendship, despite him not frequently replying to my emails.

On December 23rd 2015 CE until January 1st 2016 CE outside the masjid noor ISNF put up a large billboard sign by the road that blasphemously said, "Happy Holidays to dear Neighbors and Friends".

I took objection to this sign and emailed Mr. Qadri on the 23rd. Receiving no reply and not seeing him for salat, after the dawn prayer on the 24th I decided to tape pieces of paper over the sign with my own writing on the paper so that the sign said "<u>Try to be kind</u> to dear neighbors and friends". By Dhuhr prayer time I saw my papers getting removed by the newly elected president of ISNF Rasul Khan and Qadri personally expressed his approval of the sign to me saying how "holiday" just meant "day off of work" and "friends" referred to Muslims. I sent emails to him regarding this issue to which he replied, I marked his reply in Red, redacting the email addresses.

Email Sent Wednesday, Dec 23, 2015 at 6:00 PM

Assalaamu Aleikumw wa rahmatullaha wa barkatuhu

After Maghrib something disastrous occurred at masjid noor.

While I was leaving I saw a new sign thing by the road and it says "Happy Holidays"

So I'm hoping that some Kafir donated a free sign to the masjid and just left a message on it for us.

Although I'm afraid it might've been someone professing Islam who may have set such a filthy object up.

First it's the US flag, then this thing. What's next a cross on top? Statues? Slot machines?

Since when has masjid noor become a church?

It seems like the type of sign you told me you suggested, you didn't do this did you?

This is a complete disgrace! I think it'd feel better to get raped. I do hope you can inshallah prevent such stuff from happening ever again. Because given that it's December 23rd, and Ramadan is 6 months away, I don't think the sign refers to

Jumah prayers since holidays is plural and the word isn't eid. Muslims don't have holidays we have eids. It's haram by consensus to wish kafirs a happy holiday or congratulate them on their festivals. And there is no second opinion about it. It's haram at the least, insulting to Islam as well and everything Islam stands for, also it could even be kufr depending on whether the guilty individual is a fool or not.

http://islamqa.info/en/947

Every holiday is a religious commemoration, hence the word "holi-day" which comes from "holy day". Only God has the right to establish a specific day of the year to be celebrated annually as a holiday, because every single holiday is a religious event with religious rituals. A secular holiday cannot exist, because a holiday observed on a annual basis can only be ordained by the one who made time. People cannot invent holidays to thank God. It's God who tells us how and when to celebrate, not governments, family, friends or cultural traditions. Basically if God didn't teach you about that holiday then you know that it's not something God is pleased with. Realistically all the holidays that God hasn't decreed aren't really holidays at all, but are pay days for the economy and ways for governments to control when and what people do, literally dictating when and how families are supposed to get together whether they want to or not. Haven't you wondered why so many family's dread "getting through the holidays"? It's because those holidays are unnatural and not something we were created to do. This is how people end up *worshiping governments because by celebrating when governments allow/order them to, they end up thinking celebrations can be dictated by the government and give God's authority to others. Also most of those holidays when folks are partying is when governments do their dirty work passing oppressive laws, because they know people are too busy to notice. Frequent and diverse holidays also make populations emotionally unstable as their emotions change according to the calendar and social pressure controls their behavior. Therefore Muslims don't participate in any of the unislamic holidays.*

Please Please Please do not tell me Santa Claus is giving the Khutbah on Friday!

If Santa Claus shows up there will be a big big big problem, I'm actually concerned Santa Claus might show up in the masjid on friday that's how bad it's getting. Is the Easter Bunny going to come in Spring?

While on it the same issue applies to "pot-luck" dinners? Why can't we call them "pot-Qadr"?
This is what happens when you don't come to the masjid.

If you miss a salat in the masjid next week it might get turned into a Brothel.

Email sent Thu, Dec 24, 2015 at 4:33 PM

This fatwa mention hadith of prophet Muhammad pbuh indicating that every festival is a religious festival.
http://islamqa.info/en/1130

Also don't know if you read fatwa sent in previous email because it seemed clear to me and mentioned specifically that haram to congratulate on their specific religious festivals AND it says you can't wish them "happy festival" either. With the "happy festival" applying to all the non-islamic holidays. It says in the fatwa "as is", meaning AND it covers all holidays religious and secular yet secularism is a religion itself. The problem is that holiday is holy day, as prophet taught us. This whole thing of holidays being a day of secular rest is false. This is the Kafir definition, the Muslims didn't say that. Muslims can't use their vocabulary and definitions. The whole "Holiday" thing was basically made so people can do the same thing without officially having to adopt that religion, or so they think they can. Business close on Saturday and Sunday because Jews and Christians think God rested on the 7th and Jews have saturday sabbath while Christians did Sun-day because they worship the alleged "son of God" and made their holidays on the pagan days to make the pagans get used to following kafir holiday schedule. This is how Christians convert people they get them to celebrate their stuff at the same times and take off the same times until eventually they are doing the same things the same ways and are the same. Remember the reason they stopped saying MC greeting as much is because non-Christians didn't celebrate it, and it made a barrier for people entering Christianity and it alienated non-Christians thus hindering evangelization. Non-Christians didn't use to take off or celebrate anything at the same times as Christians. Santa Claus or Saint Nicohlas myth made non-Christians think they could have fun with their kids the way christians do without being a christian. Then they began celebrating the same day and such and now all non-Christians are taking off, therefore the Christians now press for "Happy Holidays" to be returned back to MC greeting and after that happens people are expected to then accept basic things of Christian doctrine until eventually accepting Christianity. Think about it Santa Claus is a Catholic saint yet many non-Christians tell their kids he gives them gifts and enters their house. This happened through this interfaith type of taking off the same day thing after exposure to Christian calendars.

This fatwa mentions hadith of prophet Muhammad pbuh forbidding Muslims from initiating a greeting to Kafirs. (Thus de facto applying to sign making it haram, if strict). Also this fatwa shows how it's forbidden to honor them and even offer them condolences if a loved one dies. Mentions festivals as well.

http://islamqa.info/en/32560

This fatwa mentions we cannot attend kafir festivals and mentions hadith instructing Muslims to avoid kafirs on their festivals. Also keep in mind hadith which says we shouldn't even see their fires, so the whole theory of "when living in a non-Muslim environment...." is wrong to begin with so anything that is justified because of us doing something wrong to begin with cannot be good because it requires us to do something wrong. You don't make a bad situation for yourself and then say "lets do this to make the best of a bad situation" it is because of this mentality Shaitan wants Muslims to get into bad situations. Also what leads to Kufr and Haram is haram, according to Quran forbidding us from coming near to adultery and preventing even looks and alone time. Thus tell me what happens if you die and future generations decide to just go full throttle with the MC greeting? Statues are forbidden because they lead to evil, when the ancient statues were first made they had good intentions but later on it became idolatry.

http://islamqa.info/en/3325

This fatwa says how Muslim married to Christian must stop her from going to Church and celebrating her festivals.

http://islamqa.info/en/3320

If a Muslim must stop his wife from celebrating her festival then how can we possibly say "Happy Holiday"? Shariah instructs us to say "NO HOLIDAY today" Even if one takes the kafir deceitful trick definition of Holiday, we cannot ambiguously say this because it is an encouragement and people will interpret it to mean they should enjoy their Christmas festival. If even one person gets that interpretation *then it's haram. I got that interpretation as have others. If my parents see that sign they'll say "See even the masjid says Christmas is ok, if we can't do it or it's bad then why are they telling us to have a happy holiday?*

Everyone knows Holiday is just politically correct word for Christmas because some non-Christians get offended by term Christmas. Every Christian knows this that when someone says "Happy Holidays" they really mean Christmas but they can't legally say Christmas because of secularism and putting people like Muslims in a situation of having to respond or accept their festival as legitimate. I used to be a kafir, have kafir relatives and know how they'll interpret it. Someone born and raised Muslim is less qualified to say how Christians will interpret it. And it doesn't matter, weigh the benefit and the harm.

What is the benefit?

The harm is humilitaion, disunity, disgrace, haram, bida, promoting kufr at least unintentionally, and showing love to kufar taking them as friends.

Will look for other fatwa from other sites inshallah and ask specific questions to people with pic of sign inshallah describing my actions to see what was best solution and course of action for all involved.

Mr. Qadri replied to these emails of mine, and our in-masjid discussion as follows:

Email Sent Thursday Dec 24, 2015 at 7:41 PM

Assalaamu Aleikumw wa rahmatullaha wa barkatuhu

I dont think you heard my point clearly.

*There is a difference between festival and holiday.
Holiday is a day when people are off from their work and enjoy spending time with family and friends. None of the fataawa mentions it's haraam to say happy holidays.*

What is being mentioned in these fatawa is to take part in their festivals or to congratulate them for their kuffar. This means to have a Christmas tree or have any other event related to this is haraam. To wish them good for their festival is also forbidden. And I agree to this.

ISNF is wishing the community and the neighborhood happy holiday which has nothing to do with Christmas.

*If I were to take off for a week does that mean I'm celebrating Christmas too?
What do you mean we cannot use their vocabulary. We are using their language to begin with.*

You have to be very careful when you make things halal and haraam. The prophet was reprimanded when he made honey haraam on himself.

May Allah guide us all.

My replies were as follows:

Email Sent Thursday Dec 24, 2015 at 7:43 PM

1. What were the intentions?

Was this done to please Allah? Or to please the Kuffar? Or because of fear of the Kuffar? Or because of fear of Allah punishing us if this wasn't done?

Why was the phrase "Happy Holidays" chosen? Did Muslims come up with this phrase all by themselves? No. Its a Kafir phrase and using it means imitating the kufar and it went even further than that in believing the kafir definitions. A Kafir won't tell Muslims "doing X is kufr" they just want us to be like them because of the mob mentality similar to how if many kids believe in Santa Claus then a child thinks it must be true. By us not giving them legitimacy it makes them second guess themselves just as a kid does if others don't believe in Santa Claus or accept the mythology.

http://www.islamweb.net/en/article/142713/ This fatwa from different less strict more mainstream site gives extra evidence for why we cannot wish holiday greetings or return their greetings and that it is sinful to do so, and can be kufr but is sinful without any other opinion.

Attaching link of a Church Sign to prove that Holidays do mean Holy Days, even today. To a Christian Holiday=Holy Day. So Christians will interpret it according to their definition of the word. Intentions don't make actions good. It's not just about what you say it's about how you say it and who you say it to and what they understand from what you say.

https://flic.kr/p/aVVNG2

Oh and this site "curbappealforchurches" even sells signs that say "Happy Holidays" and "Season Greetings" for churches to buy and put up. These signs are sold under the category of "Christmas Signs". So if some Christians show up at the masjid tomorrow thinking the masjid is a church I wouldn't be surprised. Literally "Happy Holidays" is the same exact sign letter for letter that Churches put up and sell to churches to put up because it's a religious sign for kufr.

http://www.curbappealforchurches.com/Holiday_Collections/Christmas_Holidays/Christmas_Signs

So clearly this is imitating the Kufar without a shadow of a doubt. Thus while before one could maybe say at best it's makrooh because it could be understood, now it is at best haram if not kufr. Now I'm not saying doing it automatically makes one a kafir because people can be foolish but Allah could consider if an act of kufr. I'm not saying Allah does but this is a huge grave risky dangerous sign. So it doesn't matter who approved it or what the systematic protocol is when it's haram and potentially kufr. It does encourage kufr. People will be more inclined to perform kufr after reading it and that is the opposite of everything Islam teaches us to do. Muslims should lead people away from kufr not make it easier for them, even if it's unintentional.

What rewards can come from this sign? The risks are that it makes one a Christian missionary and evangelist.

The word "Holiday" is a Christian improvement on the word Xmas because now people are considering it a holiday and "Seasons Greetings" refers to the Liturgical calendar Christmas "Season of Advent". It's not the season of Winter, it's the season of Advent for Christians, that's what "Seasons Greetings" means" to them "Seasons Greetings" is like saying "Ramadan Mubarak" to us.

In 2007, a controversy arose when a public school in Ottawa, Ontario planned to have the children in its primary choir sing a version of the song "Silver Bells" with the word "Christmas" replaced by "festive".

Note a Christmas song about kufr simply use "festive" as a substitute word for Christmas. They didn't change the meaning of the song and it was still about the same kufr practices, they just used a different word so as to make kufr less sectarian and more palatable to the masses.

That's what these terms "holidays" and "Seasons greetings" are it just kufr going mainstream for all kafirs instead of just certain kafirs and many Muslims get trapped in it because of kafir education system that everyone is equal and love each other for who they are regardless of what they believe/do etc.

Here again is another sight with "Happy Holidays" sign templates in the "Christmas Signs" section. https://www.esigns.com/templates/christmas-signs/

Oh and here's a Christmas card(which is haram) with a picture of a church that says "Happy Holidays". Its a Christian card "Happy Holidays" is a Christian phrase.

https://www.pinterest.com/pin/481181541408562626/

I'm not making this stuff up, it's how Christians celebrate their religious holidays which are Holy days to them. I have Christian family and they use the phrase to this day and even say "Why don't you celebrate the holidays?" Every religious holiday of theirs they complain "Why can't you celebrate the Holiday?" "Well you know it's the holidays, so we'll be going over to X's house". Or "I have to send out cards for the holidays". Or my people I know who sing in church having to practice for the "holiday concert" singing "holiday songs" of kufr meant to be song in a church encouraging kufr.

Oh and you know what the "festive spirit" is or what it means to "get into the spirit of the season"? Well just refer to the Mormonism email where I discussed the Holy Ghost/Spirit they claimed to be receiving inspiration from as all Christians believe in as either a third part of the trinity or a special

Christian spirit like prophet inside or helping/guiding every Christian.

Here is "Revolution Church's" website telling everyone "Happy Holidays" http://www.revolutionchurch.com/happy-holidays/

Even the Temple of Satan use the term as explained here, they publicly put on a performance where their angel (Christians think Iblees was an angel) drops down and produces a sign/says "Happy Holidays". The whole thing is religious too. They think saying "Happy Holidays" espouses their religious viewpoint. So all these different kafirs know "Happy Holidays" is religious except apparently for born and raised Muslims who don't really have a clue what kafirs actually think and plan for them. The Kafir plan for society doesn't include Muslims or Islam. The whole coexistence thing is a ploy to get Muslims to abandon Islam, they are simply playing us because they realize they can't defeat Islam so they have to make the Muslims feel pressured to stop practicing Islam of their own freewill. Whether they do they threw fear or friendliness they both want the same even if they refuse to admit it. No matter what Muslims do they won't be pleased with us ever, not until we disbelieve and reject Islam. Every compromise and attempt to blend in and be friendly will be interpreted as them winning us over. I've read Christian evangelist material they give to Christians on how to convert Muslims and this is their plan, friendly coexistence and assimilation until there is little difference. Every step we take they will always tell us "well it's about time you STARTED going in the right direction".

https://www.washingtonpost.com/news/post-nation/wp/2014/12/04/the-florida-capitols-holiday-display-will-include-a-festive-message-from-the-satanic-temple/

Just so you don't think "Holiday" only refers to Christmas and Easter here is the Little Bethlehem Church blog saying "Happy Holidays" in June for the other kafir holidays they celebrate which are specifically religious sectarian holidays. http://littlebethlehem.blogspot.com/2011/06/happy-holidays.html

Here's the "Shawn Church" site saying "Happy Holidays" for the "holiday season"
http://www.shawnchurch.com/news/20101218153531.html

A Christian Pastor from a MEGACHURCH in TEXAS even admits he's not concerned about people saying "Happy Holidays" instead of Christmas because he knows what it means and sees it as a way for non-Christians to celebrate Christmas and acknowledge Christmas without feeling like their Christian. Oh and he's a Fox News guest as well. So don't be fooled by the "tolerance" he knows the plan and game. Other laymen don't know the plan and that's where this whole "Holiday" being a attack on Christmas comes from. That's the viewpoint of those who aren't serious Christians or ignorant devout Christians. The ringleaders of Christianity fully endorse the term "Happy Holidays" and *they even advertise with it saying how the reason these holidays are "happy" is because of Jesus pbuh /God coming to earth. They say he's the "reason for the season" and "made the Holidays Happy". So to say "Happy Holidays" to a Christian that means you agree with the Christian doctrine that Jesus pbuh is the savior of the world.*

http://www.christianpost.com/news/joel-osteen-not-concerned-about-war-on-christmas-or-happy-holidays-111392/

Words aren't about what the speaker thinks they mean they're about what those hearing/reading them think they mean. The point of words is to communicate an idea. To do so you have to say what you mean. If you use words to which they mean one thing to you and another to someone else then you are conveying a different message than what you think. This is why when doing dawah one must know what their audience thinks, thus it's best to say Creator instead of God or Allah or Creator of the Universe if like the Mormons they think each planet has it's own god/creator. If a sign where put up saying "pray to God" people who see it will do kufr thinking that's what you meant because to them the word prayer doesn't mean salat and God doesn't mean Allah.

Of course that example is more open to dispute but "Happy Holidays" is even worse because that is explicitly unislamic. Islam literally has nothing with that sign someone who sees it would have no clue at all those where Muslims and no inclination to research or embrace Islam or to do anything good. The sign basically says "Have fun doing whatever you do however you want to do whatever you want to call it, you aren't just our neighbors but our friends too just the way you are".

That's what Muslims will also think you are saying as well. This sign's apparent meaning is evil and the hidden secret meaning is stupid and wasteful even if it's not bad but even then the message intended to be given in secret which nobody would ever guess is bad in itself. I don't think anybody at all would interpret the sign the way you interpreted it. People won't guess what that asterisk means they'll just think it's a snowflake or a star as in the star over the alleged city of bethelehem and/or cave which God/jesus was allegedly born in.

Now I could keep on adding more and more but seriously nearly every single Church website and bulletina and Church Christmas program says "Happy Holidays".

So we have a Masjid saying the same exact thing as the Churches using the same exact phrase at the same exact time in the same exact way but you expect people to think they mean completely different things when Muslims have never ever done this at all? They will say "Finally these Muslims are giving up and becoming American because we're better and Islam is wrong." If only all the other Muslims in the world could be more like them, and not wear the hijab or say our religion is wrong or go to pray 5 times a day or say drugs, pork, music, pictures, gambling, democracy, freedom is evil etc.

Finally why should Muslims even do dawah at all when the Masjid is telling kafirs "Happy Holidays"? This sign potentially destroys the effect of all the dawah done in the community thus far. Dawah practically has to start all over from scratch now. People trying to do dawah to pure prophetic Islam feel betrayed. We go out trying to bring people to the masjid and the masjid puts out a sign telling them to go to the church and then locks the doors so nobody can even come in if they ignored the sign's advice to be a happy kafir celebrating a kufr holiday.

Regarding holidays being a day of rest. This is actually exactly what religious holidays are. The Jews only took off on the Sabbath and worked 6 days a week. The disbelievers ridiculed them saying they were lazy bums and their mocked there religion because it told them to take a day off. Subsequently in Rome they had many holidays throughout the year including the Coliseum as the Greeks did with the Olympic games.

Religiously speaking the only reason people have "off days" is because of religious rituals and festivals. The Weekend is the off time because of the Jews and Christians saying God needed to rest on the 7th day and they picked different days of the week. The pagans took off Sunday because they worshipped sun-gods and solar cults. They had Spring break, for the fertility rituals, Summer break for the Summer planting rituals, Fall break for the harvest rituals, and Winter break was for the Winter rituals which led to a new "Sun" being born since the old sun was running out of light and dying, thus at winter solstice ie Christmas time the new "Sun of God" was born.

Even today every single official day off is a day off for a religious reason. There is a religious background to every holiday including government ones and for every winter break or midterm break or summer vacation this has religious significance.

So even if one were to congratulate for having days off, people get off days for religious reasons, just because some people are religious they still take off because of mob mentality and wanting to do what the crowd does. This is how governments control people's lives by dictating when they learn, when they work, when they spend time with family etc.

It is a religious sign and it is not the religion of Islam that is being propagated. It is not enjoining good rather it is enjoining evil and hindering good.

It is counterproductive, disgraceful, disunity, sinful and a bida linguistically speaking since bida means something new and since it does have something to do with religion one could say it's bida dalala but I'm not going to because it's worse than a simple bida as bad as bida is and I'll admit the bida thing regarding this may be a bit of a stretch.

Yet on top of that it causes extremism. As is evident it leads people to adopt extremely passionate attitudes and those who disagree with the unislamic position get labeled extreme. What do you think anyone at risk for extremism will do after seeing *such a sign. Lets say theoretically someone were influenced by ISIS propaganda which is technically everyone on the planet who's heard the name. What do you think such an individual would feel like and think? This type of stuff pushes people towards ISIS and ISIS uses this stuff to say "look and see for yourselves these people calling us incorrect are living with the enemies of Islam wishing them "Happy Holidays"! Now my view on them is clear that ISIS is misguided and very dangerous to Islam. But this sign polarizes the Muslim community and those who don't say anything will do so out of fear or feeling of futility. This causes people most at risk to isolate themselves because that's what Islam teaches to do in such circumstances when surrounded by evildoings. As they always say "Say yourself first"! Some Muslim might actually go live in a cave after seeing that sign. Especially considering the 25th is Juma so all those who only come to masjid on Christmas will come and see that sign and what do you think the Muslim who never prays except on eid and only comes to the masjid for "Good Friday" and Christmas (because on eid their busy working)*

Finally what do you think the young Muslim children who read the sign will think? These same Muslim kids who go to school and all their peers and teachers teach them the holidays are their specific religious rituals. Those kids aren't going to have enmity for kufar. In fact they may even start practicing these holidays themselves since they read the sign at the masjid and learned it was ok to do and be happy on them and tell others to have "happy holidays". Worse still they may even take it to mean that all religions count/lead to heaven and none are wrong.

On the other hand there is a sign which says "Try to be kind to dear neighbors and friends" what do you think Muslims and Kufar will think or do when reading that?

On December 24th I had taped papers over the "Happy Holidays" portion of the sign so that it said "Try to be kind to dear neighbors and friends" and it was taken down by the president of ISNF and the Imam gave me a lecture on obeying authority.

If one takes one sign down in favor of the other or one covers one sign up in favor of the other which do you think is really the good deed resulting in goodness and which is the bad deed resulting in evil.

Is it worse to disobey systematic protocol (of the same system who sets up an anti-Islamic thing) or is it worse to tear down a sign saying "Try to be Kind" replacing it with "Happy Holidays".

Which sign would Muhammad pbuh or Jesus pbuh take down or cover up? Would they side with "the majority" or "the authority" or "the system"?

Hypothetically which party is at more risk? Which is the bigger mistake? For one to break systematic policy to say "Try to be Kind" or for many to do makrooh, haram, potentially bida and kufr?

What gain is worth putting so many people at risk and risking such devastating effects for Kafirs, the community and Muslims?

Even if one forgets the legal ruling on which position is right and wrong. Which is the greater good and which is the greater evil?

At what point did the system become the determining factor of right and wrong and good and bad or that the system is by default the best solution?

The system has never resulted in the revival of the Ummah. If you want things to change you don't change the system because that's the problem and the solution that's been continually tried. The kafir doesnt' become a Muslim and say let me fix the church they abandon the church go to the masjid (hopefully ignore the sign telling them to celebrate Christmas) and tell those in the church to leave the church too before the calamity befalls it.

Regardless of a person's intention, if they work in a gun factory they will never ever end up producing candy. The system can only produce the results it was designed for. An Unislamic system will never ever and never ever has resulted in Islamic outcomes.

Allah will never change a people's condition until they change themselves. It doesn't say if they change the system and fix it. Each individual must change themselves and then Allah *changes the conditions and grants them the system of Islam only AFTER they abandon the unislamic systems.*

You drop the satanic luggage before getting on the plane to paradise, you don't try to make it comply with TSA regulations you just leave it behind so you can meet the desired goal.

When a sports team sucks they don't change the playbook. They fire the coach and the players and get a new coach, new players and a new playbook.

In Islam the playbook is the prophets, the problem is we aren't using his playbook but are saying lets use another teams playbook because we're playing in their stadium and their fans are the majority and they like to see teams play a certain way. So if the visiting team plays the way the home team and their fans like do they win? No! They lose terribly but worse than simply losing is that they get disunited and lose their reputation and fan loyalty. While the sports team owner is outraged and may well fire the whole team for copying the ways of the other team thinking they could beat them at their own game.

When the game is rigged only the fool plays. If you don't play a rigged game then you can complain, if you choose to play a rigged game you can't complain when you lose.

Moses pbuh refuted the kufar on the day of their festival, yet the masjid tells people to have happy ones?

Even the Jehovah's Witnesses don't wish people "Happy Holidays".

http://www.islamweb.net/en/article/156589/congratulating-non-muslims-on-their-feasts

The prophet could've done something like this but he never did as far as I know and he had more reason to do so if it were good or effective to do.

Allah is the most sever in punishment and the most merciful.

http://www.islamweb.net/en/article/155976/the-forbiddance-of-celebrating-non-muslims-festivals

If one says holiday doesn't mean holy day today, well then everything is justified such as lights and lights on trees too. People today put trees in their house with lights on them just as a pastime for fun, and they puts lights on their house for fun to make their home more bright. Yet we can't put lights on a pine tree at this time, even if we just intend to make it pretty because that's what the kufar do for different reasons, same for lights on houses. Both are imitating kufar in actions despite intentions being different. Yet the sign is even worse because it imitates via action and speech using exact same phrases and same exact signs.

Honestly if a traveler were looking for a masjid they would drive right on by and be upset thinking there are more kufar in that place too upon falsehood.

Will still try to ask those I think are qualified explaining exact specific situation but just sending this now because I think time is of the essence in removing evil.

Next and last email on this email thread I sent to Qadri prior to Christmas 2015 Khutbah:

Email Sent Friday, Dec 25, 2015 at 12:18 PM

Here is a Christian blog expressly instructing Christians to say "Happy Holidays" to Muslims because saying "Merry Christmas" will inhibit their evangelization process because Muslims don't understand what Christians mean when they speak. Guy even says that "Happy Holidays" covers ALL THE RELIGIOUS HOLIDAYS. Thus it's actually worse to say "Happy Holidays" than it is to say "merry Christmas" because "Happy Holidays" includes hannukkah, kwanza, new years, kings day, epiphany, boxing day and many more. http://mark-cannon.com/2012/12/11/do-muslims-wish-happy-holidays-or-merry-christmas/

Further proof that "Happy Holidays" is understood to mean "Merry Christmas", when you say "Happy Holiday" to a Christian they think that's what it means.

http://www.usnews.com/opinion/blogs/peter-roff/2014/12/12/theres-nothing-wrong-with-saying-happy-holidays-or-merry-Christmas

Definition of "holiday" according to etymological dictionary proves "Holiday" means "holy day" and the word "Holiday" has been used since the 15th century to refer to religious festivals. It's not a modern word at all. It's always been a reference to religious festivals. since 1937 CE in America it has meant "Merry Christmas". So for 78 years it's meant "Merry Christmas" in America.
http://www.etymonline.com/index.php?term=holiday

The U.S. Army has even used the word "Holiday" instead of "Christmas" in Muslim countries so as to protect themselves while performing kufr in Muslim lands
http://www.ibtimes.com/merry-christmas-or-happy-holidays-army-told-not-say-christmas-report-1519576

Here is a yahoo thread in which a poll is given on "Happy Holidays" or "Merry Christmas". All agree it refers to religious holidays. Christians like to think it refers to their holidays and non-Christians say it in order to cover all the religious holidays of December. Not one person thinks it refers to "taking a day off".

https://ca.answers.yahoo.com/question/index?qid=20121120104131AA3Q3ms

These are the same types of people who pass by the sign and see it.

Also fatwas specifically say it's forbidden to say "Happy festival" and I think you might have agreed. Well the definition of festival is equated to the same word as "holiday".

http://etymonline.com/index.php?term=festival&allowed_in_frame=0

There is no such thing as a non-religious holiday. And I'm guessing those who proposed this used the modern dictionary secular definition of holiday when proposing it and hoping that initially you thought it was bad idea until excuse was used. However the initial reaction is evil so even if "holiday" didn't refer to religious celebrations, which it does, but just say it didn't and all my evidence is rejected then one must look at the effect of the sign. How will people understand it? The only way to get the meaning that you say it means is if they look into the special dictionary you used (and not any other dictionary) and they looked into Islam to learn the definition of "friends" and researched Islam in depth to learn Muslims don't really consider kufar to be friends. Yet who has ever looked into a dictionary after reading a sign like that? If even one doesn't and gets wrong interpretation then evil has resulted and whether the sign has good intentions or not the effects play a decicive role in whether it is a good deed or a bad deed. The point is the real harm done outweighs the imaginary theoretically fantastical "benefits" of making the kafirs feel "happy". Seriously why do we even care if they are happy or not? It's impossible for a kafir to be happy. If you want a kafir to be happy then you invite them to Islam. Happyiness can only come in paradise or in this life via the obedience to Allah. So technically telling a kafir to be happy is telling them to do the impossible unless of course one doesn't believe practicing Islam is the only way to achieve happiness. By saying "happy holiday" regardless of what it means the masjid sends the message that happiness can be found outside of Islam by our kafir neighbors. And this is false and possibly kufr, again I'm not saying it is kufr but without Islam there is no happiness.

I don't mean to overburden with info but I'm 100% certain it's haram at the least to have this sign. There is no doubt in my mind and I'm willing to say it is haram on the Day of Judgement. I wouldn't have done what I did if there were any doubt in my mind. Are you 100% certain it's muba and not makrooh, or haram, or bida, or kufr? Personally if I were you I wouldn't take the risk. It has already divided the community and caused hard feelings amongst Muslims, so that in itself is haram enough. Think of how it has caused Muslims to argue and have hurt feelings and what is the benefit? Kufar get all the benefit of it and Muslims get all the harm. Muslims are starving to death worldwide and even in WNY there are Muslims begging for funds. Thus due to circumstances themselves spending money to tell the kufar "Happy Holidays" when local Muslims are struggling to survive on a daily basis makes it haram. Personally I've even met Muslims at Masjid Noor this december who say they and their family are sleeping in their car, which I've seen has broken window, because they have no money and no job and gas and electricity at their place was cut off. Yet the masjid spends money to say "Happy Holidays". What do you think those Muslims will feel like when they see that sign?

Finally what do you think Shaitan wants? Do you think Shaitan likes this sign or that it makes Shaitan angry? In the short, mid and long term does it help Shaitan's plan or harm it?

On that Christmas Friday a khateeb named Husam Ghanim preached the Abrahamic faiths interfaith doctrine specifically saying Jews and Christians are "our friends". Later that Christmas night another guest speaker (not Qadri or Ghanim) said they had "Christian friends". Thereupon Qadri got up and announced how for dawah(inviting people to Islam) that day (Christmas Friday 2015) he and other Muslims went door to door giving people food baskets as "gifts". Meanwhile the sign outside the ISNF masjid noor said "Happy Holidays to dear neighbors and friends". A local clipping from a News media article about the imam giving many non-Muslims Christmas gifts was later posted inside the mosque bulletin board and stayed up for several years.

> Saturday January 09, 2016
> The Buffalo News.com (/)
>
> # Opinion
>
> ### Letter: Members of mosque are great neighbors
>
> Updated: January 5, 2016, 02:17 PM Published: January 6, 2016, 12:01 AM
>
> **Members of mosque are great neighbors**
>
> The Hallmark Channel sets the standard for giving us those touching moments of family and holidays, especially this time of the year. Sometimes that makes it difficult for our lives to match up to those feelings in our busy lives. How often do we have time to reach out to a neighbor?
>
> One afternoon right before Christmas, our doorbell rang. I answered the door to find a well-dressed, attractive, well-spoken, young man. He introduced himself as a representative of the mosque on Heim Road. He asked my husband and me if we had seen the sign in front of the mosque wishing their neighbors a happy holiday and thanking them. We had seen the sign and told him how nice that was. He handed us a box of chocolates, to extend a more personal thank you for being good neighbors, and a holiday greeting card that was signed by the president of Islamic Society of Niagara Frontier. This was such a kind and unexpected gesture that it seemed like a Hallmark moment of what the world could and should be.
>
> Deborah Boehm

As a result of this blatant disregard of my advice and condemnation of corrupting the religion with innovative "Happy Holidays" greetings billboards and "Holiday gifts" in December 2015 I decided to stop taking Tajweed lessons with Qadri and sent the following email explaining why.

Email Sent Saturday, Dec 26, 2015 at 12:09 PM

Assalaamu Aleikum wa rahmatullaha wa barakatuhu

Was thinking of dawah methods with kafir family.

Now some know that I don't celebrate kafir holidays, yet they may not know why.

I was thinking of sarcastically asking you what the difference was between saying "Happy Holidays" on a billboard sign or me sending out Christmas cards saying the same and whether you thought it was ok for me to do that with only the following message on a card:

To my Dear_____(familial relation)

"Happy Holidays"

From Abdullah

But then I was distressed to learn you gave cards to kafirs on Christmas, I really hope they didn't say "Happy Holidays" or worse. Because that is a Christmas card and greeting and I know because I've gotten Christmas cards before and I know people who write Christmas cards and that's what they say on them. A card made specifically to be given to someone on Christmas is a Christmas card whether it says Christmas on it or not. Atheists give Christmas gifts on Christmas despite not considering it a religious practice.

However if you did it then there must have been a reason. Of course everything we do we should do to get good deeds. Thus if it's a good deed to have done then why didn't you ask me to join you? Don't you want me to get good deeds? Why wouldn't you ask me to join you in doing a good deed? Is it a good deed? You tell me I should get involved and then you exclude me from even knowing what's going on. How am I supposed to know to ask if the community is going to be giving out cards and gifts on Christmas day? I never even considered the Muslim community would do this and was surprised. So this "dawah opportunity" never even occurred to me and surely you know that I'm telling the truth when I say this idea never occurred to me as a possibility.

I was unaware such a thing was allowed and as you probably would guess I had an immediate inclination to presume it was haram, which may be why you kept me in the dark. However proof is required for good deeds and bad deeds. Which may also be why you kept me in the dark, because I tend to insist on proof. Yet I'm starting to wonder what other "good deeds" am I missing out on that nobody wants to share the opportunity with me? Fortunately this is something that can easily be proven as to whether it's good or bad. During the time of the sahaba the Christians celebrated Christmas and the Muslims had food and baskets and cards and letters. So did the Sahaba do this? If it was a good deed why would they neglect it? They were more concerned with softening kafirs hearts to Islam than we can ever be and had true certainty in the danger kafirs were in and were the best of propagators since they were eyewitnesses to prophethood and miracles.

Do Muslims in Muslim countries give cards and gifts to Christians on Christmas? What about in the West do any Muslims or have any ever done this?

Fatwa I see says this "***it is haram for the Muslim to imitate the disbelievers by establishing celebrations for these occasions, or to exchanges gifts, or to distribute sweets, or trays of food, or to stop work or anything like this.*** Due to the statement of the Prophet" except from http://ummuabdulazeez.com/2012/12/15/responding-to-merry-christmas-2/

To me I see it as haram but if it's not then I can do it with my family and it can make huge difference if it's good and I don't while it can also do lots of damage if it's haram and I do. So these differences of opinion are causing us to either get sins or lose out on good deeds. Also these types of differences aren't the valid types of differences to have. It's not a madhhab issue these are black and white matters. There cannot be an opinion which says it's sinful and another which says it's virtuous. They can't both be right. The prophet pbuh told us the halal is clear and the haram is clear and inbetween there is doubtful matters. However stays away from the doubtful will be safe. I think many things that have transpired recently are clearly haram and if I'm wrong and they're doubtful then they should still be avoided and abandoned for safety reasons. While if they are clearly halal then I'm wrong to be forbidding what is good. Also the Ummah will never unite upon error. Clearly we aren't united so that may be the reason why. The Jamah is not the majority, the Jamah is the majority of those upon the truth ie the generations of the salaf. 1 can be a Jamah. I'm not saying I'm a Jamah but I am saying that board approval doesn't mean its the Jamah.

How is giving a gift on Christmas not a Christmas gift? Christmas gifts are called that because of the day it's given on, intention has nothing to do with whether it's a Christmas gift or not. Also nobody ever gives a card on off-days unless it's a get well-card for an injured person or a religious holiday card. But even if it's not that is how it will be interpreted even if you explicitly say it isn't. Actions speak louder than words. I guarantee everyone who got a gift from a Muslim on Christmas was very happy indeed, because they interpreted it as victory, to which soon the Muslims will be in the Churches just like them. This is how it happens. Study Islam in America and discover why it is that Masjid from the previous centuries are no longer active, despite the Muslims never moving. The same families live in those same neighborhoods, but after they started policies similar to those being enacted today the trend towards kufr and apostasy took it's course step by step by step. The reason people give gifts on Christmas is because they think Jesus pbuh got gifts on Christmas from Middle Eastern Kings who came to visit him. That's why it started and that's why it continues. But just look at the sahaba did they ever give someone a gift on Christmas? What did prophet saws say to the Jews on Day of Ashura? He said Muslims are more closer to Moses pbuh than they are and are superior to them. Today they call that a "put-down". Christmas is a day where Kufar expect gifts from Kufar. The nation of Kufar exchange gifts on this day, regardless which denomination of Kufr they belong to. So to give gifts on this day is imitating the kufar. Seriously my family says how I can just go over and give and receive gifts and it doesn't have to be Christmas with my gifts. They'll just play games and say "It's not a Christmas gift we just want to give you a gift today and it just so happens to be Christmas." Whereas if I say "Oh yeah me too I have a gift for you and it just so happens to be Christmas *today and we both just so happen to be giving each other our gifts on the same day." Clearly that's a Christmas gift and haram. If you really wanted gifts to soften the hearts they would be given on a different day so people can see it was genuine and really had absolutely nothing to do with Christmas at all. Do you think all those who helped with giving cards and gifts didn't intend it as a Christmas gift? Do you think those who suggested a "Happy Holidays" sign really didn't intend it to refer to Christmas? Lets just pretend there were a hypocrite who wanted to corrupt the Muslim community, aren't these types of policies exactly what they would push for? Do you think Saul/Paul publicly said he was corrupting the religion of Jesus pbuh? Do you think Christians publicly said they were copying / adopting the rituals of pagans and their holidays? No it's an escalator to kufr. From my perspective the community is stepping on the escalator and the descent has begun.*

Whereas you might be happy that 1 person became Muslim on Christmas. Yet you said there is a Muslim funeral about once a month. So that's a 90%+ loss of Muslim numbers. It should be a shame that only 1 person became Muslim. Just 1? Really? Only 1? We should be having on average more than 1 per day just for that masjids community. The sahaba's image was worse than us and they antagonized kufar and they had more success.
Why? Because they didn't care at all what the community thought about them. It was about spreading Islam AND eradicating evil, not improving their standing in the community and gaining political comfort. There were no hypocrites in Mecca. So if we're in the Meccan period then that means there are zero hypocrites.

I'm not saying this stuff to cause trouble or criticize, it's not exactly fun to do and I could theoretically do other things that are less distressing if Allah willed. Yet I think it is an Islamic obligation that cerain things must be condemned. ISIS isn't the only thing that must be condemned. Many who condemn ISIS likewise must be condemned because they are in error for different reasons. It's not about uniting against Khawarij it's about condemning everything that's wrong whether it's peaceful and friendly or violent and aggressive.

Also you told me that "Nobody is saying Jews and Christians are our friends." Whereas on Friday in 2 separate lectures I heard kufar being referred to explicitly as friends. So regardless of what the "friends" on the sign was intended to mean it will not be interpreted that way by the kufar nor the Muslims. I was told several times yesterday that kufar are our friends and in 3rd grade my teacher taught me "a friend is someone who sticks with you until the end, that's why the word "friend" ends with "end" "

Can you explain these verses to me? 68:9, 3:118-120, 58:22, 5:51, 11:113

Also can you read Surah 2:109-140 because when I read those verses in translation I seem to get a different understanding than the mainstream understanding I hear. Likewise with people referring to persecution in Mecca. I thought bilal was put on sand because he spat in the idol's face and that he said "ahad ahad" specifically because he wanted to infuriate the kufar and didn't know anything they hating hearing more than that and if he did he said he would've said it. Whereas many sahaba also would repudiate falsehood and get beat as a result and were glad to get beat or even lose an eye because of it. So it seems even under pain of torture the sahaba weren't trying to "soften the hearts of the community". Likewise when Hamza became a Muslim he didn't try to soften the heart of Abu Jahl, he cracked his head open. Now I don't think that is the best approach for people to take today but there are many other instances of "unfriendly" antagonistic discourses between believers and kafirs. Likewise when Abu Bakr was beaten unconscious, or the traveler (I think Abu Darda(Dharr) who announced shahada repeatedly at Kaba to infuriate kufar) or Umar telling Muslims to proclaim Allah is greater than the kufars false gods. Afterall how did prophet pbuh announce his public dawah. By telling people they were on the road to hellfire. That was his public message from day 1. He didn't ease into it and try to display friendly neighborly manners before letting them know they were wicked and hated by God. Likewise I thought that the religion of Abraham was Islam only and didn't know he was responsible for other faiths. Christians and Jews told me he was but I never believed them, was I wrong? Also were all the battles Muslims have fought throughout all time done out of religious ignorance or extremism? I thought they were all for the sake of Allah. Such as Dawood pbuh, Badr, Tabuk, Hattin, Ayn Jalut and on and on even up til the modern day battles against the USSR in Afghanistan and elsewhere. Was I wrong? Is Jihad not a part of Islam at all? I thought scholars wrote volumes and volumes on the matter of religious violence. Where they ignorant or extreme?

If we want to speak in sign terminology. Prophet's first billboard saws would basically say "I warn you of the hellfire if you don't accept Islam". If we love Allah we would obey the Messenger *saws. Allah hurls the truth at falsehood. Allah tells us Jews and Christians will never ever be pleased with us until they make us abandon our faith. Allah did not lie when he revealed those verse and they apply to Americans in the 21st century. I testify to the truthfulness of Allah's speech. The goal is to spread Islam, not improve the image of the Muslim community. Honor comes from Islam alone, it doesn't come from complimenting kufar or being kind and friendly. When you have a masjid where not one person attends salat 5 times a day everyday(including myself) and that masjid doesn't even have 3 people for Dhuhr and Asr. And on Christmas morning when the kufar are up before fajr time opening their presents committing shirk with their many various rituals whilst Muslims who have off of work miss fajr at the masjid to the extent where a regular workday has more people show up for fajr than do on Christmas morning this is a sign that the problem is between Muslims and Allah.*

If you want the kufar to love us then cause Allah to love us and he will order mankind to love us. If Allah is displeased with the Muslims negligence then they are disgraced, dishonored and the people will hate them as well. Perhaps the Kufar persecute us because Allah is displeased with our sins and wants us to return to him instead of trying to be like them. The only way to improve the relations between Muslims and Kufar in America is to improve the Muslims relationship with Allah and the Muslims. If you try to improve the relationship with the Kufar at all costs and especially at the expense of the relationship with Allah or the Muslims then it will only result in disaster.

Consider did any of the Sahaba ever become disunited because of some being friendly to the Kufar? Consider that in trying to be nice to Kufar and instill nice feelings in their hearts towards the Muslims it is causing distress to Muslims and causing disunity and hard feelings to spread within the Muslim community. By trying to unite the Muslim community and the Kafir community it is further disuniting the Muslims. So yes maybe some kafirs will like it, but if Muslims hate it then what is the real outcome. Does Allah want us to please the kufar at the expense of displeasing Muslims? Or to please Muslims at the expense of displeasing the Kufar?

I thought the sign was too far across the line but it seems that the line hasn't just been crossed but that it's been crossed by miles while the traveler keeps going farther and faster.

I'm not even being sarcastic when I express concerns that their may be plans for a Spring Egg hunt at the masjid for the kids. At the current rate of "progress" I actually want you to promise me that there will not be any type of egg hunt in spring no matter what type of reason or justification there is. I mean they already had the Olympic Games and those are religious. The words Olympic games are games done by various Greek city-states or global states in honor to the gods of Mt. Olympia. Seriously I think an egg hunt will be proposed as a public event for the whole community of Muslims and non-Muslims and certain dictionaries might get used to get you to agree to it. Maybe not this year but I can clearly see it happening. Or maybe a Shia holiday may get suggested instead.

What am I supposed to do? Should I just keep quiet and withdraw? Part of the conditions for Muslims living in lands of disbelief is the ability to forbid all types of evil. I think it would be sinful for me to not say things going on are sinful.

I don't even know how we can use the word "Muslim community" when we don't even have enough people to perform congregational salat in the masjid! How can there be a president and board for a Masjid which doesn't even have 3 people praying in it for Zuhr or Asr? With less than 7 for maghribs? With less than a dozen-2dozen for fajr? With less than 3 dozen for isha, and that's being generous. How can there be a governing body for the masjid in which there is no bodies? How can there be elections or meetings when there is no congregational salat? Why don't they make it a condition that anyone who votes has to come to the masjid twice a day minimum?

Members of a Masjid are those who pray in the masjid. Not those who fill out a sheet and pay a certain amount of money each year. The first reason a Muslim gains a means of transportation is to come to the masjid. Yet the masjid doors aren't even open. There are more security cameras for the masjid than there are Muslims who come for salat. There are more lightposts for the parking lot than there are Muslims who come for salat. There are more toilets in the bathrooms than there are Muslims who come to salat. There are more drains for wudu than their are Muslims who come for slat. There are more paper towel dispensers than there are muslims who come for salat. There are more railings outside the masjid than there are Muslims who come to salat. Yet this ghost masjid has a "System"? Clearly the number 1 priority of an Islamic system would be to have people pray in the masjid for congregational prayers. Why bother with lighting, heating, parking, audio etc when nobody is their to see the lights, feel the heat, use the parking or hear the audio? The hasanat isn't in building a masjid or maintaining it, the hasanat comes from what happens in what is built and what is done with it.

If the prophet Muhammad pbuh were president or Imam or a board member. I don't think he would even consider talking about anything else except the salat in congregation. There is no point in having a masjid at all if people don't come to it and perform the obligatory ibada.

There may be a group calling itself the "Islamic Society of the Niagara Frontier" but where is the Islamic society of Muslims praying fard salat in Masjid Noor? Are they out on the Niagara Frontier or prostrating on the masjid floor?

Sorry if I'm harsh or excessive but I don't think I will be attending Arabic lessons from you anymore. I think you are a bad influence on me. Whether what you are doing is right or wrong the things you say and do have a negative influence on me and cause distress. So that's where I'd rather not be around such influences which have such effects lest it harm my religion.

After sending this email I quickly sent another email saying that I don't think he should read it because I was angry when I wrote it, then I went to the masjid for prayer. At the time Mr. Qadri had been dealing with a foot injury he got on Hajj earlier that year in the city of Mecca where Jews and Christians and all non-Muslims are forbidden to enter due to their disbelief/shirk. So Mr. Qadri had been letting other people lead the prayers and he would sit in the row in a chair instead of leading salat. He could have led the prayers in his chair and all those behind him would've had to pray sitting too but he decided to let others lead the congregational prayers instead until his foot was healed. Immediately after the prayer I fled as fast as I could fearing my offensive email might have hurt our relationship. But to my surprise before I could get out of the masjid, Mr. Qadri ran behind me and caught up to me at the exit despite his severe foot injury. Mr. Qadri told me he had already read my first email before getting the secondary email saying not to read it. However as I review my first email, years later, it was correct aside from a few typos and not as insulting or harsh as I feared, yet the damage to the relationship was done and at that point I stopped learning Tajweed (Arabic pronunciation of Quran) from Mr. Qadri.

Anas ibn Mālik narrated Allāh's Messenger ﷺ said:

"No two people love each other for the sake of Allāh and then fall out except due to a sin one of them commits."

Source: Al-Adab al-Mufrad of al-Bukhārī (no. 401), Grade: Ṣaḥīḥ

Al-Munāwī said in explanation of this ḥadīth:

"The punishment of separation happens due to the sin. This is why Mūsá al-Kāthim said: 'If you see your friend change towards you, know that this is due to a sin that you have committed. So repent to Allāh from every sin and the love between you shall be rectified.'"

Source: Fayḍ al-Qadīr number 7879

I would give other reminders on the topic of Holiday greetings to kuffar and giving gifts as well as other topics as time went by but this book is not meant to be a mere email record so I'm not including every email I sent condemning every bida or error done by Qadri or ISNF for the sake of keeping this book a shorter length. Yet with that said I do feel it appropriate to include an email I sent after witnessing Mr. Qadri refuse to give charity money to a traveling Muslim who ran out of gas for his car when asking for Zakat and/or Sadaqah on ISNF masjid noor property. I alluded to this event in a chapter of my biography called "Big Business Religions" where Mr. Qadri refused to discharge the collected charity funds to a Muslim who was eligible for zakat charity because the "policy" of ISNF board says you can only give out charity in check form. Since the gas station didn't accept checks and banks were closed, the man was forced to beg from the little coinage available in the pockets of those who showed up for salat at that time without getting access to the ISNF treasure chests filled with money within eyesight.

Email Sent Sunday, Feb 28, 2016 at 12:32 PM

Assalaamu Aleikum wa rahmatullaha wa barakatuhu

I hope that you can inform me of some good news regarding the oppression last night. When a traveling revert who's father was on life support was refused aid from a "islamic organization". Despite there being huge money chests, recently filled within plain view for all to see. Why does the masjid accept paper and coin if they aren't willing to distribute paper and coin? Why should someone donate to a masjid who doesn't donate to Muslims in dire need? This organization can pay to put up a Christmas sign, which congratulates all holidays including more than just Christmas such as Kwanza, hanukkah etc. This organization can pay to go door to door giving out Christmas gifts to kafirs on their holiday, as if we the Muslims were paying them Jizya. (that is what it was, that was like jizya paid to kafirs) This organization can put on a banquet and buffet to feed hundreds of kafirs. Yet days later their policy prevents helping a new Muslim who is traveling to visit a dying father? What kind of feeling do you think such a revert will have of Islam and Muslims? What do you think their family will think of Islam? You know there are lots of churches who would be more than glad to help such a person, (since that's basically their only effective form of dawah) but no the masjid doesn't. However it may be that I'm too harsh on those turning away the miskin and possibly the yatim.

So what happened to my brother? You did eventually help my brother and change your policy on following the policy right? The Muslims did practice Islam after I left right? I'm serious to ask this, I'm hoping for good news that help was merely delayed due to our sins and not completely devoid of ever occurring. What will you say to Allah when he asks you about that event and you see it written in your book of deeds and that Muslim is there on the kuntera?

Nevertheless it's good this happened because it was kind of my last straw with this unislamic environment. Changes must be made, the islamic way.

How does one go about changing masjid/board/comittee policies?

Is there a counter board or some type of boarder police?

What do I have to do to change such anti-islamic anti-muslim policies which I see being implemented?

I say "I" because I do not know if there is a "we" option available. To me I don't see no board or society and I don't know of this board or society, they are almost like some mythical phantom which gets blamed for every issue I bring to you. All I know is that there are some presidents who get put in charge as a mouthpiece once in awhile. But then again if this board exists and I went to them maybe they'd just blame you and claim total innocence. Maybe you are the board. Leadership is a diplomatic position, so you may think you have to play on all sides of the fence. I don't play political games because they are rigged and I see no difference between politics and religion. Politics is a new concept invented after the West separated the state and religion. For the majority of the world politics was considered a sub-category of religion. Thus only a religious solution is a valid option for me but I would like to know the theoretical options nonetheless. Afterall if I'm going to keep on complaining I might as well get some answers. Consistently ignoring this will only breed extremism. Muslims get radicalized because of other Muslims being unislamic and not providing options for Islam to flourish and thus out of desperation and disgust such Muslims go haywire and see the sword as the only alternative since diplomacy is made to be completely fruitless unless one compromises their religion.

Who's the board? What's the board? Where's the board? Why is there a board? When was this board created? When will the board retire? Is anyone else beyond bored with the board and willing to get on board with my plans for/on/about/against the board?

That is, besides the Lord. I just ask for logistical reasons and time management.

Does this board have an expiration date? Where it will be replaced by an entirely different political machination after it runs out of steam or time? Or is it self-perpetuating?

In either case if changes cannot be made in an islamic manner then how does one abolish the board and build a new authority structure? Do they allow an option to vote where if X decision passes there are never ever any more votes, elections, polls, ballots again? Basically is it possible to vote to ban and forbid voting?

Who are the essentials and the influentials? That's a rhetorical question, the answer is Allah.

My response to the board is "Allahu Akbar".

What is the islamic basis for this board? Or is it just a copy of American religious organizations infrastructures and dogmas? Was this board imported or made in, by and for the USA?

Institutionally the masjid bureaucracy is structurally unknown and ineffective. When these alleged meetings take place they are not in the masjid and on those days one can see there are more cars in the parking lot than there are people who pray the salat. Churches are organized where everyone knows who is in charge of what and who can change things and who is to blame for things, everybody knows the structure in and out. And the leaders are the most publicly involved in the religious rituals and services, seen and known by all, considered to be the most devout. It's basically just a ladder to climb. The more kufr you do the more control you get.

Also churches have on average 50-150 people attend a daily mass for about an hour, even though it's not an obligatory part of their faith to go to church even once a week let alone 7 times a week.

Furthermore no church would delay their church services 30 minutes in order to talk to some non-Christians. To delay salat for the sake of dawah to kafirs is anti-dawah and makes them think our religion is a joke that we don't take seriously or believe in. Because if God really wanted us to pray at certain times then we would because he is most important. Also he is the one who guides not people. To tell a kafir, "excuse me but it's time to worship our Creator I will be back afterwards" creates a serious impact on their mind that this is a serious religion that the person really believes in so much that they are willing to be socially awkward and impolite in order to pray when their religion tells them to rather than try to convert someone. That has a profound dawah effect showing that we would rather practice our religion than preach because we actually enjoy it, believe in it, implement it and aren't desperate for new members. Plus the imam is the leader of the Muslims, the leader at the time of salat. The prophet saws never delayed salat making Muslims wait in the masjid in order to talk to a kafir, as far as I know. Muslims are not in America to make friends with kafirs or make them like us. Allah has said this will never ever happen, not ever. The only way a kafir will like you is if Allah doesn't. Allah has not lied, so then knowing this do you think Allah will like one to delay the salat which is at fixed times, and split the jamat, in order to please one whom Allah has already said hates you more than you will ever know and will never be pleased with you until you commit kufr?

Muslims in the U.S. fear the kafir more than the kafir fears them. They fear being feared by the kafir but the kafir doesn't fear frightening the believer. Allah is the only being worthy of being feared. After all whence do you think fear comes from? If you don't want kafirs to fear you that much then ask Allah and he will grant it. But never ever think a kafir won't fear Islam. So if they ever don't fear Muslims then it's because we are no longer Muslims who practice Islam.

Also when did the Jaffariya center become a Sunni masjid? Last time I went there it was a shiite masjid and they disbelieved in the Quran, disbelieved in Muhammad saws, slandered Ali and disbelieved in Allah. So why do we publicy advertise them if they haven't changed? Why is MPAC headquarters in the Shia masjid? Is it MPAC, SPAC, KPAC, APAC or just a pack of problems? Which is worse to be friends with kafirs or with Shia? Isn't MPAC friends with all except the salafies?

You've been imam since January 2014. I remember we prayed on a friday then and it was just us 2. Well it's over 2 years later and what progress has been made? The first step after shahada is the salat. So we've gotten some shahadas yet still where's the progress? The people who used to come are no longer coming, I think because they moved. While those who come are in school and will move. Those who come from other cities or states move too because they can't handle the unislamic environment in the masjid and lack of a islamic muslim community. When an occasional traveler comes they are horrified and saddened. The population of those praying is aging and the youth are not filling the ranks. I don't even want to live in this country, so don't think I'm going to have 500 kids to fill the rows. Inshallah my kids won't ever pray in masjid noor, unless of course it's no longer located in America or America becomes a islamic nation. But first we need an islamic masjid before we get an islamic nation. Who will be praying in that masjid in 40 years? Spiders? Or will it be a church by then? Was that why the kafirs came to visit? Yes. There are already days when more kafirs come than Muslims do. And that's the crazy thing is that if you tell Muslims some kafirs are coming to visit the masjid then they'll show up in droves. But if you tell them the salat is being prayed or the prophets teachings are being disseminated or the word of the Creator of the Universe is being recited. Then the spiders come to weave their cobwebs. Yet the spiders will not be brought to account for all their deeds and have them weighed on the scale, nor be forced to cross the siratt, nor be interrogated in the grave and asked 3 questions by angels the faces of which are black and blue.

How can we be Muslims in this time in this place without our own faces being blue and black?

Have you not heard of what has been done to the masjid Al-Aqsa which every single prophet of Allah has prayed a salat in simultaneously all at once?

Allah's houses are being destroyed by the tax dollars Muslims pay. And they pretend they have to pay in order to live in such countries. Yet if they aren't praying the masjid then what life are they living? Can one even consider that to be living? I lived that type of existence and I would never call that living.

While simultaneously Allah's other houses are abandoned while being controlled by those who don't come to pray. More come to play basketball in winter than to answer the call of the athan.

You and I both know there is not 1 single Muslim who prays in masjid noor 5 times a day 7 days a week. And I go to visit my parents sometimes so it's not going to be me, and if you go to school then I don't know how it could be you. So what blessing will a masjid have when not a single member prays there 5 times a day every day of the Islamic hijri year?

There may even be some times when salat is not even prayed at all and the masjid misses salat.

That is an oppression to the house of the almighty. Do you think it will forgive the community?

Are there truly Muslims in America? Where? I just see empty masjids. and a bunch of people who get a long lunch break on fridays.

Of course dua is the cure but one cannot say to make dua without saying "do". Thus what do I or "we" do to restore honor to the house of Allah and implement the rules of the house owner within it?

Email Sent Monday, Feb 29, 2016 at 9:11 PM

I was thinking of something very funny.

You know according to my methodology the organizational structure that I'd desire would be for the imam to be in charge of everything, which would mean you.

So I thought that was ironic because you seem to disagree with my idea of you being in charge.

However then I thought about it and it was even funnier,.

Because if we look at the problems I have with what is going on such as the Christmas sign, giving Christmas gifts etc. You approved and participated in that stuff.

So even if my blueprint for administration was adopted I would still have a problem and many of those problems I have would still exist.

So I have a problem with my own solution to the problems.

Thus that's a fundamental problem. Either I have a fundamental problem or the majority does or it's both or something else.

I just thought that was funny how even if the boards, committees, councils and elections were all abolished I'd still likely have problems.

In such an event then our relationship would probably be even worse because then you'd get 100% of the blame whereas in this current state of affairs you are not 100% to blame, for everything. You're not even 99% to blame. Don't ask me for the true percentage because I don't know what it is only Allah knows who is to blame for what.

The first step towards a solution is identifying the problems.

The 2nd step is knowing how to find a solution and where. Fortunately all Muslims know the how and where. It's just a matter of getting the knowledge followed by implementation and the decree of Allah.

The trickiest part in climbing a mountain is the tiny steps directly in front of you. Most who mess up mess up on those tiny steps, not on knowing their goal and how to get there. Most every mountain climber can see their destination and has a map, equipment and the ability yet not all who attempt the steep ascent reach the goal which they intended.

To take those tiny steps you have to look down and see where you currently are. Then be firm and steadfast when proceeding without tripping, misstepping, falling or allowing your gaze to wander off the path.

It is the exercise gained during the journey that improves the physique of the body, being on top doesn't give one the reward of physical improvement. The spiritual reward in this life and the next therefore lies in the struggle of life e, and is not the victory sit at the top or the glorious view.

Muslims will not get honor when in power if they don't have honor without it. Muslims will not be superior when they have superior firepower if they are not superior without it. Muslims will not be safe or confident when in the majority if they are not safe and confident in the minority. If Muslims care what the kufar think in these conditions then they will care what they think in all conditions, even on the day they meet the judge of judges.

If you want to succeed on the day of judgement then you should die prepared for it so that when you are raised you are raised already prepared. To be prepared one must be mentally prepared to only care what Allah thinks of one without any care for anyone else so that way when raise one will be raised in such a state of total devotion and sincerity. Thus one will be granted total forgiveness and paradise for eternity, inshallah it's both for you and me. But those who live every second in such a condition have such an outcome guaranteed.

Habitually every Friday, despite ISNF refusing to give out money in charity to eligible Muslims they would have representatives of the board walk around during the Bayan before the Khutbah with a money bag for people to donate money to while sitting listening to the lecture. Since the Hanafi madhhab innovated this Bayan lecture prior to giving a Khutbah lecture in non-Arabic speaking lands it technically didn't interrupt the Arabic Friday Jumuah Khutbah to partake and donate, though the method in itself matches what Christians do in churches passing collection baskets around during congregational services and for that reason is prohibited anyways. Yet frequently the ignorant board members of ISNF wouldn't distinguish between a Bayan by Mr. Qadri and an actual Friday Khutbah by any guest speaker. Once a guest speaker was giving the Khutbah and the president of ISNF Rasul Khan starting going around to people with his money bag pestering people to donate and thereby invalidate their prayer. The guest speaker stopped his Khutbah and asked "What are you doing?" and then after realizing what was going on, the guest speaker insisted Mr. Khan sit down on the spot and stop doing that during the Friday prayer sermon, humorously saying there was plenty of time to get donations later and that he promised to finish his Friday Jumuah lecture before it was time for Asr prayer. Afterwards the well-traveled guest lecturer said privately that out of all the masjids he's ever been to anywhere in the world he had never ever seen somebody walk around during a lecture much less the Friday Khutbah asking people for donations. I naturally informed Mr. Qadri how wrong this was but he just looked at me justifying the practice which imitates Christian greed by explaining that technically he gives the Khutbah after the donation basket is passed around so technically it is different and not breaking the Jumuah prayer since it is during a Bayan and not Khutbah when he does it. I disagreed at Mr. Qadri allowing this but dropped the issue despite my detesting of the greedy innovation.

Another error of Mr. Qadri was ignorance of religious matters under the guise of belonging to the Hanafi Madhhab. Once after a funeral Janaza prayer, another Muslim came and asked Mr. Qadri how he broke wudu so had to miss some of it and didn't know what to do when he returned. Mr. Qadri told him to just start over and do it himself individually, which was correct. However then Mr. Qadri shockingly said how if you break wudu during an obligatory salat in the masjid, then you go make wudu and as long as you don't talk to anybody before you return to the prayer you can just return to the same spot in prayer you were in before and don't have to start over from the beginning or make up extra rakats afterward. This was entirely wrong. Everyone knows if you break wudu during prayer by farting or something else then you have to go redo wudu and you start over from the beginning and if it's in the midst of congregational salat then you make up for what you missed at the end by doing the extra rakats afterwards. So witnessing this huge mistake and fearing the person would actually follow it not knowing better, I politely said this doesn't sound right and might just be a Madhhab thing. So Mr. Qadri angrily glared at me for disagreeing with him and asking for evidence. I later learned Mr. Qadri likely got this error in fiqh from a certain book attributed to Abu Hanifa containing a report that could lead one into this error if they didn't know the report was unuseable and contradicted many authentic hadith. Even children who don't even pray daily due to their youth still know that breaking wudu during prayer means you start over from scratch making up stuff later if necessary. Yet Mr. Qadri told people otherwise. To be clear it's just a jurisprudential error but this error I witnessed is huge enough that anyone who followed this advice would have invalid prayers in such scenarios. So Mr. Qadri unwittingly was teaching people anti-Islamic fiqh that no Scholar could have mistakenly fallen into. Sure it's just a mistake, but for Qadri to call himself a Scholar became questionable in my eyes after such a travesty. In comparison in Canada the khateebs would say on the pulpit that they don't know of a single scholar in all of North America, yet according to Qadri he himself was a Scholar just because he took a six year program at a darul uloom school. Classically some true scholars would study 40 years before even giving a single public lecture and then still didn't consider themselves scholars; as its very rare and arrogant for a genuine Muslim scholar to accept the label or use it when referring to themself.

On Friday after fajr April 8th 2016, there were signs posted in the ISNF masjid noor saying to vote in the democratic party primary elections. So being enraged such a sign was at a masjid I took a paper poster sign down but then considered how I got in trouble last time for messing with signs. So I figured before taking the rest of the signs down I would try notifying the imam of the evil of the signs so he would take them down. Since if I took them down because I didn't have authority at the masjid they would likely just get put up again. I emailed the imam 4 emails that day first notifying him how voting was haram(forbidden), then apologizing for taking the signs down without permission and mistakenly thinking they might have been for a Muslim board election which has a different ruling, then retracting my apology and expressing discontent over the signs being up when I found out they and the organization that put them up were the unislamic innovative MPAC organization. The imam never replied and the signs stayed up. After the Khutba ISNF reps announced members of the democratic party were there to register people to vote democrat and many registered.

A annual interfaith "Children of Abraham" style event was also held at the ISNF property where Jews and Christians came for a tri-panel lecture series, sometimes with the heretical Shia in attendance as well. At the masjid a Jew and Christian speaker were allowed to preach/speak to the crowd and then Mr. Qadri gave a speech to the crowd with Jews, Christians, Shiites and Muslim in the audience as well. I didn't attend but as I was sitting in the Musalla area I overheard the speech of Mr. Qadri and I didn't like the speech much. During the Q &A one Christian lady asked the Muslim audience how it would be possible for her and others to adopt Muslim child orphans. She quickly said "not to convert them or anything" but to allegedly show unity and help the Muslim community. Realistically though what is a Christian lady going to do with a Muslim child? When it's time to go to Church will they leave the kid at home alone? Or will they teach it to punctually pray 5 times a day to Allah who they disbelieve in and according to Muhammad's teachings who they don't accept as a prophet? Or will they do what they think is right and guide them to worship Jesus as a son of God or God? Pathetically the Muslims heard her out respectfully despite the clear insulting suggestion of giving Muslim kids over to be raised by non-Muslims. Just imagine the outrage if Muslims went to Churches and asked for Christian orphans to raise in their houses. Theologically Muslims would feel better if Jews raised their kids than Christians because they are less astray in a sense when it comes to anthropomorphism and polytheistic practices. Then the panel was asked what the difference between Sunnis and Shia were and it led to a foolish disaster of non-explanation so as not to cause disunity amongst the panel with all 4 faiths claiming to belong to Abraham. But worst of all the sunset prayer was delayed because people who didn't attend the interfaith lecture didn't know when to call the athan because the event was ongoing within earshot. So knowing I was a bit of a known complainer and fearing instigating trouble if I interrupted the interfaith meeting by calling Athan in the midst of it, as I had done in the past, then I didn't call the athan; but another brother did. When the Athan was called the Muslims left to come to pray. After the prayer, the leader of the MPAC-WNY (Muslim Public Affairs Council)

Khalid Qazi who was a founder of ISNF and masjid noor and organizer of the Interfaith events, came up to the microphone and publicly announced he was embarrassed that the Athan was called while his non-Muslim friends were giving their speech at the masjid thereby interrupting them. Meanwhile Mr. Qazi looked directly at me most of the time he was talking thinking I had called the athan that interrupted them. I almost said something rebuking him until the former president of ISNF, Mr. Yasin, said it was haram/forbidden not to call the athan on time. As hypocritical and dangerous as such statements by Khalid Qazi were it caused a new policy for ISNF to be created where they decided whenever there were Jews/Christians or non-Muslims present to allegedly "learn about Islam" at the masjid or for an interfaith event, the masjid would put a sign on the athan clock covering it up with paper listing the times they would pray instead of the actual times we are supposed to pray with a warning label saying not to call the athan before X time or else. So basically the Muslims delayed the obligatory salat prayer under the pretense of dawah propagation and threatened Muslims in the masjid against calling the athan for the prayer to begin on time under the guise of religious cooperation with others, all the while claiming gratitude to be in America where they can "freely practice and preach Islam". After this atrocious incompetent interfaith event, I sat down with Mr. Qadri and discussed our different approaches to propagating the Islamic faith at length trying to find some common ground before we became disunited. We talked late into the night and decided to have another meeting days later to further discuss in a more organized manner what I perceived as possible creedal differences and methodological aberrations from prophetic Manhaj.

Email Sent Monday, Apr 11, 2016 at 5:04 PM

Assalaamu Aleikum wa rahmatullaha wa barakatuhu

The core question is:
"If my beliefs and message is right and you agree with me, then why does your public message sound so different than mine to the extent that I tell you I disagree with it and don't believe in it?

I think there are 6 fundamental reasons for our differences and my unease with your messages.

1. Different methodologies in that I think the Salafi methodology is the one chosen by Muhammad pbuh and I think I try to follow that whereas I think those are two pages which are not in your playbook, or your practicebook.

2. Confrontationalism

This could also be called publicity of walaa and baraa. But I will will call it confrontationalism.

I explain this somewhat in book by saying:

> *"The thing is we can all be tolerant of persons with different religious opinions but we cannot be tolerant of different religions. There is a difference between peaceful intolerance and violent intolerance and extremist intolerance and violent extremist intolerance. The first 2 are prophetic, the second 2 are satanic. There is no such thing in the prophetic religion as peaceful tolerance. Moses, Jesus and Muhammad pbut taught both peaceful intolerance as well as violent intolerance when certain situations arose. Yet I personally know some Muslims who don't understand what prophetic peaceful intolerance is. So it's more accurate to say Publicly Peaceful Aggressive Intolerance which is sometimes polite depending on the specific person or people one is communicating with. One thing many fail to understand is that while prophets were frequently peaceful, during those peaceful moments they were not always polite. The*

majority of the time prophets interacted with disbelievers they were confrontational. Sometimes the prophets were rudely confrontational but they were politely confrontational more. Rarely were prophets peacefully politely non-confrontational with disbelievers when it came to discussing religion. They would act like that only with people who were genuinely deeply interested in learning about what they believed and preached. Usually the prophets were boldly confrontational because confrontation causes motivation for the one confronted to quickly and correctly resolve the confrontation. Unfortunately many Muslims, particularly in the West, are not confrontational when discussing religion with disbelievers when they should be. While those who are might sometimes be only confrontational, too confrontational or not as polite as they should be because they lack knowledge and manners. Yet overall the world in general, due to secularism, freedom, equality, tolerance, etc, has forgotten that confrontationalism is central to religion. This causes most today to incorrectly mistake confrontational people as extreme just because they are confrontational. The true prophetic religion is only spread by theological confrontation. "

If that is wrong to tell people then correct me, and if it's right then how come you seem more passive than aggressive? Honestly has a non-Muslim in America ever told you about how they felt about you hating them and their religion? How do you know if they even know if they never say so and you never say you do? People do not assume that you hate them, they incorrectly assume only extremists hate people because they have different religious beliefs. So if they don't think you are an extremist then they most probably don't think that you hate them. Whereas to reject taghut means to reject it. It doesn't mean to disagree with it, or keep your personal opinions about it to yourself. It means the followers of taghut know you and them have a problem that will not be resolved until they abandon their taghut and embrace Islam. Public disavowal is a requirement for Muslims if they are to live amongst non-Muslims. Unless they are truly afraid for their safety, and if they are they are obligated to leave and move to another land where they can publicly express disavowal and enmity.

And of course the extremist police say that only extremists use the word taghut or use a siwak. I'm not joking I've read a book by an undercover spy called Omar Nasiri who infiltrated an Al-Qaeda camp in Afghanistan and spied in masjids and he says in his book you can tell someone is a Muslim extremist if they use the word taghut or if they use a stick toothbrush. Or if they mutter prayers with their lips, ie make zikr. Seriously those are the sign of extremism according to this internationally acclaimed undercover spy and expert on Muslim extremism. Oh and another "Muslim" reporter Abdel Bari Atwan who interviewed Osama bin Laden in Tora Bora said that they prayed fajr on time early in the morning, which he was not used to doing. So he wrote in his book that is a sign of extremism because Muslims have a large block of time to pray in and don't have to pray at the earliest times or be that strict, but he knew that they were very religious men how likely wouldn't allow him the option of sleeping in and praying later so he got up and prayed with them. Which he said was actually easy to do because he hadn't slept the night fearing that he was with violent extremists who he feared might kill him if he didn't get up and pray fajr on time.

So this is where the stuff I say I think is islamically correct but you say very similar things as the people who say the stuff that I say and/or do is extremism. So to me it's like you have both opinions except for the other side other side of the coin you tell me you don't quite believe what your statements seem to say. Yet I don't know if that's also what you are saying to the other side of the coin. Basically do you tell the other people who say similar stuff that you don't share their views. Or are they like you and really believe what I believe but everyone is just saying things that seem to mean completely different things than what they believe and Islam teaches, even going so far as to shave or do unislamic activities and promote unislamic things? Is there some secret memo which all the Muslims except me that says "Lets tell the Kafirs X and act like X even though we all really believe in Y"? I never got such a memo, so I'm just like "What the heck is everyone doing?"

3. Difference of opinion regarding political, economic and historical realities. As well as solutions to those modern realities.

This regards our views on emigration, taxation, political actions and participation or non-participation in various political, social or religious events. Ex. Flags, Potlucks, Voting.

4. Difference of opinion regarding Kufar

This applies to their status, their intentions, their religions, and their potential and how to treat them.

5. Difference of opinion regarding how to view our differences of opinion.

We disagree on how serious our differences of opinion in these matters are allowed to be and whether certain differences are valid to have.

For instance some of our differences I don't think we can islamically disagree on while others I consider to be potentially valid but to be huge major grave extreme differences.

6. Difference of opinion regarding the status of Muslims and priorities they should have

This relates to point 3 somewhat as well as takfir. While the takfirish element of this point is what makes all these differences much more important and also relates to point 5.

For instance I don't think the Khawarij are a real problem in America but think the real problem is Muslims being in America #1 and then #2 deviance, disobedience and underboard extremism of those Muslims, that is if all who claim to be Muslims can be considered Muslims.

Which I think such a statement itself would alarm you since "that's one of the signs to be on the watch for". Yet I tell you this type of stuff and you don't show alarm which makes mes wonder if there really is alarm but you don't want me to get alarmed at your alarm. And that makes me get alarmed, because if I'm right then why do these differences persist? And *if I'm wrong then why do they persist without you proving me wrong? Which again relates to number 5 as the cycle continues and the plot thickens as events take place and more info is learned.*

It is my personal opinion that you are not as confrontational with Muslims and non-Muslims as you should be. Whereas that is the root cause of extremism. Because extremism and ignorance of all types is not confronted with equal zeal it leads some types of ignorance and extremism to make gains against other types of ignorance and extremism. Whereas if you have the knowledge then if you just add extra passion then presto that solves the problem as long as one can maintain such energy over time without becoming extreme or letting the passion become unhealthy. If you are not confrontational then extremism will flourish because they will be confrontational, especially in democracies where whoever has the most Charisma is thought to be the most correct. Because the fundamental issue is the ignorant people consisting of disbelievers and Muslims of all types of extremism and ignorance have more passion and emotional zeal than many of those who are more knowledgeable. All the prophets had both the knowledge and the enthusiastic passion to consistently inflame the passions of believers and disbelievers alike. You could not possibly interact with a prophet without some serious emotions getting stirred causing one to take action whether they were believer or disbeliever.

Thus the people of knowledge must get more passion and energy than the underboard extremists such as the murjiya and get more confrontational than the overboard extremists like the Khawarrij.

So for you I suggest more emotionalism + more confrontationalism + more energy to make sure one doesn't get burned out or let the passion be blinding or corrupting or cause arrogance or negligence.

That last bit is my advice, take it or leave it and/or pass it on to others who could benefit from it.

We had the meeting as scheduled but no great breakthroughs were achieved. Although Mr. Qadri did confirm in these meetings that he knows the last verse of Fatihah refers to Allah being Angry/Wrathful with Jews and Christians primarily being astray and deviant. However we seemed to be stuck on an issue dealing with Love and Hate, which is a vital aspect of Islamic Creed.

So I emailed the following explaining my position after hearing a remark of Mr. Qadri saying to "hate the sin but not the sinner" which is dangerously ignorant to say publicly let alone believe as a creed.

Email Sent Monday, Jun 13, 2016 at 6:07 PM

Assalaamu Aleikum wa rahmatullaha wa barakatuhu

Before voicing my opinion and religious belief I will cut to the conclusion.

Please provide me with 1 ayat of the Quran or 1 authentic hadith or 1 statement of a sahabah which teaches "hate the sin but not the sinner". This belief and doctrine is not from Islam, in my opinion. Following are my reasons and some proofs as to why which I've included in my book. So I am expressly writing in my book that Islam teaches to hate the sinner as a person as well as to hate their sins. (there is a difference between kafirs and Muslims though) However again I think we have different definitions of kafir. I think you seem to frequently use the technical meaning of kafir with the farmer definition instead of the shariah definition. Whereas for me everyone who is sane and mature and has not said the shahada is a kafir, generally there may be some exceptions like one who doesn't know the phrase or physically cannot say it so there might some exceptions but I think you understand what I mean in that if one does not consider themself a Muslim then they aren't. Ignorance doesn't free one from the kafir label, unless one is an ignorant Muslim. The word "non-Muslim" does not exist in Arabic, as far as I know, and the Sahabah called every "non-Muslim" a kafir or a mushrik or an enemy of God if they were upset. The kafirs didn't like being called this, but Muslims called them it anyways even though the kafirs didn't like the term. There are different levels of kafir but all who are not Muslims are kafirs. Hypocrisy applies to both groups and can range from being a sin to a type of kufr. Some kafirs who die in total ignorance devoid of opportunity to embrace Islam get a special test but they are still legally kafirs. Whereas to prove the farmer definition is invalid, inheritance is sufficient. You would not say an ignorant non-Muslim can inherit from a Muslim because they aren't really a kafir because "a kafir lingustically refers to a farmer who hides something in the ground". Thus if they can't inherit from a Muslim relative then they are kafirs, or insane or criminals or maybe some other loopholes; but you know what I mean and this is trailing off topic. First we must establish the principle of hating a kafir before defining a kafir.

Before including what I write in book I think I should address another related matter. Frequently you say we should act like the Muslims did in Mecca. But they were in Mecca 13 years and they acted very differently at different periods. At first they whispered Islam in secret. Obviously we are not whispering so we can't use that time as our example. Once Umar joined they went public and they expressed enmity and even got into physical confrontations in Mecca. Politically they were stating a revolution and they publicly expressed hatred even before Umar became a Muslim, and he was number 39, 40 or 41. Thus I conclude that if we have more than 39 Muslims then publicly expressing hatred is the way. But then you might cite the incident of Abu Hurayra and his mother. That was in Medinah though, not Mecca so you can't use that if you are to say Muslims in the minority should act like we're in Mecca. Furthermore Abu Hurayra's dawah to his mother didn't work. She only became Muslim because the prophet pbuh made dua and Allah guided her. The kind treatment didn't do it for her. Whereas the public expression of hate as I think Abu Dar had for his tribe did work and there are many examples of the sahabah having intolerant interactions that led to conversions. Plus in Mecca Hamza wacked Abu Jahl in the head and was not reprimanded by the prophet saws for doing that. Bilal spat on an idol, which led to his famous torture and was not reprimanded for doing that. When Muslims would express hatred for Islam at the Kaba and get beat up, and do so repeatedly the prophet pbuh did not stop them or say it was "unwise". Umar got repeatedly beat up on his first day as a Muslim because he made it clear he now hated all who weren't Muslims and was their enemy. Although this is another issue, I'm just going into it a little to show that expressing hate does not hurt dawah, it actually helps especially in areas where people don't think religion is important. All religions thrive off of hatred. It is because of hating disbelievers that people try to convert them, because one hates hating people. The greater the hate for non-members, the greater the psychological need to convert others to your faith.

Yet if they don't hate and hate does not affect their interactions or attitudes they will not care to do what is necessary to change the religious demographic they live in. So I guess I'm saying "embrace the hate". Allah loves those who hate for his sake and express their hatred publicly.

Below is book excerpt, Please correct if wrong since if you don't my beliefs may be published:

> "Tragically some people espouse a doctrine of "hate the sin, but not the sinner". This was not taught by any prophet. It is not taught by Judaism, Christianity, Hinduism, Buddhism or any traditional religion and most certainly it is not taught by Islam. Some Christians may think Christianity teaches this but those who think this don't know the bible. This "love everybody no matter how bad they are" doctrine is the very doctrine of Satan himself and I can prove it is satanic. As an example consider the "sinner" known to history as Adolf Hitler. Now do Muslims love Adolf Hitler but hate his sins? No we hate him and his sins. The same applies to the Shia Iranian Ayatollah Khomeini. Likewise for Osama bin Laden. The same rule goes for Ghandi, the Popes and Martin Luther King Jr. Muslims even hate Abu Talib, who was the uncle of Muhammad pbuh and his guardian since the age of 8 who raised him and protected him from his

enemies until he died when Muhammad pbuh was 50 years old. I must admit that Abu Talib was very kind to Muslims and helped them very much, but he never embraced Islam because he feared his idolatrous family members would make fun of him. Thus Abu Talib died as a disbeliever despite Muhammad's deepest desires that he embrace Islam. As a result, even though Muhammad pbuh really cared about Abu Talib and was greatly assisted by him throughout his life he made it publicly known that Abu Talib will be in the hellfire forever and he didn't attend his own uncle's funeral. Muhammad pbuh wished Abu Talib had become a Muslim but he didn't, so Muhammad pbuh hated him even though he always treated him kindly as his closest relative. Likewise despite Abu Talib never harming Muslims and even aiding Muslims and Islam, all Muslims hate Abu Talib because he never accepted Islam and died as an idol worshipper. He was a very moral man but his sin of disbelief requires him to be hated. So because Allah hates him Muslims hate him too. Nobody would dare to say "I love Abu Talib but hate his sins", this would be blasphemous for a Muslim to think, unless they were a complete fool and didn't know better. I covered this principle of hate and it's limits on page 350-351, but it is important to reiterate *for Muslims. There is not a single verse in the Quran, not 1 authentic hadith and no statements from any companions of Muhammad pbuh which teach this doctrine of "Hate the sin, but not the sinner." Whereas there are many verses in the Quran, many hadith and every single Sahabah taught Muslims to hate people based on them being disbelievers alone. Sins also justify hating someone, but different sins are given different values and good deeds counterbalance the sins as well. Although it is a tilted scale where belief or disbelief determines the final outcome. This is how it is with God too. God hates all sinners because of their sins, like disbelief. Whereas God loves all believers because of their good deeds, like belief. Yet the weight of our scales constantly fluctuate as long as we are alive and circumstances can change the weight of our deeds/sins. For example repentance can forgive one's sins while to disbelieve eliminates any and all credit for one's good deeds. While major sins and minor sins can erase some good deeds and some good deeds can erase minor sins, with repentance being needed for major sins and belief being needed to forgive the sin of disbelief. Yet major sins can become disbelief and minor sins can become major sins so it's a very complex relationship each individual has with God and it fluctuates until we die. Regardless though God loves those on the side of belief and hates those on the side of disbelief, and aside from these two criterion God hates sinners for their sins. Although as it concerns believers God's love for them outweighs the hate God has for them because of their sins. God might still punish them for those sins but there is still love there, but the disbeliever has no love from God until they believe. However humans are not God, but the revelations and prophets God sent us tell us to love what God hates and hate what God hates. Thus God wants us to hate the sins and to hate the sinners, even if they are believers, but with believers our love for their belief likewise outweighs our hate for them because of their sin, so we love believers more than we hate them. Yet the true slaves of God hate all sinners, even themselves. Of course prophets are the exception because since God forgives all their sins it means God does not hate prophets thus believers cannot hate prophets even an iota nor any other specific person God expressed his love for; although such a love has not been made known for anyone on earth today. Therefore technically we should all hate everybody a tiny bit, because they sin but if they believe then our love for them is greater than the hate, while if they disbelieve then our hate will overpower any emotional affection they or Satan may inspire us to have towards them. Yet again I must stress that having hate does not mean being nasty or hurtful. It is a prophetic hatred that is peaceful in most instances, except during war. The "Hate the sin, but not the sinner" doctrine is not from God, his revelations, nor his prophets, but is the doctrine taught by Freemasons which was incorporated into the composite faith of Americanism and adopted by interfaith secularists and the religiously ignorant. It might sound clever, cute and tolerant but it's a satanic false doctrine. Unfortunately once I heard this doctrine preached by a public speaker in a masjid when commenting on a Muslim extremist shooting up a club of sodomites. Afterwards in private I informed the Muslim speaker that this doctrine is not Islamic and asked him for a single verse from the Quran, authentic hadith or a statement of a sahabah to justify such a doctrine. I then sent him what I wrote about this doctrine being unislamic in this book. Thus far I've not been given any proof that justifies their statement, nor have they refuted my position so since they haven't told me I was wrong when I asked them too then it can only mean that I'm right, on this issue of hating the sinner and the disbelievers as persons because of their sins.*

Muslims agree the companions of the prophet pbuh were much better than us and practiced Islam the best since they were taught directly by the prophet pbuh. Also the Arabs at that time had extremely strong family ties, they would fight wars for their family members even if they were wrong, just because they were family and loved each other. However when Arabs in Mecca embraced Islam they were horribly persecuted. Why? Is it because the early Muslims were bad mannered? No they had the best of manners and best behavior, better than all Muslims alive today. Why then did the super close Arab families have such animosity towards the Muslims? It is because of the animosity and hatred the Muslims expressed for idolatry and idolaters. They made their hatred known and got persecuted for having such religiously intolerant and politically/economically/socially threatening ideas that forced a spiritual, economic, political and social clash.

For contextual reasons on page 350-351 I had the following info:

> "Off topic let me explain the hate relationship, because some claim Islam teaches hate. Let's say you "love" your spouse, they tell you they hate so and so because of such and such. Now if you say anything that's not in

agreement with them you'd be in big trouble. If you said "oh but I love so and so" you might be left without a spouse or kicked out of the house. It's impossible for a person to love something and simultaneously love what their beloved hates. The heart cannot have conflicting loves. Even on a personal level, many times spouses eating together in a restaurant tell the server, "I'll have the same thing they're having" because they love what that person loves and hate what that person hates, so they automatically trust they will be satisfied eating whatever that person chooses to eat. The same goes for nationalism, when one has "love for one's country" that also means hating who that country hates, which is typically determined by who the government says to hate. Yet when it comes to God frequently people have a delusion that God doesn't hate anything ignoring all the evidence to the contrary. As it relates to Islam, a Muslim loves God; therefore a Muslim loves what God loves. However there are things God hates, so if a Muslim really loves God they must also hate what God hates. Some examples of what God hates include: Satan, the friends of Satan, corruption, sin, idolatry, falsehood, tyranny, oppressors, injustice, greed, liars. Who in their right mind wouldn't hate these things? You cannot truly love God until you hate what

God hates. If God makes clear his hatred for ____ and you say "oh but I love ____" do you think God will love you while you love what he hates? Loving what God hates may make God hate you and is tantamount to you hating God. A person cannot love God and the prophets of God while loving the enemies of God and the enemies of the prophets. If you were to love an "enemy of the state" the state would consider you an enemy and punish you, so what do you think God will think of and do to someone who loves his enemies? Examples of enemies would be: the Pharaoh who rejected Moses pbuh or the Goliath who fought David pbuh. The same goes for hating the prophets, someone who hates or slanders even one prophet would be hating God simultaneously; whether they know it or not. A true friend wouldn't be a friend with your enemy, if they were no sane person would keep them as a friend. This is a leveraged relationship, in that the more you love God the more you hate Satan, and the more you love the friends of God (the prophets and believers) the more you hate the enemies of God (the friends of Satan and the disbelievers). Examples of specific people whom we are obligated to hate today would be the antichrist and the peoples of Gog and Magog. Some think one should just hate the sin but love the sinner. This notion is wrong. For instance no believer would say: "I love Pharaoh, but I hate what he did to Moses pbuh", or "I love Goliath but I just hate what he did to David pbuh" or "I love the antichrist but I just hate the sins that he commits." One cannot separate the sins from the sinner who did them. Now of course this doesn't mean if someone on God's team sins then they should be hated as enemies of God. Different sins result in different amounts of hate. Think of it like 2 rival sports teams. A sports fan loves everyone on their team and hates everyone on the rival team by default. No matter what a player on the rival team does that's good the true fan will always hate them because of their team. Likewise the sports fan will always love their team's players even if they do bad things, in such cases they will hate the bad things their team's players do but their love for the players supersedes the hate for their team members mistakes. Whereas their hate for the rival team overpowers any good that the rival team member may do. Thus believers love all believers and hate all disbelievers, while they may have some hate for believers but such hate is due to their sins only. Therefore one is to love the believer, and hate the disbeliever, love the good deed and hate the sin. Whereas religion is the heaviest weight that determines the main attitude one will have, so whether someone is a believer or a disbeliever accounts for over 99% of a believer's attitude towards that person. So it's similar to how a sports fan hates their team when they make a foolish mistake and or lose the game, but that hate is very miniscule whereas the hatred for the rival team(s) is always strong even if they where to beat another rival team and in doing so ended up benefiting the fan's team some way. Regarding religions take Mother Teresa and Mahatma Gandhi, currently these are revered by many as having been pious virtuous people, yet one was a Christian and the other a Hindu. Now in God's view there is no way both could ever be loved by God if they were on different teams. They both could be hated if those 2 teams were rivals to the believing team but it's impossible for God to have loved both and thus a believer can never love both regardless of how many good things they may have done; a believer would have to hate one or the other or both. Those people in the highest ranks of paradise are the prophets because they are the best friends of God who hate Satan and disbelief and disbelievers the most. While those in the lowest level of hellfire are the best friends of Satan who hate God and belief the most. May we be registered amongst the friends of God and not the friends of Satan. The

English translation of the New International Version of the Bible also teaches this:"

After the first paragraph I included from chap 24 in email, in later chap 24 I write :

"Whenever a prophet was sent to teach the religion of God, it disrupted society on nearly every level. Every person in every community was in an uproar and socially distressed that an intolerance for the ancient and popular ways of believing and living was being expressed by the followers of God's prophets. The pagan complaint was always the same in that, "Everyone was getting along just fine in perfect harmony until this "prophet" starting spewing hatred for our religions and customs. They are publicly judging us as evil teaching our own flesh and blood to hate us and saying we have to accept their religion and practices or burn in hell for eternity. Personally they are very moral and pious, but polite and peaceful as they are their teachings are very offensive and intolerant. They are saying that God hates those who have a different religion than them and that their followers should hate non-members just as their God does." All religions thrive off of hatred. It is because of hating disbelievers that people try to convert them, because one naturally hates hating people they live and

interact with. Yet if they don't hate and hate does not affect their interactions or attitudes they will not care to do what is necessary to change the religious demographic they live in. So for a religion to spread it's members must publicly espouse hatred for all who don't belong believe as they do. Everyone knew the prophets hated disbelief and disbelievers and that's why the disbelievers gave importance to their message of Islam, because the hate preachers demand attention. You can't hear someone saying "I hate you because of your beliefs" and then completely ignore their message. If you preach hate then people will listen and it forces the matter to be decided as either you are right or wrong, but whatever you are the matter will be known by all as important to discuss and decide upon. Without the public expression of hate then Islam is not important for the non-Muslims to worry about. Nobody likes to be hated, if disbelievers knew Muslims hate them for being disbelievers they will see they have an important decision to make and have motivation to make it. But if you don't preach hate then they don't care since you aren't bothering them in anyway, because it's not personal. The hate must be personal to cause persons to make important personal decisions regarding their choice of religion. If it's not personal people don't think it's important. So they don't care if you hate their religion, but if they know you hate them personally then there is a potential for a serious conversation that will result in serious actions one way or the other. But remember expressing hatred must be done the prophetic way, because we aren't hating for personal reasons we are hating for God's sake. Thus we express hatred for disbelief and disbelievers publicly because God likes such public enmity for what and those he hates. So that Muslims in the West today who act worse than the Sahabah do, to people who have place less value on social ties than the Arab idolaters did means that logically we should be getting persecuted much worse than the early Muslims did. Yet we are not because most Muslims are not letting the disbelievers know we hate disbelief and disbelievers the way the early Muslims did. Honestly many Muslims don't care as much as they should that people disbelieve in God and are on the road to hellfire. They don't see it as their personal problem and neglect their duty to help guide their fellow human being. This is why Islam is not spreading as it did back then, because Muslims are afraid of having dramatic religious confrontations that disrupt social pleasantries. Many fear persecution of people more than they fear concealing the truth which God has commanded Muslims to make known, publicly to everyone in every place. (Note I did not say every time is the best time, certain times are better than others, but the place and the people don't matter.) The problem is ignorant hate preachers and extremist hate preachers give hate preaching a bad reputation. The key to being a "hate preacher" is to do it the prophetic way, otherwise it would be dangerously satanic. Such is it with most things in life, we either do it correctly the prophetic way or the satanic way. All prophets were "hate preachers" but the way they did it was different than the way many today do it, yet there was public hatred there. Everyone knew the prophets were not pleased with those who rejected their prophethood or believed in another religion. Thus the disbelievers were not pleased with the prophets, even if they didn't combat the true faith. However the prophets didn't care if anyone was pleased with them, their job and our job is to worship and please God. The prophets didn't pretend or hide their true feelings from people, they felt how God felt about them and their falsehood, said how they felt and treated them the way God said to treat them. We must do the same today."

Now that's what I wrote but I'm still looking into this to check to see if my beliefs are extreme. I don't think they are thus far. Currently still reading pdfs by Muhammad Saeed Al Qahtani about Wala and Bara according to the aqeedah of the salaf. Which is the aqeedah of all Muslims, since madhabs don't have different aqeedahs, or so I'm told. In part 2, which I've attached, his chapter 7 lists 20 types of "Alliance with the disbelievers" which are forbidden in Islam. They are:

1. Contentment with the disbelievers

2. Reliance on the disbelievers

3. Agree with Points of Disbelief

4. <u>Seeking the affection of the disbelievers</u>

5. Inclining towards the disbelievers

6. <u>Flattery of the Disbeliever's faith</u>

7. Taking of Disbelievers as Friends

8. Obedience to the Disbelievers

9. To Sit with Disbelievers who Ridicule the Qur'an

10. To Give the Disbelievers Authority over Muslims

11. <u>Trusting the Disbelievers</u>

12. <u>To Express Pleasure with the Actions of the Disbelievers</u>

13. *To Draw Near to the Disbelievers*

14. *To Aid the Disbelievers in Wrongdoing*

15. To Seek the Advice of Disbelievers

16. *To Honour the Disbelievers*

17. *To Live amongst the Disbelievers*

18. To Collude with the Disbelievers

19. To Revile the Muslims and Love the Disbelievers

20. *To Support the Ideologies of the Disbelievers*

Then after lengthily explaining each type he writes:

Acceptable and Unacceptable Excuses:

Some of those who ally themselves with the disbelievers excuse themselves saying that they were afraid for their jobs, material well being, social status and so forth. These are all unacceptable excuses and reveal nothing more than a fondness for this world and its pleasures. Allah does not excuse anyone who openly acknowledges loyalty to the disbelievers, obeys them willingly or endorses their religion, except for those who have been forced. He says:"Whoever disbelieves after Faith, except for those who have been forced and whose hearts are reinforced with Faith, and who opens his breast to disbelief, on them is the wrath of Allah and theirs is an awful punishment. They *preferred the life of this world to the Hereafter. Allah does not guide a disbelieving people" and He it said,*

*"The believers shall not take the disbelievers as allies in preference to the believers. Whoever does this shall never be helped by Allah in any way, except if you indeed fear a danger from them." As for feeling love in the heart, this can not be forced upon anyone. Inclining inwardly towards the disbelievers can not be the result of coercion since no one knows what is in the heart of another. As long as, (the heart is reinforced by Faith) as Allah says, it is impossible to truly favour them. Whoever does is always a disbeliever. If <u>they</u> <u>**overtly declare support** for them and **act accordingly**</u>, then they are disbelievers whose fate is eternal damnation. <u>But if,</u> while favouring them in their hearts, <u>they **neither declare it** **nor act upon it**</u> and appear to live according to Islam, <u>then they are hypocrites</u> whose fate lies in the darkest pit of hell.*

Now to me I feel that some people are "overtly declaring support" for disbelievers. This is not allowed, even if kafirs get killed by criminals. Also I feel a US flag being in the masjid is an overt declaration combined with an according action, at the very least it is honor to the disbelievers of their religious icon which is a religious icon as defined by the US Supreme Court. We can be a hypocrite doomed to hell even if we don't declare or act upon such sentiments. Yet to me it seems that not only do such forbidden sentiments exist but they are combined with public declaration and actions. Plus paying taxes speaks for itself, that is an overt action of financial support. However one may be forced but such "force" is very rare and most direct taxation is voluntary. I'm not going into takfir, I'm just saying my beliefs are that the beliefs being publicly promoted and espoused at the masjid are false, forbidden and satanic.

So please correct me if I'm wrong but it is my religious belief that it is obligatory to hate the sinner, especially if they are a kafir. It doesn't mean kill them or harm them. But we must hate them vehemently and express such hatred publicly. Or if one is a coward then they can be silent without any statements or actions of alliance. But Islam will not spread until we believe and apply it without fear of consequences. If they don't like being hated by us then they can change their religion and become Muslims. At the very least they will care about Islam. If we don't like saying we hate them then we can change our geographical location. When Muslims lose their hatred for what and who Allah hates then they lose this world and the next. If they say "you catch more flies with honey than vinegar" you say we ain't trying to catch people but guide people with something sweeter than honey for those whom Allah favors/guides and something more bitter than vinegar for those whom Allah allows to go astray. Flies are better than the kafirs who we try to guide, but we try to guide for the hasanat *and only to please Allah. Even if we do a bad job Allah will guide whom he wills, we cannot prevent them from accepting Islam. We must at least stop preaching doctrines that are contrary to Islam but pleasing to a kafir ear.*

Another character entered my life around this point in time. This new character's name was Joel and he was a non-Muslim who I met in the masjid that was interested in learning more about Islam. Joel also, like me, had trained to be a Catholic Priest and almost became a Benedictine monk before he learned about the falsehood of Christianity and Catholicism due to the information he was exposed to. I would typically meet with Joel on a weekly basis in the masjid, without a schedule, and we emailed back and forth. A few months later Joel also decided to become a Muslim. Prior to him nobody I personally invited to Islam had accepted the message to my knowledge, so I took seriously the responsibility of teaching my newfound friend what I knew, but he was a very smart person to start with and was a fast learner who seemed eager to implement Islam. I had met many other reverts/converts to Islam but all of them had become Muslim before I met them so I felt this was a special friend because of the chance of getting partial credit myself for any good deeds he did in Islam due to inviting Joel to Islam's prophetic truth.

During Ramadan 2016 in response to an Orlando, Florida gay club being shot up by ISIS the local Western New York ISNF masjid noor put up a billboard outside the masjid saying they pray for the Orlando victims. I and others took objection to this haram sign as it is forbidden to pray for dead kafirs regardless of how they died. Eventually the billboard was removed from the premises days later, likely after the renting agreement expired.

My condemnation of their condemnation was as follows, and you might notice I don't include Mr. Qadri's replies when I share my emails that I sent to him. That's because I wasn't getting any replies. At the time that seemed fine since I was seeing Qadri nearly 5 times a day it didn't seem like a red flag. Besides some phrases from emails I sent to Qadri would be quoted by him in his public lectures. So, I did not require email replies and since Qadri would use my email material as some of his own then I didn't care to get credit for some of his preaching. I felt Qadri was reading my emails but just didn't have time to respond scholastically to each email.

Email Sent Wednesday, Jun 15, 2016 at 8:35 PM

Assalaamu Aleikum wa rahmatullaha wa barakatuhu

I saw a sign outside the masjid.

It looks like a sign of the end of time.

I think I already refuted it in my prior email before it was put up.

Surely you know the praying for kafir dead is wrong and consoling kafirs in such a way is not part of the sunnah.

We both know the unislamic intentions behind the sign. Just doing something for Islam does not mean it's permissible or that it's helping Islam. Such signs may be put up in response to extremist attacks but personally such signs themselves to be extremist attacks.

Did you know Muslims are getting killed every hour?

Do you care about them? Really do you really care?

Because they need money for food and water since their

oppressors in multiple countries restrict their food and water supplies.

So whatever you think about the sign from a religious aspect, of which it's so haram to me I don't even want to have to explain all the reasons because it'd be repetitive and voluminous even for me, just consider the financial aspect.

Allah will ask those responsible what they did with every penny they were responsible for when the Ummah was crying, starving, bleeding and dying. Those oppressed Muslims will be there on Qiyamma raised in a state of abandonment. They will be waiting on the Kuntera preventing people from entering paradise until their are recompensed for their rights which we violated by paying for such signs instead of taking care of the rights of our true brothers and sisters who are the real victims. We are making Muslims victims by attempts to please the kufar.

No dead victim is going to see that sign, and I don't think any family member of a victim is going to see that sign.

Who is that sign for? What is it's purpose? Is someone going to become a Muslim after seeing it?

To me it's a big fat expensive "I'm sorry. Please don't think we are terrorists anymore."

This is NOT what the prophet saws did in Mecca nor Medinah. This is NOT the Sunnah.

Honestly do you think that Muhammad pbuh if he were the Imam would approve such a thing under the circumstances the

Ummah is in today? Would Abu Bakr? Would Umar? Would Abu Ubeidah?

Why do you think none of the reverts ever suggest such interfaith pandering? Because we know what the kafirs think of it. The signs won't even have the effect people think they'll have. So the "benefit" only exists in the warped Muslim mind and it really isn't a benefit it just further gives you an inferiority complex. Consider my whole family consists of Kufar. I don't get extra points with them for having the attitudes and beliefs I have and if your style is Islamically correct then I would be more inclined to use such an approach then you because I would in theory get more worldly benefit from such an approach than you would. But I don't take that approach because it is wrong, if it's right then prove it to me and I'll take it because it'd be a lot easier to do in theory. Yet in reality it's not easier because the prophet saws always took the easier path of permissible options and his dawah was not like your dawah or ISNF dawah. Just saying theoretically I'd be more likely than you to convey your dawah approach and message. So then why don't I? There are more reasons for a revert to use your approach than a non-revert so why don't reverts use it? We could and we choose not to for very important and Islamic reasons. We are not trying to make things difficult for ourselves, we are trying to practice Islam but Muslims are making it difficult and you can verify this by asking reverts whether Muslims help or hinder their dawah.

When fatwas were passed in the Muslim world permitting Muslims to come to America, they did not tell Muslims they could come to America and do such shameful crazy nonsense. Imagine if you were living in the Middle East and got 1,000 people and wanted to come to America for dawah and went to a scholar there and said "We're going to build a masjid in America and during Ramadan we're going to spend money to put up a sign that says _____" We both know every single scholar would tell such a group 1. Don't go. 2. Don't put up such a sign. 3. Study Islam so you understand how Islam says we are to feel, view and treat the kufar as well as how to do dawah according to Islam.

Are you an American or are you a Muslim? The citizenship/passport doesn't determine either.

Honestly ask and answer yourself as to whether you felt more stress hearing a bomb was dropped on Muslims in Syria, which is happening every day. Or whether you felt more distress hearing sodomite kafirs got killed in Orlando. If you are a Muslim the Muslims getting killed in Palestine, Syria, Mali, CAR, Kashmir, Afghanistan and Allah knows best all the other places should be much more disturbing and distressing than an American shooting of kufar.

Ask yourself which headline affected you more?

Which news reports cause more emotions?

Which crimes cause you to take actions that you wouldn't have taken otherwise?

Which crimes cause you to say things you wouldn't say if they didn't happen?

Which crimes cause you to make duas which you wouldn't make otherwise?

Which death affects you more in your personal and public life?

The death of a Muslim living far away or a Kafir living in a non-Muslim Western country?

If you felt more distress because the shooter was called a Muslim then you really don't feel genuine distress but are just distressed because of what the Kufar will think of you. Personally I'm guessing (not accusing) you don't really care as much about the Kafirs dying as you do about what the living Kufar will think of you, the Muslims, or Islam as a result of those kafirs dying. This is a problem. All must stop caring about the Kafir opinion and only care about Allah's opinion. You should not even care about my opinion either, not that I'm saying you do. Although Islamically a Muslims opinion is much more important than a kafirs, they are not equal. Yet human opinions are nothing to Allah's.

Surely that sign is a sign of the end of time. A minor sign that is wrong in a major way.

However what was worse was a sign inside the masjid which was put up before another Interfaith Abrahamic pluralism type of gathering which said stuff about how Islam condemns all hatred or inequality based on religion, sexuality, gender etc., and worst of all if I correctly recall that "no faith has a monopoly on salvation". To which I thought it was kufr/disbelief because Islam does teach hatred for kuffar and inequality for various reasons including those the sign said it didn't and every Muslim is obligated to believe that no salvation is found outside of Islam. I felt obliged to email again.

Email Sent Thursday, Jun 16, 2016 at 8:01 PM

Assalaamu Aleikum wa rahmatullaha wa barakatuhu

I'm very worried.

In my opinion there are clear cut statements of Kufr on the ISNF paper on the easel right outside your office.

Did you read that? I'm convinced that even you will agree there are statements of kufr on it which Muslims are not allowed to say.

I'm not going to quote it because if you read it then you should know. But if you read it and you don't then I might have a problem praying behind you. I really think you have to read that paper. Either it has statements of Kufr that must not be said/written or I'm an idiot extremist.

It is now at that point, either it's kufr or I'm stupid.

If I'm mistaken, which would be better for the Ummah for me to be in the wrong in this regard rather than have the others wrong, then we must have a long talk because I must not understand Islam.

To be clear I'm not saying those making the statements are kafirs, ignorance is an excuse.

But I am saying that paper says stuff that is haram and kufr, please rectify the situation by correcting the misconceptions of Muslims. Whether the misconceptions are mine or others.

Either I have to stop my dawah because it's unislamic or others have to adjust/stop their dawah.

Somebody clearly is doing haram dawah, maybe both but the 2 sides are teaching contradictory messages. Islam cannot teach what I believe and say and what ISNF is saying.

Someone must be corrected, if it's me then hurry up and correct me already. If it's not then hurry up even more.

After I emailed and personally told Mr. Qadri my views on June 17th, 2016 we met at the very unislamic easel sign, and he laughed at it taking a picture of it with his phone after I said these public statements are disbelief in Islam. Immediately we had a private conversation in his office and Mr. Qadri said Islam doesn't teach hatred for anybody and that God loves everybody. I asked, *"What about Pharaoh?"* and he said God loves pharaoh too. This statement of his was kufr/disbelief so afterwards I emailed fatwas explaining it's obligatory to hate sinners, even Muslim sinners and fatwas forbidding the "Abrahamic faiths" interfaith movements. I didn't consider Qadri a kafir though, just confused and incorrectly mistaken. So, I sent fatwas in email and continued admonishing him including a list of grievances which I desperately wanted to solve.

Email Sent Sunday, Jun 19, 2016 at 11:21 AM

There are things which I've considered that has led my attitude towards you to change.

I will list in number form although the order is not the order they have come in.

1. You yourself admitted the sign at the road is wrong and "will be changed". So we agree it is wrong, yet it has not been changed. So it's haram and you permit it despite believing it's haram. You said it would be changed over 24 hours ago? Yet when I changed the Christmas sign, improving it adding an islamic message to be kind and nice, that gets changed within hours. So why this double standard? How come my islamic improvement to a haram sign gets changed? But the haram sign takes so long? Do you think Muhammad pbuh would permit that sign to be up for over 24 hours after knowing it's wrong and getting an assurance that it'd be changed? So what is the deal do you follow Islam or do you follow the ISNF system? Because you know it's haram, so why does the evil persist? A Muslim would just cover it up with a blanket because the harm is greater than any benefit. Why can't you just put a blanket on it? Or do you truly want people to get the wrong message? Have you considered that perhaps people tell you stuff when they think something else, in a similar fashion to how you tell me stuff? Maybe they tell you they hate kafirs but really don't and are just saying that to you so you let them promote their true beliefs, have you thought of that? If people thought it was wrong they would change it as soon as possible. If they believed it was right, then they would delay as long as possible. Afterall isn't that what happened to my paper sign? That got changed real fast. But why? Was what it said haram? No. My sign wasn't haram or wrong, it was just not ISNF's doing. So a halal sign gets changed because it's not according to ISNF desires but a haram sign stays even after they promise to change it? Why hasn't a blanket been put over it? Can you imagine what Umar would've done? Really consider why was my sign changed so fast but a sign that they know and get told is haram gets left up so thousands can continue to see it. Why didn't they leave my sign up for over 24 hours before taking it down? Islamically speaking this sign should've been changed faster than they changed my sign, because this is worse than mine even according to yourself. So not only is the sign wrong, as you say, but the way the wrong is being fixed is wrong. Meaning the whole dang system is wrong!

2. You yourself know the statement on the easel is unislamic and false and indefensible. BUT I didn't even say the worst parts of it. You can check your picture that is on your phone, whether you

took that because you thought it was a joke or for documentation purposes I don't know. However if you check it, you will see it says Muslims "don't discriminate on the basis of religion". Whereas we do, allah does and shariah does. So that is a haram statement, we do discriminate based on religion, that's one of the only things we can discriminate based upon. Inheritance? Marriage? Jizya? Zakat distribution? Umar divorced his wife just because they were kafirs, that was the only reason, just for religion. Islam is built upon religious discrimination. Thus it's a lie to say it's not and a denial of Islamic truth and shariah. Yet that's not even the worst part, or maybe it is. At the end it says something to effect of Muslims consider hate to be evil and condemn all hatred. Thus you got condemned by ISNF and you don't even know it. You said "hate is there" ISNF says hate is evil and no Muslims hate at all and Muslims pray for the "defeat of evil hate and intolerance". Check it yourself, it's also on the ISNF website. Now I consider that to be a statement of kufr to reject hate altogether and I think even the teachers who taught you in South Africa would agree and say such a statement is haram and must not be said or written or publicized by Muslims in the USA. But you take a picture of it with a smile. That's not funny. Do you think it's funny that I think such things are statements of kufr? What would Muhammad pbuh say of such a sign? Do you think he'd find it funny if a Muslim thought such a thing was kufr or haram? Do you think he'd take a picture of it in the manner you did?

3. You believed the evil Christmas sign I covered up was okay. I was thinking of asking for a fatwa during Ramadan because I'm so convinced it is haram that Ramadan would be best time for a repentance to be accepted by Allah and easiest time for you to repent for your part in it, but then this fiasco happened and it just gets worse.

4. You claim to love the Muslims and have hate for the kufar. Yet when Muslim travelers in dire need come to the Masjid you tell them "check only, no cash". This is not an expression of love. But not only that, you also give Christmas presents to the kuffar with the wealth of the Muslims. AND publicly announce it with pride even though scholars say this is haram and possibly kufr and I sent you the fatwas. You spent the wealth of Muslims to give Christmas gifts to kafirs. Is that "loving the Muslims and hating the kufar"? Also that same day you witnessed several instances of Muslims saying kafirs were their friends, and even heard one say this while saying his kafir friend publicly doesn't trust him. Thus you have Muslims saying "My kafir friends don't consider me a friend." It's supposed to be the other way around. You told me nobody was saying this stuff but they did and they do and Muslims hear this. What are they supposed to think when you don't refute it? Everyone must think you agree, obviously that's how I get inclined to think even when you tell me otherwise. So what of those you don't tell otherwise, like the youth or the women or etc?

5. You teach the doctrine "hate the sin, not the sinner". This is a kafir doctrine not from Islam. There is no ayat, hadith or statement of sahabah teaching this concept. If you believe this then why not love Satan? He is just another kafir sinner. Allah says hate him as well as the other kafirs and take them all as enemies. So why distinguish between human sinners an jinn sinners? Is this what Abu Hanifa taught? No. Abu hanifa did not believe in "hating the sin but not the sinner" and the Hanafi madhhab doesn't teach this either. And again I don't think you were taught this in South Africa either. Did they teach you this doctrine in SA? Or did you get it from the kafirs when you came to the USA? Or did ISNF, MPAC or WNY Muslims teach it to you? Because it's not part of any traditional religion and even Christians reject it. This is a political modern doctrine it is not Islamic, so bring your proof from Islam if you think it teaches this. Why did no classical scholars teach this? Do you know Islam better than them? What happened to taqleed? Or is it just follow the scholars unless it's politically unpopular?

Just give me one proof from Islamic Quran or Sunnah that teaches this explicit doctrine you have.

6. You don't have Islamic bumperstickers despite me explaining why they are so important and perhaps even necessary. Yet you claim to love kufar so much it forces you do dawah and make dua for them to be guided? If so then where is your bumperstickers if you really care? If you worry about paint then I can give you magnets to glue to bumperstickers so no paint need be effected. I

can even give you extra bumperstickers I have. So where is the dawah when you drive? Are you afraid someone will know you are driving Muslim? Do you want them to think you are a kafir? Muslims cars should be distinct from kafir cars. You claim you want to spread Islam, but just not when you drive? You already know the car insurance is haram and gas can be haram. Hate for what they say about Allah should make you defend Allah to try guiding them. The "love" doesn't make you do the dawah when you drive, only the hate for them to be ignorant and kafirs will force one to take the risk of kafir road rage. Because you'd hate them to blow kafir kisses and be uninformed.

7. I have heard from filthy kafir liars that you collude with them in conspiracy saying things about someone that they didn't know you said about them and would not have liked you to said about them which you never said you said about them to/with their kafir enemies. While my source is a filthy kafir liar who is worse than a skunk their information seems to be of the type that could only be obtained either through email surveillance, jinn, Allah or yourself. So do you collude with kafirs and keep secrets with kafirs against the Muslims? This would be allying with the Kufar, and backbiting. Such a thing is haram and possibly disbelief.

Thus I doubt whether you are trustworthy because if you conspire against a Muslim and keep secrets with their kafir enemies then how can I trust you to talk to you? How can I present a "statement of hate" to see if it's right or wrong if you are an ally of kafirs and violate the trusts?

8. You claim to love the Muslims and want to do dawah yet how long did it take to review the sections I asked you to review in my book? Not mad about it, it's better book because of delay but it's just a factor I've considered on this list that adds weight to an overall verdict and character analysis.

9. You don't read my emails. So again why should I even bother trying to communicate? But that's okay, the thing I wonder though is if you read the emails kafirs send you? Do you ever not read a personal email which a kafir sends you? Do you not respond to kafir emails?

10. You claim to love the Muslims but you don't reply to their salaams. When an email is sent with the salaams it is the right of the Muslim that their salaam is responded to. Now I understand you likely get thousands of emails, and I've probably sent hundreds, so it is perhaps unrealistic to expect every email to be read and fully replied to even though the prophets and Kalifhs would have, it is kind of a job of being a leader. However Muhammad pbuh not only replied to every salaam but he made salaam first and he was much busier than you. So what excuse will you give to Allah when you are asked why you didn't respond to the salaams the Muslims gave you in emails. (Also remember already discussed how WAS is not the same.) Prophets and Khalifhs never abbreviated the salaams. Now I'm not saying you

have to, it's up to you BUT if you are going to claim to "love Muslims" then you should be responding to every single digital salaam you get in full. Even if you just copy paste a response stating it's a copy past reply to their salam this I think is the minimum a "friend of the Muslims" would do.

11. When you meet another ex-Catholic former Seminarian you don't bother to tell me for dawah opportunities. That's just another thing that makes me wonder how, whether and why should I trust you? This is minor thing but still boggles me, and lends credibility to the horror story I heard about your conspiracy with a kafir secretly backbiting a Muslim.

12. You condemn the deaths of kafirs but not the deaths of Muslims when killed by kafirs, unless it is the popular thing to do. Examples are abundant you publicly condemn Muslims in North Carolina getting killed (do you even know what happened to their murderer, or did you only care temporarily?) yet when a hospital gets bombed by the US in Kunduz Afghanistan in 2015 no condemnation is heard even though it's condemned internationally. Yet if the Taliban kills people at a military school in Afghanistan you condemn it, even though it's exposed as a hoax where a kid who died years earlier at a sandy hook shooting has his picture listed as the dead which the Taliban allegedly killed at a "military training school". Why the double standard? Or do you consider hospitals to be legit targets when the US bombs them? If you condemn all crimes then condemn all crimes. Not just the crimes that are politically important and popular to condemn.

ISNF likes to say they "condemn all acts of violence" but they don't, they just say that whenever they condemn the stuff the US government wants them to condemn. When was the last time they condemned the US military for it's war crimes in Afghanistan, Iraq, Syria, Libya, Yemen, Somalia, Pakistan etc etc. No they don't condemn it, they tell us to go pay taxes and register to vote for kafirs and wave the flags saying "I shall not hate". (You did tell them at that rally that "the hate is there" didn't you? Was the hate there that day in December? Because I don't think anybody at that rally got the message since they were preaching the opposite.)

13. *You delayed the salat of the masjid to associate with kufar, yet claim to love the Muslims and hate the kufar. If you love the Muslims and hate kufar why would you have done that? Have you not heard of when the prophet saws turned away from the blind man to preach to filthy kufar? That was not delaying salat, that was just postponing an answer to a question and the Muslim didn't even know. What kind of leader of the Muslims chooses to talk to kafirs over leading the Muslims in their salat on time? What is such a leader leading us to do? To "love the Muslims and hate the kufar"? They may say they do but what do their actions say? Lets just say such a person didn't have a tongue and you could only judge them by their actions, what would one think of them? How can a Muslim trust one who has these characteristics?*

14. Other things I think are doctrinal errors, like the surah falaq difference of opinion on ayat 2, taqleed, madhhabs, the claim that Muhammad saws knew the mutashaabiyyat, democracy, voting, taxes, living amongst kafirs, having the flag at the masjid, potlucks, MPAC, ISNF, WNY Muslims, Shia, education of Muslim children, girls olympics, basketball court, paying religious teachers, paying imams, collection plate on friday, masjid divider and females' TV etc. (But that stuff is basically typical for everyone I know. Thus these issue aren't particularly unique to you, but they all contribute and they are magnified because I warn/argue with you and you know more and have more responsibilities.)

In conclusion I strongly disagree with your concept of wala and baraa and think it is incorrect. This is an aqeedah issue and not a fiqh issue, so when it's differences in aqeedah that's a big thing in which no differences are allowed. Also I think you do some bidas, like the beads, the dua after fajr, the recitation of Quran for dead people thinking the rewards can be donated to them. But the bida ideas are separate. Of course there are some good things and good qualities I like, but you already know how I'm a criticizer more than a complimenter.

The main point is that concerning this difference of ideas of aqeedah, from my perspective you would either be a disbeliever or ignorant/confused. Or I'm wrong and extreme, as I've heard kafirs say people who collude/conspire with them say about me. Now I don't want to make takfir and probably am not *qualified. Also I want to pray in the masjid so I really don't want to come to a conclusion that you are disbeliever but we do have a difference in aqeedah regarding walaa and baraa. So since I don't want to think you've gone outside then I have to think you are ignorant/confused in this matter to avoid takfir. Basically I have to think you are ignorant to keep praying at the masjid. But if I think you are ignorant/confused about walaa/baraa then I cannot voluntarily learn from you because this would be dangerous. Also it's dangerous anyways because of the effects you tend to have on me. So that's where I don't really want to talk to you less I find more that I dislike/disagree with that makes things harder to pray at the masjid. Also I don't really want to talk to you either if you have such an opinion about love and hate.*

However I know this can be a plot of Satan to disunite and isolate ummah. So I do want to give you my "Statements of hate" to be reviewed because I think it refutes and would correct the issue. but 1. I don't think you are trustworthy. So if you disagree with me or think I'm extreme then I'd be risking my book, especially if you collude with the kafirs and keep secrets with them. How am I supposed to know this whole thing isn't an act and that you have not reported me and recommended I be put on a list? How do I know you aren't just waiting til I get ready to publish book and then alert enemies of Islam to quash it? Afterall if you think I'm extreme and that my book is extreme, logically you would try to stop it from spreading extremism. That's what I do to you, so why wouldn't you do it to me? Isn't that part of your contract?

Islamically it would be your duty if you thought I was extreme and would corrupt the Ummah. Thus why should I share things that may be extreme or controversial, or things you think are extreme, which could lead to such results? Why fall for the bait so I get labeled even more? Or risk my book by sharing info/ideas with you? Furthermore if I share a lengthy example of how I teach hate and disavowel for the kuffar you probably won't even read it anyways so why waste my time? I could use my time on book before you report me and collude with the kufar to imprison/silence me rather than trying to prove/explain my position to you. And then maybe you think it's exteme for me to think you'd do that, but that's what the policy they have is. They say report and deport. Isn't that the ISNF and MPAC policy too? Isn't that what the FBI say when ISNF invites them to preach and intimidate the Muslims at the masjid? So if you think I'm extreme and wrong about walaa and baraa then basically it'd be game over unless Allah decreed otherwise.

So that's where I don't know whether it's wise for me to share with you my "statements of hate" or things in my book because I don't trust you. If you can't be trusted to lead the salat on time when you are present then what can you be trusted with?

Yet I'm saying I don't trust you, so isn't that a contradiction? Why tell you this stuff if I really feel that way? 1. Allah protects whoever he will and Qadr is already written. 2. Because there is either heaven or hellfire and if you have the incorrect belief regarding walaa and baraa as I think you do then you could end up in hellfire and what would my excuse be for not warning you? It is not because of love that I warn, it is because I hate this unislamic belief and hate to see you suffer for it in the next life. Also because you spread your beliefs to people many others follow your path. Privately you may agree with me and say you hate but publicly Muslims may think otherwise. Just consider, I'm hearing you say what you say to me with my own ears and I know you've read some of my book and didn't disagree with certain things, and I still think you don't hate the kufar. Other Muslims don't know that stuff about you, an don't know Islam, they just hear what you say publicly and what ISNF says, and MPAC and they think that stuff is Islam. They aren't thinking "Oh they're just saying that for the cameras, they really hate kafirs, democracy, freedom etc." They don't even know to grow a beard, do you think they know aqeedah? Kids at sunday school don't know aqeedah so why would the adults?

From my perspective most people coming to the masjid have wrong beliefs, like their beliefs about taxes, democracy, living with in land of kufar, so to me it's crazy here, I'm nearly in apocalyptic mode. Yet that type of attitude leads to extremism. Thus the Muslims around me have an effect that pushes me towards extremism because they are so unislamic from my perspective. Yet if I cut myself off then I got nothing but kafirs around me. So both sides are pushing towards extremism and kufr. So this is how extremism happens, it's because of Muslims telling reverts how to treat kafirs when these Muslims don't have experience or know what Islam really teaches about kafir, kufr and their politics. If there is anything reverts know, it's how to treat kafirs and what they must reject and what they don't have to reject (or most should know the 2nd and 3rd, sadly too many don't and some don't know any). Yet generally that's the thing we tend to learn first, because it's a living necessity we have to thoroughly learn. Reverts spend more time learning about Muslim-Kafir interaction in Islam and have more interactions than the Muslims who tell us we don't know Islam and are extreme. If I don't know what Islam teaches about kafirs and kufr and hatred for both then how can I know anything? Do you think I didn't look into it and just decided to be a jerk out of laziness or fun? I'd say that's one of the only things I know but foreign Muslims come here and tell native revert Americans that we don't know how to do dawah or live with kafirs. Its the only thing we know about Islam. These Muslims come here and tell us "There is no islamic country for you to move to so you have to stay here. Now you have to accommodate the disbelievers and can't call for shariah or tell the kafirs to become Muslims or change their system." But who has the right to make that call? Who are these foreign non-American immigrant Muslims to tell native reverts what we are to do politically and how to do dawah? They tell us we are right to have changed and become Muslim and then they tell us not to change anyone else or our system. They should either tell us where to go for Shariah or let us establish it here. We became Muslims because we want Shariah and the Muslims come here and tell us "No shariah there and no shariah here. We have to live with the non-Musims under kufr." Well then why did we even become Muslims if we aren't going to live under shariah or with Muslims? Why can't we just turn the kafirs into Muslims and abolish our own system? No the Muslims don't want us to convert our nation they just want the kafirs to like them and live comfortably under kufr, and they want us to stop trying to change our nation and our former allies who became our enemies after Islam. We changed teams and then the Muslims tell us not to play the game but to cheer for the opponent.

But do you know what? That will never happen. The kafirs will never ever ever stop thinking Islam teaches hate. No matter what you say or do. You've done it for years and years and years and years and they still think Islam teaches hate. Do you know why? Because it does.

You can't convince the kafir Islam doesn't teach hate because Islam does teach hate. You can't convince the kafirs that Islam isn't against freedom and democracy because it is. It is. So stop wasting time lying about Islam. Even kafirs can tell that the Muslims don't know their own faith. Muslims will gain nothing until they begin to hate the kafir and kufar and express this publicly.

Who do you think knows how to do dawah? Those who were kafirs and became Muslims or those who were never kafirs and never learned kufr was false or had to make a decision to reject it and choose Islam but were given islam spoon-fed since birth? Who is more likely to know how to help one transition from kufr to *islam? Those who never did it themselves or those who did?*

If Islam really didn't teach hate, the kafirs would know it by now, it wouldn't take this long to get the message across. The message doesn't stick because it's not the Islamic message. I can prove this, was looking and found dozens of ayat in just chapter 6 and 7 of Quran proving hatred for kufar being publicly expressed is the prophetic method. There are so many ayat that I don't want to send you a list because if I take the time and get dozens and dozens of ayat proving my position and you reject it then I wouldn't be able to pray behind you. I'm not just saying that, I could give you a very long list inshallah but it would take a lot of time because there are so many verses and I would not want to risk the consequences for me if you rejected the evidence.

Also where do you think I and other reverts get this hate for kafirs and kufr from? If the Muslims are all telling us to be nice and kind and vote then where did we get this idea that Islam teaches us to hate and express that hate publicly? Did we get it from our kafir families? No. Did we get it from the Western Muslims? NO. We got it from Islam, that's the only place we got it from and the only reason we accepted it and preach it. Thus it is my duty to warn you in an attempt to rectify the issues and dangers.

I think Allah would prefer I send this email and that Satan would prefer I don't send it.

If I were wrong and extreme then I'd have to send so as to get corrected and not isolated. Whereas if you were wrong, then someone must inform you and personally I don't know who will because I think many are wrong about walaa and baraa in this extreme locality.

Whomever Allah guides then none can misguide, meaning hate does not harm dawah.

So if you want me to send you my "Statements of Hate" then let me know via email because I don't want to learn from or talk to you if you still have the belief about walaa and baraa which you had the last time we spoke.

Three days later I sent the following email explaining as gently as I could why I wouldn't be praying behind Qadri until he repented from his unislamic beliefs/sayings.

Email Sent Wednesday, Jun 22, 2016, 9:54 AM

This is for explanation so you don't worry and to clarify my increased worry about you.

1. I haven't prayed Taraweeh because I don't feel comfortable praying behind you for nawafil. But why then not pray a taraweeh behind others? This is because when I was praying the whole set it was because I heard if one prays Taraweeh behind imam until they finish including witr then it counts as if one prayed the whole night. Yet if I'm not praying behind you then I won't get that. Thus when considering that I don't know what is being said for the most part during the recitation and have much to learn and do and have sore feelings towards you and other Muslims because people pay taxes so it makes me feel isolated then I figured it would be more effective if I used my time doing other things. Also praying Isha and Fajr in congregation counts for praying the night anyways. The sunnah of taraweeh involved the sahabah knowing arabic and understanding. It's not necessarily a sunnah if you don't know the arabic.

2. Learning more about Walaa and Baraa has not improved my opinion of you but made it worse.

I have learned 3 things which I think you have forgotten.

1. The shahada does not count unless one has enmity and expresses enmity for all kufr and all kafirs. (of course lack of expression may possibly be excused if fear for life exists)

2. Allah does not love any disbelievers at all. Not even a little. Does Allah provide for them? Yes. Does Allah love good deeds? Yes. Does Allah give them rights? Yes. But Allah does not love them. For example Satan is a disbeliever, Satan is provided for and even given rights yet Allah does not love him at all. As such there is no proof to suggest Allah loves kafirs and there is proof that Allah hates them all. Loving a good doer does not mean he loves a kafir, because the kafirs good deeds do not count because of their kufr. So realistically they are not a

gooddoer, even if they do a good deed, because their deed doesn't count. Yet Allah is so merciful they still get their reward in this life for that good deed because of justice and to encourage them to do good despite his hatred for them. A perfect example of this is the Satan who told Abu Hurayra about what to say before going to sleep for protection. Satan told Abu Hurayra the truth and Islamic knowledge, this is a good deed. Yet does that mean Allah loves the satan because of this? NO! But it was a good deed and Allah loves good deeds and good doers and the devil did a good deed. Likewise even Pharaoh did good by raising Moses pbuh but Allah did not love him for that just as Allah did not love Abu Talib despite him protecting the prophet saws and assisting him, nor the father of Abraham pbuh, nor the son of Noah pbuh who served his father, nor the wife of Lot pbuh who raised good Muslim children. He hated them all even while they were doing those good deeds. You have to qualify for Allah's love, kafirs do not qualify. Good deeds don't earn Allah's love without faith, just as good deeds don't earn paradise without Allah's mercy.

Since you said Allah loves disbelievers, this troubles me, because this is not an islamic belief, as far as I've read. Allah hates all disbelievers regardless of their knowledge of Islam or attitudes towards Islam. Many scholars have said this using Quran and Sunnah as their proof. In the past it was an issue of takfir, except few people had an issue with it because the Freemason doctrine of human brotherhood and equality had not proliferated nor be incorporated into the composite combo faith of Americanism.

3. It is obligatory for a Muslim to hate all disbelievers and have no love for them. This does not mean they cannot have mercy, justice or kindness but they cannot have any love for them at all. It is obligatory to express disavowal and hatred from all types of kufr and all types of kafirs publicly, unless if perhaps there is serious threat of loss of life as in a sword is literally on your shoulder blade or a laser pointer from a gun is on your head.

4. Actions alone can constitute disbelief even if one inwardly believes and feels or says things that are correct. Meaning that making statements or doing certain actions can take one outside of Islam even if one believes in all the correct things and privately says all the right stuff. Essentially what I'm saying is that expressing hatred for kafirs and kufr is obligatory BUT there are exceptions that may permit a Muslim not to express hatred publicly. HOWEVER it is absolutely forbidden to express any love for kufr or kafirs, whether privately or publicly. Unislamic political systems are included in types of kufr. Now don't misunderstand me thinking I'm saying "praying for families" is disbelief, one can and should make dua that kafir families are guided to Islam. Yet such ambiguous statements are extremely dangerous because the halal meanings are not conveyed and the haram and kufr meanings can and are conveyed. Kafirs don't know what you mean and even the Muslims don't know what is meant. Thus it can be haraam to convey messages which will have incorrect meanings when one knows the incorrect meaning will be conveyed. It's not haraam in every instance, like Abraham pbuh

saying he was sick. However it is very dangerous and risky. I'm not saying that conveying a message that gets interpreted in a way that would constitute kufr, if the person meant it, is kufr itself. But if messages of kufr are being conveyed even though one doesn't believe in those meanings or that's not the intention, I do think this is haraam. It could be kufr but I'm just saying it's haraam because I didn't do the research to see if such a thing is kufr. Whereas thinking something that's haraam to be halal and boasting about it, aka publicizing it, is disbelief. So as long as the Muslims know such statements are haraam then it's just haraam, if they don't know it's haraam then if could be disbelief but I'm not saying that because I have not researched that in depth. Yet regardless the statements being made cannot be made and they cannot be portrayed as halal. If you say what you say and ISNF makes the statements they make that's one thing, but neither can say it's halal. Saying such "dawah" is halal makes it into even a bigger sin, that could raise it to kufr, if it isn't already, which I'm not saying it is or isn't but there are indications I'm just being safe and not wanting to say whether it is or isn't at this time.

5. Not all disbelief = disbelief in Islam. Ex. Those who drink alcohol disbelieve but they are not disbelievers necessarily. Sunnah implies that there is a disbelief that is less than disbelief, a hypocrisy that is less than hypocrisy, a shirk that is less than shirk, a corruption that is less than corruption, and an oppression that is less than oppression. Yet unfortunately in this regard we, or at least I, may be talking about the type of disbelief that takes one outside of Islam. But just establishing the principle that not all disbelief is the disbelief that nullifies Islam, there is linguistic disbelief and then religious disbelief.

Now I have not given proof from Quran and Sunnah or Salaf in this email but the proof is there, I just don't want to send all kinds of info to you over and over because I want to keep contact to a minimum. Unfortunately though I feel as though I've heard you say things that are statements of kufr. It doesn't make you a kafir, but I just don't feel comfortable praying behind you because basically I'm making excuses and there is a limit to how many excuses can be made and how far they can go. Whereas personally I don't know if I'd ever be capable of making takfir on someone who leads prayers even if there was overwhelming evidence. So I have to consider my own reluctance to make takfir, that can't influence my actions such as prayer behind someone. Also there is the issue of my mother and you keeping secrets. 1. Being alone with my mother would be haram. 2. Looking at her would be haraam. 3. Saying what she says you said would be haram. Although none of that would be disbelief. Yet the keeping secrets bit is red flag for me. Whereas since I made it clear I didn't want you to talk to my mother and she indicated she reminded you of that then you should have told me even if you promised otherwise. Such a promise of conspiracy with a kafir would not be a valid or permissible promise to make in my opinion. I don't think it is permissible for a Muslim to keep secrets with kafirs against other Muslims. It feels like that would be allying with

kafirs against Muslims, check the 20 types I sent in a prior email, especially if the secrets involve revealing confidential information the kafir could not obtain otherwise and involves sabotaging another Muslim's dawah efforts and reputation. However my mother is a liar, a known liar and enemy of Allah so I did not believe her, at first. Although after hearing what you said about walaa and baraa it seemed plausible. Yet when I mentioned this in my prior email there would only be 3 possible reactions:
1. Apologize and repent if it was true. 2. Ask what the heck I was talking about and inform me it was false, if it was false and you didn't know anything about such a thing. 3. Don't say nothing. However choice 3 indicates guilt or ignorance, meaning either it is true and you don't feel sorry about it or you didn't read my last email which is simply not a good indication and does not inspire good feelings. Thus it seems you either ignored me or are guilty of betraying me, and are not contrite if guilty.

Anyways I simply find it very hard to pray behind you knowing the things you've said. I'm not saying such a prayer would be invalid but personally it's too hard for me to do. Thus I considered not going to the masjid anymore because my parents don't want me to go to buffalo and it's impractical to go there. However it is extremely dangerous to not go to the masjid and is surely a plot of Satan and can lead to extremism or disbelief. But there is a solution. I will simply come and pray at the masjid at a different time than the congregation times. Maybe earlier or later depending on the time, that way I will still pray in the masjid but won't have to pray behind you. Just letting you know so you don't worry when you don't see me at congregational times.

I'm worried about you and clearly someone is wrong on this issue. It'd be better for me to be wrong, because if you are then that's a bigger problem for the whole community as many hold similar beliefs as you've expressed. In theory it'd be easier for me to get fixed. Yet I currently think my opinion on love/hate is the Islamic position and cannot let it go without proof but the more I look the more proof I find to back it up. For example Why did Moses pbuh angrily pull the beard of his brother Aaron pbuh who was a prophet? Because he did not express public enmity for kufr and kafirs. So Moses pbuh expressed enmity at him for not expressing enmity.

I may compile a list of Quran verses proving hate and expression of hate is obligatory but such a list will take a long time. I do not plan on telling anyone of my dispute with you because I believe leaders should be advised in private, even though this is a public issue. Yet if/when I compile proofs from Quran, if you still reject them then such a policy may change. I'd rather never make this a public issue though, but eventually if people see me praying always at different times if they ask me why after I've sent proof for the Islamic position then I would tell them why I pray at different times. I don't plan on making a big public disturbance but if in such a situation after I send proofs then I would just say how I disagree with your beliefs on walaa and baraa. I wouldn't go on a big speal, I hope, I am unpredictable though so I can't say with *certainty what I'd say. But then again this plan of mine may change depending on how much and what proof I learn of and/or find. Because surely you can agree there are certain aqeedah issues which if you were wrong on then different levels of opposition would be appropriate, ex. if you say Jesus pbuh was crucified, or deny the life in the grave, or qadr so I don't know what the appropriate level of opposition is for this yet but it is an issue worth a significant amount. I just don't fully know how big of an issue this is or how clear it is yet. So I can't say where it will go because I don't know, although violence can surely be ruled out at least when we are in a land like this. So don't think I'm any type of physical threat or anything, we are in america there are laws to follow regardless of what one's aqeedah is. I'm not saying if it weren't america then I would be, I'm just saying no matter where it goes I firmly believe it will never get violent here. Yet that should not make you complacent and think Allah does not punish people who deviate. Of course I know such assurances themselves can be misinterpreted as threats, but that's not why I say that stuff, the tone doesn't really get conveyed via email. I'm just saying that since I would not use force here then I expect a similar courtesy, in that you would not use force against me, such as kafir forces if you think I'm extreme. That is what some imams have been known to do to practicing Muslims. In America a Lebanese Muslim was even threatened with the police and called a terrorist once simply because when visiting a US sunni masjid he wanted to lead a salat since the masjid's imam didn't know tajweed for fatihah. So at the end of the day if I am an extremist, then you already know that on US soil I'd be the peaceful type. Not like the peaceful underboard types which I think you and others might be, but still peaceful in this country.*

So there 4 main types of extremists

1. Violent Overboard. (ex. honor killings)

2. Peaceful Overboard (ex. ISIS propagandists)

3. Violent Underboard (ex. Report and Ban people they think are too strict or extremists, or tow cars of Muslims thereby harming Muslims and funding kufar for the sake of kafir traditions, which Muhammad pbuh wouldn't have done)

4. Peaceful Underboard (ex. friends with kafirs, promote tolerance and love for everyone and almost everything, interfaith, Abrahamic faith promoters, pro-democracy)

Basically my belief is as follows:

"Hate the Sin and the Sinner" (but you love them more than you hate them if they're a believer.)

AND

"Love the Good deed, but never a kafir"

That's the rhyme so it's easier to remember.

Further explained and clarified as:
Express enmity for kufr and every kafir.
Express love for Islam and every believer.

Hate all evil and evil doers.

Love every good deed, but only love Muslim people.

Harm who Allah says, When Allah says, How Allah says, Where Allah says, 4 the reason Allah says. And if you don't follow Allah's commands and restrictions on harming then you get harmed in this life and the next.

Be Kind to who Allah says the way Allah says and be harsh to who Allah says the way Allah says. Hatred can be polite and harsh, every situation requires a different type of expression of hate. But no kafir qualifies for love under any circumstances in any place or time. Kindness, sometimes, but kafirs don't qualify for love at all and Allah commands us to hate them all publicly.

So despite not making takfir I felt uncomfortable praying behind an Imam that said hate was not part of the religion. I would go to the masjid and if Mr. Qadri was there to lead then I would hide in the wudu area waiting and then later pray by myself, if Qadri wasn't there I would join the congregation. I did this to protect the community from learning of our dispute and to protect his reputation from harm so he could repent more easily.

In the interim while disputing this deviancy, there was a flyer on the masjid for Muslims to enjoy the "Festival of the Moon" at a Karaokee event located at the "Trinity Methodist Church". I wrote with pen on the sign which mentioned music would be played at the Church festival that "Music is haram". To which my other revert friend Abdul Haq guessed I had done it and expressed his approval to me. I also emailed a condemnation to Mr. Qadri of that musical festival at a church being advertised at a mosque but it's something length does not allow to include despite being a serious travesty on its own and Mr. Qadri himself publicly saying on Eid the year before that music is sinful. So how a flyer for a musical event at a church gets posted and stays up at a masjid where the imam forbids music says a lot about religious authority at that masjid. Meanwhile Mr. Qadri never replied to a single email of mine which I sent trying to reconcile although we did talk a few times. Once when talking with Mr. Qadri, trying to resolve the dispute of whether Islam teaches hatred for kuffar we were interrupted by Khalid Qazi founder/leader of MPAC-WNY which is a deviant democratic interfaith group and he is also a founder of ISNF which owns masjid noor in Amherst/Getzville, NY and masjid taqwa in Niagara Falls, NY. Khalid Qazi wanted my email but I refused to give it to him and he then got angry and asked what made me think I had the right to take down his sign, to which I replied he had to be more specific because I take down lots of signs that are sinful. (I didn't know whether he referred to me covering the Christmas sign or me taking down just one of many signs saying to vote in the democratic primary election.) Anyways that interruption with Khalid Qazi prevented me and Qadri reconciling and after that Qadri would rarely speak with me and never emailed me though we would give each other the salams when passing each other. I was still going to the masjid 5 times a day but I politely silently refused to pray behind Qadri when he led due to him incorrectly saying to me privately that God loves everybody and God loves Pharaoh and that Islam forbids hatred of people.

After that conversation with me, Qadri and Qazi, I decided to go to the newly opened masjid in Niagara Wheatfield as an alternative. I liked it for awhile and the imam Mr. Agwa told me how he got previously fired as ISNF masjid noor imam, a few years earlier, because he removed people from the ISNF board because they sold alcohol. Yet they didn't accept being removed from the board so he got fired instead. Then he used the money he earned at ISNF to buy his own new building to make into a masjid. One Tunisian friend I had met at the ISNF masjid, named Khalid, would pray at the new Niagara Wheatfield Islamic Cultural Center. Khalid explained it was called a cultural center because they would never have gotten the permit to buy the building if they had called it a mosque. It was interesting going there because I had previously been in the very same building before as a non-Muslim when it was a restaurant prior to becoming a masjid. However I eventually had an issue with this imam too because he told me it was recommended to take interest from banks in America and then give it to charity as interest is forbidden in Islam. I did not make takfir of him and didn't refuse to pray behind him but just thought it was a big jurisprudential fiqh issue of Mr. Agwa's and decided to go back to masjid noor to resolve the issue with Qadri, since Qadri's masjid noor was much closer to my house anyways.

Being at a stalemate I tried my earnest to end the dispute with Mr. Qadri, as I wanted to pray in congregation once more and didn't want to argue further. The following email proves such:

Email Sent Wednesday, Jul 6, 2016 at 8:53 PM

Greetings

Allah commands mankind to establish salat in the masjid, in congregation with those who bow down and prostrate.

I have not been doing that because I don't feel it is proper to pray behind you after having heard, disagreed and discussed things that you've said publicly and privately.

So basically my attitude towards you is coming between me and a command of Allah.

However this situation can be improved a bit.

From past experience neither of us are people who pray in the masjid 5 times a day, 7 days a week, 29-30 days a month, 354 or so days a year. Therefore IF you don't pray 5 times a day everyday in masjid noor then for those salat that you are not leading I have no excuse not to participate in the jama. Thus I should and must pray those salat in jama which you are not leading, because Allah commands us to establish salat. Especially considering how sometimes there are not 3 people for a Jama, so if there is a salat that you aren't there for AND I'm not there for then that is 2 less people and it may result in a salat that does not get performed in the masjid with Jama. Such an event is unacceptable, and if such a thing happens the whole community is sinful and should just move to the Muslim lands if they cannot establish salat. Afterall doesn't everyone always say they came to America to practice Islam and "establish salat"? If so then the Jama must take place, for it not to take place once is simply unacceptable for people who call themselves Muslims or an Islamic Society. Such negligence of salat is oppression of the masjid and the masjid will demand it's rights from the Muslims on the day of Judgment and list every day and time the Muslims failed to pray salat in Jama in it as Allah deserves and orders. But even if there are 3+ without you or me then I still must attend as an individual responsibility AND because the more Muslims in the Jama the more reward there is for them all. Thus by me not going and you not going all the other Muslims would be getting less reward, at least theoretically because we don't even know whether Allah considers us as Muslims or not. We'd like to think that and hope for such but so do lots of people who are not, yet taking what is apparent apparently less people for salat means less reward for the Ummah.

Now the problem is I don't pray behind you so I don't go at the times you lead at, so as to prevent further fitna. But from past experience you have a schedule I've noticed where you don't pray every salat in the masjid. Therefore my idea is that I can pray in Jama for the salat that you don't lead.

Although you might wonder whether me praying with people routinely at the times you aren't may lead to suspicion and fitna. Well I do not believe I have established proof to justify publicizing my personal disagreement with your aqeedah. I believe I've established sufficient proof for you to change your belief, but not enough to have my disagreement with you publicly known. So if anyone asks me why I don't come for the other salat and/or only seem to pray in Jamat when you aren't leading then I will simply reply saying something like:

"It is the Qadr of Allah that determines how many salat I pray in congregation. You should worry about your own salat and be grateful Allah blesses you with so many more than me and may Allah give us both many more and increase their quality bringing them to perfection and accept our most recent since it may have been our last before getting asked the 3 questions in the grave. May our next salat be our best, thus far and then if their is any more they should be better and inshallah in congregation."

Thus I will not mention my dispute so there is no need to fear loss of reputation in the sight of people or fitna. Also the greater fitna is having less people for salat in Jama when you are not there and me missing a single salat in Jama. Allah commands us to establish salat in the masjid in congregation! Thus I must pray those salat in the masjid in congregation.

The issue and reason for my email is that I do not know with certainty every single salat that you won't be there to pray in congregation. So I would appreciate you informing me of any and all future salats which you know in advance that you will not be there to lead in congregation. Then I can pray in Jama for those at least. By sharing such information it would be part of establishing salat on your part, because establishing salat doesn't mean just doing it yourself but calling others to it as well, which is why there is an athan, iqama and audible sounds during the prayers. The harm of not informing me is greater than the benefit that'd come from informing me. It is not that you are helping me and making it easier to not pray in Jamat behind you, it would be you helping to establish salat on earth as best as possible.

Alas though, you may not want to inform me for some reason which I'd guess would be unislamic. In such an event I have a solution and inshallah will still be praying those salat. BUT my plan B solution would cause fitna.

Plan B would be for me to simply go to the masjid at all the times because I know there is a tiny % chance that one of them may be led by someone other than you and it would be worth it to try them all because I'd be catching those rare opportunities by basic probability inshallah. With this method though then I would be there for the times you do lead even though I don't pray behind you at this moment. Thus such a scenario could cause fitna. However I would try to minimize this by pretending I broke wudu and then going to make wudu that takes as long as it does for you to finish salat. Wudu is sunnah to do b4 salat even if one still has it and to take measures to prevent fitna is sunnah too. You can also fully try to make salat even if you inform me that you won't be there for X salats and if you show up to lead then I will do same wudu thing so there is no conflict and you can lead if able. Yet if you don't inform me of which salat you know you won't be there for so I can coordinate, then when coming for every salat and pretending to make wudu every time you lead people may get suspicious. I could try to alleviate that suspicion but it would be very hard, especially when you yourself have said that people complained to you about me accidentally breaking wudu during salat once in a rare while. If they were talking to you about me having genuinely broken wudu a couple times, what would they do if every single salat you lead they see me break wudu for as long as the salat is? Anyone would get suspicious no matter what they got told, it's just too suspicious. But if you don't inform me ahead of time of which salat you won't lead then I'll be trying to go for each one and that will be my way to avoid praying behind you while making as little fitna as possible. Cannot say the fitna is too great to justify such behaviour because Allah has said to establish salat in masjid in congregation. So in order to do that as best as possible without me praying behind you I'd have to go to all salat and then excuse myself if you led while holding those walaa and baraa ideas you previously expressed. If I'm there for every salat then sometimes people might pressure me to make athan for a salat that you will lead. Now that could be awkward for me to make athan and iqama and then refuse to pray behind you, but to minimize fitna I'd do the wudu trick but again that would get very suspicious very quickly.

In conclusion I'd appreciate if you informed me of the any and all future salat times you know in advance that you won't be present for so I can attend and do salat in Jama for those times. If you do then I will not come at the times you expect to attend but will come at those you expect not to attend. If/for those salat you inform me you don't expect to attend but do end up attending then I will use the wudu cover unless you can suggest a better solution. Whereas if you choose not to inform me then I will try to come to all and do wudu cover whenever you are there, unless you have a better idea to suggest. I think this is best way to improve the situation and establish salat in masjid in congregation as Allah has commanded the Muslims to do.

Take heed of 8:70-75 as well which in an attempted english translation means:

> O Prophet! (Muhammad)Say to the captives that are in your hands: "If Allâh knows any good in your hearts, He will give you something better than what has been taken from you, and He will forgive you, and Allâh is Oft-Forgiving, Most Merciful." (70) But if they intend to betray you (O Muhammad), they indeed betrayed Allâh before. So He gave (you) power over them. And Allâh is All-Knower, All-Wise (71) Verily, those who believed, and emigrated and strove hard and fought

with their property and their lives in the Cause of Allâh as well as those who gave (them) asylum and help, - these are (all) allies to one another. And as to those who believed but did not emigrate (to you O Muhammad), you owe no duty of protection to them until they emigrate, but if they seek your help in religion, it is your duty to help them except against a people with whom you have a treaty of mutual alliance, and Allâh is the All-Seer of what you do. (72) And those who disbelieve are allies of one another, (and) if you (Muslims of the whole world collectively) do not do so [i.e. become allies, as one united block under one Khalifah (a chief Muslim ruler for the whole Muslim world) to make victorious Allâh's religion of Islâmic Monotheism], there will be Fitnah (wars, battles, polytheism) and oppression on the earth, and a great mischief and corruption (appearance of polytheism). (73) And those who believed, and emigrated and strove hard in the Cause of Allâh (Al-Jihâd), as well as those who gave (them) asylum and aid; - these are the believers in truth, for them is forgiveness and Rizqun Karîm (a generous provision i.e. Paradise). (74) And those who believed afterwards, and emigrated and strove hard along with you, (in the Cause of Allâh) they are of you. But kindred by blood are nearer to one

> another (regarding inheritance) in the decree ordained by Allâh. Verily, Allâh is the All-Knower of everything. (75)

2 points here in that 70 refers to captives where IF Allah knows of ANY GOOD IN THEIR HEARTS then Allah will give them better. Who were those captives and what did Allah give them? They were apparent kafirs and IF Allah knew of ANY GOOD IN THEIR HEARTS then they would be given "something better". That "something better" was Islam. Meaning this applies to all kafirs wheareas if there is any good in their heart then Allah will guide them to Islam. Those who are not Muslims therefore have no good in their heart at all. And what is the status of one who has zero good in their heart according to Allah? Does Allah love them? No. Should Muslims? No. We take what is apparant. If they are apparantly non-Muslims then we have no love for them. Whereas the incident of sahabah slaying a man after shahada and prophet saws said how he is not sent to look in people's heart has to do with the apparant. Apparantly the guy slain said shahada and apparantly embraced Islam and was thus loved by God. If there is no apparant shahada then Muslims cannot love such a person until they have knowledge of their apparant Islam. If they are apparantly Muslim then such a person cannot consider them kafir until there is apparant proof to indicate kufr by their statements and/or

deeds AND ignorance/confusiion is no a valid excuse for them. Because even an apparant sign/statement/deed of major kufr can be done without apostasy IF one is ignorant or confused. But if say someone is saying Jesus pbuh is divine and was crucified, you might be better off not praying behind them even though they might just be extremely ignorant and confused. Because if one prays behind such confused people then it sets evil example and eases ability of kufr to proliferate AND how else is the person to know they are ignorant or confused if everyone just tries to be extra polite and act normal like what they are saying/doing/believing in doesn't contradict/oppose Islam. If Bida is staunchly rejected by Muslims as the salaf rejected it then what about ignorance that would constitute kufr if not for the person being ignorant/confused? Surely the bida is less dangerous because the bida believer/practicioner is not all in hellfire for eternity, although it depends on the bida.

Regarding verse 72 it means "if they seek your help in religion, it is your duty to help them". Well informing me of the times you don't expect to lead salat in masjid will help me to establish salat in masjid in congregation and thus help me in religion AND help the other Muslims because in theory if I attend then all who pray get more reward because more Muslims in salat means more reward. While even if I'm not a Muslim it still helps other Muslims in their religion because

I'm a body and psychologically having more bodies praying salat gives one confidence in the numbers who also believe in what you believe in and pray when and how you pray, whereas Muslims esteem and confidence is important to bolster in the land who has a mutual alliance with Shaitan, Kufr and Kafirs against Islam, Muslims, Jibreel and Allah. The bit about emigration applies to both emigrating from evil and from dar al kufr, then and now and in the future. It is not a special rule just for Muhammad pbuh or for the muhajirs during his time. Emigration from dar al kufr to dar al islam will always exist and so will emigration from evil deeds to good deeds. It is only the specific emigration from Mecca to Medinah that has been abrogated at the time of the conquest of Mecca when it became dar al islam and will remain dar al islam until the Muslims are no longer on the earth.

Now maybe you have reformed since Ramadan and now expect to pray every salat in masjid on time. If so then you may get sick sometime, or go for Umra or Hajj or Jihad or to reconcile Muslims which would mean you wouldn't expect to pray in masjid on time for congregation. In such an event I'd appreciate being informed so I can pray those times in salat in masjid in congregation.

Otherwise I will assume you did not read this or choose not to inform me and will proceed with wudu cover plan. However I was thinking with wudu plan, I could still do that because then

I would be present to hear the athan and maybe say athan and get reward for that. However those types of reward I do not think justify the possible fitna of the wudu cover method. If you think they do let me know, but personally I don't think possiblity of those rewards justify using wudu cover but the possibility of catching a salat in masjid in congregation when you aren't there does.

Or you could just change your beliefs, or I could change mine, so I could pray behind you again.

But in the meantime I think this would be the best for Ummah and please Allah / enrage Iblees.(that's how it goes, you can't please Allah without enraging Iblees and you can't please Iblees without upsetting Allah) If one of them loves you the other one hates you. And even if Allah hates someone Iblees still hates them. So it is really just a matter of whether Allah loves one or not because Iblees hates everyone, to different degrees. Whereas if you read 22:38 of which in various attempted english translations means:

> *Truly, Allâh defends those who believe. Verily! Allâh likes not any treacherous ingrate to Allâh [those who disobey Allâh but obey Shaitân (Satan)].*
>
> *Verily Allah will repel from those who believe: verily Allah loveth not any treacherous, ingrate.*

> *Verily Allah will defend (from ill) those who believe: verily, Allah loveth not any that is a traitor to faith or shows ingratitude.*

One can deduce that Allah does not love nor like an ingrate who betrays Allah, other translations say ungrateful instead of ingrate. This is every kafir not just those who broke the treaty. How? Because before we were born all humans swore an oath to worship and obey Allah, it was a contract every person made and this is mentioned in the Quran and authentic hadith. Thus every kafir has broken their treaty with and betrayed Allah even if they don't remember making it. But if you don't accept that then there is the clear definition of who/what is an ingrate or what is ungratitude? To be an ungrateful ingrate is to disbelieve in Allah and disobey Allah instead choosing to worship and obey Iblees which thus merits Allahs hatred and eliminates Allah's love. Who disbelieves and disobeys Allah and voluntarily chooses to worship and obey Iblees? Every non-Muslim, because to disobey Allah is to obey one's nafs or Shaitan and to obey one's nafs against Allah is to obey and worship Shaitan. To be clear a sin itself doesn't take one outside Islam but it is a type of minor kufr. To disobey is a type of disbelief similar to how to obey is a type of belief. Allah loves obedience yet all who obey are not believers nor loved despite obedience being a type of belief because even the Quraysh obeyed in some manners by not committing sodomy or saying Jesus pbuh was God yet they were not believers and Allah specifically says how he does not love them despite some obedience, even mentioning some by name like Abu Lahab. Yet minor kufr does not result in eternal hellfire nor justify takfir nor does it eliminate Allah's love. However when it comes to a non-Muslim since they are not obeying Allah by following his prophet Muhammad pbuh and the Quran by doing things like salat, zakat, fasting, hajj, shahada etc. then automatically they must be disobeying Allah and obeying Shaitan and thereby worshipping Shaitan to an extent that constitutes major kufr "kufr akbar" which necessitates Allah's wrath and hatred and eliminates any possibility of love until they accept Islam and reform. This is because without Islam such a person is a kafir, there is no such human who can be a non-Muslim and non-kafir at the same time. Hypocrites can be Muslims or Kafirs, there are different types of hypocrisy but there is no hypocrite who is neither a Muslim nor a kafir(non-Muslim). 2 categories of people 2 religions and 2 eternal permanent destinations with 3 questions in the grave that have 2 possible outcomes. One is either obediently grateful to Allah as a believing repentant sinner who Allah loves, or one is a disobedient ungrateful ingrate sinner who Allah does not love but hates, although a Muslim who delays repentance is still loved but it is sinful/hateful to delay repentance and they are playing on the fence over the hellfire and major hatred if they persist in not *repenting for their sins as Allah commands. One cannot say this verse only applies to Allah not loving those who break treaties, because Muslims break treaties and it doesn't make them apostates hated and not loved by Allah. I think breaking a treaty or betraying a trust may be a type of minor kufr but I don't think it is major kufr, but I could be wrong on that bit. So the Quraysh breaking the treaty was just their final straw of betrayal against Allah via betraying his rasul saws and to fully motivate those who may have not fully understood walaa and baraa to wage jihad. Allah had to be explicit about this hatred and lack of love because in context it was an order for Jihad and some Muslims might not have went forth against their families if they didn't have this extra explicit clarity about what the position of Allah was regarding them. Allah didn't love them before and then stop loving after they broke the treaty, he did not love them and hated and went to not loving and hating even more so much Jihad was called for. See Allah hates different kafirs to different degrees which means we treat them differently accordingly but Allah has no love for any kafir(non-Muslim) and neither can we. Thus is just one of many verses that demonstrates how Allah hates every kafir and does NOT love them at all, whereas as Muslims we must have same belief and attitude. But don't worry about how kafirs will react to such an Aqeedah because the very verse which teaches us to have this hateful attitude without love also assures us that truly Allah will defend and protect the believers from those kafirs whom he doesn't love and commands us to hate without having love for them.*

Or at least that's my understanding, maybe I'm wrong, maybe we both are, maybe my interpretation could be wrong despite the aqeedah and beliefs derived being correct.

Later in summer 2016, Qadri and Husam Ghanim who gave the Abrahamic faiths Khutbah on Christmas 2015 (saying Christians are our friends/brothers) talked to me about the issue of hating kuffar. This three-way meeting occurred because I went to Jumuah thinking Qadri would not be giving Khutbah that day, and then when I saw he was I left and waited in my car until it was over, since it was too late to drive elsewhere. In hindsight this was a mistake as if forced one can pray behind an innovating disbelieving leader and then repeat the prayer afterwards, but I did not know that intricate part of Islamic jurisprudence at the time and didn't want to fake it or hear Qadri preach anything more deviant. During this three-way meeting between Husam Ghanim and Mr.

Qadri wherein they promoted an anti-hatred pro-love agenda, I proved them both wrong but they didn't accept the truth. During this three-person conversation, Husam Ghanim mentioned how he did not believe in the Dajjal(antichrist) as existing or coming because he isn't mentioned in the Quran. I rebuked and reproofed him citing hadith saying the Dajjal is a despicable character not deserving of direct mention in the Quran (though he is mentioned indirectly) but Husam Ghanim said he doesn't accept hadith which contradict the intellect. Whereas scholars like Ibn Qayyim refuted this very heresy from more than 200 perspectives in his book As-Sawaiq al Mursalah. The alleged reliance upon intellect that rejects divine revelation is such a false principle that the person who makes such a statement clearly has no intellect to be making such a claim of choosing intellect. While I waited for Qadri to reproof Husam Ghanim surprisingly Qadri shocked me by saying sahih bukhari has weak hadith. The lunacy of this statement is known to nearly all Muslims of all ages. Shah Waliullah even wrote a comment about those who make such comments strongly condemning such idiots saying, *"As for the two authentic books of Ahadith (Bukhari and Muslim), scholars of Hadith sciences are unanimous that the Muttasil(Connected) and Marfu(Traceable) contained in the twain are absolutely Sound and Mutawatir(Continuous) up to their compilers and that anyone who belittles the two is an innovator (Mubtadi), following a way other than that of the believers."* I do not know if Mr. Qadri also disbelieved in the dajjal/antichrist or not but he did not support me in reproofing Husam Ghanim who ignorantly argued on Qadri's behalf regarding love/hate. Still I cautiously did not do takfir of anybody. Yet I remembered this extremely ignorant error of Husam Ghanim who expressed the deviant philosophy of the Quraniyoon sect and personally decided to never pray behind him either until he repented from his disbelief in the existence and coming of the antichrist and his anti-hate mistake as well. However it never became an issue because I never saw Husam Ghanim lead another prayer at masjid noor again for it to be an issue between us. After this incident I would silently publicly stay within the Musalla prayer area when Mr. Qadri was present to lead instead of hiding when he led the salat, then I'd pray separately afterwards. This was because I was tired of hiding and was only doing so to protect Mr. Qadri's reputation and feelings and hide his deviance from the public. Yet since others now knew of our dispute I figured secrecy was no longer available and I hoped a solution could be found sooner this way if people knew I wasn't abstaining from prayer in congregation due to negligence or circumstance. If approached I planned to say why I wasn't praying in congregation hoping Mr. Qadri would take time to have dialogue and change his errant position instead of blatantly ignoring all my email communications.

One friend of mine named Payraw spoke with me and we eventually got on the topic of hating kuffar and he also ignorantly said similar to what Mr. Qadri said about hating Kuffar being forbidden, despite in reality it being an important obligatory part of the Islamic faith. So I told my friend Payraw I could not pray behind him either after hearing his statement until he repents too, because I cannot be just if not praying behind Mr. Qadri for the very same reason and then praying behind you when you are both identically mistaken. However despite being a college student younger than me, Payraw had much better manners and reasonability than Mr. Qadri. He was hurt emotionally by my refusal to pray behind him and I was hurt too because it reduced the few salat I could pray in Jamat at the masjid even more. However Payraw talked to his Dad about our disagreement and his Dad spoke with me about it. We agreed that until Payraw and I agreed then Payraw's Dad would lead the two of us in prayer so as not to cause either of us to be hurt or miss salat together. So for the good of the two of us Payraw was willing to step aside from his unofficial position as auxiliary prayer leader after Mr. Qadri to let his Dad lead us, thereby hiding our disagreement and maintaining maximum occupancy for prayer in the masjid by everyone. Soon afterwards I brought the fatwas I had previously emailed Mr. Qadri in paper format to Payraw in person and I showed him what the Scholars said about hating non-Muslims within the confines of Islamic manners and justice. Payraw then agreed with me all in the span of a few days argument and accepted that Islam teaches hatred for disbelievers when he read the reasoning and scholastic reports. However other Muslims disliking the public dissonance were asking me to leave the masjid and go elsewhere if I wasn't praying behind Mr. Qadri. I then explained the dire situation our conflict was causing to Mr. Qadri.

Email Sent Saturday, Aug 6, 2016 at 2:32 AM

I was told that I should not come to the salat if I'm not going to pray behind you because by me not praying behind you it causes disunity, distress and distracts the Muslims from their salat.

I then also extrapolated this to mean that I shouldn't come at other times to pray at the masjid either because there would be a chance of being seen not praying behind you and thus it could cause distress to Muslims for them to know I'm praying at other times in the masjid.

Causing distress to Muslims is a very serious sin.

Yet if I don't pray in the masjid then it has negative impact on me and also I would be missing the salat behind others who I do pray behind aside from you and the other guy whose views you've seemed to picked up. Regardless I know that you don't lead every salat and that sometimes it's led by people I do pray behind, thus I have to attend those salat and since you don't tell me when those are then I have to go to each one so as not to miss any. Last week there were 3 who I didn't pray behind, however now there are only 2 because one clarified our misunderstanding was due to the english language.

But with you I don't know if it can all be attributed to english misunderstandings and you haven't sincerely communicated to me to clarify or reconcile. Thus I simply don't know what you believe but based on what's apparent I have reasons that inhibit me from praying behind you.

Maybe that's takfir via action maybe not, I don't know.

Yet if I'm to be going to each salat so as not to miss some salat then since I can't bring myself to pray behind you having heard what I've heard and not having reasons to think you've changed your beliefs or were misunderstood by me then this will result in times you come where I secede. Now there are various ways I could abstain. I could either leave and come back after the salat or sit somewhere else in the masjid so as to remain in the masjid without leaving it. Yet preferable as the sitting elsewhere in the masjid may seem this will cause distress and distraction to Muslims. So I think in such an event when you lead I will just leave and return later inshallah. However I can't say I'm always going to do that because right now I don't know what you believe due to recent development of you possibly not knowing how to communicate with me in english. Last week I did not consider the possibility of you not being able to express yourself to me in english. Thus as such possibility exists I do not want to openly oppose via sitting method however if you are persistent in not explaining your beliefs or trying to reconcile then eventually I may return to public sit-out method despite the distress it may cause to Muslims.

However there is one thing we can agree on and that is to minimize the distress of the Muslims. I don't think we have done that and could've handle our dispute much better. Thus I have 3 suggestions for us to reduce distress of Muslims even if neither of us changes our positions.

1. Communicate directly without any side chit chat to others about it. Ex. When you have a problem with a spouse you don't go telling everybody about it. Even if it were a Christian spouse. Whereas bond of Islam is stronger than marriage thus ppl should learn of spousal disputes before they do of disputes between Muslims. Our problem is with each other's beliefs, if we extend this and involve others it is likely to only add to problem. You were the first to involve others in this but I think it's best not to involve any more lest it cause further disunity and/or distress. If dispute is mentioned to 3rd party for advice the 2nd party themselves need not be.

2. In case of scenario where it is you and me and another Muslim for a salat then I propose we both unanimously insist the 3rd party lead the salat because otherwise it would not be 3.

3. You could also not lead the salat until this dispute is resolved so that way I could pray in Jama and there would be more people. I know that is much to ask and is offensive and unkind but there is precedent for Muslims in the past giving up rightful leadership to preserve unity and avoid distress. Ex. Hassan gave up the Khilafah to Muawwiya to avoid distress and disunity. So if Hassan gave up Khilafah then there is precedent to temporarily let another lead so as to increase the numbers of those in the jama. Of course this is an undesirable scandalous practice and terrible precedent but at the end of the day we are supposed to establish the salat. So if less people pray with you leading and more people pray with someone else leading then which is truly the greater good? For

Muslims to be united in salat with more focus behind someone else or for there to be less people with distraction behind you or one who knows the most Quran? Again I apologize for suggestion and know it is evil thing to suggest but it might be better if we just prayed side by side so as to increase the numbers of people in the rows. Sometimes to establish the salat may mean to not lead it even if one is in the right and is most qualified to lead. There are priorities to consider and reducing distress and disunity is a very big priority. Sometimes the best leaders are those who choose not to lead for the greater good, example Abu Ubaidah letting khaalid take the lead in several battles despite Abu Ubaidah being the true leader appointed to be in charge. Plus Abu Ubaidah let Khaalid lead the salat despite knowing he had been appointed as the leader because the benefit of Abu Ubaidah not leading the army in salat was greater than the benefit of him leading.

I know #3 is a bitter fix and apologize for the hurt feelings and for suggesting such a thing but until we can agree then it may be what Allah wants most, at the least I feel I must suggest it rather than not. Yet as a disclaimer since you brought that other guy into it now I have problems with things he said so I don't feel right praying behind him either because of the stuff he said that is even unrelated to the issue I have with the stuff you said. So now I have 2 different problems with 2 different people of which it used to be just 1 with 1, then 1 with 2 until you brought others into it making it 2 with 3. Although as it stands now I have 2 with 2 and I'm hoping I only have the ones as previous discussed with you but again now I don't know what you believe but apparently it is different than me. Yet it's possible to label the other person as ignorant so as to pray behind him, maybe, because I have not established the proofs against him but then again there are some things for which no proof is needed, like knowing that democracy is incompatible with shariah, so it gets hard to just constantly consider people as too stupid to be kafirs. That is the islamic policy for many instances though, regarding Muslims only not with kafirs, but there are exceptions where ignorance does not excuse kufr so it's a very tricky subject that is dangerous to dabble in but you brought others into it who I didn't want into it and even said I didn't want in it. Thus bringing others into this has only increased the problems.

At the least I think we should follow #1 suggestion so as to contain our mischief. More who get involved the more problems that tend to arise. That's why democracy causes so many problems.

After we are resurrected we will be brought to account for all the distress this dispute caused to the Muslims so we must minimize this and resolve it as soon as possible. We must always be aware that even in islamic disputes over the deen the devil wants us to cause undue unjust harm to each other and *everyone else in how we conduct ourselves. So lets not let the devil dictate our dispute, demeanor or anything we do.*

Eventually, four days later, I emailed Mr. Qadri of ISNF masjid noor an ultimatum saying I would go to a scholar overseas with our dispute if he didn't communicate with me by the end of the day to resolve it. I gave this ultimatum due to an offer from friends overseas in Saudi Arabia and Qatar who said they would ask Scholars there what we should do. Within 30 minutes of sending the email ultimatum to settle our dispute by the end of the day or else I'd contact an overseas Scholar, my house phone rang and it was Mr. Qadri's full name on caller id so I answered it and thought it was Qadri's voice, but the voice asked to speak with my mother and when I said she wasn't available the voice said he'd call back. I gave benefit of the doubt and went to Asr prayer thinking it must not have been Mr. Qadri despite the evidence because I couldn't comprehend how Qadri as an imam could call and talk to me on the phone but want to involve my non-Muslim mother in our aqeedah creed disagreement refusing to talk to me when he heard my voice as I heard his. Between Asr and Maghrib I sat-down and waited outside Qadri's office hoping to talk to him while Qadri and other ISNF leaders had a meeting in his office. The meeting went all the way until Maghrib sunset prayer and nobody came out as I waited outside the office making dua. After Maghrib, which Qadri and ISNF members came too late to join, as I was about to leave Qadri talked to me and said he didn't read the fatwas I emailed him and we got closer in our positions with the possibility of linguistic confusion being discussed as a possibility. So with such new information about his self-proclaimed excuse for ignorance and my technical failure to present proofs via email I decided to pray behind Qadri again until proof could be presented to him in a manner which I knew proof was received by him. I did think it odd though that Qadri said he didn't read any fatwa I emailed him though I was publicly praying by myself in the masjid instead of praying behind him. Seemed like a sincere person would at least read the fatwas alleging his position heretical especially when it caused publicly visible disunity. So I had stopped praying behind him on June 22nd, 2016 until August 10th, 2016 and that whole entire time he didn't send one email to me and only really had 3 conversations to resolve the troubling disagreement despite being a paid public leader of the mosque and community.

A few days later my parents came home unexpectedly saying they had a meeting with Imam Qadri, the president of ISNF Rasul Khan, and founder of ISNF Khalid Qazi, and according to my parents they said how I was too strict/extreme and that Islam teaches love and not hate. After further investigation and probing of my parents, I learned that during that earlier ISNF meeting while I waited outside Qadri's office on August 10th, he called my house again to schedule a meeting with my parents and the ISNF figureheads and it was supposed to be secret. So, Qadri called my house phone in the presence of ISNF board members to schedule a secret meeting with my non-Muslim parents at the very exact same time as I was waiting outside his office hoping to discuss our personal dispute, of which ISNF board members saw me waiting outside his office prior to entering themselves for the meeting wherein they called my house. Also I later found out that during this secret meeting with my parents Qadri asked my mom to spy on me and report all the lectures I listened to with her to him but not to tell me she was reporting to him. Yet bad as this is I found excuses for him giving Qadri the benefit of the doubt forgiving him without confrontation. Though in retrospect to call and schedule a meeting with my non-Muslim parents while he knows I'm waiting to talk to him outside his office seems very insincere and devious. Additionally to have me on the phone and want to talk to my non-Muslim mother when I don't pray behind him seems very insincere if he wanted to resolve the dispute as I did. Yet I did not let any of this stop me from praying behind him even though Qadri hadn't repented yet, because I felt he had not received my proofs via email and thus he was just ignorantly mistaken and perhaps too busy to communicate via email or too busy to read my lengthy explanations as I had expected him to.

Then one day I sat down with Qadri with the same printed fatwas I showed Payraw and asked Mr. Qadri his opinion on them. I then emailed a friend the following on August 31st, 2016 which puts our conversation in better words than I can recall:

Assalaamu Aleikum wa rahmatullaha wa barakatuhu

I talked to Imam today and showed him fatwas I sent you links to b4 and first one he read with he agreed with it. It was
https://islamqa.info/en/154606

So then we talked further about definitions of words and how one shouldn't use "love" but say care about or biological affinity for disbelievers or "natural love" but never use just "love" because this equates love for Muslims with love for non-Muslims. While they are not the same. Also explained the non-Muslim definitions of love and such so he understands that what he says gets misunderstood to be kufr because of the language and environment despite him meaning otherwise so it is best to be more specific with word choices and extensive in explanation. Also explained the christian notion of loving everybody thinking all are children of

God and Jesus pbuh allegedly died for all and such. Also warned how future generations can be led astray by using the "love" expression just as Satan misled people before Nuh pbuh that led to idolatry.

Explained how kafirs misunderstand hate and love as 100% love equaling blind loyalty even if the beloved is wrong and hate as being unmerciful genocidal racist hatred. While Islamic hate is different and the Islamic "love" is different. But when we say love they misinterpret, while if we stress we "care about" and hate then they understand what we mean because we show genuine care for them so the hate is understood as not extreme but a just hatred that can be kind or polite depending on how they are.

Mentioned too how the very same fatwa he read on paper and agreed to I had sent him before asking him to look at via email so that I could pray behind him if he agreed and such but he never replied. So I thought he disagreed. He said he never read it and seemed as though it was his first time reading and we explained why I prefer big long emails over talking and why he does talking and not emails. Thus he agreed with the fatwa but just never read the fatwas I sent while I thought he was reading them all and rejecting them all but he just don't read emails. So I was having a one-way conversation giving proof upon proof upon proof thinking all the proof was rejected and none of the proof was even examined and we weren't talking to each other in person. Shaitan got me I suppose.

Also established how all non-Muslims are disbelievers and are to be hated as a result to different degrees and that all are at war with Islam spiritually but not physically. Meaning since all are at war then you cannot be friends or "love" anything in the general sense of the word but one cannot harm most since they are not physical military combatants. Examples Mother Teresa is at war with Islam and Muslims but not to the extent of deserving treatment as a physical military enemy. Or priest preaching or church choir or average person going to church and just giving money to church constitutes war worthy of hatred but not war worthy of physical harm.

Thus different levels of hatred established and hatred for and the disbelief of all non-Muslims established and agreed upon,

Essentially miscommunication and misunderstandings led to problems.

Also talked about ISNF condemning all hatred and he said how he disagreed with their thing and talked to person responsible. Whereas I thought he agreed with it 100%.

So we agree I think but just disagree on vocabulary and things to emphasize when doing dawah

Also left fatwa with him to read later as it was time to pray

Issue seems to be resolved inshallah, it feels resolved.

Later in reading the Seerah(Biography of Prophet Muhammad) with my mother and how it clearly teaches hatred for non-Muslims and how the munafiqs(hypocrites pretending to be Muslim) would act, my mother warned me not to trust imam Qadri and be careful what I tell him. However since she is a Christian disbeliever I don't trust her so I rejected her warnings thinking they were meant to disunite Muslims and that I knew Qadri better.

Another oxymoron occurred when I told Mr. Qadri he should remove the deviant Kharijiesque author Sayyid Qutb's book "Milestones" from the masjid library because it teaches and promotes radical violent revolutionary extremism. Literally that book is like the constitution for groups like ISIS and Al-Qaeda wherein the author makes takfir of all Muslim rulers and even designed the black flag with white lettering later used by such Khariji groups. So I told Mr. Qadri you should get this book out of the mosque and destroy it lest it's deviant teachings spread and count as sins for you. Qadri refused saying it was donated and thus stays.

Another public error I found Qadri made in his talks was that he would say unislamic phrases like "Islam doesn't teach violence". Mr. Qadri actually said that 10 days after teaching Muslims how to slaughter animals for eid sacrifice. So I will not bother citing my lengthy angry email refutation of that modernist catchphrase, but suffice it to say Qadri had already read an early version of my book "Proper Jihad" prior to making that completely inaccurate pacifist pandering statement. So publicly Qadri says Islam has no violence, which is incorrect, whereas privately he simultaneously allows the books written by the grandfather of ISIS and Al-Qaeda to be present in the mosque for anyone to read. Thus Qadri was inevitably going in both extremes simultaneously. Which is almost funny how he was in error on both extremes of the spectrum. Whereas Mr. Qadri also made takfir of several Muslim rulers of Arabia making khuruj(rebellion) of the tongue, saying they were disbelievers in my presence during the earlier mentioned conversation where he refused to label the Roman Catholic Pope a disbeliever. Qadri's reasoning for these Arabian Muslim Rulers being disbelievers was because of not ruling by 100% Shariah, which is merely sinful and not necessarily disbelief, yet another ruler of a country called the Pope who rules the nation known as the Holy See / Vatican State Qadri refused to label as disbeliever despite him being an even worse ruler from an Islamic perspective and a non-Muslim too. As time went by these errors and contradictions of Mr. Qadri became larger and more extreme.

Around this time I got a pleasant surprise in the masjid when one day I saw my friend from Canada, Ahmed, in the ISNF masjid noor in America. Ahmed was the same friend that taught me how wrong suicide bombings are and why they are unislamic evil. It was about two or three years since I'd seen him, we had not communicated since then and neither of us expected to see each other there. Ahmed was there doing research for a newsletter article to compare the difference between Islamic preaching in America versus Canada and he wanted to interview Mr. Qadri for his perspective as a salaried Imam in America. So Ahmed and I had a long conversation catching up and I explained some of the errors I had seen in the ISNF propagation, like the "Happy Holidays" sign. We then exchanged contact information but I never ended up seeing what Ahmed wrote in his article. Regarding the topic of articles, occasionally ISNF would publish community newsletters. At one point in the past Mr. Qadri actually asked me to write the ISNF articles since he knew I was an author; as I had given him my early biography draft to review in 2014. Although I told Mr. Qadri rather than exclusively write all of ISNF articles myself, it would be better if anyone/everyone from the Muslim community could submit an article to him to review for accuracy and then he picked the best each month/week for the newsletter. This way if there is a wider pool of submissions we can as a community get the best of the best articles, as long as there is a systematic filterer to filter out errors. As you might've guessed none of my article submissions ever got picked to be printed in the ISNF newsletter despite Mr. Qadri's personal request for me to write the articles for them. That's no point of contention between us. I just mention it because for Mr. Qadri to have personally asked me to write the ISNF newsletter articles in the past makes his later behavior toward me all the more shocking and bizarre.

Days before the 2016 American presidential election Qadri said in the masjid during his Bayan before Khutbah, that Muslims in America have a duty to vote in the election. Whereas since months earlier ISNF had promoted people to register in the masjid to vote in the democratic primary, despite not endorsing a candidate verbally it was clear the female Hillary Clinton was his implied endorsement versus Donald Trump. I emailed Mr. Qadri evidence this pro-voting statement was forbidden for him to do, especially to do from the pulpit, and gave him the benefit of doubt of repenting though he never publicly recanted. In comparison during the 2024 American election race the week before voting took place the Imam of a different proper masjid said that regardless of whether you believe voting is sinful or not sinful the masjid is not the place for any partisan voting promotion. The masjids only exist for worship to be done within them and cannot be hijacked by politics or business interests or cultural interests, especially non-Muslim politics to promote non-Muslim personalities or agendas or platforms. Therein lies the difference between innovators and others is that innovators or deviants manipulate Muslims under religious auspices for anti-religious or sacrilegious purposes utilizing religious garbs, reasoning and environments to do so. Sadly on the voting day in 2016, Mr. Qadri didn't even show up for all of the daily prayers. In fact, I went to the ISNF masjid noor to pray on voting day and only me and my friend Payraw were there to pray the obligatory prayer which require a minimum of three people for it to be considered a congregation. So on the eve of the first Trump election selection, all the Muslims of the thousands of members of the ISNF community except for two people decided to not go pray their obligatory prayers in the masjid. How many do you think went to vote? Which is more important for Muslims, voting for non-Muslims trying to exert a drop of influence in a crooked game that not even the majority religious groups can win? Or praying as their prophet said to do as a community in congregational prayers? Every scholar agrees that even if one is deluded to think for some crazy reason they were allowed to vote at all, then it is forbidden to miss prayer in the masjid to do so, even moreso when one considers voting is sinful in most cases to begin with. So Muslims in America leave worship in the masjid in order to participate in allegiance to non-Muslim sinners in a religious ritual of deluded illusion. Yet then say they are glad to be "free to practice Islam".

In November 2016, one night as Qadri was walking away after prayer I told him *"I don't think I will tolerate another Happy Holidays sign this year"* and he just replied *"I don't think you should think out loud."* From then until almost Christmas I worked via email and getting friends to help with trying to convince Qadri that saying "Happy Holidays" on Christmas in billboard form was not permissible. We even collected 17 different alternative messages that could be put on a sign/billboard to convey Islam. My friend Payraw, then president of the MSA (Muslim Student Association) at the University of Buffalo, helped me and persuaded Qadri in a 3-way meeting that "Happy Holidays" is forbidden to say since even secular schools don't use it. I was surprised Qadri was convinced due to Payraw's simple statement when Mr. Qadri didn't believe me the year before in my emails that he read and responded to or in talks I had with him on the subject where I dissected the matter in depth. That was the first time I considered Qadri had potential to lie to me about his beliefs or be two-faced. Then we discussed the topic of obeying those in authority versus forbidding evil by the hand/tongue/heart. I thoroughly later explained in email to Mr. Qadri my position on the matter but sadly Mr. Qadri wrongly convinced Payraw that ISNF and him as "Imam" were what the Quran refers to as *"those in authority"* and that hadith refer to him as an "Imam" to which obedience is due even if they are oppressive or upon sinfulness. This was a tricky deception on the part of Mr. Qadri because the Quranic verses about "those in authority" and "Imams" mean Scholars and political national governmental leaders, they do not refer to a random salaried prayer leader at a single mosque, let alone one such person in America a place where there are no religious regulations set up to qualify "Imam" candidates. An Imam is somebody whom can legally militarily declare and wage Jihad and signs peace treaties who controls the affairs of the Muslim government. If you were in a Muslim nation nobody would ever consider the local masjid prayer leader to be an "Imam" in any capacity outside of prayer rituals. Yet those basic prayer ritual "Imams" in Muslim countries are much more qualified and knowledgeable than the "Imams" in American mosques as there are strict governmental criteria to pass before one is allowed to even apply to be considered for such governmental positions in Muslim nations. They go through years of training and testing after they become qualified to even apply. Most "Imams" in non-Muslim countries don't even qualify to apply to be considered eligible for a prayer leader position in a Muslim country. Basically in America they just ask if you have memorized the Quran and if so, then masha'allah they've found their treasure to put on the pedestal so they can pray taraweeh during Ramadan without their leader looking out of the book. Whereas the main organization in this narrative, ISNF, is merely a tiny microscopic faction of ignorant Muslim immigrants and descendants of immigrants that got together with some money and built a building incorporating into a non-profit organization and then unislamically held elections for some positions in that organization. Simply put, the leaders of ISNF or their prayer leader is not who the Quran and Sunnah defines as "those in authority"; not even by a long shot. They are just owners of a couple pieces of infrastructure without any real religious or political authority over Muslim masses. The real authority in America is the national government and then the state governments that divide into various counties and cities/villages. One cannot take verses in the Quran that apply to political military leaders and heads of State then say, "*Since we're in America and have so little political power then the democratically elected board members of the local masjid and our "Imam" are those whom the Quran means as "those in authority" to whom obedience is due.*" That position is almost more laughable than heretical Shiite beliefs regarding their "imams". And even if in an impossible alternate universe that were the case then still obedience is only in that which complies with the goodness of Islamic Shariah. It doesn't mean evil mistakes are allowed to be performed without criticism or stern face to face forbidding refutation. I never got to explain this to Payraw though because I figured emailing Mr. Qadri the evidence was more of a priority and I didn't have Payraw's email. Some of the evidences for the obligation of forbidding evil to be done by someone in all circumstances are as follows.

Narrated An-Nu`man bin Bashir:

The Prophet (ﷺ) said, "The example of the person abiding by Allah's order and restrictions in comparison to those who violate them is like the example of those persons who drew lots for their seats in a boat. Some of them got seats in the upper part, and the others in the lower. When the latter needed water, they had to go up to bring water (and that troubled the others), so they said, 'Let us make a hole in our share of the ship (and get water) saving those who are above us from troubling them. So, if the people in the upper part left the others do what they had suggested, all the people of the ship would be destroyed, but if they prevented them, both parties would be safe."

Source: Sahih al-Bukhari 2493

Shakyh Muhammad Abdu related:

"No Muslim, the Quran assumes, can be ignorant of the acts categorized as good and wrong. Such knowledge is not at all difficult to obtain. What is good in the Quranic sense is recognized universally as good. In the same way, *the forbidden acts are those of which every person instinctively disapproves. For knowledge of these directives one need not study specialized [scholarly] works... Enough guidance in this respect is provided by the Quran, the Sunnah and people's own consciences. No one can manage to remain ignorant of it. A Muslim is supposed to know it well. Those who interpret the duty of enjoining right and forbidding wrong in general terms appear to imply that an ordinary Muslim may not know or appreciate the difference between right and wrong acts. Such a viewpoint is certainly not in accord with the spirit of the religion of Islam...*

The duty of enjoining the good and forbidding the wrong is, in a certain sense, more desirable than that of performing the hajj pilgrimage. Only Muslims who can afford it are asked to perform hajj. However, no such prerequisite is required for this duty. It can be performed by all."

(Tafseer al Quran wa Hakeem [al Manar] volume 4)

Imam Ash-Shatibi said:

"Generally speaking, inviting others to what is good and right is obligatory and its fulfilment is compulsory on all. Some Muslims ---not all--- are capable of it. Those who are incapable should encourage and assist the capable ones. In other words, those who are capable are to perform it, while those who are incapable are required to persuade the capable ones to perform it. Both the capable and the incapable are thus entrusted with the responsibility of its performance."

(Al-Muwafaqah fee Usool Ash-Shariah)

Ali al-Qari said:

"Without doubt, enjoining what is good and right and forbidding what is wrong is a collective responsibility whenever there are a number of people capable of doing it. However, when there is only one person who possesses the knowledge necessary to carry it out, the duty to do so becomes an individual obligation."

(Al-Mubeen al-Mu'een)

Imam Ghazali said:

"One who acts as a silent spectator to the committing of wrongdoing is a transgressor. He is commanded by the Quran to forbid wrongdoing in every possible way. It is, therefore absurd to consider the permission of the ruler as a prerequisite for the fulfillment of this responsibility.

When the ruler himself is to be censured as part of this duty how can his permission be regarded as a prerequisite? The fact that the scholars and pious Muslims have reprimanded the rulers, as needed, proves by itself that no such permission is required. Moreover, if the ruler disapproves of some acts which are indeed good, this in itself amounts to committing a wrongful act. In short, the permission of the ruler is not at all necessary."

(Ihya Uloom ad-Deen volume 2)

Jalaluddin Umari said in "Maroof and Munkar":

"One may exercise discretion in ascertaining certain details of the Shariah. However, as far as the fundamentals go, there is no room for discretion. Anyone calling into question the very fundamentals of Islam cannot be referred to as one who is exercising discretion. One must certainly put a stop to the defiance

of basic Islamic teachings. Any digression from the Sunnah and the Shariah is considered to be a form of innovation. Al Ghazali made the following observation: (in Ihya Uloom ad-Deen):

> *'All innovators and their innovations are to be found, exposed, and stopped, even if they claim to be on the right path.'"*

Imam al Juwayni said:

"Every citizen in the Islamic State has a right to forbid what is wrong subject to the condition that it is by persuasion and does not entail bloodshed. Should the situation be grave, the matter must be left to those who are in power." (Shar Muslim an-Nawwawi)

Uwais al Qarni said:

"No doubt enjoining right and forbidding wrong have left the believer with no friend. Whenever we enjoin right upon the people or forbid them to do wrong, they offense our honors, and find assistants from among the wicked to support them. They indeed charged me with the most hideous slanders. But by Allah, I will not cease to enjoin right upon them and forbid them to do evil."

Source: Siyar Alam An Nubala 4:19

Imam Barbaharee said:

"From the Sunnah is that you do not obey anyone in disobedience to Allah; neither the parents nor the entire creatures. There should be no obedience to any creature in disobedience to Allah. Do not love anyone upon it (disobedience to Allah); you should hate all that for the sake of Allah."

Source: Sharus Sunnah point 169

So these innovative "Happy Holidays" signs were a clear evil well-known to commoners and Scholars alike, but ignorantly promoted by Mr. Qadri and ISNF until the head of the Muslim Student Association, Payraw, "persuaded" Qadri with much less effort and evidence that I had presented which failed to change his mind. Anyways I was glad progress seemed to be made on this issue of the ISNF sign. Despite Mr. Qadri finally agreeing the "Happy Holidays" sign was wrong the year before, in the end of 2016 ISNF put up a big billboard saying "Seasons Greetings from the Islamic Society" which for all intents and purposes is almost equivalent in impermissibility as the Happy Holidays to our friends and neighbors sign of 2015; but still it was an improvement thus I left it alone despite personal disgust with it after mentioning this too was bida to Payraw. One of my revert friends Abdul Haq thanked me for persuading Mr. Qadri to have not put up the same sinful sign as last year, yet I declined taking credit because the fact is Qadri only changed it for Payraw.

Shortly after this sign was put up and then eventually taken down when the contract expired an alleged "Scholar" from Atlanta, Georgia, USA came to visit the masjid to give a lecture. This lecture was all about "People whom Allah dislikes". The entire lecture consisted of the speaker listing verses of the Quran that say "Allah dislikes X people or X attribute" and he cited his sources in Arabic and English. I was elated because this surprise lecture vindicated my position regarding the summer dispute with Mr. Qadri and others wherein they falsely mistakenly taught that "God loves everybody" and "its wrong to hate". Even though the speaker used the term "dislike" I made it a point to publicly ask him in front of the entire masjid if I am correct to use the term "hate" instead of dislike. The speaker said I was correct. Again I asked a question publicly whether, *"Is it correct to believe that it is obligatory to hate all disbelievers and that Jews and Christians are all disbelievers, and even some sinful Muslims are hated according to their level of sinfulness since some of the attributes you mentioned apply to Muslims too? But our love for Muslims outweighs our hatred of them due to sins whereas we are forbidden to love non-Muslims due to their disbelief outweighing any good they do?"* The "Scholar" said I was exactly correct and that was the happiest I had ever been in that masjid, especially since Mr. Qadri was right in front of the speaker in the first row hearing how I was right and he was wrong regarding our dispute; although I hid his sin despite not being able to hide my prideful smile as Mr. Qadri stared at me. Sheikh Ibn Uthaymeen was asked a similar question once and he replied,

> *"If we have a believer, he has sins and he also has faith, what is our position towards him? We have allegiance to him according to [what he possesses of] his faith, and we hate him due to what he has from sins and disobedience…this believer who is a fasiq(rebellious sinful person), we love him due to what he has of faith and we hate him due to what he has from sin. And what is amazing is that some people hate the sinful believer more than they hate the kafir(disbeliever). This is a problem! This is turning the facts and reality upside down. We must hate the kafir(disbeliever) with all our heart, because he is an enemy to Allah and His Messenger and an enemy to us…"*

Then I let others ask questions on the topic before asking my final question to the "Scholar" from Georgia whose credentials I didn't know. I asked him in a less specific manner what the ruling was on meetings of "Abrahamic faiths" where people get together claiming to all belong to Prophet Abraham. This was my smoking gun against the interfaith agenda. Already the Scholar publicly said how Hatred was obligatory and Love was forbidden and that Jews and Christians were disbelievers. Yet in response to this question he seemed not to understand the reality of what was going on or why I asked the question, because he merely said how since some people become Muslims as a result it is hard to prohibit it entirely but dawah should be done "with wisdom". Obviously the "dawah"(inviting people to Islam) was not done with wisdom by ISNF or MPAC, especially since they would include the Shia heretics in their interfaith gatherings sometimes too. But alas I failed in adequately asking the question accurately depicting the scenario of the community so the Scholar didn't have enough information to forbid the Interfaith events as I hoped. Still to have Mr. Qadri witness that I was correct in what I taught him while he was wrong and have the others who knew of our dispute learn this too, like my friend Payraw and his Dad, was a victory in my book. Later that month when my Mom visited the masjid one day, Payraw's Dad even talked with my Mom and labeled me saying I was a "Good Man"; despite being only 24 years old. That was the first time I had ever been complimented to such an extent by someone I argued with and whose very son I had refused to pray behind just months before. Mr. Qadri didn't congratulate or thank me for having taught him or corrected him regarding our dispute and in fact seemed uncomfortable regarding the comments said by the "Scholar" they themselves had approved and invited to lecture. I say this because the very next day I believe I overheard the then Secretary of ISNF at that time and Mr. Qadri saying how Qadri should give a special lecture on the topic of not hating people because the kids who listened to the Scholar answer the questions last night might get confused. That's when I worried that the correct Islamic Scholastic position might not have sunk in overnight. It seemed to me the only thing Mr. Qadri picked up from the lecture was that Muslims have to preach "with wisdom" as he parroted this statement many times since then while teaching oppositely unwise things. So naturally I sent him a private email of correctional advice.

Email Sent Friday, Jan 13, 2017 at 1:10 PM

Assalaamu Aleikum wa rahmatullaha wa barakatuhu

I noticed you stressed preaching with wisdom to "non-Muslims" as you call the kuffar.

You used the word wisdom a lot and it's same word used by other Imam when describing how to correctly do "Abrahamic faith dawah". But is your definition the same as his? Or mine?

I don't think the ISNF dawah in the past was with wisdom and I think it would be wise if they did not do the "Tent of Abraham" this year because they aren't qualified to do dawah to christians and Jews simultaneously correctly with wisdom in my opinion. Every intelligent religious preacher knows if you are going to preach effectively it's best to preach to people of 1 faith. For example when Muhammad pbuh preached to Christians did he have the Jews there too and preach to both groups at the same time? No. He kept them separate because that is wisdom in preaching to them since each has different issues and if together when preached to they are less likely to agree with Islam when they see others who don't agree with it for different reasons. So for Muslims to voluntarily want Jews and Christians in same place to do dawah is foolish and ineffective if the goal is for both groups to become Muslims. Why do you think Christians don't invite Muslims and Jews to church at the same time? Because they can't preach Jesus to us both at the same time because we have different issues with their version and will use the other non-Christians as proofs that Christians are wrong if we feel doubt. Particularly in a democratic society 2 non-Muslim groups vs. 1 Muslim seems proof to them that Islam is wrong. But if you are in a 1 on 1 situation, then conversions can happen. Ideally ISNF wouldn't do Abrahamic faith thing at all because Muhammad pbuh never did this so if it was effective he would have done it as would Muslims pre-WWII and pre-Israel. This "Abrahamic dawah" is a post-Israel phenomenon so Israel can avoid a holy war that defeats them. It wasn't preached prior to Israel. Seriously Muhammad pbuh never preached this "We're all children of Abraham" stuff and he lived in a tribalistic era. So if it was ever "wise" he would've done it, but he didn't. Yet if ISNF still wants to do the "tent of Abraham" don't do it this Ramadan. I know they've done it each Ramadan X years in a row and that's why it's wise to not do it this year. Opting out reasserts control over the event. Christians and Jews can't just expect a free meal every year, if Muslims want to do that it's on Islamic terms for Islamic reasons not because of tradition and social expectations. The Christians and Jews today feel entitled to an annual free meal that makes them certified as tolerant and interfaith pluralists. Not doing it makes it something Muslims are in control over and shows there is a limit to interacting. For the Muslims who wonder why no Abrahamic meal they can be told we simply aren't qualified to communally preach Islam wisely to Jews/Christians without diluting Islam, at this time. By cancelling the event for a year ISNF can have extra time to get wise to do communal dawah and it sends a polite message to Jews and Christians. By skipping a year its lets them know that there are more important things to Muslims than inter-faith nonsense. Politely ISNF can just tell the Kafirs that they want to take a year off without seeming extreme or intolerant and that will create a safe distance between kafir and Muslims so next time when there is wise politely intolerant pro-Islam preaching it's not as much of a shock. It also shows Muslims *that its not the quantity of dawah that matters, and we aren't concerned with kafir attitudes and we only do dawah if its wise and effective. It's not to be a yearly pro-tolerance entertainment exhibit. To have yearly "Abrahamic faith" events shows its not effective because if it were they'd become Muslims and you wouldn't be having an annual get together because they'd be Muslims. When Muhammad pbuh had Jews and Christians doing dawah, he didn't say "Ok come back next year same time, same place. And the year after that and the year after that forever and ever." Instead before leaving he asked them to make a dua with him to curse those upon falsehood. When the "Abrahamic tent" disperses do you ask them to make the dua the Quran says to make? Do you ever plan on doing that? After how many years of dinners will the dua be made? If never then this is not the prophetic type of dawah.*

Anyways I agree with you that Muslims must preach with wisdom but you aren't defining it for them. We can agree the Muslims in America don't have wisdom. They are expecting you to teach them how to preach with wisdom but then you just say "Preach with wisdom", without making them wise. To get wisdom about how to say things to kafirs the right way, you gotta have experience in saying it the wrong way first. You gotta piss a lot of people off to learn how to preach the intolerant truth politely. If Muslims have never pissed people off they don't know what they can say and can't say or how to say what they want to say in a way that gets the polite response they want regardless of what it is they are saying. Also remember the reaction of the kafir to your preaching is not necessarily a reflection of your preaching. Pissing them off doesn't mean you preached without wisdom, the truth pisses many people off and nothing but false pleasantries will please them. So if politeness is the goal this is not wisdom. The goal has to be conveying the prophetic message WITHOUT DILUTION appropriately. It's better to piss em off than to dilute Islam. Never dilute Islam for the sake of politeness, just work on hate preaching politely. Don't limit the hate in any way just package it more politely. Wisdom doesn't mean not to express hatred, it means to get them to accept hatred voluntarily through wise justification. Many think hate is unwise or even unislamic. So when you stress wisdom don't forget to give real examples that display wisdom. Many may mistakenly think hatred is unwise.

For example you have to say "As an example Kafirs say X and You reply X." and you can't just make this stuff up you have actually use real dialogue from real kafirs. Otherwise it's just theory. And the theories many Muslims have about "wise preaching" are grossly incorrect.

Hate for religious reasons makes religion important and religious differences important.

Persecution increases your attachment to your faith.

Hatred from another towards you makes you think about converting, persecution makes you firm.

Hate preaching gets converts, Persecution inhibits conversion. Display hate but don't persecute.

Many Muslims believe in freedom, equality and love for kafirs and think such things are "wisdom".

Rather than stress "preach with wisdom" I think Muslims must be told that "You Muslims don't have wisdom to spread Islam in this country and that's why it hasn't been spreading. Lets face it you didn't come to this country to convert the Americans to Islam did you? And you aren't staying in this country to convert them or establish Shariah are you? Learn Islam. Take the time to learn and practice. You have to live the Shahada before you can teach it to others." We need less Muslim preachers today because the foolish ones doing the "wise preaching" are harming the wise preaching done by others. In America it'd be better to specialize than decentralize. We are after quality not quantity. Dawah in dar al-kufr is not meant to have the masses become Muslim. Inshallah that could happen but there is a limit to what is realistically expected in dar al-kufr. Whenever prophets preached in dar al-kufr only a minority believed. Their preaching was to the masses but the masses were not really the targeted market, their preaching was not tailored to the masses and as such it was effective to a certain extent. If the preaching is tailored to the mass mainstream appeal then it will fail because while Islam is for the masses the masses will not accept it in dar al-kufr. If you try preaching for mass acceptance in this country then even the minority who would've accepted Islam will turn away from it because that's not prophetic preaching. Must have realistic goals. The end goal is 100% Muslim population, but you aren't going to get that by preaching to 100% of the population. You have to preach to a minority then they preach to a minority who preach to others and others. There is a chain reaction. To get a strong core to start with you need a strong "radical" message. The average person won't become a practicing Muslim in dar al-kufr. We'll accept those people as they come but we aren't targeting them because they aren't going to be doing the dawah because they will only become Muslim via a diluted dawah and that's why they'll practice a diluted version of Islam. If you want fully practicing Muslims doing dawah to the fullest you have to preach the full undiluted intolerant version of Islam full wisdom. "Preaching with wisdom" just means polite preaching and anyone from any faith can do that. Christians "preach with wisdom" but they don't preach full undiluted fundamentalist Islam.

I think perhaps a class should be created to teach Muslims how to do dawah correctly to the various types of kafirs. Each faith requires a different type of dawah. Each denomination of each faith requires a different type of dawah. AND you need to have analysis abilities because most kafirs don't know what type of kufr they believe in so you have to preach to what they believe and not what they tell you they believe. For some religions I might be able to teach how to do dawah, somewhat, but currently I don't have the time to dedicate to such a project. Maybe in the future inshallah. Yet if you are going to do dawah in the community, a simple lecture every few months is not going to be enough training. Many Muslims really need to be trained, you haven't trained them to do dawah and they don't have wisdom. So "Preach with wisdom" is an empty phrase that doesn't teach them what to do. They aren't going to "preach with wisdom" just because you drilled it into their heads because they don't have the wisdom, they just have a catchphrase and by you telling them to "preach with wisdom" they think they have it since you told them to preach. Hence they'll keep preaching however they want but think it's wisely because you told them "preach with wisdom" and they remembered you said that, thus by remembering that they'll think they're doing that when they're not. They don't know *they aren't qualified to do dawah wisely and you are making them think they are. Yet before being trained they need to believe in core principles of Islam and many don't even have that. Most Muslims in this country are only Muslims because they are ignorant, which prevents takfir. Simply put Muslims can't preach what they don't believe and practice, if they believe in unislamic concepts like freedom, democracy, equality, love, interfaith they will preach that and if they practice democracy, nationalism, capitalism, conformity, hedonism then they will preach that. Ignorant people are incapable of preaching with wisdom even when they are told to do so because they aren't wise. ISNF is full of ignorant people who will "wisely preach ignorance" to people thinking they are wisely preaching islam. Wise people don't need to be told to preach with wisdom because they do that naturally.*

Since you tell them to "preach with wisdom" it means they aren't qualified to do good preaching. You gotta teach them the wisdom. You don't teach them they need wisdom, they are coming to you to get it and you are saying they need to use it. But they don't have it to use it. You aren't saying they don't have it and you aren't saying what it is. So I don't think you are wisely teaching people to preach with wisdom. Teaching to preach is different than telling to preach. Are you teaching or are you telling?

The Muslims must slow down with the preaching and work on the practicing, preaching comes with practicing not before practicing. No non-practicing Muslim ever does successful preaching. The practicing Muslim only preaches because it's part of practicing, not because they want to preach or want others to practice. So any non-practicing preacher isn't really preaching Islam. One who is free can never preach slavery. Only a slave can invite people to be slaves effectively. Muslims here aren't slaves in their lifestyle thus they can never preach the slavery that is Islam until they become true genuine strict slaves of God. A slave doesn't preach how the audience likes it or wants it, they preach the way their master says to do so, hate/intolerance and everything. If Muslims can't even utter the words hate in the house of Allah they definately don't have it for kufr or kafirs and won't preach it when outside the masjid. If people aren't willing to preach hate preaching amongst Muslims in Allah's house how will they do it outside Allah's house amongst Satan and his allies? The purpose of preaching is to please Allah. Honestly I don't think the local Muslims even know that. They preach to give Muslims a better image or "rights" or to improve relationships. Some, usually reverts, preach for converts. But who preaches for Allah's sake? With wisdom means to please Allah, not to preach politely. Sometimes preaching politely is foolish to do and unwise.

Fire/brimstone preachers are effective despite being impolite because it's a wise way to preach.

Just take the violent extremists as an example. How is it they can get people to literally blow themselves up? Do they do that by preaching stupid stuff like a fool? No they "preach with wisdom". Preaching with wisdom is not the problem, the problem is preaching nonsense in the name of tolerance, freedom, equality, unity, democracy and love but calling that Islam.

In January 2017, I figured it would be best to have another meeting with Mr. Qadri and my parents and me this time. And this was the first time I really confronted Mr. Qadri about the secret meeting he had with my parents during summer 2016 wherein he said to them Islam teaches love for all and that I am wrong to hate and such. I approached Mr. Qadri saying how whatever he told my parents has messed them up and hindered my dawah and that I don't think it was islamic for him to have talked to them secretly along with Rasul Khan and Khalid Qazi when we had our problem earlier when he could've just talked to me directly. Mr. Qadri said,

"When we had that problem with you not praying we couldn't get through to you and we tried to talk to you so we only talked to your parents because we didn't know how else to solve the problem of you not praying with us and lots of Muslims were complaining about you not praying with us. So we talked to your parents because we weren't able to communicate with you after having tried every way we could." Whereas in reality he didn't email me once, nor talk to me on the phone when I answered his call and only barely talked to me in person at my behest three times in nearly three months, so upon this statement I knew that Mr. Qadri lied to me.

Also I had been praying behind Mr. Qadri for four entire days, 20 prayers, before the secret meeting took place, so if not praying behind Mr. Qadri was the reason for the meeting it should never have happened. Thus it was a lie by Qadri to my face. Therefore after that I felt upset with Qadri so I figured to utilize my angry emotions constructively and try to stop his minor bida of congregational dua (supplication) after fajr by privately advising him its bida and such. I gave him a private note after fajr salat saying not to do it because it's bida. Mr. Qadri read the note and did it anyways. He just told me it's not bida and walked away. I went after him and talked about it and Qadri expressed his dislike for Salafi Scholars and Salafis. (which I thought was another bad sign) Mr. Qadri kept making congregational dua after fajr and so I would make dua out loud against/refuting his congregational dua, verbally asking Allah to guide people away from the bida of congregational dua. Nobody said anything to me about it. I emailed Qadri fatwas saying it's bida and suggested that he read hadith after fajr instead thus replacing it without losing face on something all agree is good/okay/better. Qadri could only quote a Sufi Shaqili alleged cult leader Nuh Ha Meem Keller as saying it's okay and not bida. Then I talked again with Qadri and he felt I was disrespectful so he stopped talking to me and walked away. Another time we talked again about it in the masjid about being bida or not and in reply to my proofs he simply said, *"You have no friends."*

and walked away. Which I thought was wrong for an Imam to say such in an argument over fiqh since it was a direct insult and at all because Allah and angels and Muslim Jinn are friends of believers even if they have no human friends. I followed Qadri to his office and sincerely apologized for upsetting him and he agreed to talk with me but didn't apologize himself. Then I asked him to read hadith instead of congregational dua after fajr and Qadri said no and that doing hadith readings only after Isha is enough and he is too busy to do a hadith reading after fajr. Then in his office in my presence Mr. Qadri read the fatwas in email that I sent days before and said he didn't read them when I sent them because he knew the arguments already so he skimmed them. After reading the fatwas Qadri simply said, *"That's why I don't like Salafi scholars because everything is bida with them."* I was shocked at such "dislike" for the best of the best of the Muslims but kept calm. Another time Qadri had heretically said *"We are not Ahl-Hadith."* but I had figured he didn't mean such things literally but was mistakenly saying such due to some groups in India and Pakistan being mislabeled "Ahl-Hadith" when they are otherwise. Ahl-Hadith and Salafi are basically synonymous terms and both labels can apply to all the Muslim Scholars and Muslims upon the prophetic creed and methodology. So for Mr. Qadri to have said such stuff before about not being "Ahl-Hadith" and then also express "dislike" for Salafis was a huge red alarming warning flag of deviance and ignorance and arrogance.

Abu Haatim said:

"A sign of the people of innovation is their battling against the people of Narrations(hadith)."

As-Saffaareenee said

"And we are not focusing on mentioning the virtues of the people of Hadith, for indeed their virtues are well known and their merits are many. So whoever belittles them, then he is despicable and lowly. And whoever hates them, then he is from the backward party of the Devil."

Source: Lawaa'ihul Anwaar

Abu Uthman As-Saaboonee said:

"The signs of the people of innovation are clear and obvious. The most apparent of their signs is their severe enmity for those who carry the reports(hadith) of the Prophet."

Source: The Aqeedah of the (Pious) Predecessors page 101

Abdul Qaadir Al-Jeelaanee said:

"As for the saved sect it is Ahlu Sunnah Wal Jamaah and there is no name for Ahlu Sunnah except one, and that is the people of hadith."

Source: Al Ghunyatut Taalibeen

Abu Haatim Ar Raazee said:

"A sign of the people of innovation is their hatred of the people of narrations(hadith)."

Source: Ibnut Tabaree in As-Sunnah

Imam Ash Shaafie said:

"Stick to the people of hadith, since they are the most correct from amongst the people."

Source: Siyar A'laamin Nubulaa

Jafar bin Ahmed bin Sinan said: 'I heard my father saying:

'There is not a Mubtadi' (innovator) except that he hates the companions of Hadeeth. And if a man innovates a Bida then the sweetness of the Hadeeth is torn out from his heart.'

Source: Siyaar 'Alaam an-Nubala

Mr. Qadri then said he thinks that making congregational dua is more important than teaching a hadith. Qadri refused to teach hadith instead of the dua which I said was bida and risky to do even if he thinks it's not bida, and that for the sake of unity he would stop but Mr. Qadri stressed he thinks the congregational dua supplication he says is that important it's worth it but reading hadith is not. I really tried to get Qadri to read hadith instead of dua any way I could. I even said if he wants to do the dua and the hadith that's his decision but he should at least do hadith after fajr even if he still makes the dua. Yet Qadri just didn't want to teach hadith after fajr even with the dua too and couldn't give me any reason I considered Islamically valid. I even asked if it's just because I suggested it and he doesn't want to lose the argument or something so that's why he is saying no? But he just flat out said how he just doesn't want to teach hadith after fajr. That was all he could say was that "I don't want to." and for him that's reason enough to not recite hadith after fajr even when I ask and expound the benefits of it. Lastly I even asked him in the name of Allah with tears falling off my face to teach hadith after fajr too, even if he still does the dua which I say is bida. Which I thought for sure he'd say okay because he himself publicly stated when someone asks for something from you in Allah's name then you have to say yes. But instead he said he'll consider it. I was upset Qadri still didn't say yes, then he said, "*You should be happy I said I'd consider it, before you asked in the name of Allah I wasn't even considering doing a hadith after fajr.*" Then I told Qadri this is why I don't think he's sincere and then he says I'm disrespectful and you can't just say someone isn't sincere to their face the way I do to him, he said it's unislamic to do. By this time I recognized that was Qadri's pattern when arguing, whenever he loses he says you argue disrespectful in a way unbefitting a "scholar" as he calls himself. Anyways I waited to see if he'd read hadith or not and he didn't, for several days Qadri didn't despite saying he'd consider it. He kept doing the dua though. I emailed evidence that Umar would beat those who made congregational dua in the masjids and that Umar made individual dua and told ibn Abbas to make individual dua and nobody ever even suggested making congregational dua thus proving it's a bida. Also Imam Shatibi, a Muslim Scholar from Spain who died in 1388 CE, in his book Kitab Itisam devoted many pages, paragraphs and chapters to this specific bida explaining many ways and reasons why congregational dua is sinful bida. Its not just a few sentences or pages, but literally entire chapters of Ash-Shatibi's book explained in depth why congregational dua is bida; as is most synchronized congregational acts of worship that have no prophetic precedence. But I did not read that book by this time so I used what evidences I knew of at the time. Suffice it to say on a fundamental basis only an arrogant person would perform congregational dua routinely especially when advised to stop as its bida. It's because the person thinks their dua supplication is special and so important for others to say Ameen to and hear that they would even contemplate doing such an act publicly in the first place. Also Angels make dua for those who study hadith, even if they aren't sincere in their studies of it and are just overhearing for other reasons. So if Mr. Qadri even knew the hadith about the angels supplicating for hadith students then he is basically saying that his individual dua is so valuable that it is better for the community than them learning their religion from the Prophetic Hadith and having multitudes of Angels supplicate for their goodness. Such a position is undoubtedly in error even if congregational dua wasn't bida as they foolishly claimed. I asked Qadri if he read the extra evidence I emailed him and he said he did but he still didn't change his position. So on February 2nd, 2017 before Mr. Qadri made dua after fajr I told him face to face publicly in front of people how, "*I privately advised you making congregational dua is bida because Umar bin Khattab would beat those who did it in the masjid with sticks. So this is sinful bida that you are publicly doing and any who follow you in doing this would be sinful and all bida is rejected.*" Then Mr. Qadri raised his hands and made dua silently then gave me a mini-lecture in front of everyone else on respecting "difference of opinions" saying how if I don't like the way things are done and keep spreading disunity then I should leave and stop coming to the masjid. I made it clear that there is no reason for me to leave and that what I'm doing is right and he is publicly doing bida making all who follow sinful and even if he disagrees he should stop for the sake of unity and if he's right and stops arguing that is better for him to do. Yet Qadri said he will continue and I said I'll continue to forbid you. I did not mention my idea of him teaching hadith after fajr publicly because I was hoping he would do it and by me pressuring him publicly to do so it would be less likely for him to do since it'd seem like he was giving in to me. Thus even when publicly correcting him I was his friend with his best interests in mind the entire time hoping for goodness for him. If Qadri had started teaching hadith the next day, nobody would have known that Qadri gave in to my ideas they would've thought he came up with such a good idea all by himself. Instead of taking that route, Qadri publicly said in front of everyone in the masjid that if I continue "*ISNF will take some steps*" threatening me. Also this was not the first time Qadri said I should leave the masjid if I didn't like something. Mr. Qadri privately told me before I should leave the masjid if I don't like things that go on there but this was the first time Qadri publicly said I should leave the masjid in front of others. Nobody else said anything to either of us but I got quite a few glares.

I decided I would just continue as is, but since Mr. Qadri was openly choosing to commit minor bida in clear contradiction of private and public advice to cease with verification of the evidence being read by him, I made one adjustment. I would go to pray in the masjid behind Mr. Qadri and then after the prayer I would close my eyes until I was sure that Mr. Qadri left, despite him praying right in front of me most of the time. This was because I was disgusted and didn't want to see him lest I lose my temper or be exposed to seeing further innovations or errors that I would feel compelled to correct/condemn if I saw with my own eyes. However I think it bothered Mr. Qadri's ego that I would pray behind him yet refuse to look at him before or after the prayer. I did this for several prayers not looking at him or speaking to him. After a night prayer that same day after praying a night salat together (February 2nd 2017) Payraw, me and Qadri had a 3-way meeting to resolve the new dispute between me and Mr. Qadri. Basically they double-teamed me and said that because I'm not a

Scholar, don't have certification, don't know Arabic fluently and don't "have a teacher" then I'm not allowed to have an opinion or say the opinions of others are wrong regardless of whatever proofs I bring to support my claims. They said my opinion is invalid because "you don't have a teacher or ijazas". I explained how I can't give fatwas or impose my opinions on others but I can still possibly come to a correct opinion without being a Scholar, knowing Arabic or "having a teacher" and it all depends on an opinion by opinion basis as to whether my method at arriving at an opinion is correct and if the proof is authentic and supports the opinion. Things got a little heated because I went into saying how even if I'm not qualified if I see evil/wrong and it isn't being corrected or stopped then somebody has to say something and it's obligatory for the wrong to be refuted by somebody. Thus that's why I condemn their interfaith junk. Then they got on my attitude towards kafirs and spreading disunity between Muslims/kafirs and among Muslims. I said how unity is not the purpose of Islam or the prophetic dawah but the purpose is to distinguish the truth from the falsehood, and the right from the wrong, the good from the bad. To do that is to disunite mankind and Allah says how mankind will never cease to differ and if he wanted he could have made us all one nation, but we aren't because he doesn't want unity at the expense of what is true/right. Then they said how you have to be united with Muslims, and I taught them that's if they are good and doing the right stuff, not if they are wicked doing wrong things in that case it's best for disunity lest everyone be wrong and go astray. They thought unity is most important echoing the popular innovative deviant Ikhwani Muslim Brotherhood principles. I thought truth and following the prophetic Islam correctly was more important. Then they said how my dawah leads non-Muslims away from Islam and the Quran says "if you were harsh with them they'd turn away from you" and you are harsh with people and no one you preach to will become Muslim. I said those verses were about prophet not being harsh with Muslims after the battle of Uhud and that for kafirs(disbelievers) you are harsher with them as Quran says how you will find them harsh with the disbelievers and merciful with each other (or something to that effect perhaps not in that order). This led to us talking about Jews/Christians and Mr. Qadri had trouble with me labeling them and all non-Muslims as kafirs/disbelievers. And I had trouble with Qadri having trouble with that. Qadri said something like *"not all non-Muslims are kafirs some of them are Mushriks so you can't call all of the non-Muslims kafirs"*. He said Christians were Mushriks(polytheists) and not kafirs(disbelievers). I said they are both, got upset and said how every Mushrik is a Kafir but not every Kafir is a Mushrik, a Mushrik(polytheist) is just a certain type of Kafir (disbeliever) who does a certain type of Kufr (disbelief). Then he asked what about Jews and Christians are they all Kafirs? I explained as calmly as possible that non-Muslim is synonymous with kafir and he said "no it's not" and I think he might have additionally said not every non-Muslim is a kafir or disbeliever. So I was saying how yes they are and there are only 2 categories that exist: Muslim and Non-Muslim or Muslim and Kafir stressing again how all non-Muslims are kafirs. I said how anyone who isn't a Muslim is a kafir(disbeliever) by default. In reply Mr. Qadri said, no a kafir is someone who deliberately takes the seed and hides it, (so a kafir is a special category where they know the truth and intentionally hide it but all non-Muslims aren't kafirs). He didn't say that parenthesis part at that time but he said that before in conversation to me so he didn't need to because I knew what he meant when he started the "kufr is to hide and a kafir is one who hides" linguistical trick. So then Mr. Qadri asked if all Ahl-Kitab are kafirs? I said how there are Muslims considered to be Ahl-Kitab, like Salman Farsi and Abdullah bin Salam (over the 2016 summer during our dispute he told me Salman Farsi wasn't a Christian but a fire-worshipper and never a Christian, which proved to me his ignorance especially since you can't understand Quran Tafsir without knowing that, but he has since accepted/remembered that Salman became a Christian before becoming Muslim). This is something many Muslims forget, those Ahl-Kitab Christians and Jews who became Muslims, were still occasionally called Ahl-Kitab during the prophet's lifetime and Allah refers to them as such in the Quran in some places. Not every Ahl-Kitab verse is about non-Muslims, some of them are about Muslims who converted. (Like the ones about Ahl-Kitab who prostrate when the Quran is recited, or say "even before this we were Muslims", or even the one where Allah says "Ask the people of the Scripture if you don't know or doubt." that verse isn't telling Muhammad to ask Jews or Christians if he is a prophet (as Christians today falsely claim) it was telling him to ask those Muslims who used to be Jews and Christians if his features were described in previous Scriptures and such. Then the Muslim reverts confirmed it, most Jews/Christians denied it.) So after explaining how some "Ahl-Kitab" are Muslims, (I might be in that category), I stressed that the Ahl-Kitab who don't say the shahada(Islamic testimony of faith) or become Muslims are all kafirs. So every Jew (religious not ethnic) and every Christian is a kafir and it's obligatory to believe this and say it. I had already sent him fatwas before saying this on January 13th 2017 and other times as well because I feared he might've thought that. I challenged Mr. Qadri to call every Imam in Western New York and they'll say the same and how everyone says this and you can make takfir(legally label as an apostate) of someone who doesn't believe Jews/Christians are kafirs or that non-Muslims aren't kafirs. Yet Qadri didn't seem to believe me. Instead Qadri asked me, *"Can't you marry Ahl-Kitab? You can't marry kafirs but you can marry Ahl-Kitab so how can they all be kafirs? Can you marry Ahl-Kitab yes or no?"* (he was testing me to see if I would say "No you can't marry a Christian or Jew lady it's haram!") I just said yes you can marry them subject to certain conditions but you can't love them and you have to hate them and they are kafirs. Just because you can marry them doesn't mean they aren't kafirs. Yet sadly Qadri disagreed with me on this, thinking Christian/Jewish women aren't kafirs because you can marry them. Even though he knew Muslim women are forbidden from marrying Christian and Jewish men, because they are Kafirs and he had been to Mecca where Jews and Christians of all genders are prohibited from entering due to their kufr/disbelief. Then Qadri even expressed doubt over the important fundamental fiqh decree prohibiting Muslims from inheriting Christians and Jews or any disbeliever despite the numerous sahih hadith mentioning it as being forbidden for Muslims to inherit disbelievers or any non-Muslim or "person of other religion".

It was narrated from 'Amr bin Shu'aib, from his father, from his grandfather, that the Messenger of Allah (ﷺ) said:

"People of two different religions do not inherit from one another."

Source: Sunan Ibn Majah 2731 Grade: Sahih as well as Sunan abi Dawud 2911 Grade: Sahih, with the wording variation of Ibn Majah cited above.

By not knowing this core fiqh matter due to his Aqeedah error Mr. Qadri is ignorantly allowing people to inherit when it is sinful and legalizing the illegal transfer of wealth under the guise of it being allowed due to his own corruption and ignorance about hadith and Islamic creed. Mr. Qadri even specifically said that there are three categories: Muslim, non-Muslim and Ahl-Kitab. I insisted there are only two, Muslim and Kafir. Sadly when I asked Payraw for support during this new on the spot dispute over core fundamental creed Payraw said that he doesn't even know what we were talking about. Payraw had zoned out after we continued going back and forth and missed the huge error of Mr. Qadri and the new dispute we had. So despite there being one other witness besides me to this heretical debate by Mr. Qadri, I was the only one who realized the gravity of the error and remembered well enough for it to be admissible in a Shariah court of Law. That night I felt I couldn't pray behind Mr. Qadri again until he recanted this grievous heresy and told him such in email where I said he is either a fool, OR a disbeliever OR a Munafiq pretending to be Muslim and in all three cases I felt and said such a mistake disqualified him from being the imam of a masjid. Qadri didn't reply to that email. But I do have proof confirming admission of his heresy in that Qadri replied to another one of my email admonishments which I sent the next day:

Email Sent Friday, Feb 3, 2017 at 10:56 PM

It seems you define kafir as one who deliberately hides as a farmer does.

This is the linguistic Arabic meaning but in Islam words have different definitions.

Such as Zakat, Salat, Jihad etc all have a linguistic meaning that differs from its Shariah meaning.

Perhaps you forgot this.

If we say a kafir refers to the one who hides deliberately like a farmer then does that mean Allah is telling us that all farmers who deliberately hide their seeds in the soil will burn forever in hellfire?

No. Doing the Kufr of planting seeds does not take one out of Islam nor is an act of disbelief.

Yet in Islam Kufr means disbelief not to plant a seed like a farmer and the kafir is the disbeliever and not the farmer.

This is definition of Kufr and it's various kinds:

https://islamqa.info/en/21249

All non-Muslims, Christians and Jews are kafirs and anything who think not or doubt are as well.

This is why ISNF dawah is so dangerous and unislamic since many like you seem not to know this and thus you don't preach Islam as the prophets did or have the hatred Islam requires for non-Muslims because many don't even think non-Muslims are kafirs and think only extreme enemies of Islam are kafirs and that some/most non-Muslims are good, which is another statement of kufr.

Not to add to the list of issues but you still didn't recant from saying "most non-Muslims are good people" which I explained is impossible and contradicts verse 8:70 on January 29th email.

Why don't you say all non-Muslims are kafirs? Or all Christians and Jews are kafirs? And that no non-Muslim is good? That's what Islam teaches. If I'm wrong it is your job to correct me just as it is my job to correct you. Are you going to let me go to the hellfire because I'm a jerk when I write and speak to you? I'm asking your opinion and position requesting you to correct me if I'm wrong.

If I'm an extreme idiot tell me why so I can change. Don't hide the truth from me like a farmer.

How can you do dawah to non-Muslims if you won't even tell me if I'm wrong or if you disagree?

Remember when in the masjid I said how we seem to be on two different roads with Islam between us in the middle and Khawarijism on the other side of me and Murjism on the other side of you? We should both be closer to Islam today than we were that day. Were we not brothers then? Do you only advise those who are polite and respectful even if lack of advice means they will burn in the hellfire forever?

You know it is true at the end of that day that one of us is wrong and made a mistake. I think it was you and I don't want you to burn forever in the hellfire because I didn't teach you correctly. If it is me please correct me because I see us going apart and we both that will not result in both of us in paradise and if one of us is in hellfire and the other isn't we will wish we warned each other. Warn me if I'm wrong or repent if I'm right. Neither of us can be indifferent to each other.

You say you want to understand me I explain who I am and try to explain why/what I believe and do. Do you turn away from the blind man who asks for advice and refutation?

If I'm a Khariji or takfiri and asking for refutation/correction why don't you do so? Is it not obligatory to refute a deviant who personally asks to be refuted?

If we believe the same thing then why don't you say so? The sin of Iblis was arrogance and pride. None of us is safe from kufr. Believers are to be mirrors to each other I inform you of your flaws and you should inform me of mine. Or do u imitate Christians and turn the other cheek? If I am extreme and you know it and I burn in hell because of it I will testify that you concealed the knowledge of my errors and refused to refute or inform me of any/all errors.

Verily if you are a believer it is known how you will respond, if a munafiq and/or kafir it is known.

Allah is the Judge and Allah sent the Furqan, even though the disbelievers hate it so much.

Whatever you do I inshallah have done and will do my duty and Allah is the Wali of the believers and the disbelievers/ all non-Muslims verily have no Wali neither in this life nor the afterlife.

The Qadr is written and Allah determines who the true Khalilullallah's and Abdullah's are yet as it is now I don't see how both of are names could be truthful, but regardless like it or not I might as well tell you I think/feel the name Khalilullah is a bida not permitted to call oneself by Shariah. You may call yourself whatever you please, but what Allah will call us is what matters.

Mr. Qadri replied as follows:

As SalamuAlykum Mr. Yasin, Khalid, Abdullah or Gregory.

At this point I will tell you that Br. Payraw and I have tried and spent alot of time with you to understand you and your way of practicing Islam. Our discussion (or at least mine) was never fruitful and went on and on for hours and sometime days. Im at a point that im not ready to discuss further with you on any topic because of your disrespect, disregard, and your attitude towards me, the entire community and maybe even the ummah at large.

I will suggest that if you dont agree with what I believe and preach, then instead of verbally abusing me, calling me a Kafir, fool etc and spreading fitna in the Masjid why dont you please share your concern with a local Imam who can help me understand.

Finally, I will conclude by saying that if you continue to cause fitna in the Masjid then the board will step in and take action.

May Allaah guide us to the straight path. Aameen.

Case closed.

Khalilullah.

After that email response I continued sending emails that were even proofread by friends(so they weren't "disrespectful" according to Mr. Qadri's standards), trying to reconcile but I'd never get another email reply from him.

On February 6th, 2017, my maternal grandfather Joseph went to the hospital with pains in his chest. At the time I had finished reviewing a book he gave me to read and wanted my feedback on. It was a book written by a former Shiite Somali woman who falsely claimed she was an "Ex-Muslim" and said reasons why she hates Islamic falsehood and gave a plan on how to reform it to fix Islam and its alleged "flaws".

The author said to "reform Islam", Muslims must be tricked or forced into disbelieving/discarding these 5 key points of their 1400+ year old faith in the name of "Islam" itself, so they think these points are not part of Islam.

1. The Quran's infallibility and Muhammad's status of absolute authority regarding religious

matters, they say the hadith must be discredited and rejected before the Quran is. Then the Quran must be rejected as a man-made book not from God as it claims.

2. The investment in life after death being more important than investing in this worldly life before death.

3. Shariah as being the best and only legal system allowed by God and the idea that it is ordained by God and applicable for the modern age.

4. The empowering of individuals to encourage good and forbid evil, by both tongue and hand.

5. The imperative to wage military Jihad.

Those are the 5 points this self-alleged apostate from Islam say will destroy the Muslims if they adopt all or any of them. I say alleged apostate because the individual who proposed these 5 points to "reform Islam" claims they were raised as a Muslim who apostated. However they never fasted in Ramadan, and they didn't start praying until they were 16 when they started practicing Shiism. So Islamically speaking they were not a Muslim, then became a Shiite then apostated from heretical Shiism and today go around claiming they are a Muslim apostate denouncing Islam telling people how to destroy it; or as they say "reform" or "renovate" it. They explicitly use these terms because they know if they say destroy then it will never work as their plan involves getting Muslims to destroy Islam. The 5 points are what they list in their book written for disbelievers to read in order to hate/reject Islam and join the "reformation efforts". Later in the same book they explain how to get Muslims to adopt and practice the 5 points so as to destroy Islam without them even knowing it. When "Muslim reformers" are preaching the 5 points to destroy Islam, or the non-Muslims pressure Muslims to adopt the 5 points, they are never to tell the 5 points explicitly for what they are but use the following points which are identical in meaning but camouflaged via language. The enemies of Islam say to get Muslims to finally permanently destroy Islam then Muslims should:

1. Ensure that Muhammad and the Quran are open to interpretation and criticism.

2. Give priority to this life, *along with* the next one. Basically you have to focus on the here and now more than the afterlife, live in the real world in the present and work for it.

3. *Reconcile* Shariah with unislamic laws and dispel the notion that Shariah is superior to every other type of law. Muslims must learn to *adapt* Shariah with unislamic laws *and compromise* on things. Shariah must become flexible and adapt to the times as well as the non-Muslims' political systems.

4. End the practice of "commanding right and forbidding wrong" on the individual level. Make it an exclusively institutional responsibility. Also stress that people have the freedom to believe and do whatever they want and nobody has a right to judge them or treat them differently or negatively based on their beliefs, speech or actions. Freedom and Equality means you have to keep your opinions about right/wrong to yourself, respect people's privacy and avoid judging them according to Islamic values but view and treat everybody as equals. Love the sinners, don't judge them or criticize them, or try to get people to change. They say Muslims have to learn to tolerate different religious beliefs and cannot just dismiss them as invalid because they are unislamic. They teach that interfaith is the key to destroying the Islamic faith. This is because Christians and Jews have learned they cannot effectively coerce someone to convert if they haven't cooperated with them beforehand

becoming emotionally and socially dependent or intertwined. Christians/Jews get you to love Christians/Jews first before the person loves Christianity/Judaism because nobody can ever voluntarily love or adopt their faiths without having love for Christians/Jews first. Hate for non-Muslim people is the preventative factor between Muslims converting to other faiths. Therefore the enemies of Islam emphatically preach that "love all, hate none" doctrine.

5. Abandon the call to Jihad. First stress Jihad is only defensive. Then teach that Jihad is only a spiritual struggle, violence is never justified and offensive Jihad is unislamic/sinful. Lastly teach that Jihad was historically useful but in the modern age of freedom and democracy it is extreme, obsolete and incompatible with civilized morality. Essentially the final step is to persuade Muslims that the prophets would never have fought anybody if they could have voted in elections.

Now I paraphrased the points a little but in essence those are the points proffered by the top enemies of Islam to get Muslims to destroy Islam. Whereas if you go to America or other countries, this is exactly the stuff disbelievers pressure Muslims to believe, practice and preach. It's also exactly what the misguided sects and heretical innovators teach Muslims to believe in and practice in this modern day and age. You have the enemies of Islam preaching one message to "reform(destroy) Islam" and then some people come to a masjid and teach the same exact message but say they are Muslims and/or Islamic. Then Muslims hear that filthy anti-Islamic message and go around telling everybody that's what Islam teaches and they actually think by doing so they are teaching Islam to people just as Muhammad taught it. Therefore when a rule about Muslims not waging war against Islam if they live in non-Muslim countries exists, one must consider all the different elements and aspects of a war;

including the political, economic, social, moral, verbal and ideological aspects. Not every warrior gets their hands bloody or physically fights. Some "Muslims" in dar al-kufr could be ideologically or methodologically at war with Islam. While being "financially at war with Islam" is something I won't define. Yet if you consider the enemies of Islam and their 5 points to be a war strategy then some Muslims in the West who preach such stuff could Islamically speaking be considered spiritual enemies of Islam. The extremists say they should be killed in vigilante fashion for that. I don't, but think that they should be properly peacefully educated and if they refuse to change or desist then they must be refuted, denounced and prevented from preaching in the name of Islam or advertising in masjids or to Muslims. It is important to know how an individual need not be on the military battlefield to be "at war with Islam". They could be a theological warrior against Islam while claiming to be Muslims due to ignorance. That is the danger of living in Dar Al-Kufr that could make one a disbeliever and that danger is even greater in Dar Al-Harb. Yet sadly many Muslims are unaware of these dangers and thus fall into the danger zone unknowingly, then label those strict Muslims who stress how important it is to live in Dar Al-Islam or Dar Al-Muslim as extremists or unrealistic. Some Muslims don't even think their unislamic non-Muslim majority nation is Dar Al-Kufr or Dar Al-Harb at all, I've even heard speakers at masjids in America who ignorantly say where they live is Dar Al-Islam.

I had typed up my refutation of this anti-Islam book for my grandfather yet found myself face to face with "Muslims" and was going to a masjid 35 times a week where they shockingly preached what this enemy of Islam said was what the "reformers" should do to kill Islam. I was conflicted as to which was the priority after learning of Mr. Qadri's new heresy. Since establishing prayer with as many people as possible is a duty owed to Allah and I could not pray in congregation behind a heretic whose heresy amounted to disbelief then I figured fixing the flaw within the masjid leader was top priority that weekend instead of returning the book and sharing the 20+ page refutation with my atheist grandfather. Surprisingly grandpa Joseph died the very same Monday as he entered the hospital, merely four days after I had the debate with Mr. Qadri as to whether Jews and Christians were disbelievers. I was taking care of my grandmother while grandfather was in the hospital when we got the call from my Uncle Art that grandfather was resuscitated and about to die in a few hours according to the doctors. So me, my Grandmother, Uncle and a male and female cousin all got into the truck to go to the hospital to say our goodbyes. Now my priorities shifted and the top priority was to help my atheist grandfather become a Muslim before death. This would not be easy as he had sarcastically claimed to be a prophet himself during the summer when I told him he has to follow the religion of the prophets to enter paradise. Anyways my parents met the caravan at the hospital and I was concerned over how my father and maternal uncle would react to me attempting to convert grandpa to Islam on his deathbed, as they seemed to be the most Islamophobic members of my family at the time. Yet the hospital said we all couldn't visit Joseph at once so only a limited number of us were permitted. My grandmother Florence, my Mom, me, and my cousins Natalie and Jarod were allowed to enter first as a group. So I'm thinking there is a chance for success because aside from a one-on-one conversation, I got the least Islamophobic crowd I could hope for under the circumstances, or so I thought. On the way to say our final goodbyes I stressed to my Mom within earshot of cousins that *"if he doesn't die as a Muslim, I'm not going to the funeral, and you yourself already asked the mufti from Mecca about it being forbidden to attend"*. When we arrived my grandfather spoke to us all first. He started saying we don't know what pain feels like and we wouldn't ever complain about anything if we knew what he was feeling at that moment, and that was despite him being medicated with lots of morphine and painkillers. Then Grandfather Joseph said how *"there must be some super-human type of being up there."* He then addressed his grandchildren saying he married his grandmother while they were both virgins and recommended we abstain from sex outside of marriage. People often think they will spew words of wisdom on their deathbed, but usually when you are about to die you are not in a mood or capacity to intellectually communicate the wisest words of your life. If you want to advise someone wisely, do so before you are near death because you are likely to forget any gems you might've had due to the painful scary unexpected once in a lifetime experience. Finally Joseph concluded by saying he loved us all and prayed for us everyday. This I knew was a lie because as long as I knew him he was staunchly atheist and mocked the concept of God. Aside from one single ritualistically invalid prayer at a mosque and occasional culturally demanded church services he was anti-religion thinking they were financial scams. Whenever I broached the topic of religion with him he often turned to atheist philosophy and was the main unnamed philosopher I refuted in my book "Religious Equality Refuted". Anyways since it was his deathbed and he seemed to acknowledge a "super-human" in the sky, I ignored his lie about praying for us everyday; despite it's clear falsity since he didn't believe in any prayers or accept a deity to pray to in the first place aside from Christian crap which he rejected. So I began my address to him apologizing for not taking the time to discuss religion with him as much as I should have; despite having played the Quran in English audio to both my maternal grandparents and him having read several Islamic books and having several debates with me. I paraphrased what Prophet Abraham said to his disbelieving father explaining how God gave me knowledge which had not got to him. As tenderly as possible I explained how Muhammad's uncle Abu Talib was on his deathbed in an identical scenario and

Muhammad invited his uncle to testify there was nothing to be worshipped except Allah/God the Creator and if he said that then Muhammad would testify on his behalf that he believed without him even publicly saying Muhammad was a prophet because Muhammad knew he believed that already but feared their pagan relatives reactions and rebuke. I continued that Abu Talib feared to become a Muslim on his deathbed because of his relatives and then died and Muhammad said he would be in hellfire forever as a result and would've been in paradise forever if he became Muslim. Furthermore I said how although he shouldn't blindly follow, he has run out of time to research and must make his decision on which religion he will choose. So after reminding him he had read a translation of the Quran and is not ignorant, finally I begged my grandfather to say the Shahada to become a Muslim, which I said in Arabic and English. I additionally told him that he is literally on his deathbed and wouldn't even have to perform any of the five obligatory daily prayers to enter paradise because he will be dead before it's time to pray. At this the nurse gave me a look because I don't think anyone told him or was supposed to tell the patient that they are on their deathbed, and his vitals monitor started beeping. I waited for a positive reply and the room was entirely silent as everyone waited to see what grandpa would do/say. He didn't say anything and turned his face away from me in silence just thinking to himself. It had always been his belief that he could just wait until he died to find out the truth whatever it was and then belief after resurrection from the dead would cause him to go to paradise. Such a foolish philosophy was refuted in depth in my book which I recently mentioned. I did my best to stress that he's not getting any second chances and has to make a decision as to whether he wants to die as a Muslim or not. I began to fear he would give a negative reply or that my relatives would mistakenly think he was other than an atheist, recently converted to a belief in a "super-human type of being up there", which is far worse than what is expected of a baby to believe let alone for a 96 year-old intellectual as himself. So now focusing on my present Christian relatives and preaching indirectly to them and the jinn that accompanied them, because I don't like deathbed preaching and don't plan on doing it again on their deathbeds, I said to my grandfather Joseph *"You know their religion is wrong."* This time my grandfather looked at me and spoke. Grandpa Joseph clearly said, *"I agree with you."* However this response is not enough to be a Muslim and likely was just him agreeing Christianity was wrong as all of the others present except for me were Christians. So I figured this was him just confirming he knew Christianity was false/wrong and that he wasn't dying as Christian. So I stressed that agreement is not enough and that he has to testify and become a Muslim or else he will burn in hellfire forever. He again turned away and was silent ignoring me and everyone else. Nobody said anything and it became evident he wasn't going to say anything more on the topic. So I begged him, despite Islam being a prize honor to be chased rather than a charity to be accepted grudgingly, yet I desperately didn't want Joseph to die as an atheist kafir. Yet Joseph didn't say anything else and I realized he was arrogantly refusing to speak not out of direct disbelief or any problems he had with Islam, but he just doubted and the Greek and European philosophers had thoroughly poisoned his mind into thinking his non-commitment was an educated plan instead of guaranteed doom. Thus I turned away likewise and politely said something like, "*Okay, I tried offering you the opportunity to embrace Islam and become a Muslim, now I'm done.*" So I turned away and walked out the door never to see him again and he died a few hours afterwards. In hindsight I should've had a flashcard or note and written the shahada down on it leaving it with him just in case he changed his mind, but it was my first deathbed dawah attempt so I didn't think of doing that. His loss and my gain in the experience and effort and lessons learned. Meanwhile Joseph gets punished painfully in the grave after failing the 3 question test by the angels Munkar and Nakir, and will reside in the hellfire eternally after everyone is raised from the dead on Judgement day due to dying upon other than the singular monotheistic prophetic faith of Islam. I don't make the rules, Allah does and makes it clear in the Quran and before that through the teachings of previous prophets that anyone who dies upon a religion other than Islamic monotheism will have it divinely rejected from them and be punished as a result unless they had a legitimate excuse of ignorance such as never being exposed to Islam. Negligence to learn however is not an excuse and my grandfather wasn't even unexposed, he was just stupid due to consuming philosophy literature. Despite being an avid reader of non-fiction who even had several books delivered to him in the mail on the day he died, on his last day before death Joseph spent hours watching the football championship instead of doing something useful. As a sidenote, professional sports are a tragic waste of time on a massive scale, even unprofessional sports are generally not worth the effort. After teams lose some people even have a mental health crises and recently on the news after the local team lost a playoff game they were advising people to check themselves into therapy over the trauma. Such a culture or mindset is deadly and you should never be someone who wastes their life on games of any kind. It's just not worth it. People will play sports and games until you die, and on the day you die you will have a chance to enjoy games or do goodness to save yourself from the hellfire. Don't be like the millions who die wasting their lifespan. You don't know when you will die and even if it is a long time from now, you will regret any time invested in games of amusement or entertainment.

The next day when the family told my grandmother Florence her husband had died, my mother broke a promise to me to not say blasphemous stuff. Had I known my Mom would say what she said then I would not have even been present. Despite Joseph dying saying that he agreed with me that Christianity is wrong, and being anti-Catholic as long as I knew him, even though Christianity itself teaches non-Christians like Joseph go to eternal hell, my nominal Catholic mother told her mother that my dead grandfather has gone to heaven. My grandmother Florence reacted by tearfully wailing, *"God is no good!"* several times despite the apparent "good news" which was entirely false regardless. This expression of my wailing grandmother in itself is apostasy from every religion in the world that every religion in the world condemns as a mortal sin of heretical disbelief that must be contritely repented from before the criminal dies or else it's eternal hell for them. So I was forced to correct her blasphemy and said *"You can't just say that God is no good because of being sad."* But this time, unlike at Joseph's deathbed, many more relatives were present and they chastised my polite correction. They said I should just let her grieve, thereby showing incorrectly indirectly they care more about her than they do about God. For example if God declares that anybody is no good then their relationship to me doesn't matter I'm going to say they are no good. If someone says God is no good, it doesn't matter who they are I will try my best to defend God from their evil speech though God is far above needing any protection. My relatives condemnation of my correction was actually another blasphemous sin that's similar to the level of how "Happy Holidays" to a polytheist is equal to pleasure with disbelief. So approval of blasphemous sorrow is a comparable form of pleasure with disbelief. Basically the death of my atheist grandfather caused my Christian grandmother to become a disbeliever even according to Christian standards. What's worse is some Christian relatives even supported her in this act thereby disbelieving alongside her by supporting her heretical cries of insulting the divine. Needless to say my relatives didn't want to get into a debate about religion at that time with the only Muslim in the family, so I decided to flee from the situation as Islam commands one to do when Allah or his ayat are ridiculed and one is powerless to change the dialogue. So as politely as possible I explained I have to depart and cannot be there to console them under those circumstances.

On Friday February 10th, 2017 my family held a Christian funeral for Joseph, despite him not being a Christian when he died, and I did not go since he died a disbeliever and the rituals involved disbelief in Islam. Instead I went back to the mosque to pray. There was a guest speaker leading the Friday Jumuah prayer and I noticed Mr. Qadri sitting in the front row and sat right next to him before Jumuah Athan was called as he was reading from the Quran. I had brought paper fatwas(Scholastic legal rulings) with me which explained succinctly how all Jews and Christians and non-Muslims were disbelievers/kafirs which also said how those who had Mr. Qadri's belief cannot be Muslims. The exact source and fatwa text I personally placed in front of Mr. Qadri is as follows:

https://www.thesunniway.com/articles/item/263-calling-a-kafir-a-kafir

Question

Respected Mufti Sahib, Someone that says that we mustn't call a kaafir as a kaafir as because what if he died whilst reciting the Shahadah. As we know on the same token a Muslim may be a Muslim but we don't know how he will die. Please enlighten us with the proper Islamic ruling

Answer

Only an ignorant person can make such a comment. All throughout the history of Islam, the magnificent scholars have unanimously agreed that it is a part of Imaan (faith) to know a kafir as a kafir and a Muslim as a Muslim. This is the reason why in their books they have a section named Baab Al-Murtad. All the books of Aqaa'id (Beliefs) and Fiqh (Jurisprudence) have included this section and clearly clarified that whoever did such and such or said such and such is a 'kafir'.

In Bahare Shariat, it says:

"To regard a Muslim a Muslim and a kafir a kafir is from the necessities of faith."

Sadr Al-Shariah further writes:

"Although we cannot say with certainty regarding a specific individual that he died as a Muslim or (may Allah protect) as a kafir until the state of his death is proven by Shar'i evidence; however, this does not mean that one may doubt the kufr of someone who has clearly committed kufr, because doubting the kufr of a clear kafir makes the person a kafir." He further writes: *"Judgement in the hereafter will be based on the state at the time of death, but the hukm (rule) of Shariah is based on the apparent. For example, if a kafir such as a Jew, Christian or idol worshipper died, it cannot be said with certainty that he died as a kafir; but it is the command of Allah and His Messenger (peace and blessings be upon him) for us to regard him as a kafir. We must deal with all his matters in his life and after his death as we deal with the matters of every kafir such as: the matters of association; marriage; Salah Al-Janazah; shroud (kafan for the deceased); and burial. When he has committed kufr, then it is an obligation that we know him as a kafir and leave his state of death to Allah (whether he died a kafir or a believer); in the same way as a person who is an apparent Muslim and has not made any statement or committed any action against Imaan (faith), it is an obligation that*

we must know him as a Muslim, even though we do not know the state he died in."

The tremendous Scholar Qadi Iyad in his *Shifaa'* writes:

"There is a unanimous consensus upon the kufr of he who does not regard the Jews, Christians or anyone who separates from the religion of the Muslims as a kafir; or he who hesitates in calling them kafir; or he who doubts in this matter. Qadi Abu Bakr (Al-Baaqalani) said: This is because the tawqeef (Shar'i evidence from the Quran and Sunnah upon which none can speak with their own opinion like the number of units in Salah) and the consensus (of the Ummah) both agree upon their kufr; therefore, whoever hesitates or has a doubt in calling them kafir, has rejected the evidence and the tawqeef. Only a kafir would reject or doubt in such a matter."

From the above, one can understand how ignorant a person must be to feel so confident that he is prepared to dispute and differ from not only all the giant scholars all throughout the Islamic history, but also against the unanimous agreement of the Ummah. Yet, he does not wish to stop there; he takes this dispute against Allah and the Messenger of Allah (peace and blessings be upon him) that he will not call a kafir a kafir.

Qadi Iyad further writes in his Shifaa':

"He is a kafir who does not regard those who believe in other than Islam as kafir; or he who hesitates or has doubt in this matter; or he deems their religion correct, even if he himself claims to be a Muslim and apparently deems the rest of the false religions incorrect; he is a kafir for making apparent what he made apparent against that."

Is it not clear that black is black, white is white, water is water, fire is fire, a book is a book, a pen is a pen, a man is a man, a woman is a woman, a child is a child, a Jew is a Jew, a Christian is a Christian, a Buddhist is a Buddhist and a Muslim is a Muslim? Of course it is! Then why is a kafir not a kafir?

If you look in the Quran and Sunnah, you will find that Allah and His beloved Messenger (peace and blessings be upon him) rendered many nominal Muslims kafir. These were people who swore that they were Muslims, performed Salah behind the Prophet Muhammed (peace and blessings be upon him) and even took part in Jihad *side by side with the Sahaabah (Allah is pleased with them); but because they uttered a sentence of kufr, Allah and His Messenger (peace and blessings be upon him) rendered them kafir. It is mentioned in Musannaf Ibn Abi Shaybah, Ibn Munzir, the Tafseer of Sheikh Addi Bin Abi Haatim and recorded in Al-Durr Al-Manthoor, by Imam Jalal Al-Deen Al-Suyooti, regarding a man who lost his female camel and came to ask the Messenger of Allah (peace and blessings be upon him) for help. The Messenger of Allah (peace and blessings be upon him) advised him to go to such and such a place and that he would find his camel there. Upon this some people said:*

"Muhammad says that such and such a person's camel is in such and such a place; what does he know of the gayb (unseen)?"

These were people who had declared that there is none worthy of worship but Allah Muhammad is the Messenger of Allah; they performed Salah behind the Prophet (peace and blessings be upon him); and they fought in the battlefields under the banner of Allah. When the Prophet (peace and blessings be upon him) was informed of their statement, he called for them and enquired why they said such. They replied: "We were only joking and playing."

Allah, the Almighty and Wise, revealed a verse of the Quran upon this; this is the sixty fifth verse of Surah Al-Tawbah:

"Say O Beloved: Are you joking with Allah, His verses and His Messenger? Do not make excuses, you have become kafir after your Imaan (faith)."

There are several other verses in which Allah has declared some who accepted Islam and became Muslims as kafir, due to an act or a statement. Even in the Hadith, the Messenger of Allah (peace and blessings be upon him) foretold us of people who will be nominal Muslims, yet will not be Muslims. This Hadith in Bukhari Shareef is an eye opener, and one should read it again and again. Sayyiduna Ali (Allah is pleased with him) narrated that the Messenger of Allah (peace and blessings be upon him) said:

"A time will come upon the people in which nothing from Islam will remain but its name; nothing from the Quran will remain but its written form; their Masaajid will be full but empty from guidance; fitnah (corruption) will be released from them and in them, it will return."

In the time of Sayyiduna Ali (Allah is pleased with him), he regarded the khawaarij as kafir and went to war against them; and then there were those who said Ali is worthy of worship. Thus, Sayyiduna Ali regarded them as kafir and ordered for them to be burnt in fire.

This continued all throughout the history of Islam where the Ulema regarded groups who deviated as either misguided or kafir based upon their actions, statements and beliefs. The Messenger of Allah said:

"When fitnah or innovation becomes apparent and the Scholar does not express his knowledge, then the curse of Allah and the Angels and all the people is upon him."

If we were to follow the ideology of this person, where we do not call a kafir a kafir, because we do not know what is in his heart or in what state he will die, then this would mean that we must not call a Muslim a Muslim, because we do not know what is in his heart or in what state he will die. This would also mean that he cannot call his own father a Muslim or even the Sahabah (Allah is *pleased with them) cannot be called Muslims and the pious predecessors, like Imam Abu Hanifah and Imam Shafa'i and Sheikh Abd Al-Qadir Al-Jeelaani, cannot be regarded a Muslim anymore. In the same way, Khumeni cannot be called a kafir, nor can we call Salman Rushdie or George Bush a kafir.*

May Allah protect us from such ignorance and keep us firm on the path of the pious predecessors.

Allah knows best and He is most Wise.

I put this paper in front of Mr. Qadri and asked him if he read this fatwa I had emailed him. Mr. Qadri confirmed reading it before but said nothing else and would ignore me purposely refusing to say anything, similar to how Joseph had done on his deathbed. I left the paper fatwa sitting in front of his prayer spot not removing it. To further avoid resolving our dispute Mr. Qadri stood up and left me by walking to another part of the masjid to avoid me while I remained sitting in the front row preparing for the Friday Prayer led by the guest.

Some days after our last email interaction I began publicly not praying behind Mr. Qadri. When it was time for salat, if Qadri wasn't there I'd pray in congregational jama and if he was then I would silently wait until they were finished and pray by myself afterwards. One time after Mr. Qadri led the congregation in fajr prayer, I finished praying alone separately and turned around to see the former ISNF president, Mr. Yasin, who had hired Mr. Qadri just standing and looking at me as he was about to leave. I looked back at him and wished he would come ask me why I wasn't praying with the rest to possibly resolve the dispute as I knew he agreed with my beliefs. Regrettably Mr. Yasin turned and left, and then I took off my hood to see if anyone else was left in the masjid who I could speak with. I saw it was only me and Mr. Qadri and he quickly got up and exited after seeing Mr. Yasin leave. That time I realized if I had approached Mr. Yasin we could have had a private three-way talk with me, the guy who hired Mr. Qadri as masjid Imam, and Mr. Qadri to resolve the issues. I have always regretted missing that opportunity and Mr. Qadri's insincerity is known from that incident because if Mr. Yasin had talked with me he could have fired Mr. Qadri perhaps. Thus Mr. Qadri didn't want any such talk and fled the scene soon after. If I knew it was just the three of us there I would've suggested we talk it out, but I was wearing a hoodie that day and couldn't see who else was present and thought it was a huge crowd. Mr. Qadri was not wearing a hoodie and knew he could've had a private chat with me and Mr. Yasin to peacefully settle our dispute in creed, or even a chat with just me and nobody else after Mr. Yasin left, but he refused to do so and fled as fast as he could without looking bad in front of Mr. Yasin. Thereby I lost a great opportunity at a peaceful dialogue as was destined to be missed.

Eventually I left masjid noor and would go to masjid huda in Lackawanna, NY to pray as my friend Abdul Haq had done and suggested since he said it was much better and scholastic upon the proper manhaj. Masjid huda was much better with more Muslims, knowledge and practice applied with much less corruption and innovation. But they didn't have an imam. A guest imam Scholar Jalal Abual Rub who had translated Ibn Kathir's Tafsir of the Quran into English was serving as the guest imam and he would give lectures every single day. Abdul Haq brought me to Jalal Abual Rub asking him what I should do about my dispute with Mr. Qadri. In reply Jalal said to just stay at masjid huda when I told him about the situation. Sheikh Jalal told me that despite it being disbelief in Islam and an incorrect position, sadly the majority of American Imams have fallen into this heresy, so I should just stay at the masjids which don't believe that heresy or promote it. I also asked Sheikh Jalal about Hijra(emigration) and the topic of moving to a Muslim country and whether Scholars would ever say every Muslim in America has to leave en masse. He answered me that it should be the goal of every individual Muslim in America to migrate to a Muslim country but they have to do it smartly with a plan to ensure they will be able to stay once they go. Jalal said you can't just get a plane ticket and go because then that foreign country will deport you since you have no job or place to stay. The situation is further complicated because most countries don't currently offer citizenship and getting visas can be an ordeal, yet despite the difficulty still every Muslim in America should be making a plan to move out as soon as they possibly can. Jalal also told me that when he first came to America to teach Islam to people, originally he was born in Palestine, he made a rule for himself that he would never ever work for a non-Muslim and humiliate himself via employment under a disbeliever. Jalal reported that this rule of his was very hard upon him and he was even forced to be homeless some time and sleep on the streets as a result of his strict rule but he survived never having broken his self-imposed condition. Since first becoming Muslim in 2011, I had been averse to paying taxes to fund the USA military fighting in Afghanistan and elsewhere against Muslims, as shown somewhat in my previously included emails. After research on the matter I learned it is sinful and potentially disbelief to pay non-Muslim militaries who are fighting Muslims. Naturally if one is oppressively forced the sin is much reduced but that doesn't reduce it entirely to being sinless and since depending on the intention of the taxpayer giving such money could amount to disbelief then it is dangerous even if there is leeway under the claim of oppressive necessity. Most people if oppressed try to leave the oppressive environment, they don't celebrate being American and in America and then when it's tax season say "Oh I'm oppressively paying against my will and hate it truly." If they hate it then they will want to stop somehow by legally moving to another country and then revoking American citizenship, since America is one of only two countries in the world that tax its citizens globally even if they live in other countries. However taxation is a very taboo subject wherein the Khawarij extremists who tend to make takfir of Muslims en masse mistakenly say if you pay/support a disbelieving ruler then de facto this "approval/support" amounts to apostasy.

Khawarij groups like Al-Qaeda and ISIS promote this error and thereby end up killing civilians since they consider them combatants due to funding militaries of non-Muslims. This topic of taxation confused me for a long time myself because within a Muslim heart there is natural guilt in funding such militaries that are killing your co-religionists and many Quran verses and hadith warn against doing this making it forbidden. The best book I found on this subject was a book, as destiny would have it, also partially worked on by Jalal Abual Rub called *"A Critique of the Methodology of Anwar Al-Awlaki: And His Errors in the Fiqh of Jihad in Light of the Qur'an, Sunnah and Classical to Contemporary Scholars of Ahl Us-Sunnah"*. Mr. Awlaki was a peaceful although heretical American Ikhwani Muslim prior to being unjustly incarcerated by America post 9/11. He got radicalized further due to the trauma of being in prison and after his release he became a Khariji leader of Al-Qaeda in Yemen. In Awlaki's last video prior to his death via drone strike in 2011 he crazily said Muslims in America should basically kill anything/everything they can. Such an extremist terrorist idea was clearly erroneously overboard because he didn't even consider the Muslims living in America as safe from his wrath either. So as someone who hadn't been employed for six years from the time I quit rap music in 2011 onwards after embracing Islam, I hadn't paid any taxes nor did anything to merit such a target on my back even if Al-Qaeda was in any way sensible in such illegal unislamic tactics. Yet for those feeling guilty about American taxation without knowing the Shariah ruling in depth it would be easy to be misled by eloquent speakers into the extreme of Al-Qaeda thinking any who pay is apostate or conversely the extreme of the popular Murjiah deviant heretics who think no matter what sin you do, including paying taxes to kafir militaries, then it doesn't impact your faith or relationship with Allah. The truth is in between in that the taxes are sinful. How sinful they are depends on the individual's circumstances and their ability to legally avoid through migration or other measures. For some it could amount to disbelief (major or minor) and for others it could be a major or minor sin and for others it might not merit any sin and Allah's forgiveness is sought regardless of the scenario.

After hearing this scholarly advice about my dream/goal of moving to a Muslim country and committing to strict rules while in non-Muslim territory, I decided my rule would be that I would not pay taxes to the USA military until I either moved to another country or the war in Afghanistan was over. This was 2017 and despite Mr. Qadri not even knowing a war in Afghanistan was ongoing, when I asked him about paying taxes to the USA military, I felt the war and my conscience prevented me from funding the USA side in anyway until the eventual Muslim victory which I hoped for. The trouble was that I had been unemployed for 6 years, no nation was allowing Muslims like me to just come and permanently live in their country without a skilled profession or educational reason, with the exception of ISIS. Yet since ISIS were clearly scholastically labeled as Khawarij heretical extremists I didn't want to go there. Likewise if you don't know Arabic or the language of the land and have no relevant military experience you are going to be a burden rather than an aid to any military Jihad, and many alleged Jihads are not even legitimate. Realistically if you have no combat experience and don't even know the language of the country you aren't going to be helping anybody by inserting yourself into a warzone "for the sake of Allah". Often extremists take advantage of this naivety and recruit non-Arab foreigners without lingual or military experience and end up being the only ones accepting of such unqualified jihadi candidates, thus fools of a feather flock together. Essentially if you want to wage Jihad in this era, learn Arabic first so you can access the Scholars to learn what Jihad even is and which modern groups are and aren't practicing Islam correctly. The first step of Jihad is studying Islam. So learn Arabic so you can properly learn and practice and be prepared if ever needed. Muslims don't need uneducated idiots fighting on our behalf because the damage they do is worse than that done by our enemies. All those who ended up joining the Khawarij groups like Al-Qaeda and ISIS ended up hurting the cause of Islam and Muslims despite whatever they intended. Ignorance nullifies Sincerity making it sinful in reality in all scenarios.

Surprising when I told my parents my plan to move to a Muslim country explaining my limited options and that I would likely need a foreign college scholarship, explaining ISIS is the only "country" currently taking all Muslims promising them free passports and jobs automatically, my non-Muslim parents surprisingly suggested I go there because they were sick of paying for my groceries and gas. However despite several other non-Muslim relatives also offering me one-way plane tickets to move to ISIS territory so I'd be gone from America if I hated it so much, I refused to take them up on the offers because ISIS were heretical extremists which puts them in a similar category as ISNF in my view. The main difference being that ISNF is a different brand of non-violent heretical Muslims. But both unwittingly work together in deviating people from Islam, and they coincidentally fuel each other as those disillusioned due to groups like ISNF often turn to groups like ISIS while those disillusioned with ISISesque terrorist groups often turn to peaceful anti-terror groups like ISNF in a see-saw transfer push-pull rotational cycle.

Anyways since I felt I couldn't pray behind Mr. Qadri until he repented, and my parents were fed up with funding my nonprofitable yet to be published writing career, I decided my best opportunity to move to a Muslim country would be through a college scholarship to learn Arabic overseas. I already had been advised and encouraged to apply to Islamic Universities overseas by people in Canada and America, but I prioritized writing books to share Islam with my family first. That was a destined mistake perhaps because I might have been better positioned to write after attending an Islamic Shariah study program overseas as the knowledge available in America was highly limited. The main problem as I saw it was that my name was still Gregory Heary. I figured I would legally change my name to Abdullah Bin-Kevin and then apply for college overseas in Muslim countries and have a better chance of getting a scholarship with an Islamic name than my unislamic one. In the meantime, to avoid indirect funding of the USA military by contributing to the national income tax pool, by buying food products from taxpayers which contributes to their income, then I would make it a secondary rule of mine to only eat imported food and boycott all American products and stores. The gas I used was not taxed by the USA since my parents got it from the nearby Native American reservation which is technically a separate country. In April 2017, I finally scheduled my name change appointment in Court to take place in June 2017 and limited myself to eating pasta from Turkey and dates from Saudi Arabia as my only two foods that I could afford to import, while getting drinking water from my parent's well. I also minimized my usage of electricity, unplugging the house refrigerator and had plans to go off-grid and only use public internet resources to save on electricity costs so as to contribute as little as possible to American GDP. I informed my friends of my migratory, name changing, dietary plans and they suggested following the advice of Sheikh Jalal regarding my dispute with Mr. Qadri who was unanimously upon clear heretical error.

Since I lived far from the Lackawanna masjid, I tried going to other masjids in Buffalo. Once I unwittingly went to a heretical "Nation of Islam" Black Supremacist mosque whose most notorious false prophet Elijah Muhammad actually used to preach in Lackawanna, NY prior to Malcolm X (before he became Sunni) persuading Elijah to shift their base to Buffalo, New York. Mistaking this Masjid Numan for a Sunni masjid I went there for one Friday prayer but after seeing the brochures and flyers on the wall never ever returned. After researching I found out there were only two masjids in all of the Western New York claiming to be upon the pure prophetic Islam according to the original Salafiyyah, one in Lackawanna and the other in Buffalo. Today as I write eight years later there are four total, as far as I know, that claim Salafiyyah. Some are better than others but in all there is goodness. Some of them even offer daily lecture classes as their administrators disseminate the knowledge of the religion and offer free carpool services so people can get free rides to the masjid. Sometimes there are even classes multiple times a day as compared to other mosques where they have neither classes nor people to even pray there. In comparison to masjid noor which didn't even have 3 people for most of the daily prayers despite having thousands show up for Friday Jumuah, in Lackawanna they not only prayed at the correct minute everyday without delay but they'd have hundreds of people for every prayer as well. Additionally I had been going to the tiny Salafi masjid in Buffalo for several months before discovering where the donation box was, because getting money is not a big part of their program.

Consider that I didn't even know how to even give money to the Salafi mosque in Buffalo until I had been going there several months and nobody ever asked for donations for me to discover how to donate earlier. Is there any other comparable religious place of worship where you can attend for several months and not know how to donate money? Sadly learning how to donate money is probably the only thing you learn at other places of worship. Most importantly I'd actually learn things at the Salafi masjids and have my faith increase as the brothers were both sincere and smart.

Still I could not forget my dispute with Mr. Qadri. I wanted to reconcile because I didn't feel right about the situation, or how it stood with me basically abandoning the masjid that I knew would not meet the minimum requirements to have congregational salat without me there; despite its size capacity to hold thousands every weekly Friday prayer. So, I continued to email Mr. Qadri but to no avail.

Email Sent Monday, Feb 27, 2017 at 8:56 AM

Greetings Brother I have 4 things to apologize for.

1. I am rude to you for unjustified personal reasons.

2. I am unable to patiently politely teach you what I know/think effectively.

3. I am not 100% sincere when I try to teach you things or communicate with you.

4. I struggle to make short messages.

Due to the above we greatly miscommunicate and anything I say tends to get rejected or ignored by you simply because it's me saying it the way I say it. Sometimes I'm wrong but sometimes I'm right and on those occasions when I'm right because of my insincerity and unislamic mannerisms it can cause you to reject what is right because I either don't know how to say what needs to be said or I don't care to be careful.

I fear our latest conflict is one of those times. I was frustrated and had fury building up for awhile towards you and this caused my patience to expire and I became rash and impatient with what I perceived to be ignorance on your part. My theological correcting became personal more than it should have. I am sorry for this and hope you forgive my lack of ability to communicate with you effectively. We do have differences regarding taqleed, ijtihad and madhhabs so these differences tend to exasperate every argument since we are fundamentally on different branches arguing over leaves. Yet because of the way we argued I think we are now on different trees.

Surely Allah loves those who try to reconcile for his sake and since our difference deals with deen then there is even more reason to reconcile. Had we just hated each other for personal reasons we should try to reconcile but now we have religious differences that amounted to takfir. Sorry I fostered such a situation. I think we must try to fix it. It is best to try and fail many times than to fail to try many times.

If I am right then it may be my fault you are wrong and if you are right with me wrong then it may be your fault I'm wrong because we fail to teach the each other why we see the other to be in error. The safe thing is to try to correct each other until it finally works. If we both try to talk with kafirs about Islam when they don't even want to know then how can we not try to reconcile with each other when both of us care about Islam and Muslims? Regardless of our statuses we each deserve to be corrected by the other more than the non-Muslims whom we try to correct. Teaching the ignorant/arrogant takes priority over the infidels. Each of us is closer to Islam than those who have never said the shahada.

As you know I made takfir of you for saying that Christians and Jews(religious) are not kuffar and that non-Muslims are not all kafirs, including the non-Muslim ahl-kitab. I also accused you of hypocrisy, being unqualified to be an Imam, insincere, foolish, being a liar and an innovator. The final 6 are irrelevant regarding praying behind you. But the issue of takfir for the beliefs you expressed about non-Muslims and Ahl-Kitab is great and inhibits congregational salat for me when you lead. Either I was right to do it or wrong. If wrong then I'm ignorant and need to be corrected and hope you can correct my errors inshallah. Now regarding the way I express myself to you I was wrong to use the wording I used but the conclusion I still think to be right though the way I communicated my notion of your error was incorrect. I fear that emotionalism may prevent you from realizing why beliefs as you expressed were/are kufr akbar of a degree which justifies takfir even without conditions being applied or prevent you from correcting me if it isn't. I have researched takfir and would like to share some of what I've learned with you so perhaps inshallah you may understand the specific type of takfir I made and why so perhaps inshallah we can resolve this and I can pray in jamat behind you once more with all our errors being rectified. Also how can you correct me or the many others like me if you don't know the reasons for my/our ruling on you? In the future inshallah I plan to send you 2 emails. One explaining the types of kufr and why all non-Muslims are kafirs and the types of kufr which your *statements about them not being kafirs amount to. The second about the various types of takfir, when they can be made and when they can't be and the specific type and the reason for which I made Takfir un-Nass on you.*

Please don't be unjust. It is unjust to flee from correction and it is also unjust to fail to correct me. Every Imam is a shepherd and will be asked concerning their flock. If I made a mistake I made a mistake, if you made a mistake then you made a mistake. At the minimum one of us has made a mistake, by not discussing this our mistakes will likely persist and we will not repent from our mistakes until we realize they are mistakes. The sooner we get corrected the sooner we can repent and be united on the road to paradise and get rewarded by Allah for reconciling. I want you to correct me if I am wrong. So far I think I'm right but you seem not to agree so I think/feel I should correct you. This is a very serious matter and Satan has plots to isolate us from the truth. Really if I don't get corrected by you then who do you think is going to correct me? And if you are wrong and I abandon you then who will correct you? I apologize if I'm partially motivated for egotistical reasons but if I think you are a kafir that means I think you will go to hell if you die in the state I currently think you are in. Personal disputes and wrongdoings aside I don't want that to happen to you. I just want to better understand Islam and the same for you. Going to a different masjid and abandoning you will not solve your problem or my problem. Brothers don't abandon each other, even when they hate each other and hate to talk to each other. I hope to reconcile with you soon inshallah. This latest dispute of ours is a test we both can be better from or worse from depending on how we react. Do not make the mistake which Jonah pbuh made. Because not only are you not Jonah pbuh and unlikely to get the mercy Jonah pbuh received but it's possible that you unlike Jonah pbuh could be in the wrong. Don't let anger at me keep either of us stuck in our errors. For you to conceal knowledge of my errors is for you to oppress me. Allah tells you to forbid my evil and I ask you to let me know of any evil I do, if my charge against you and your evil is untrue then explain to me why it is. If true then repent. Either way a stand-off is not the solution that leads to reconciliation and forgiveness.

Ibn Hibban said: "The best brothers are those who wish the most well for one. It is better to be hit by a person who wishes well for you than to be greeted by a bad one."

I apologize if my words sting but the truth also stings when it is contrary to what we believe/think. But please don't reject the truth of my words because of the extra sting I add to them. Also do not fail to teach me because I am difficult to teach/correct when I think I'm right. The command to establish salat doesn't just apply to you individually but it also applies to you helping others, like me, to establish salat in jamat at the masjid. I will try to teach you inshallah what I think you need to be reminded of, please let me and then teach me what is wrong with my understanding if anything is wrong and teach me what is wrong with the way I try to teach you regardless. If what I say is correct then you should accept it wholeheartedly as should I if whatever you teach me is correct. But teach and be taught we must do, as difficult as that may be.

I want to reconcile so we are on the same page in agreement working together towards paradise mutually benefiting each other but that requires communication both ways.

Email Sent Thursday, Mar 9, 2017 at 10:09 PM

I want to pray salat in jamat at the masjid and my iman(faith) suffers a lot when I don't.

Because of the beliefs you expressed to me and your refusal thus far to discuss them with me or change them as I believe you should then I am unable to pray behind you as previously said. In that knowing what I know about you, knowing the rulings regarding persons like you with beliefs as you've expressed to me and knowing the rulings regarding those who know those 2 things my salat behind you would be invalid even though the salat *of others who don't know what I know about you + the rulings about you is still valid.*

Until our conflict is resolved I would hope you could have someone else lead when/if I'm present for salat at the same time as you so that way I can pray in jamat too.

Can you put personal pride, prestige and protocol aside so I can pray in jamat in the masjid?

Or could you tell me why I'm wrong to think your beliefs are wrong (if they are)?

I want to pray salat in jamat at the masjid.

I can't because of your unislamic beliefs.

So 1. You could change those beliefs to the correct beliefs.

2. I could change my beliefs after you explain to me why my beliefs about your beliefs are wrong if they are.

3. You could let someone else lead the salat when the two of us are both present for jamat at the same time so that way both of us can pray in jamat without causing communal conflict/stress without either of us having to suffer the loss of iman that comes with not praying in jamat.

One Friday at another masjid I heard a sermon about reconciling with Muslims before Ramadan begins. So after over two months absence I returned to ISNF masjid noor, after emailing Mr. Qadri prior to my return with intentions to reconcile listing further ideas on how we could resolve our differences amicably. Surprisingly and against Islamic rulings, there were non-Muslim guards at the masjid. (Things had corrupted without me there just as I feared.) Anyways I prayed tahiyatul masjid and waited until Mr. Qadri was done talking with his friends and asked him directly face to face to talk to him but he refused and walked away ignoring me.

So I decided to try a different tactic. I looked up his phone number on the masjid bulletin board and called, left voicemail and texted it. Then I left notes in his office and on the front and back doors of his house saying how I want to be friends and reconcile with him but can't until he agrees non-Muslims are kuffar, shirk is kufr and Jews and Christians are disbelievers. I got no response and he didn't come back for prayers at the masjid that day either. After isha night prayer I waited outside his house(which is next to the masjid paid for by ISNF) just reciting Quran not knowing what to do because I didn't want to pray separately causing a scene if he showed up for fajr morning prayer but I wasn't going to abandon going to the masjid for fajr. Finally I got a response via text at around midnight from Mr. Qadri that he refuses to ever discuss anything with me because I'm too disrespectful and unthankful with him saying there is hadith that those unthankful to people are unthankful to Allah. Later my friend Payraw, who I hadn't seen in months, told me in the masjid that Imam Khalilullah Qadri said to him that all the Imams of WNY all told Qadri that he shouldn't talk to me anymore even to say that he agrees "Shrik is Kufr, Mushriks are Kafirs and that non-Muslims are all disbelievers" so I pray behind him again. Suspecting this ridiculous alleged community unity against me to be a deceptive lie from Mr. Qadri to Payraw I needed proof. Therefore I tried personally emailing all the Imams of WNY to see if they knew of our dispute and said to Qadri what Payraw alleged they said. I got 2 replies. One from the Lackawanna guest imam Jalal Abual Rub who told me in person before not to go to that ISNF masjid when I asked him in person what to do if the imam of a masjid says Jews and Christians are not kuffar. In the email Jalal Abual Rub sent me he said he didn't know the imam and never spoke to him about me and that I should just pray at masjid huda if things are as I say. The other reply was from another ISNF imam of their other masjid in Niagara Falls saying my email was too long to read and to condense the message to four lines or else he wouldn't bother reading it. I condensed it to four lines as requested but didn't get a reply. Although the very same day I sent that email out the other ISNF imam came to masjid noor for one of the prayers, but Mr. Qadri wasn't there and I showed up late so I missed praying with him. As I prayed alone after the others were leaving I noticed the other ISNF imam was talking to ISNF board members and I think it was about me and my dispute with Qadri. They were discussing amongst themselves within my earshot how could they prevent or ban me from coming to the mosque. Some said I hadn't done anything illegal or violent so it was difficult for them to concoct a plot that could get me banned, but this was what I heard them discuss while I prayed. However by the time I finished praying nobody was left in the masjid and nobody talked to me as I had hoped; despite talking about me in extremely sacrilegious mannerisms.

I decided because masjid noor was closest to my house and sometimes there were not enough people for jamat, especially on days Mr. Qadri doesn't attend all 5, that if I stopped going it would mean that sometimes a masjid would not have enough people to have jamat prayers in congregation. Especially since I had sometimes prayed the obligatory salat there all by myself because nobody else would show up. I figured there was a real possibility that if I didn't go to masjid noor then they will not be performing all 5 salat daily. This was because Qadri didn't attend all 5 prayers every day, 35 times a week, despite being paid to be the prayer leader, and despite living next to masjid; at least from 2014-2017. Plus I hoped for reconciliation and repentance on Mr. Qadri's part, so I had to fix the problem so the repentance of Mr. Qadri or myself would solve the disturbance.

As a paranoid precaution I decided I would only utter Arabic aloud at the masjid despite not knowing Arabic fluently. If anyone asked why I wasn't praying behind Qadri I would show them my printed out email evidence of him being upon heresy and his last reply to me and hope they would arbitrate for us so his error would be corrected. I would bring a folder with me of my evidence nearly every time I came to the masjid five times a day with written explanations of why I'm only speaking Arabic and not praying behind Qadri until he recants his heretical position or is fired. I did this because I was scared and didn't know how to fix the situation that had been ongoing for 3 months, or longer, and Qadri was boycotting me communication wise despite me being the most frequent masjid goer besides him. Often over the course of 2014 to 2017, it would be just me and Qadri for salat so to be ignored by Qadri for so long just because I insisted Jews and Christians are disbelievers in Islam and that I won't pray behind him until he agrees with that was very hard to bear. Furthermore because I was white, revert and wore Turban and Islamic dress daily while most of masjid noor demographic was indo/pak, clean-shaven, suit-wearing liberals then I was basically a loner at the masjid simply because the demographic is mostly college students from the University of Buffalo and medical professionals who don't attend the masjid much or know much about Islam. Plus being naturally paranoid, non-confrontational and shy further compounded my problems.

The idea of only speaking Arabic was because I heard a motivational speaker mention a story of a woman who only spoke Quran verses yet was able to survive. However Imam Jawzi related in one of his books that using the Quran in such a way is not piety but innovative sinful bida and abuse of the Quran misusing it for things it's not meant for. Yet I didn't at that time know this was bida to only say Quran and mistakenly saw it as virtuous, therefore I figured if I only speak Arabic, since I only know Quranic ayat, salams, Islamic phrases and dhikr then I could only end up saying good things. Therefore any "steps" Qadri said ISNF would take against me could not materialize if I was only saying Quran and Dhikr in the masjid. Thus I incorrectly thought limiting my vocabulary and language would help me get support from Allah and safety from saying/doing anything that could remotely be seen as evil. In reality I was confused and chose an innovative method of desperation that would lead to disastrous consequences. All Bida even if done with pure intentions always leads to great calamity no matter what.

With this new strategy of only speaking Arabic, one day while Qadri gave tajweed lessons to kids I recited Quran verses relevant to our dispute alongside them almost as a weapon in a rather loud voice hoping such recitation would move his heart to reconcile or repent or stop ignoring me. He continued to ignore me despite staring at me and then I overheard him backbiting me in his office to one of my revert friends, Anthony, as I left the masjid that day after my friend and him decided to have their customary tajweed lesson in his office in order to be away from my loud recitation.

My friend Payraw and his Dad had a private meeting with me to try to resolve situation with me not praying behind Mr. Qadri. But as Payraw's Dad was clean-shaven and from Iraq and since I wasn't speaking English the meeting ended up with him thinking and accusing me of being extreme for wearing Turban everyday in America and then he angrily cited how ISIS triggered Shiite killing of Sunnis in Iraq. And since I couldn't speak English due to my innovative vow of only Arabic, all I could say was Arabic Quran verses. In reply I said the Arabic word "Qadr" explaining that it was Destiny. But Payraw's Dad did not like my new communication method and didn't want to look at my folder of evidence to understand my position so then the meeting ended without me being able to prove to Payraw that Qadri lied to him or was leveraging him against me in his last email to me as a means of isolating me from the community. At this point I was trying to rely solely on Allah for help because I had been thoroughly isolated by Mr. Qadri's plotting and my self-imposed limited Arabic-only communication.

The very next day on May 3rd, 2017 at Fajr dawn prayer, exactly three Gregorian months after his previously displayed email reply, Mr. Qadri came late after the iqamah was called for someone else and still led the prayer despite the hadith of Jesus returning to earth during the time of the Mahdi where the Mahdi will lead Jesus in prayer because iqamah is called before Jesus arrives to prayer in the mosque in Damascus prior to killing the antichrist. This was a big deal for me because Mr. Qadri wasn't there and the iqamah was called for someone else to lead us all and people knew I don't pray in congregation when Mr. Qadri is there but I do when he is not. Then astonishingly Mr. Qadri came late and led the prayer thereby intentionally depriving me of praying in congregation and contradicting the prophetic authentic hadith too regarding praying behind whoever the iqamah is called for even if a better candidate comes later.

At that point I was furious and afterall that had happened over the last three months and the three years before that I thought Mr. Qadri must be a Munafiq(fake Muslim/enemy of Islam). But only knowing little Arabic vocabulary, being furious and put on the spot about to miss out on congregational prayer due to arrogant oppression mixed with fools not knowing better, I could only think of one thing to say, "Munafiq". So I publicly angrily called him Munafiq, which is the word for a non-Muslim disbelieving enemy of Islam who pretends to be a Muslim, and stepped back out of the prayer line thereby making public takfir/excommunication. I was silent while they prayed then I read Quran afterwards and prayed fajr alone. Nobody said anything to me. I then texted Mr. Qadri how /why he was wrong to have led the salat when he came late knowing I wouldn't pray in jamat if he led. At home I tried to inform other Imams and Masjids via email about the situation so Mr. Qadri could get fired. At this point I knew that his foolishness and heresy was no longer excusable because he was deliberately acting against well-known Islamic doctrines and practices and wasn't innocently confused nor apologetical. In the process I temporarily lost my phone containing my text message evidence because I forgot where I had plugged it in to charge. As a result, I had a panic attack that felt like a heart attack that I thought was a jinn attack since I never had a panic attack before. This was because publicly making takfir of your former best friend and tajweed teacher and prayer leader in the masjid is very stressful and not something to be done lightly, if ever. So I knew I needed all the evidence I could gather and since I misplaced my phone while typing the emails I freaked out thinking nobody will believe me because I lost my phone containing valuable text message evidence confirming his kufr and refusal to interact or repent from any mistakes despite advice and evidence. It was at this point my nervous mental breakdown was triggered.

Everything before this was all documented and nobody can claim any insanity on my part prior to this point. In my emails to all the masjid organizations in WNY at that time I added a charge of a magic attack by Mr. Qadri to my charge of him being a Munafiq due to not believing Jews/Christians are kuffar/disbelievers because I felt nearly immediate heart attack symptoms hours after making takfir and at the very moment I tried typing up emails asking other Imams to get Mr. Qadri fired from his position at ISNF. I felt I was going to die during my panic attack and had minutes left to live while typing those emails telling the rest of the Muslim community leaders about what was going on. Even as I typed I could only use one hand to type because one arm was paralyzed. Panic attacks are painfully scary and unhealthy and I was under extreme stress and probably nutritionally deficient too since I had only been eating pasta, dates and water. Therefore I began to suspect perhaps the symptoms of my panic attack were related to Qadri doing magic because of what I said about him being a Munafiq.

After Asr prayer that same day May 3rd, 2017 I overheard Payraw telling Mr. Qadri about my vow of silence and that I'd pray behind him again if he said shirk was kufr and all non-Muslims were disbelievers. Yet Mr. Qadri pretended to Payraw he had no idea why I don't pray behind him though I knew Mr. Qadri knew because he told me so before in email and text messages that he knew why I wasn't praying behind him and he disagreed with my beliefs. Other ISNF members upon hearing for the first time why I don't pray behind Mr. Qadri said, *"We can't say Christians are disbelievers because we are married to Christians and love them."* Mr. Qadri did not correct them. I then went over to them and broke my vow of silence and publicly informed Mr. Qadri of his earlier error of leading fajr prayer that day despite the hadith of Jesus praying behind the

Mahdi when Jesus comes late after Iqamah is already called. Mr. Qadri laughed in my face about leading earlier that day even though doing so was wrong and doubly wrong because he knew I would pray separately if he led. Then I got distracted by another ISNF member who was saying Jews and Christians are not disbelievers before angrily storming off. So I went out following this commoner trying to correct his mistaken creed individually since I figured I can correct/expose Qadri further later but I might not see this other ISNF guy again who was a commoner upon error. I did not make takfir of this commoner because after dialogue I realized he knew almost nothing about Islam despite having Muslim children in the tajweed class I interrupted. This guy said I must have learned my religion from Abu Jahl and Abu Lahab (two polytheist Quraishi relatives of Muhammad who ferociously fought Islam tooth and nail) because they hated Muhammad and Muslims so therefore because I teach hatred for Christians and Jews and call them disbelievers then

I must have got my religion from Abu Jahl and Abu Lahab. Such an ignorant insulting statement was so foolish that it's funny. It's like saying because Prophet David killed Goliath he must have learned his religion from Pharoah and not Moses because Pharoah killed people. By the time I finished talking separately with the common fool, then Mr. Qadri and everybody else had left the masjid. Mr. Qadri was not excused in my opinion for being upon the same error as the commoner because Mr. Qadri had memorized the Quran and been Islamically educated and informed, put into a public leadership position, called himself a Scholar and confirmed reading the fatwa rulings on the matter and was refusing to discuss the matter due to ego. The clean-shaven pant dragging common fool was clearly too stupid to understand what he was discussing and I doubted the man even ever read the Quran once in any language. So since people are not equal they are not to be treated equally even if they make the same exact mistakes.

Later I was praying by myself after Isha on May 3rd, 2017 and while I recited Quran in Isha qiyaam Mr. Qadri took a microphone and loudly said publicly, *"Will someone please tell this brother to stop bothering us. La hawla wa la quwati illah billah."* because apparently my recitation in qiyam was too loud for the crowd to hear him while he was reading hadith. I found this appalling because at Masjid Huda when people came late to prayer their guest Imam Jalal Abual Rub remained silent the whole time waiting for their prayers to stop before starting his own scheduled lectures. Also before our dispute when I asked Mr. Qadri in the name of Allah to read hadith after fajr, he refused. So I knew Mr. Qadri didn't care that much for hadith. And since he knew 100% how to end the dispute with me, by Qadri saying others should talk to me in such a public fashion it was further proof for me that he persisted upon heresy. Payraw told him earlier that very day that I would pray behind him ending the argument if he just said Shirk was Kufr, Mushriks were Kafirs and Jews and Christians were disbelievers. So what purpose does Qadri saying someone else should tell me to stop bothering him serve if he didn't still believe in the heresy? He could have concealed the whole affair and told me privately that we agreed or just talked to me himself to discuss a solution if he disagreed. Furthermore I could not islamically respond to him at that time because I was busy praying isha prayer and he knew that. So it was essentially a public verbal assault while I was praying with him disguised as the concerned innocent patient victim. And he issued his retort while I was reciting Quran aloud, which contradicts further hadith that I didn't know until recently which forbid overspeaking of the Quran especially in masjids.

After that I decided I cannot go to ISNF masjid noor anymore because the community had turned against me and I cannot fix the situation. It was at such an extent that people would pass by me praying alone and say to the few people I considered friends, like Anthony, *"Don't talk to him he's ISIS!"* meanwhile I can't respond to the slanders because of being busy with obligatory prayer. So in 2017 CE to be in a masjid praying alone while the community is publicly calling you a member of the violent terrorist Khariji group ISIS is very dangerous. Especially when the non-Muslim national government is openly at war with such a organization hunting down its alleged members. It's basically like having people say "Arrest him!" when you are trying to pray peacefully in a position that the religion forbids you to interrupt your prayer to respond to slanders no matter what dangerously false charges they levy against you.

At this point I figured I would try to learn Payraw's email from a mutual friend we both knew from the masjid who was living in Saudi Arabia that I had informed about the situation who had agreed with my creed. I sent a long word document to this friend requesting Payraw to come to my house to visit me and my parents so Payraw can see my evidence and hear my parents testimony of Qadri's secret meetings during our 2016 dispute and learn his true character. I asked Payraw if he could help get Mr. Qadri fired as nobody would listen to me but since Payraw was frequently the alternate prayer leader and the MSA president then perhaps people would listen to him. In this long document I had our mutual friend email to Payraw I also crazily asked him to spy on Qadri and report what he says about me and stuff so I could compile more evidence. I also said I didn't want Payraw to tell his father about coming to visit me because I didn't trust his father after he seemingly thought I was extreme or pro-ISIS. Basically I went crazy at this point into a paranoid near domino takfir mode almost. This was because the panic attack I had hours after calling Qadri munafiq caused brain damage and insanity would come and go intermittently and my paranoia increased. I would heal this insanity and the muscle spasms I'd feel with reading the Quran just thinking its magical jinn attacks from Mr. Qadri using jinn via magic to try to stop me in order to secure his position as ISNF masjid noor imam. Now I know most of my email to Payraw was wrong, hyper-paranoid, crazy and likely gave an incorrect impression of me being Khariji especially since Qadri and other ISNF members were openly claiming such about me. Also since I had been only eating foreign imported pasta, dates and water my nutritional imbalance mixed with extreme traumatic stress on it's own, plus lack of sleep, could cause insanity without any magic being involved. Yet an insane person cannot often think clearly in the midst of and in-between episodes of delusion. In hindsight I could have just emailed our mutual friend to forward my evidence to Payraw but I couldn't think straight at that point and felt if Payraw visited me and saw and heard the testimony from my parents then he would realize how Qadri is two-faced and tells lies.

Mr. Qadri knew full well I was not Khariji or Al-Qaeda or ISIS because he had read early editions of my books which refuted the Khawarij and their deviancy. And my emails to Qadri themselves condemn ISIS and Al-Qaeda too. But because I never talked to many people at masjid noor and the only issue which most people witnessed publicly was me not praying behind Qadri ever since the day I publicly reprimanded him for making congregational dua, most people probably thought I made takfir of him for making congregational dua after fajr. If that was the case then it would have been me in the wrong for declaring Mr. Qadri an apostate for a minor innovative sin. Yet there was a whole other story which only a handful of people knew about and Mr. Qadri twisted this lack of public knowledge about our dispute over creed to his advantage. Nearly nobody knew about Mr. Qadri saying Jews/Christians are not disbelievers or that shirk(polytheism) is not kufr(disbelief) and that mushriks(polytheists) are not kafirs(disbelievers). I didn't tell people of our dispute because I was thinking it would cause fitna(tribulation) where people would have to choose me or Mr. Qadri and I didn't want them to choose wrong due to partisanship and then I'd have problems with others too. So I figured concealing Qadri's error until we could reconcile was best. Since for three months Qadri refused to reconcile, I got desperate because I couldn't pray jamat at the masjid closest to my house and nobody would speak with me because they likely thought I was extreme not praying due to the congregational dua issue. When I stopped talking in English the matter compounded fast and I medically came down with psychosis/insanity from the stress of trying to reconcile with Mr. Qadri plus the brain damage of the panic attack I had after I uttered the word Munafiq plus the nutritional imbalance. At the time under the circumstances I concluded Mr. Qadri had done magic to me. It was already a logical evidence-based conclusion the guy was pretending to be Muslim and hiding his true beliefs from the public, so when you are faced with that kind of person and then when you oppose them trying to get them fired and get symptoms similar to magic then it's sensible to deduce the heretic is resorting to magical attacks to keep their position. One month later in June 2017 I would be hospitalized and medically diagnosed with psychosis but at the time I did not know what that was. Thus recognizing unexplained bouts of hyper-paranoid insanity coming and going with increased frequency ever since the time I publicly said Mr. Qadri was a Munafiq, I thought it was magic from him, specifically a type of magic called sihr al-junun.

That was the situation I found myself in days later without a reply from my attempt to email Payraw indirectly, having people in the masjid saying I'm ISIS while I'm praying alone within earshot and thinking my recent bouts of insanity and physical feelings of prickly tremors were from Mr. Qadri doing magic to me. On Friday May 5th, 2017 I figured that Payraw was not going to email me back and probably shared my insanesque email with ISNF or Qadri and since they were already publicly accusing me of belonging to illegal criminal terrorist organizations then I figured it was only a matter of time before they tried framing me and involving American non-Muslim law enforcement. Logically if they think I'm a terrorist and say so publicly then it's a duty to inform the police even if the original accusers know it's a lie, the lie was spreading and someone would be dumb enough to report me without informing me sooner or later. While showering for the Friday prayer without knowing where to go for it I got two random phone call messages from both my parents saying they loved me dearly. With my paranoia at it's peak I figured that was them tipping me off that I had been reported on the news and the police were on their way to take me to terrorist interrogation and lock me away in prison forever. So, under such a presumption that if ever my parents were going to tip me off then that would be how they would do likely do it, then I figured I was now a fugitive wanted by the law framed by ISNF for belonging to ISIS which I was innocent of. But I wasn't going to wait for the police to kick down the door guns blazing. I took my laptop and some food and some extra layers of clothing and left the house figuring I couldn't drive anywhere lest my license plates show up on radar and I couldn't be seen on any cameras under the impression a warrant had already been issued for my arrest. So I took some cash and silver coins and walked to a nearby park for dogs that was on a mini-island in the middle of the Erie canal and decided that was where I would live as a homeless person, until my name was cleared. I had little time to prepare everything and then I started to think of how to clear my name from the charges. I decided I needed internet access so I could send my digital evidence exposing Qadri and the lies he told the Muslims in the area hoping they could defend me before the impending arrest. I didn't want to use a public wifi though because of fear of getting caught on camera. Then some dogs started harassing me at the park and I got hungry so I decided to move locations. I decided to do the unexpected and that the last place police would look for an alleged Muslim terrorist on the run would be a church. And though I had no intention of apostasy from Islam I figured I could just talk to a priest and explain I'm trying to get a fake Muslim Imam fired and he accused me falsely of being ISIS and I was hoping to use your property to hide and utilize the wifi to upload my evidence to clear my name before I get arrested. That was my new plan. I asked another park goer if they could take me to the nearby church and they declined even though I offered to pay them with a silver coin upon the methodology of the people of the Cave. Then I figured this guy might report me. So I fled and ended up walking to the nearby church myself under the radar and sat down at a bench near a statue thinking if I was thinking everything through correctly anticipating what might happen next. As I contemplated and was disgusted by the idolatrous statue, I realized I had gone crazy and that everything I stood for is in opposition to the polytheism of Christianity and that seeking help from disbelievers is not something I was willing to do and likely would not result in goodness if I tried anyways. I had always been a staunch opponent of Muslims seeking help from non-Muslims due to the Quran and Hadith teaching the opposite of that, yet there I was sitting on a bench near a statute alleged to be of Jesus' mother. What would I do when it was time to pray the next daily prayer? Can't do that in a church with images and crosses. Then I reconsidered my plan and decided that perhaps I was under the influence of magically induced insanity that made me think the police were after me when it wasn't so. Plus I was very hungry and wanted to eat so I decided to walk back home and take my chances with the perceived threat of arrest. After eating I felt much better and realized it was definitely a crazy idea to think a church would help me in my situation, if anything they'd report me or try to convert me back to Christianity rather than help me get a heretical Muslim leader fired. So I thought how in the world could my mind have ever imagined such a scenario/plan was so logical and true? Certainly I was insane and something must have caused it. I diagnosed my insanity as bewitchment and tried to treat it as if it were magic since it is known Islamically how to treat such afflictions. It turned out I was not reported to the police or at least nobody was coming to get me as I feared. So I typed up a long email to the mutual friend of mine and Payraw, who lived in Saudia

Arabia, explaining what was going on and that Payraw never emailed me and my belief magic was done to me by Qadri asking for advice on what I should do. Before I could send the email, I noticed it was almost time to pray the dawn prayer. So I figured rather than wait to get arrested if/when ISNF do eventually report me under false pretenses then I would bravely go to the mosque myself and explain to the community in person that Qadri has heretical beliefs and refused to change them for the past three months. Furthermore I would explain that because I tried to get Qadri fired then I think he's doing magic to me to stop me from exposing his heretical errors to the Muslim community so he is fired as Islamic law requires.

On May 6th, 2017 before the fajr dawn prayer after publicly desperately accusing Mr. Qadri of being a magician and munafiq for saying Christians and Jews are not kuffar, I asked Qadri publicly and this time begged everyone else present to let another lead us in salat so I could pray in jamat too. Devastatingly Mr. Qadri and the congregation refused to have someone other than Mr. Qadri lead salat despite being informed of his heresy, although my claims of magic didn't help persuade them. There were only about a dozen people there. Payraw and his Dad were absent. Whatever the number the situation was as follows: If Mr. Qadri the imam on salary leads prayer then X number of people will worship Allah in unity minus one. If someone else other than Mr. Qadri leads in prayer everyone will worship Allah in unity in a greater number. Religiously speaking which is better in the sight of God. Having 19 or 20 people pray to him together? How on earth could it be better for 19 total with Qadri as a leader to pray rather than having 20 total pray together? How arrogant and special would Mr. Qadri have to consider himself to insist on leading salat under the circumstances? Logically Allah wants as many worshippers as possible and this is what the prophets taught. It is a fundamental aspect of establishing the salat that if you can do so in greater numbers with other leadership then you do so. Having Qadri lead in such a scenario is actually preventing Allah from being worshipped in a manner Allah deserves, so it is actually a step of bigoted partisanship that rather than establishes salat/prayer is the opposite and is an anti-worship of God despite the appearance of people gathering to worship God. Basically by excluding me so Qadri could lead they are saying Qadri's right to lead prayers is more important than the right of Allah to be worshipped by as many people as possible. So Islamically I was entirely justified and correct in begging the community to have someone else lead the prayer for that moment so I could join, as I had explained Qadri's heresy and his refusal to communicate prevented me spiritually from praying behind him. I would pray next to him shoulder to shoulder, foot to foot, if I had to but I was fed up with missing out on praying together in the community because of Qadri arrogantly leading the prayers and refusing to communicate. If you recall in 2015 when Mr. Qadri had a foot injury, despite being most qualified to lead salat he chose not to and prayed sitting in a chair with others leading the prayers for several days. So it's not like Qadri would be sinful or wrong in any way for letting another person lead the salat because he had done it before many times with much less reason. This was an emergency crisis matter that he didn't want to resolve and I begged for someone else to lead until we resolved the matter. I wasn't saying fire Qadri on the spot, I just said let's all pray together behind someone else for this one short prayer and then afterwards me and Qadri can finally settle our argument once and for all peacefully by talking it out. Instead Qadri arrogantly took advantage of the ignorance of the congregation and insisted on leading despite me refusing to pray behind him since he had beliefs rendering his prayer invalid. If I prayed behind him knowing what I knew my prayer wouldn't count so I wasn't going to pretend and waste my time and validate his leadership when Qadri islamically deserves exposure, censuring and termination from his position. It's one thing to oppress me and exclude me from praying in jamat, but it's a whole other thing to reduce the number of people praying to Allah in Allah's house. Thus I looked at it for what it was, someone preventing Allah from being worshipped as best as possible. Truly Allah deserves the best effort in quality and quantity from the community and they were refusing to have the quantity be as large as it could be because of liking Qadri so much and hating me. So I lost my temper and then publicly said to Qadri, *"May you die before you finish the salat if you lead."* And then I stepped aside and behind the rows while they prayed, but this time instead of remaining silent, as I always had done everytime before, I recited the Quranic verses of surah alaq aloud during fajr hoping Allah would kill Qadri via my ruqya style recitation of Quran during the jamat over his recitation which I was beginning to think was infused with magic. I believed if Qadri dies on the spot from me merely reading Quran verses then that will be divine undeniable proof I was right all along and Allah answered my curse on him immediately thus proving almost miraculously that he really was a fake hypocrite defrauding Muslims. However, Qadri kept praying longer than normal not dying, as I kept reciting and crying. This in itself was forbidden for him as well as me. I was totally insane at this point and wrong to be reading Quran during their salat as it contradicts authentic hadith, but Mr. Qadri was wrong too by prolonging the prayer when there was a clear medical emergency or at the minimum a disturbance. The prophet Muhammad would cut short his prayer for babies crying out of mercy, but Mr. Qadri is not a person of mercy it would seem. After fajr ended a guy ran up to me and shouted at me saying to leave them alone and stop disturbing them and their prayers. So I tried explaining how Mr. Qadri is a Munafiq doing magic to me and then as I was outnumbered and disbelieved I finally acquiesced and said I'll leave and never come back. So I left without even praying fajr myself at the masjid, praying elsewhere, despite knowing the hadith forbidding leaving a masjid after the athan is called without praying, because I felt so unwelcomed.

I later realized that my reciting Quran during fajr was wrong and goes against hadith. Yet even still my reading Quran verses while Qadri read Quran in salat is less sinful than him publicly saying, *"Will someone please tell this brother to stop bothering us. La hawla wa la quwata illa billah."* with the microphone while I was reading Quran aloud in salat during Isha days earlier. So Qadri publicly did worse to me when I was praying in the masjid than I ever did to him but his overreading of my Quran wasn't seen as evil despite it being in reality more evil than my overreading of his Quran recitation. I interrupted his Quran with Quran, he interrupted my Quran with personal speech of deceptive persecution. Plus he did it days earlier while sane and I did it while in the midst of a psychotic episode. The key difference was our social networks and positions and that I wished death upon him. Yet to be clear I never ever threatened him with any violence. This distinction is important. For example someone swearing angrily saying "F*** you!" is very different than threatening to rape someone sexually. Nobody could say that uttering such a vulgar phrase was a threat/attempt of sexual assault. Just like how nobody can say me wishing Qadri died if he led the salat was any way a threat that I would physically use violence against him. Furthermore in my emails to others, and even to Qadri himself, when trying to get Qadri fired I always stressed that despite his apostasy I disavowed using violence inside America and was peaceful even though the punishment for apostasy in Islam is execution by the Muslim government. There is absolutely no vigilante implementation of the law in Islam. Heretics know this and take advantage by fleeing to countries where they cannot be harmed unless it were by vigilantes, of which those who believe in and practice Islam are forbidden from vigilante violence in all cases. So basically no matter what heresy anyone falls into, they are diplomatically protected in America even if they deserve the death penalty for heresy according to their religion or other religions. Furthermore I later apologized to Qadri via email explaining I had psychosis at that time thinking sihr al junun was done to me by him during the incident. Yet because of that one incident of me reciting Quran aloud while Qadri led fajr prayer, I got banned from masjid noor hours after the incident by Mr. Qadri himself via text message. During our texting back and forth I threatened to curse Qadri daily/nightly for the rest of my life for doing magic, being a heretic and preventing me from worshiping in congregation and then banning me from the mosque. Qadri oddly never ever denied doing magic nor ever said that he agreed with my beliefs regarding creed so that there was no reason for us to be arguing or having an issue, in reply Mr. Qadri texted me back that I'd never ever get married. Which in actuality is a type of fortunetelling regarding unseen destiny which is sinful to say/do. So he just added another heresy to the list of his errors. And how would Qardi know I would never get married unless he was doing magic to prevent it and if he wasn't then why would he text that to a Muslim if he was a Muslim Imam wanting goodness for them instead of a hypocritical Munafiq as I alleged. His two-facedness was extremely evil and apparent to me. Sadly though it was hidden from the community who thought he was a literally a saintly friend of God as his first name was legally innovatively "Khalil-Allah" despite in reality acting like he was a "Khalil-Shaitan".

So while still getting bouts of insanity, including extreme ringing in my head while texting Qadri, amidst my traumatization I retreated to the Lackawanna masjid hoping for help and healing from what I thought was magic and for reinforcements and support in my quest to get Qadri to repent or be fired. Surprisingly I met a Muslim taxi driver who had talked to me before when he stopped in ISNF masjid noor to pray. This taxi driver translated my problem after viewing and reading my papers of email evidence to the other people in the masjid, everyone there said if what I claimed was true about Qadri's denial that Jews and Christians were kuffar then this was clear disbelief in Islam. They also said I should talk to an administrative leader called Anwar. Yet I didn't know who Anwar was or what he looked like. So I waited and then my revert friend I met in ISNF masjid noor, Abdul Haq, came for congregational prayer and he saw me. I explained to him what happened and that I need to talk to Anwar so Abdul Haq introduced us to each other. This meeting with Anwar took place May 6th 2017, the very same day I called Qadri a magician and read Quran and got banned from the mosque by Qadri via text message.

Firstly Anwar told me his opinion of "Khalilullah" (Friend of God) Qadri was that he was a "Liberal Sufi" type of Imam that dilutes Islam a bit to suit liberal tastes. I explained what happened earlier that day and me being banned from the mosque by Qadri and how I never planned to ever go back to that masjid but just wanted to share my email evidence to learn if I was wrong or if Qadri was wrong. Anwar upon hearing my plans to abandon Qadri and curse him forever stressed I forgive and "Never curse someone". I explained how sometimes even prophet Muhammad cursed people but despite me being correct on that point, I must admit Anwar was correct when he told me "You never stop the dawah no matter what." I had never been more pissed off in my life and certain that someone living was doomed to hellfire for eternity, and I even said in the mosque before I left that Qadri will burn in hell forever since I figured he was a magician heretic. This was incorrect of me to do regarding the unseen future, just as Qadri was wrong to text I'd never get married, as I did not have a proof that Qadri will die upon magic or heresy, yet even still from the moment Anwar said that until now I realize Anwar was right on that point. Anwar also said if the stuff I was saying was true then Qadri was undoubtedly a disbeliever but he just wanted to check with Qadri first and I told him this was a good idea. Later Anwar incorrectly said how you "hate the sin but not the sinner" and I corrected him and explained the love/hate relationship in depth and how 99 drops of hate for a sinful Muslim was outweighed by 1 drop of Faith.

While 99 drops of good were contaminated by 1 drop of Kufr for which was why I hate Kafirs as Islam says. Anwar agreed with me and thanked me for the explanation/correction. Then Anwar said that based on what he knows of the Imam then he would love to reconcile and that I would be of more benefit to Muslims if I prayed at ISNF masjid noor instead. I said I was banned and promised I'd never go back and Qadri is not the kind guy who Anwar imagines him to be and for months refused to even communicate about possible reconciliation. Anwar though advised me to return to the ISNF masjid noor and just talk it out with Qadri. I said that I was done with trying with him and that he refused to accept what I had to say so since he didn't want to be my friend then I was done with him. Anwar told me that one can never be done doing dawah or stop asking Allah to guide/forgive him and that even if he don't seem to want it we don't have the right to stop doing dawah. Anwar totally agreed that anyone saying non-Muslims weren't disbelievers would be a disbeliever and that shirk was kufr and that all mushriks were kafirs. Regarding Payraw's story about Qadri contacting all Imams about me, Anwar said that he had never talked to Qadri about me and only knew of our dispute via my emails which Sheikh Jalal forwarded to him and personally meeting me that very day. Although regrettably I did not show Anwar my folder of evidence despite having it with me when we met. Instead I tried to email Anwar my entire record of email correspondence with Qadri from 2014 to 2017 to prove I was not ISIS as people at ISNF were saying and not extreme when making takfir. Basically I was playing defense trying to clear my name when I should have been playing offense. Especially since there were over 150 emails in a three-year timeframe then it was not a good idea to try vindicating myself prior to proving Qadri guilty. So after sending Anwar hundreds of email records I later realized he was too busy to read such evidence. I figured if I was just honest and gave all my evidence as a court matter requires then justice would be done. But people in America don't have time to examine the whole truth as justice demands.

This same day May 6th, 2017 during the night I got an email from my dear friend Joel who had converted to Islam after our discussions on the subject. Adding further stressful trauma to my life, Joel said that he was no longer interested in being a Muslim. I devoted several sincere hours and days to dialoguing back and forth to find out why this sudden surprising change. At the root cause it was because after becoming a Muslim his fellow islamophobic co-worker got into a physical altercation fighting him, so he ended up getting fired and was having a difficult time getting a new job. That was his main reason, not any glaring issue with any doctrines or practices because I answered all his questions and even he himself admitted that he couldn't handle the pressure of being Muslim in America despite it being convincing far beyond any other religion. I asked Joel if it was anything I had said or done, as Qadri claimed my dawah led people astray, but Joel said that was not the case at all and that I did nothing but help him and we even stayed in contact via email for a few years after he apostated. Anyways May 6th, 2017 was quite a traumatic eventful day to have been prevented from worshipping in congregation despite my pleas, then banned from a mosque by my best friend turned nemesis via text message and then find out my first Muslim convert friend which I influenced was apostating. Surely that's enough to make any sincere Muslim go insane, especially when one adds the personal stress of making takfir of anyone let alone a former friend/teacher/leader even if there is no magic involved, but especially when you add in the nutritional imbalance and lack of sleep I was getting due to typing many long emails to people.

As Anwar advised me, I returned to ISNF masjid noor on the next day May 7th, 2017 to try to talk things out with Qadri. I prayed tahiyaatul masjid, and sunnah prayers and nobody else was yet there for salat. Next the burly non-Muslim Sunday School security guard asked me to talk outside. I said we can talk in the masjid with no issue but the guard insisted we talk outside in private. So after I went outside of my own choice the guard simply said, "*You're a good person but the imam banned you because you threatened him and the cops will be called if you ever come back to the property.*" I left and never returned to this day. Later in May 2017 on the phone with my Christian mother when Qadri was banning me to he, she asked him, "*Why are you even talking to me about this when I'm a disbeliever?*" and after all that and the alleged ignorance of our dispute and doubts of others that I misinterpreted Qadri's statements, my mother told me Qadri laughed at her question telling her, "*I don't consider you to be one even though your son does*". So even when Qadri audibly hears a known Christian tell him clearly that she is a disbeliever in Islam, he refuses to believe they are disbelievers. Clearly Qadri was a fool deluded by the devil.

On May 26th, 2017, the first day of Ramadan that year, then ISNF president Rasul Khan sent a letter to my parent's house and the Amherst police chief officially banning me from the masjid saying I was no longer welcome at masjid noor and that local law enforcement was notified and would comply in preventing me from returning.

Executive Board:

President
Rasul Khan

Vice-President
Attiq ur Rahman

Secretary
Shahid Mehboob

Treasurer
Tajudeen Kariapper

Members
Sarah Syed
Fazal Wahab
Sadiq Ur Rahman
Nasir Dara
Azhar Hussain

Council of Trustees:

Chairperson
Yusuf Fazli

Secretary
Shahid Ahmed

Members
Ashraf Balti
Ghous Yasin
Mustafa Syed
Humaira Hashmi
Arjuman Haroon
Osman Duaellah
Quyyum Fazili

Imam:

Masjid An-Noor:
Syed Khalil Ullah Qadri

Masjid Al-Taqwa
M. Hanin Zaman

Sunday school:

Principal:
Syed Khalil Ullah Qadri

School Board President:
M. Abdelhadi Ghazi

Mr. Abdullah Bin Kevin (Greg Henry)

1280 E Robinson St,

Tonawanda, NY

MR. ABDULLAH BIN KEVIN:

After careful consideration of the incident involving Mr. Abdullah that occurred at our Masjid (located at 745 Heim Road) during midday Prayer Service on May 07, 2017 at approximately 1:00 pm, the Executive Board of the Islamic Society of Niagara Frontier (ISNF) have come to the decision that you (Mr. Abdullah) will no longer be welcomed at our Facility.

This has not been the first incident at the facility involving you, rather it has been an ongoing issue with you for the past several years. On Sunday, May 7, 2017, you were advised by our Security Personal that you are no longer welcomed on our premises.

All Local Law Enforcement Officials have been properly notified of the current and past incidents that you are involved with, and they have offered assistance with regard to this matter, if needed.

Please consider this letter as an official notice from the ISNF, advising you that you are no longer welcomed to attend any Services or Activities at the Islamic Center (745 Heim Rd, Getzville, NY).

Sincerely,

President
(Mr. Rasul Khan) 5/26/17
Islamic Society of Niagara Frontier

CC: AMHERST POLICE CHIEF

Masjid An-Noor: 745 Heim Rd, Getzville, NY-14068,   Masjid At-Taqwa: 40 Parker St, Buffalo, NY 14214

Regarding this letter my last name was spelled wrong as was my address. More importantly though I was banned by Mr. Qadri on May 6th, 2017 for what I did at fajr dawn prayer that day, it was not for coming back to the masjid on 5/7/2017 as the letter says. And I came back at 1:30pm did Sunnah prayers and peacefully left when the Sunday School security guards asked me to leave, before Dhuhr which they do at a delayed time of 2:00pm on Sundays because of Sunday School. Most importantly the letter says, "*it has been an on-going issue with you <u>for the past several years</u>*" whereas it simply was not. The issue with Qadri saying ahl-kitab were not disbelievers and shirk was not kufr started February 2nd, 2017 and then I left for 2 months or more and the only real issue was that on May 6th, 2017 I had read Quran aloud while Mr. Qadri was leading fajr and wished death upon him. It was a one-time incident and I was medically insane at the time thinking Qadri was a magician and I publicly said he was a magician before he led the prayer, thus clearly I was insane at that time or not in a sound mindstate or at the least deserved a trial or Shariah investigation into my reasoning/intentions/mindstate. I never got an opportunity to explain myself nor defend myself. So that this banning letter says it was an ongoing issue for several years shows personal motive behind the ban which Rasul Khan probably had since December 23rd 2015 when the "Happy Holidays" sign was covered up by me, which I saw Rasul Khan personally take down my taped papers from the billboard "Happy Holidays" sign. The ignorance regarding the details of the issue and incident also indicates Rasul Khan was blindly banning me because "Imam" Qadri did and told him to. Lastly that Rasul Khan involved the Amherst police sending them a copy of such a letter seems unislamic to me and out of proportion. Ironically they sent that letter to the same exact police station I prayed in front of years earlier where I told the police the reason I was praying outside their station was because the local ISNF masjid doesn't pray on time or practice Islam correctly. Rasul Khan never once asked for my side of the story, or tried to solve the issue by any other means. In fact, I don't think we ever had a single talk about any issues because Rasul Khan, despite being ISNF president, would rarely go to the masjid and I only remember talking to him once in 2015 or 2016. Our only incident of ever speaking to each other was me asking him one question related to where all the Christian Unitarians went when they all left quickly after Jumuah prayer despite supposedly being there to observe for a dawah experience according to the announcements. (Yet they left immediately after before any Muslims could talk to them so I merely asked where they all went because I was trying to do dawah.) So aside from that one time, Rasul Khan never talked to me a single time regarding any issues, yet banned me from the mosque citing an ongoing issue for several years. Banning me was his first resort to solve the issue that was going on for 3 months, not several years as his ban letter to police claimed. Whereas literally the issue itself of me reading Quran while they were praying was a one-time mistake not an "on-going issue for the past several years".

I continued to email and text Qadri since the text message ban on May 6th, 2017 and his last replies were on May 26th, 2017 which was Ramadan 1st; the same day Rasul Khan penned the banned from masjid letter. In English Mr. Qadri ignorantly and slanderously said I was "Al-Qaeda/ISIS", despite both those Khariji groups fighting each other thus making dual membership impossible and him having more in common with them than me due to his takfir of Muslim rulers which I do not do. Then Qadri's final message was in Arabic, he sent the last verse of surah kafiroon which in English roughly translates to *"For you is your religion, and for me is my religion."* Whereas ironically during our private discussion about his speech during the Abrahamic faith interfaith debacle, I told Qadri he should've recited the whole chapter of Surah Kafiroon to his audience explaining it's tolerance instead of Surah Fatihah which he recited without even explaining the tafsir of the last two verses, which he correctly confirmed knowing they were about Allah being angry with Jews and Christians being deviantly astray. For full context Surah Kafiroon is as follows.

قُلْ يَٰٓأَيُّهَا ٱلْكَٰفِرُونَ (١) لَآ أَعْبُدُ مَا تَعْبُدُونَ (٢) وَلَآ أَنتُمْ عَٰبِدُونَ مَآ أَعْبُدُ (٣) وَلَآ أَنَا۠ عَابِدٌ مَّا عَبَدتُّمْ (٤) وَلَآ أَنتُمْ عَٰبِدُونَ مَآ أَعْبُدُ (٥) لَكُمْ دِينُكُمْ وَلِىَ دِينِ (٦)

Say, "O disbelievers, (1) I do not worship what you worship. (2) Nor are you worshippers of what I worship. (3) Nor will I be a worshipper of what you worship. (4) Nor will you be worshippers of what I worship. (5) For you is your religion, and for me is my religion." (6)

After the official ban from ISNF, at the Lackawanna masjid Anwar had a different attitude towards me altogether. He told me I should just drop the issues with Qadri and ISNF letting them be in peace. He also told me that I should publicly apologize to Qadri and ISNF, and if I do so then perhaps the ban would be lifted so that "if I was sincere I'd apologize publicly". I said I would if I'm proven wrong Islamically, and he got excited, but his hopes faded when I stressed it has to be islamically proven and anything wrong I did islamically I'll apologize for publicly but I won't apologize for doing what is proven to be Islamically obligatory or correct. I asked Anwar and my friend Abdul Haq together if they'd side with me if I had scholarly support and Anwar said no because none would ever support me because it's not Islam that I'm preaching, despite previously agreeing with me that if what I had said was true then Qadri was a heretical disbeliever in Islam. Then I realized my claim of Qadri being a magician was unproveable and hindering my genuine case. So I dropped the charges of magic saying how it is an unproveable charge but that I have conclusive proof of Qadri's heretical kufr and he can merely be asked about his beliefs to confirm or refute my claims. Truly the matter is almost as simple as that. For if Qadri is not lying about his beliefs, as Munafiqs are capable of doing, then you can just ask him what his beliefs about shirk, Mushriks and Jews and Christians are. If he answers incorrectly then correct him and see if he changes. If Qadri persists in error and refuses to learn then he is a non-Muslim and if he repents/changes then we have to accept what he says at face value and treat him accordingly but be cautious to make sure he acts in accordance with his newly stated Islamic beliefs. The only real problem would be if Qadri lied and said he always believed the same as me, that Jews and Christians were kuffar, shirk was kufr and Mushriks were kafirs and that he never said otherwise to me as I claim to have heard with my own two ears. Then there would be a problem because his entire factually proven and experienced behavior for four months from February 2017 to June 2017 and even prior to that would be unexplainable since his deeds would contradict this theoretical claim. In response to me insisting my claims of Qadri's heresy were true, my friend Abdul Haq informed me that he had just recently spoken to Qadri's own father in the Lackawanna Masjid and that Qadri's father is a staunch Muslim who believes the same as me that Jews and Christians are disbelievers, that shirk is kufr and mushriks are kafirs. So I was overjoyed that my enemy's own father is on my correct creed. I figured if I could just find Qadri's father then I could tell him of his son's crimes against Islam, Muslims and me personally and surely he could set things right with his son. Yet sadly I was never able to meet Qadri's father to this day, despite him allegedly having the same creed as the guy his son boycotted and banned from the masjid due to alleged extremism. But I have hope that someday his father may fix him or his descendants will, because the Quran itself as well as the Sunnah teach what I preached. Similar to how Muhammad when asked by angels to order them to destroy Taif responding by saying perhaps their descendants will become Muslims, I have similar hope that Qadri's descendants will become Muslims properly because the very sources of the Quran and Sunnah teach what is correct despite Qadri's distortion. Even if Qadri corrupts his kids, there is high hopes for future generations because families of heretics and innovators expose their descendants to more of the Islamic truth than non-Muslim families do. So since there is so much exposure to the creed of Salafiyyah, then by all trying to follow Islam then the future belongs to the truth no matter the efforts of the enemies of it today. Munafiqs eventually end up increasing the numbers of Muslims because they breed with us and Allah removes the nifaq from the descendants of hypocrites as Allah wills. In fact, the Salaf used to say that if it weren't for Munafiqs then the Muslim armies wouldn't have enough soldiers to wage war and the city streets would be empty.

Conclusively together Anwar and Abdul Haq said ISNF appoints their own Imam and ISNF likes Qadri so it doesn't matter what I say/do and I'm not qualified to say he should be fired or is kafir or insincere etc. Privately as a friend Abdul Haq told me that the FBI had visited the Lackawanna Masjid and been around asking questions about me. So this is probably what caused Anwar, as a masjid administrator, to be more skeptical of my claims and distanced trying to end the struggle. Especially since a short while prior to me coming there the Lackawanna masjid actually had reported a community member who was a genuine ISIS heretic that was plotting violent terrorist attacks. Shamefully despite having no role in the reporting process or any connection with the Lackawanna masjid the previously mentioned character Khalid Qazi, founder of ISNF and leader of MPAC-WNY, made an appearance after the arrest of the ISIS guy in Lackawanna with the local TV station in front of Masjid Huda to twist the story into an interfaith propaganda point. Qazi also said other suck-up anti-terror catchphrases in his broadcast sadly mixed with heretical unislamic doctrines too. Such performances actually fuel radicalization amongst true sincere Muslims with little knowledge who are smart enough to know the interfaith agenda is stinky. Basically people like that just show up for the cameras to speak with foolishness trying to portray a version of Muslims they think will help us achieve better treatment. Despite Mr. Qazi saying on TV that the arrested suspect didn't even attend the mosque, that ISIS guy actually did go to the mosque daily, and Khalid Qazi is the one who rarely goes to the mosques that he himself built. When the ISIS guy refused to repent from dangerous Khariji ideologies and was attempting to divert others in the community from genuine Islam the community reported him as a last resort to stop crime and he was caught buying guns and plotting attacks on civilians. This same Khalid Qazi guy was brought up in my discussion with Anwar about ISNF and Qadri. To my surprise despite Anwar disagreeing Qadri was heretical as I claimed, Anwar told me himself that Khalid Qazi was going against Islam promoting homosexuality and other things. He even showed me a video of Qazi's statements on that topic, saying that the Lackawanna masjid is even going to cut ties with Qazi if he doesn't stop and repent. So the funny thing is the "Muslim guy" on TV in front of Lackawanna masjid saying stuff on behalf of Muslims, is actually condemned by that very masjid and community for being an unislamic heretical extremist himself; but they don't put that report on the TV stations. Anyways since Qadri and ISNF members were accusing me of being part of Al-Qaeda and ISIS, which is contradictory because both those Khariji groups fight each other, so it's either one or the other not both, it is understandable that at all costs the admin of the masjid wanted to avoid another news report of a case of terrorism. Sadly though that "at all costs avoidance" led to a lack of sincere advice and pursuit of truth and justice at my expense. Naturally this news from my friend that the FBI was building a case on me after I was publicly accused by ISNF members of being linked to terrorist ideologies increased my paranoia further. Since insane episodes were coming and going more frequently as my nutrition levels worsened and my sleep decreased, especially since it was Ramadan, then I eventually began thinking everyone who didn't believe my claims was somehow in on a magical conspiracy. The psychosis triggered by the panic attack in May compounded this magical plot theory further to the point where if someone even looked at me in a way that was other that friendly, or acted too friendly by offering me food or some small kindness, I thought it was part of a magician conspiracy they were a member of in order to stop me from exposing the truth about Qadri.

Despite the masjid ban there was hope of a possible face to face showdown with Qadri outside of his own home turf. This was because Qadri was scheduled to give a lecture at the Lackawanna Masjid on June 11th, 2017. I was upset he was being given a platform there after my truthful charges were levied against him but figured I could confront him publicly at that time exposing his heretical deviance to all, that is if he even had the guts to show up. I didn't quite know what I would do though because knowing what I know about his deviance and hypocrisy, it's spiritually dangerous to listen to his lectures while if I interrupted and caused a scene then it would surely backfire. Also if I sit quietly sinfully listening waiting to "ask a question" at the end he would ignore me or slander me as an extremist. Plus I couldn't pray behind him knowing what I know, so if I wait to pray after he likely led the prayer he may leave before I finish. Also if I interrupt and stop him from leading the prayer, since his prayers are invalid due to heresy, then it would cause a big disturbance forcing everyone to immediately pick a side in order to determine if they would pray behind him or not. Whereas Anwar had already warned me to behave so as not to get banned from another masjid too. So I was formulating various plans in my mind as to what exactly I would do when/if Qadri came to the Lackawanna masjid I sought refuge in after the ban. Being a transparent person, I also emailed Qadri some of my more merciful pro-reconciliation dream plans, though they were filled with psychotic magical conspiracy wherein I tried to entice him with promises of forgiveness if he snitches on who other magicians in the community were so we could join forces upon his repentance of heretical kufr to combat all the magicians of the world, since a crime as Qadri committed required a huge repentance to offset his sins.

As all this was going on, my appointment for my legal name change with the County Court was scheduled for June 8th, merely three days prior to my upcoming showdown with Qadri. So I had a whole lot going on all at once with very little to eat except imported pasta and dates and water for the last two months, and the fasting month of Ramadan had recently started up. As such I would frequent the mosques I wasn't banned from and read Quran. The new guest imam in Lackwanna was informed by my friend Abdul Haq about my claims of magic against Qadri, but we never spoke directly about it. Abdul Haq said the guest imam could perform Ruqya, Islamic exorcism, on me if I wanted. However since I was capable of reading Arabic Quran myself, as Qadri taught me, I felt strong enough to exorcise myself from the magic. The only problem was that I was reading Quran loudly emotionally while doing Ruqya on myself in the mosque. So the guest imam came over politely asking me to lower my voice a bit and I complied. Eventually though as insanity increased I would physically gyrate when the guest imam led the prayers reading the Quran in Arabic. Such was just one symptom of magic I identified. Another time after I texted Qadri the challenge Noah gave to his people in the Quran, my arms went limp while in the mosque soon after sending that text. I automatically thought Qadri must've done magic upon receiving my text because both my arms were never totally paralyzed like that before nor since, but the cure was quick to come as I recited the Quran verses relevant to cure such a magic attack. Other symptoms were present indicating magic as well, with my friend Abdul Haq himself being convinced magic was done to me but just not by Qadri. While although Qadri was my top suspect, I admit it is possible someone else could have done magic as well on his behalf, even without permission or orders from Qadri, because many in the Indo-Pak community sadly go to sorcerers who disguise themselves as holy men offering to do magic or curses or other things via jinn facilitation but they disguise the reality for their ignorant customers. Some even claim to do exorcisms when in reality doing magic to their patients, so they get a lifelong customer constantly in need of "blessings". I then began "getting signs" to follow and perceived "inspirations" which I thought were from Angels or Allah. This would cause me to get lost while driving following the signs and I eventually decided to only speak Arabic again, similar to how prophet Zechariah went silent when he got signs.

My new major insane idea was that Allah was going to simultaneously send a flood and rain stones from the sky upon America and only true Muslims who had legal excuses preventing them from migrating to Muslim lands would potentially survive. I guessed this would occur on June 11th, 2017 the same day Qadri, the presumed magician who was proven heretic, was giving his speech in Lackawanna masjid after I had informed them of Qadri's heresy. So without speaking English I tried to warn people in the mosque as best I could by just reciting Quran and I played my Quran mp3 player loudly. The guest imam came over and asked me politely to turn the volume down as it was disturbing others in the masjid. I said no. Now if you recall this is exactly the alleged reason I got banned from ISNF mosque, for reading Quran too loud and disturbing others. The only difference was I did it during dawn prayer and this time it was in-between prayers while people were reading Quran individually. Yet this guest imam, who ended up becoming the regular imam in 2019 or 2020, just left me alone. He didn't even ask me twice or give me a warning or nothing. It wasn't an issue. I was disturbing people by reading and playing Quran audio loudly despite hadith prohibiting that, yet the manners of the people there were exemplary. After feeling I satisfactorily did my best in Arabic to warn the community of the impending apocalyptic storm, I left the Lackawanna masjid leaving my mp3 player in the mosque playing at maximum volume and there was no issues. Though I was even crazier at this stage and accused several in the community at Lackawanna of being magicians with even flimsier evidence than I did with the heretic Qadri, they didn't ban me nor show harshness at all. Afterall I'm just reading the Quran, even if it was too loud, how can you punish someone for reading Quran? Especially without peacefully discussing any solutions with them? One could only rightly do so if one had proof to do so from the Islamic Shariah law. This is the difference between sincere Muslims upon Salafiyyah and insincere ignorant innovators of other sects who exploit circumstances of all kinds to promote devilish agendas *"for Islam and Muslims"*.

Ever since my grandfather Joseph died, four months earlier, days after my creedal dispute with Qadri started my mother had been the primary caregiver of my 95+ year old grandmother who lived next door to where I lived. Yet since my grandmother couldn't be left alone then essentially my mom was with her 24 hours a day except for breaks when other relatives would take a shift for a few hours. I would help out occasionally as well. When I got officially banned from the ISNF mosque my mom told me a detective came to grandmother's house thinking it was where I lived, trying to forbid me from going to the mosque and get more information for his case. I do not know whether this "detective" was an ISNF contractor they hired or whether it was an FBI agent. However my mom said that as this detective interviewed both her and my grandmother asking them about me, after they explained my historical change from Catholicism to Islam and my beliefs and practices as they knew them and how I'm not a dangerous terrorist as ISNF claimed, this non-Muslim detective investigating me reportedly said, *"After talking to you, I don't even have to talk to him anymore."* This saddened me because I wanted to talk to this detective so the truth could be told and perhaps I could teach him about Islam so he'd become Muslim lest he go to hell after death. Anyways soon after my grandfather died the ashes of his cremated body were placed within my grandmother's house. Firstly cremation is against the Christian religion and was traditionally for thousands of years a shameful punishment for dead Christians who illegally sinfully consumed usury, which banks call "interest" today. Biblically Jesus himself violently whipped Jewish Rabbis in the temple in Jerusalem for doing usurious transactions. Thus for thousands of years Christians would burn the bodies of usurers as a special punishment for them, until the Templar Knights legalized usury and interest banking during the Crusades. Regardless from a Muslim perspective such burning of the body actually hurts the dead person extra and is sinful mutilation which is felt by the individual person. More importantly from my perspective since Muhammad said not to make your houses into graveyards, which is traditionally interpretated as not making them as places void of prayers as graveyards are forbidden to pray salat in, then I had tried to avoid entering my grandmother's house as much as possible because they had a dead body in it. It was essentially my grandfather's graveyard and given the evil condition his soul departed in it was extra taboo to me to be in the vicinity of the corpse of such an enemy of Allah who undoubtedly was being punished in his grave screaming at a frequency humans cannot hear. What was worse than that was that my grandmother would have the TV on almost as long as she was awake. Whereas since music and looking at women uncovered is sinful in Islam then there is no place for most American TV programs in the life of a practicing Muslim. Personally, I moved my parent's TV into the garage in 2011 and hadn't watched any TV from 2011 to 2017. So being exposed to television at my relative's house after six years without it was very stressful as they were ignorant of the sin of music, non-niqabi women or fiction. Every second around TV I felt like I was being exposed to poisonous filth and wanted to flee the scene. TV isn't automatically sinful, but it is generally a dangerous waste of time even if not sinful and since most nearly every program involves music, non-niqabi women or other evils like fiction or gossip generally TV is considered sinful by practicing Muslims. As far as I know there are no Islamic programs on TV in America at least, so Muslims have no business paying for a TV or watching it if they were serious about practicing their religion correctly. Anyone who believes they have limited time to live and will be judged by God for everything they did will not waste time on TV. As I was gaining more confidence from the psychosis and upcoming identity/name change, I finally told my mom under no more circumstances will I, as Abdullah, enter grandmother's house as long as grandfather's remnants are there and they are watching TV. I made it clear if you want me then turn off the TV. Which is more important TV shows or human life? Since she often needed assistance and knew I was under immense psychological pressure and persecution finally my mom gave in and said she would remove my grandfather from the house and turn off the TV whenever I visited. This day was June 6th, 2017 and by this time I was only getting about two hours of sleep a day as compared to my normal six hours because it was Ramadan and I'd go to the extra voluntary Ramadan Tarawih prayer at night then go home and only have about two hours before I had to wakeup to go back to the mosque to be able to attend the dawn prayer because Lackawanna was so far from where I lived. Yet I was supercharged with energy, despite fasting, due to anxiety and persecution and suspicions filling me with adrenaline. I was taking precautions against magic, including eating seven ajwa dates daily before the dawn prayer which are proven to protect one from magic due to prophetic hadith. However on this day, June 6th, I was only able to eat six ajwa dates because the time to start fasting came about before I could finish eating my seventh. So technically I was more vulnerable to magic on that day out of all the rest, it was also the

4 month anniversary of my grandfather's death. Somehow my insanity peaked on this day and I would go outside my house naked for brief moments in the backyard trying to prove myself to be following imagined tests from God or instructions from angels. I also had other sinful psychotic experiences that I won't mention but clearly in hindsight I was crazy that day. I knew it too because craziness passes momentarily as one goes back and forth between sanity and insanity, however in my sane moments I was convinced the crazy sinful moments were due to magic or jinn attacking me and not medically related to my brain being damaged from the panic attack, extreme stress and nutritional imbalance. Anyways I became certain my mom and grandmother were possessed by jinn so I performed an Islamic exorcism peacefully by reciting Quran, to which they'd laugh not understanding Arabic, thus making me think it was devils laughing prodding me on. That day I noticed my grandfather's ashes were still in the house, just hidden in a different

place, so I got upset at the trickery and said I will remove them since my mom said she'd take them out. At that my mom got violent physically assaulting me as I tried to take my dead grandfather's ashes outside the house onto the porch. Since such violence was a surprise, I deduced the jinn I thought was inside my mom was violent all of a sudden due to the box alleged to be my grandfather not really being my grandfather's ashes but being magic related paraphernalia inside. This is common in magician practice where they will give somebody something and tell them to wear it on their body or put it in their house and never open it or the power will be lost, when in reality it is known the person would destroy the magic and discard it if they opened it to see the satanic inscriptions on it. Thus under the presumption this box was a taweez, since nobody ever opened it before to see what was actually inside I decided to take it home and open it. During the violent struggle to which I defended myself as peacefully as possible, my Mom, who I thought was possessed, gave statements that her son was in the box. So fueling my suspicion further and being stressfully pushed to the brink of insanity again I wrongly concluded my grandfather must've done a magic spell on his death bed after we left trying to stay alive and as a result somehow the antichrist was in the box. This is because Christians wrongly think the antichrist is the devil's son, and since my mom mentioned I can't kill her, though I wasn't trying via my Quran recitation nor via defending myself from her punches and kicks, I wrongly deduced Satan/Iblis/Lucifer was possessing my mom confessing that the antichrist is in the box. This theory contradicts sound Islamic creed and prophetic hadith about the Antichrist so without a doubt I was wrong and crazy to think this but I had mistakenly unwittingly mixed my previous Christian dogma about the antichrist with insanity which was a terrible concoction. So as my mom realized she could not overpower me she went to call the cops as I went to the house I lived at next door. I opened the box finding ashes and considered flushing them down the toilet before the cops came. Instead I ended up pouring blessed ZamZam water from Mecca into the bag of ashes and mixing them with Ajwa dates while reciting Quran figuring if anything magic was in there then that would eliminate or neutralize the magic. Which today my twisted humor almost finds it funny because my grandfather would often frequently threaten me and other relatives that he would *"piss on our graves"* after outliving us, when his ashes were the ones that nearly went down the toilet and got disinterred. Then the cops arrived and I explained my mom was possessed and I was merely doing Islamic exorcism. They asked what was in the bag and I said water. Comically both of these cops used to listen to my Christian rap music which I made before I was Muslim and they knew who I was, and I went to school with one of the officer's sisters. Yet despite my version of events, after finally confessing the sediment in the bag was what my mom claimed were ashes of grandfather which I claimed was likely magical stuff the police decided a hospital van should be called. So I grabbed a book of supplications to read during the journey, as the police said I had to go to the hospital for five minutes just as part of protocol before they left me alone. I naively believed this was to be a five-minute hospital visit, or else I would've brought a bigger book. In the van I had to pray the afternoon prayer as best I could while traveling. At the hospital, after praying the Sunset prayer I had some aggressive interactions doing ruqya with other patients some of whom were Islamophobic, and after I tried to turn off the TV I was quickly given an injection and locked in a room. I then realized this would be longer than a five-minute visit as the police had promised me.

I was hospitalized on June 6th 2017 for 6 days and missed my legal name change Court appointment on the 8th and my potential showdown with Qadri on the 11th. I felt extremely fatigued due to the meds they made me take and just sat in my room most of the time staying away from other patients, being smart enough to know if I talked much with others I might not get out. I was diagnosed with "Paranoia and Psychosis" and given a very ancient medicine to take with a 30 day supply, no refills and no follow-up appointment with any doctor, but a recommendation to see a therapist. The therapist I was assigned to was female so since Muslim men cannot be alone with women they aren't married or related to, then my Mom would come with me for appointments.

After getting out of the hospital, I could hardly move due to the strong drug they gave me. When filling out medical paperwork I had to have my Mom fill it out because I could not move the pencil or even sit in the waiting room chairs properly. I was now sleeping about 20 hours a day with severe pain from the fatigue, which made it hard to pray my five daily prayers though I did so lest I become a disbeliever. As Muhammad explained, as did Umar on his deathbed, that the difference between being upon Islam or Polytheism is the performance of the 5 daily prayers. Thereby excommunicating via takfir all who don't pray their 5 daily prayers without a legitimate excuse such as menses or postnatal bleeding for females. While in the hospital, I received a letter from my paternal Aunt Sue, who was a Baptist Christian. She responded to my annual Ramadan letter to family wherein I said I was legally changing my name and training to be an Islamic exorcist. In her letter Sue said to never ever communicate with her by any means ever again and that she loves me but to never ever communicate with her again due to my Islamic progression to the point of changing my name. As rude and Islamophobic as Sue was in her final letter to me breaking our family ties, she was technically more "loving" than Qadri or ISNF was to me when they broke our ties. At this time, I sought Muslims out in the local community to perform an Islamic exorcism on me because I was convinced that magic was the cause for the insanity and the pain/fatigue. Abdul Haq, convinced it was magic as well rather than medical, sought help for me in that regard too. So, I was eventually put into contact with an imam named Ismail who was in Buffalo. Prior to going to visit Ismail, I asked the seemingly knowledgeable salafi brothers at the salafi masjid in Buffalo to do ruqya on me but they felt inexperienced and correctly suggested it was better for me to do it myself thereby strengthening my relationship with Allah being safe from mistakenly relying on others. Yet still I figured Ismail might be able to help since he was positively recommended. I asked the Salafis in Buffalo if Ismail was Salafi because if he was deviant then it would just cause more problems and be less likely to result in a cure. They said they didn't know. However since Ismail was on vacation I had to wait; but I could not wait. I was in such a funk that I could barely read any book, I couldn't drive or move and even asked people if I should go to the police with my accusation of magic against Qadri to have him arrested or to tell him to stop it because I was that desperate. I would even desperately text Qadri begging him to stop doing magic to me promising that if he stopped the magic then I would leave him alone forever. Yet Qadri would not reply. Eventually I decided I would go to Mr. Agwa at the Niagara Wheatfield masjid. Since he was fired by ISNF when he was the imam at masjid noor opposing their deviance I felt he was a good candidate for assistance. The elderly Mr. Agwa graduated from Al-Azhar University in Egypt and I went with my Dad for Mr. Agwa to do an exorcism on me. I explained what happened about me making takfir of Qadri and ISNF banning me and me going insane with suspicions of magic being done to me. Overall the exorcism took about an hour and afterwards Mr. Agwa confidently said that indeed magic was done to me. It seemed to Mr. Agwa the magic may have been done by Qadri because it was well known that the Darul-Uloom organization from which Qadri got his "Islamic credentials" from used to teach people magic as part of their curriculum. I didn't know this about the Deobandi Hanafi group Darul-Uloom but independent research verifies that magic spells are taught by their senior leaders in their books but they don't call them magic spells. Instead the Darul-Uloom scholar's books, most of which are in the Urdu language, will say do X if you want to curse your enemy or cause a certain type of illness, and therein their books describe magical rituals but they are mislabeled as Islamic saintly discoveries, or wazifas, which at best are fabricated innovated superstitious nonsense if not magic or polytheism. Darul-Uloom is well-known as a Deobandi organization whose founders like Ashraf Ali Thanwi would actually teach magic spells in some of their books. Most original Darul-Uloom material is in Urdu so it is inaccessible to many in the Arab Muslim world and the English world, although I have seen myself such superstitious spells written in the English translations of the founder of Darul-Uloom's books and those who are trustworthy and know the Urdu language say what exists in the Urdu books is even worse than what has been translated. To be clear not all of Darul-Uloom or Deobandis are heretical to the point of apostasy or magically inclined. In fact, the previous headteacher of Darul-Uloom Muhammad Anwar Shah Kashmiri who died in 1933 CE, even wrote a book called Ifkar al-Mulhidin detailing the definitions of Islamic Faith and Kufr/Disbelief. So even the traditional Darul-Uloom teachers taught, despite whatever other flaws they might've had, that Christians and Jews were disbelievers and that anyone who doubted such was a disbeliever too regardless of whether they claimed Islam or were Ahl-Qibla. So the very leaders and founders of the Deobandi school of thought who Mr. Qadri claims to blindly follow are in agreement Qadri has Zandaqah Heretical beliefs. So where did Qadri get these from? Nobody knows, Satan is the originator, yet Qadri falsely thinks and claims everyone believes his heresy and I'm the minority due to Salafiyyah when in reality no Muslims of any denomination are with him in his mistaken interfaith belief. Qadri's heretical error is so novel and new that there isn't even a scholastically agreed upon name for those who adopt his heresy because it is unheard of and has so few known adherents. Qadri was so wildly wrong that there isn't even a label for his blasphemy because it is so crazy. And that's why Qadri refused to discuss it with me at all costs because he feared embarrassment and exposure. Therefore having symptoms of magic when I tried to get Qadri fired, I assumed magic had been done by him or on his behalf. Due to his unislamic creed, character and manners it makes sense such a person could resort to such evil methods or have friends who would do so even without his orders. Anyways Mr. Agwa as imam of Niagara Wheatfield mosque told me to stay far away from his former employer organization ISNF and that he personally has nothing to do with Qadri, who he suspected had indeed done magic to me based on the experience he had when doing Ruqya exorcism on me. My dad, Kevin, witnessed this exorcism and diagnosis of magic.

Next, I went to Ismail because though sane I still felt pain and fatigue that made life unbearable. Despite my tale, Ismail seemed to be friends with Qadri and refused to believe my accusations of magic or takfir due to his heretical beliefs. I didn't care though, I just wanted Ruqya to be fully cured. Instead Ismail told me he didn't want to do Ruqya on me and that he thought I was mistaken on what Ruqya is and that Jinn don't speak through patients as some Islamic exorcisms on the internet show. Whereas this in itself shows Ismail's ignorance as it is well proven that in some cases Jinn do speak from inside the afflicted and Scholars of the Muslim world like Ibn Taymiyya have affirmed this and even condemned those who deny it. So at that I knew Ismail was not Salafi, but I was desperate and insisted. Yet Ismail persistently refused to do Ruqya even as a precaution and instead said he thought it was my Qareen that was whispering to me all my assumptions. Now a Qareen is a devil who Satan assigns to every person to incite them to do evil sins. So I couldn't understand why if Ismail himself believed the Qareen was influencing me as he said he wouldn't do an exorcism. As we had been talking almost an hour, Ismail said he didn't have time and he suggested I stop taking the pill the doctor gave me to see if that fixes the symptoms. At that point I didn't even care about exposing Qadri because I couldn't endure life in that condition.

Since Ismail wouldn't do Ruqya, and Abdul Haq advised against going back to Mr. Agwa because Abdul Haq didn't believe Qadri could be a magician as Mr. Agwa testified was a likely possibility, then I tried finding someone online. I found few resources in the USA and none that I could get to in person. I found one guy offering remote Ruqya whereby he would do "Jinn catching" via a proxy host person. They explained this innovative method, which I later learned was sinfully unislamic bida, as being practiced by having a volunteer human allow a "Muslim" jinn to go into them whereby the Raki would then talk to the Jinn and get them to travel to me and bring back the jinn inside me to that volunteer's body where the Raki would then perform the exorcism on the jinn that was allegedly in or harming me. Even if legitimate this method is against the teachings of Islam and contradicts the Sunnah of seeking aid from Allah alone, involves trusting untrustworthy invisible jinn, oppressing others and is risky and opposes the prophetic method of exorcism. In actuality Ruqya is supposed to only be done in person and legislatively there is no payment for such services unless and until the person is cured. If someone ever asks for payment before curing you via exorcism it is likely a scam, and even if they do cure you with Allah's help then still payment is not Islamically mandatory. However I was desperate and the person disguised all the rest of their website with genuine Islamic information and data trying to make their case. We chatted on Skype wherein prior to paying, also a warning flag though not necessarily sinful, and prior to performing this "Jinn catching exorcism" the person asked my mother's name. Now this is not necessary at all and is a warning sign of a magician because some types of magic require knowing the mother's name to be done. I knew better but went through with the transaction anyways because of desperation and assurances that it wasn't a bida innovation as I began to suspect. After being informed the jinn catching was performed we had another chat on Skype to discuss what happened. This alleged Raki, who might've been a magician in disguise, told me that magic was indeed done to me by somebody but there is no way to ever prove it. Since magic is done primarily with invisible jinn agents or devils then the human courts have no way to get jurisdiction or even analyze evidence if any exists. That was disheartening to hear. Even though I had two apparently Muslim exorcists say magic was done, to learn that it is a nearly non-prosecutable crime, especially where I live in America, my hopes of justice faded to be postponed to the afterlife. This person also told me that regarding my symptoms I would have to see doctors for several years before getting better. This shocked me because I had never mentioned anything about any hospitalization or medicine or doctors to this guy. I had just said I think magic was done to me by a heretic, but this guy was saying I needed to see doctors for years despite being perfectly healthy prior to the insanity occurring which I didn't even tell this guy about. Therefore I scheduled a psychiatrist appointment to see what was going on through that end. I had already halved the dose of the pill when Ismail suggested stopping the medicine altogether, and it improved my condition mildly. At this point I stopped taking the pill altogether with my Parents' consent, days before the psychiatrist appointment to see if anything would improve without the pill being taken.

The psychiatrist asked me why I was visiting him, so I just started saying what happened from 2011-2017 and why I converted to Islam from Christianity and why Christianity is false and how I got into a dispute with a heretic who did magic to me. This doctor said I was not yet cured from psychosis due to thinking magic was done to me. This doctor then prescribed a different anti-psychotic medication that was supposedly much newer and less strong. However years later I learned that #1 immediately stopping any anti-psychotic medicine as I had done cold turkey was dangerous and could cause something called "rebound psychosis" that is due entirely as a result of pill withdrawal but is often misdiagnosed as being regular psychosis or mental illness. While #2 immediately switching to a new anti-psychotic medicine just days after being on a different one which was stopped cold turkey can also cause psychosis/insanity because of the chemical cocktail of imbalance in the brain chemistry being changed. However I felt nearly normal again, in fact I felt supercharged after stopping the old pill and not knowing the risks involved figured I'd give the new pill a try as the doctor assured me it's much better than the ancient medicine I was originally given.

During this time I had persuaded my Dad to start reading a translation of the Quran to better understand Islam and what was going on with my situation. As a result of this exposure to Islamic literature, one night without even having gotten to the fourth chapter of the Quran translation he was reading I asked him if he wanted to say the shahada and become Muslim. I could tell he was awestruck by the Quran's language, information and miraculous nature. To my surprise my father accepted and said the Shahada in Arabic testifying that *Ash-hadu an la ilaha illa Allah, Wa ash-hadu anna Muhammadan Rasulu-Allah* which in English means: *"I testify that there is no deity truthfully worthy of worship except Allah and I testify that Muhammad is the Messenger of Allah."* I was overjoyed and everything that I went through was now worth it for my dad to have accepted the truth. There was just one problem, he didn't know much about Islam as he had not even gotten to chapter 4 and the rapid changing of anti-psychotic medicines led me to become insane again. Whether that was because psychosis hadn't gone away or because of rebound psychosis or magic or whatever, I being overstimulated by my dad's shahada wasn't sure if it was truly him becoming Muslim or a jinn inside him. So I did Ruqya on his food and drink reciting Quran over it and proceeded to do a peaceful Ruqya exorcism on him just to be sure. During this he got scared due to me emotionally reading loudly in Arabic and ran into the bathroom and called the cops. When the cops came I then had a genuine bout of insanity due to the stress of once more having cops at my door while I was trying to pray Maghrib outside. I was then handcuffed for running away from two scary police officers toward one other police officer to embrace him in a hug and get protection. My dad explained to the cops I had just gone off a pill and started a new pill days before. So I was taken to the hospital that same night as my dad became a Muslim.

In July 2017 until August 2017 for 26 days I was hospitalized. During my intake, another patient was loudly cursing all the prophets by name, clearly possessed as I thought. I talked to this patient and he almost was ready to become Muslim but was having trouble concentrating due to the drugs the nurses gave him after he tried to escape and hurt his fist punching a nurse in the face, or so he said which I didn't see. Despite his trouble concentrating he said if anyone messes with me then he would beat them up to protect me. Anyways being insane at the time according to me having delusions that contradicted clear Quran and hadith, which I won't mention, I thought I must be talking to the jinn inside this guy and the nurses must be or have devils in them to be preventing this guy from becoming Muslim. Clearly the guy was shouting profanities at prophets before I spoke to him, so I knew I wasn't that good at preaching for such a guy to convert to Islam that fast. But a devil could since I had been reading Arabic Quran to this patient doing dawah to his jinn that I thought was in him. Thus I figured it was his jinn saying the nurses or devils of the nurses were preventing his shahada. So despite being allowed to pray in a private room for the sunset prayer, I figured it was a warzone. For the nighttime prayer I went to the place I felt most of the devils would be, the bathroom, and I gave the athan call to prayer to infuriate them and get ready to pray myself. The nurses opened the door and told me to come out of the bathroom and stop yelling nonsense. I continued the athan and then left the bathroom and began to pray not telling anyone what I was doing beforehand. Now since the nighttime prayer is audible out-loud and must be done in Arabic, to the patients and hospital staff who didn't know Arabic or Islam then I was totally loony. So the male nurses seeing me prostrate, likely thinking I'm banging my head on the floor or in danger, told me to stay down and were holding me down. I got back up continuing my obligatory prayer and after the nurses kept trying to make me stop I followed the advice of the hadith of Muhammad which says to fight someone if they repeatedly stop you from praying by going in front of you more than three times, because surely they are a devil if they persist. So I started punching and kicking the nurses surrounding me and called on my almost Muslim co-patient to defend me as he promised. As you might've guessed, that patient didn't lift a finger and I got defeated. They stuck a needle in my butt and took me to a room and tied me down with restraints since after getting a few good punches and kicks in I tried escaping the hospital. So as I was tied to a bed in painful restraints, I restarted my prayer and finished it because worshipping Allah is that important that you do it on-time no matter what because Allah deserves it. Legally I was hospitalized for insanity and Shariah doesn't require an insane person to pray until they are sane again. Yet even being totally crazy as I was, I knew you had to be stupid to stop praying. Literally for a man to miss doing his obligatory salat, he must be crazy, unconscious or else he has no legitimate excuse. I was legally medically crazy but I still did all my prayers even in restraints because you gotta be stupid crazy to not pray your prayers. So even a medically crazy person won't typically stop praying their prayers because they don't know or consider themselves crazy. What then does that tell you about a regular non-insane individual who neglects to pray one of their daily obligatory salat prayers? To me I went crazy yes, and many may criticize me for publishing such an experience in detail, but the person who claims to be Muslim and doesn't pray their prayers is beyond any level of crazy I ever experienced. So I have no shame explaining my craziness in detail, rather those who don't pray should be ashamed because they are even crazier except they have no medical excuse so crazy is not the correct word. The correct description for them is lazy stupid and evil in their negligent mistaken devilish delusion.

During my first weekend in the 2nd hospital Mr. Agwa, who did exorcism on me before and said Qadri did magic, visited me and did some more exorcism by reading Quran and giving advice. Later in the initial psychiatric ward I met a Nigerian Muslim who knew some of the Quran who said his family was killed in Nigeria. We bonded and got transferred together into another unit for people that were being admitted for long-term psychiatric care. I was examined with a brain scan and then sent to a private room to have my blood drawn. Previous blood tests done at the hospital showed my liver had deadly amounts of toxicity, likely from the ancient medicine I was initially prescribed or from magic. So I presumed this was magic and that I would die in this hospital and nobody was telling me. I explained to the female phlebotomist how I preferred a male phlebotomist so as not to be touched by her because Prophet Muhammad explained it's better for an iron rod to go through a man's head than to touch a woman unlawful for him to have sex with, thus prohibiting as sinful any physical contact between non-relatives of the opposite gender. The female asked her supervisor but there were no males available to take my blood. I appreciated her asking to fulfill my dying desire to not be touched by her and expressed hope she might be forgiven due to the circumstances if she eventually became Muslim. The phlebotomist then began to cry because she knew how serious the matter was for me and that I was in serious medical danger of dying despite being just 25 years old. I then reassured her that Muslims have no fear of death because we know exactly what happens step for step and are blessed with the true prophetic religion and expect eventual forgiveness from God. Actually on the contrary, I was happy I was dying because I expected it was going to be an abdominal related death, which is martyrdom for Muslims, combined with magic attacks from a proven heretical Munafiq Qadri, which would be martyrdom too. So, I'm in the best mood I've ever been in my life, only regretting I didn't get to publish any of my books and did less sins, so I told another nurse my email login/password so she could login to my account and get the most recent drafts of my books to somehow send to my family members so they could possibly read my stuff after my death. This other nurse said she might become Muslim after she retires the next year. The main fear I had was my books would not be utilized to benefit people despite all the work I put in and despite desiring goodness for my theoretical readers I would have to suffice with Allah guiding them without me getting any chain-reaction reward for such efforts. The hospital staff then transferred me to the most severe psychiatric ward in the hospital, and county, for the most dangerous cases of mental sickness; the notorious Floor 4 Zone 3.

As I entered and told my tale regarding the allegations of magic and the confusion that led to me fighting the nurses during the intake with the Psychiatrist, the accompanying nurse called me "buddy". So naturally I gave him a lesson on how as a Muslim with you being non-Muslim it is impossible for you to be my friend or "buddy" when you are an enemy of my Lord by disbelieving in Islam. I said if you want to be my buddy then become a Muslim and if not then don't use that label. If you want to be a nurse be a nurse but don't pretend to be my friend when you oppose my religion thinking it to be other than absolute truth. Such a "friend" cannot help me even if they tried because fundamentally you don't know what's good and bad, right or wrong, true or false; so accepting your help would harm me and thus I reject your friendship until you embrace Islam. Ironically despite my assertiveness this nurse, Joe, ended up being one of the most helpful and understanding out of all the rest. The other patients however were dangerously crazy. I shortly realized

I am not going to die and that I am being held in the hospital against my own freewill; literally as a prisoner. One other patient who came to 4 zone 3 the same day as me was named Sean, he would become my new nemesis. Sean seemed to have been in prison before and had a large Nazi Swastika tattoo over his heart. As I read the Quran from memory and tried to invite the hospital staff and other patients to become Muslims, Sean would do all kinds of crazy ritualistic invocations to unknown names that seemed like magic. I diagnosed him as being a Nazi magician or having a magician jinn inside of him. Thus I would do Ruqya exorcism peacefully on him and all the other patients, reading Arabic Quran verses. The unit therapist however didn't like me publicly diagnosing other patients as possessed by devils. In one conversation while publicly advising the unit therapist to become a Muslim herself and if she refuses then to at least testify that I presented Islam to her so on the Day of Judgement I don't get punished for not conveying the message of truth, she blatantly refused saying,

"*I'm not giving you that satisfaction.*" Meaning the "satisfaction" of her telling God about me trying to persuade her to become Muslim after she is raised from the dead. So I cried my eyes out in tears over her impending damnation and sorrow that disbelievers will be so painfully punished without mercy despite our sincere attempts at peaceful dialogue, and that I might be punished for my lack of persuading presentation of prophetic truth. She said if you can't accept that then you're going to be depressed forever. So I cried and cried leaving a puddle by her feet because I knew she was right on that point. I am going to perpetually depressed if there is even one single person punished in hellfire especially if I failed in conveying the Islamic truth in the best way I could. This has stuck with me ever since then and I'd rather be depressed for life over what made prophets depressed, to the point of near deadly stress, than be happy. And that realization made me happier because that means perhaps I'm closer to being on the right path if someone being non-Muslim makes me depressed. It's the people who are satisfied with illegitimate evil religions existing in the world preaching tolerance and equality among religions that are diseased in their heart and mind. The therapist said she has Muslim friends and they aren't like me at all and don't want her to convert to Islam. So, I explained they might not be practicing Muslims like she thinks, especially if they don't want you to become Muslim to be safe from hellfire, and Muslims can't be friends with disbelievers anyways so you might think you are friends with them but if they think you are a friend then they aren't Muslims. The therapist said legally you can't tell people to change their religion because of Separation between Church and State. So I said that's Church and State, not Mosque and State, it's good for the government to be separate from the Church because Christianity is a false religion, but Islam is different. And I further began to educate her saying, *"It's you who can't tell me to change my religion as a medical professional according to evil secular American law. I'm in here against my will and allegedly crazy. So I can say anything I want to say and if you don't like it then you can let me out of the hospital and I'll leave!"* Sean was eavesdropping on my lengthy public conversation and insulted me saying how Greg's crazy thinking there's only one god and only one true religion. After saying that Sean started invoking Hindu deities. The therapist laughed in agreement with Sean's supporting her and mockery of my belief in Islam being the only true faith, despite him then acting and barking like a dog at me. Then the therapist said she thinks in her professional opinion that I'm a Radical Extremist just like the mosque I got banned from says. So while in the hospital I called the mental health whistleblowing organization hotline for mental healthcare abuse and had a case opened up on her. During the case investigation while people came to interview me in her unit they didn't think she had abused me mentally in any illegal manner by labeling me as an extremist so the case didn't result in any convictions. But she sure did shut her mouth around me after she knew she was under investigation. Yet calling the authorities on the hospital staff didn't get me out of there either. During my imprisonment, I requested my parents bring my ISNF letter of banishment to the hospital so I could present my case to the hospital doctors explaining how and why magic was done to me that made me insane, and they also brought food and books. This ISNF letter was not interpreted the way I hoped by the hospital staff. The hospital thought since Rasul Khan falsely stated *"it has been an on-going issue for several years"* that I must have been crazy as they witnessed in the hospital for years without being detected since I lived alone at my parent's house next to my grandmother's house without anyone to observe me. This letter from ISNF later led to a misdiagnosis due to a misunderstanding of facts. Inside the hospital 4 zone 3, I felt I was religiously persecuted on the one side by a Nazi magician and the other by a prejudicial liberalist therapist misinformed about Islam by "moderate Muslims" likely from ISNF too. So while being imprisoned I figured since they think I'm crazy and I might lose my tiny book of

Arabic/English supplications my parents brought me, I might as well write my supplications from the dua book I had in Arabic on the walls of my room for easy reference. The patient in my room before me wrote prayers to devils on the walls of the bathroom which I washed off, so I figured I'd write in marker on the walls of my room supplication to Allah so I could read them easier and maybe a future patient could benefit. As you can guess the hospital staff didn't like seeing the Arabic written with marker on the wall, especially because they didn't know what it said. Instead they directed me to write on the chalkboards and white boards to express myself. So I did that too. However Sean took offense to my Arabic writings and would always scribble them out and draw Nazi Swastikas in various forms to cover up the spots I had written on. I explained to one of the female nurses how the Swastika is an ancient symbol in Indian magic before it became a Christian symbol of the cross before it was adopted by the Nazi Adolf Hitler. This female nurse and Joe the nurse seemed to nearly believe me when I was diagnosing some patients with being possessed and I told them to check out Islamic exorcisms on youtube to see what I was up against and I explained the difference between Muslim exorcisms and all others and how all work and why all can work despite Islam being the only true faith. This has been discussed in more detail in other books of mine but basically devils want people to disbelieve and by leaving through the exorcism of a false religion then it makes people believe the falsehood is true. In Islam jinn are sometimes encouraged during an exorcism to become Muslims just as humans are encouraged. Sometimes it happens, sometimes not, but the jinn in Islamic exorcisms are exposed and superstition is eradicated. The female nurse and Joe both said that they couldn't understand some of the things they had witnessed between me and others. I overheard some of the non-Muslim patients and nurses discussing me through the walls of my room once saying that they sincerely thought I was some type of saint or friend of God, despite me openly trying to convert the hospital to Islam. So even while I was crazy in the hospital my good manners with people I hated led them to have good impressions. But those people were also crazy so don't think I'm some saint or friend of God due to the speech of lunatics when Allah knows my sins.

While in the hospital I would write letters to some family members with the limited means I had. One reply I got came from a maternal Aunt Chris. She said she was praying for me to get better. Now as a Christian Mushrik who believes in a trinity deity and a son of God/demi-God form of Jesus, I did not want any prayers made to Jesus on my behalf. To illustrate how this felt imagine a Christian in the hospital being told by a Hindu relative they are praying to their elephant idol Ganesh daily for them to get better. It's outrageous! So, I wrote a letter reply back forbidding such polytheism in the gentlest way I could in the red marker I had explaining how I'd rather be dead than have her perform shirk/polytheism on my behalf which will not improve my condition in anyway but will only be a placebo for her conscience that will be punished by God if she doesn't repent and become a Muslim before she dies. My letter was apparently gossiped about and my mom later told me other relatives joined in with their prayers even though I didn't want any. It's funny how forbidden and ironic such a scenario was. I'm basically hospitalized almost solely for the reason that I believe Christians are disbelievers due to worshipping Jesus instead of Allah and declare that an alleged Muslim prayer leader of a mosque who thinks otherwise is a disbelieving heretic, who banned me from the mosque primarily for my beliefs and hatred of Christianity and Christians among other hates as well which caused the insanity that I'm in the hospital for. So essentially to accept Christian polytheistic prayers to an anthropomorphic Jesus is the last thing that I desired in that condition. They expected me to say thank you. That's even worse than someone saying "Happy Holidays"! Plus the very act of comforting others by saying "I'm praying for you", is a bida innovation only done by insincere and arrogant people. If you are praying, do it privately; you don't need to boast and brag. In reality people have more faith in the statement "I'm praying for you" healing the person making them feel better than the prayers that are allegedly uttered. Such prayer trees are bogus hoaxes if not polytheistic sins to false deities. If Muslims did them they are still forbidden because it is against the Sunnah to expose sincere actions of worship. The angels join in with the secret supplications made by Muslims on other Muslim's behalf they don't do that if the Muslim brags about supplicating for others. While the companion of Muhammad, the Sahabi Abdullah ibn Masood, said, "*A silent du'a(supplication) is seventy times better than a loud one!*" Which is a proof that refutes the innovative concept of congregational dua which is what triggered the conversation that caused the aqeedah dispute with Qadri in the first place. For those who truly care to use the power of prayers to Allah alone for the wellbeing of others they would be better off doing it secretly. Anyone who insists on publicly sharing they are praying supplications for others to benefit is bragging false piety thinking it's good manners due to false cultural practices and standards. If they pray to anyone other than the Creator Allah alone then they are guilty of Shirk/polytheism and sinful. And it is such an important matter that it was worthy of refuting despite being in the midst of an insane ward warzone. Such is the truth, it is not always sweet to those upon falsehood as it can cause bitterness when foolishness is exposed no matter how gently the preacher corrects someone.

In the psychiatric ward, Sean and I would constantly be reciting words against each other but he would get naked and spread filth on himself and act like a dog and do all kinds of "crazy" things which only seemed sensible to do if a jinn was whispering in his ear that he would do magic for Sean if he humiliated himself in such a fashion. For he was doing exactly what it is credibly reported some magicians do privately to gain magical abilities. Once Sean repeatedly made invisible knots of a hangman's noose then blew it at me repeatedly trying to simulate hanging me with invisible strings. I interpreted such as death magic spells. Yet despite being much more muscular than me and even getting into violent fights with other patients, Sean would become increasingly afraid of me the more we interacted. I knew magic was involved with him and would say this publicly in conversations to him while preaching Islam. The nurses didn't know what to do with us. Then one night Sean was praying devilish prayers for a black dog to reinforce and help him. The very next day an African-American patient entered our unit, his name was Kalon. Now Kalon and Sean immediately seemed to team up against me despite Sean having a Swastika tattooed over his heart implying racist attitudes, he preferred this black Kalon over everybody else despite all the other patients being Caucasian. In my interactions with Kalon he would intensely stare at me for long periods so much it hurt me and I believed it was evil eye. I was more polite with Kalon though and, as I did with Sean, I'd offer/share food I had done Ruqya on with them. This softened the heart of Kalon very much. Once while Kalon was doing evil eye on me and my parents through the window while we had a visit in another room, at the same time as Sean was shouting curses at me, Kalon asked a nurse if he could eat some of my food which was stored in the kitchen. To which the nice female nurse asked me if I wanted to share and I replied not today. Kalon got furious and as he saw me eating whole wheat pita bread pieces I did ruqya on he kept asking everyone whether I was eating leavened or unleavened bread almost as if his life depended on knowing the answer to that question. Kalon then shouted I was trying to kill him with a shotgun shot to the chest and that he ain't dying like that. As my parents were leaving Kalon approached them with evil eye staring and I told him to stop because it's forbidden to look at a woman one isn't related to. So Kalon apologized saying he didn't know, despite having been so aggressive towards me minutes before Kalon obeyed me upon command. Kalon in a later exchange would ridicule my Arabic recitations of the Quran. So at a later time, thinking he might be possessed I offered to do Islamic exorcism on Kalon. Initially he allowed me, then as I read Quran verses in Arabic Kalon got very scared running away invoking ancient pagan Egyptian deities to protect him. When the nurses asked what happened, I told them the truth and that everything was videotaped by hospital cameras if they don't believe I was just peacefully reciting Quran in Arabic as usual. To which Kalon shouted, *"He's ISIS! He's a terrorist! He's dangerous! Lock him up! Get him away from me!"* But the nurse Joe, the one I told would never be my "buddy" until he became Muslim, calmed Kalon down reassuring him he was safe and that Greg is very peaceful and is not part of ISIS. Then Kalon cried asking why he had been sent here. On the next day I spoke to Kalon privately alone as he was spinning in rapid circles in a rolling chair in a dark room with just the TV on. I turned on the light and told Kalon that I know you're doing magic to me and I advise you to stop it and offered him forgiveness and friendship if he becomes Muslim. Kalon cried and admitted he was doing magic and promised to stop trying to harm me. Kalon asked me how I knew when nobody else could tell and thought he was just crazy as he wanted them to think. So we had a long conversation and Kalon told me he became an official Freemason at a lodge and learned Hebrew in order to do magic. Kalon actually did know the Hebrew language fluently despite being African-American. Later in the future after we emailed each other and I checked out his website I saw his actual official Freemason membership certificate. Kalon was also an aspiring Hip-Hop musician who released an independent album the year before we met. Although Kalon didn't become Muslim in the hospital we discussed a lot about magic and he explained how the Hebrew text of the bible was how he would do his magic as well as Hebrew Kabbalistic rituals. I had previously read theories that certain parts of the corrupted Hebrew bible were used in magic spells and rituals and Kalon confirmed this was true. Many Jews or Christians may be surprised by this but Hebrew itself as a language did not exist until long after prophets Moses, David and Solomon. Those prophets and their scriptures were never in the Hebrew language originally. It was only when Jews corrupted the prophetic faith that they then translated into Hebrew and pretended it was always in Hebrew to cover up their corruption. Whereas the New Testament bible texts are in Greek, a language which Jesus never spoke. Scholastically speaking nothing in the bible at all is considered original divine revelation because it's not in the languages of the prophets they portray aside from all the anthropomorphism and slanders in those books Jews and Christians call holy. Kalon was very knowledgeable about word symbolism and secret meanings of words and the number of letters in a word and mathematical calculations. I explained my case against Qadri and how I suspected magic was done to me by him or others for his sake with or without his knowledge. Kalon explained how magicians tend to live longer, age slower and how he planned to only ever use magic again to fight magicians. I asked him how I should go about defeating my magician foes. Kalon explained from his experience magicians were like criminal street gangs who are at war with police, society and other criminal gangs all at once but they cleverly hide their reality to most people, are paranoid and get viciously dangerous when they feel threatened. They have no unity and are enemies to each other with nearly each magician having a different religion or deity/jinn they worship to get their powers although they often hide their real religion from the public. Kalon said I had very powerful stuff I was using already and he wanted me to teach him. Kalon told me that when he encountered me, even though he didn't know Arabic, he couldn't beat whatever I was reciting so he couldn't help me with anything. Kalon thought the Arabic I recited was the strongest magic he ever encountered. Previously when we battled Kalon said he would get mad at me and demand I speak

English or translate the Arabic ridiculing the Quran because he couldn't beat the Arabic of whatever it was to get any magical hits to stick. I explained I'm only reciting Quran(the word of Allah) and supplications to Allah in Arabic because literally I don't know any non-religious Arabic myself as a language to say anything other than Quran or purely monotheistic supplications. So I was only saying religious monotheistic stuff prophet Muhammad taught the world. Lastly I warned Kalon that magic is forbidden sinful disbelief that dooms its practitioner to eternal hellfire and advised him to become Muslim and abandon magic, to which he promised to research. After this Kalon considered me his friend and we would interact as almost friends would despite me maintaining my religious hatred of all non-Muslims due to their kufr. Kalon and I even teamed up against Sean with our recitations and a later Spanish speaking patient who I suspected of being a magician too. This Spanish speaking patient, Larry, would only speak English in the form of musical song lyrics, everything else was Spanish. When I first met Larry I was reciting Quran at the dining table and he sat down stared and angrily pointed his finger at me, so I did Ruqya called the Athan and asked if his finger indicates the shahada or Tawheed; then extended my finger to try to touch his pointer finger to which he recoiled in fear. Larry was even filthier than Sean and Sean never even did any naked stuff until Larry started doing naked stuff. So I upped my game and would write various Dhikrs in Arabic throughout the hospital and then throw out the writing utensils so nobody else could write anything magical or evil and so the hospital would take a financial hit and have to buy more markers/chalk. Eventually due to Larry we were not allowed to have garbage cans anywhere because he'd make the place a filthy mess with his rituals so any garbage had to be given to nurses immediately. Now I don't know much about Larry or if he was doing legitimate magic for sure, although Larry told nurses he was threatened by my writings on the walls. Kalon seemed to think

Larry was a magician too despite none of us understanding his main language. As I was soon to be transferred, I decided to wash off all my Arabic writings to prove to Larry that power is not in writings or reading but only in Allah and that I don't need writings for protection or power as magicians think they get with writing/doing spells.

Next, I was transferred to Floor 5 Zone 2 as the hospital staff thought I improved mentally. There were other patients in 4 zone 3 but none of them did magic. The demise of Sean came about when the nurses/doctors admittedly didn't know what was making him do all the crazy stuff they witnessed and medicine was having no effect. I said of course it has no effect because magic is involved since he was either possessed or doing magic. Sean agreed with me yet he was put into his own restraints in a separate locked room of the hospital with the staff fearing he would harm me. After being in restraints awhile and going back and forth outside the unit and back to have many tests done on his brain, Sean would scream out for me to stop doing magic to him. I explained speaking through the wall I didn't do any magic to him. Though I did unbeknownst to Sean previously curse him and Kalon might've done magic. (though I didn't tell Sean about my curses or Kalon's abilities) I took pity on Sean and his sincere cries for help and would pray conditional English supplications to Allah's various names within Sean's earshot for him to be healed from magic so he can repent from his crimes and become a good blessed Muslim who goes to paradise. Last time I saw Sean he was being sent away to have brain surgery because the doctors had no explanation for his bizarre behavior and medicine had no impact. My mom said she talked to Sean's dad in the waiting room often, not knowing we were rivals inside, and Sean's dad told my mom someone was suspected of giving him a drug hidden in a drink in order to take him out so they could take over his business. Yet that doesn't explain the stuff I personally seen and heard from Sean in totality to discount any magical involvement. Allah knows best the truth of it.

On Floor 5 zone 2 there were no magicians unless you count one guy who claimed to be able to see people's chakra auras. He claimed they were like lightsabers with everyone's energy bursts surrounding them fighting each other. He didn't like me and I didn't like him. We didn't interact much but he eventually got carted away after trying to assault another patient, wherein a nurse who was a former Marine had to body slam him on the ground in order to get him to stop being violent. The most memorable nurse in this zone was a former Marine African-American who fought in Afghanistan against Muslims. He understood some of the stuff I did and we privately talked about Islam while he monitored me trimming my mustache, as we weren't allowed to use scissors except with special observation since many people in that zone were suicide attempters. One co-patient even got electroshock therapy due to depression and a suicide attempt. The former fighter against Islam turned nurse admitted Islam made more sense than any other religion, so for him it was a matter of how only one faith can be true because he had been brainwashed by the Freemason Equality dogma prevalent in American politics. I explained the benefit for humanity in the existence of false religions in that it makes life more bearable and less evil even though the morality of such false faiths is lacking and incomplete in many regards. Basically if it was just Islam and nothing else the world would be a much worse place, but God allows false religions because they make disbelievers who will never accept Islam under any circumstances better people who are less harmful. Yet this mild moral character they have is not accepted by God because of the major flaws and errors such false faiths teach. Hence Satan utilizes this wise allowance by God to confuse fools further similar to how a student may be confused by a multiple-choice question on a test and think incorrectly that multiple answers must be acceptable just because they are allowed to be chosen as an answer. Yet everyone knows no matter how good of an answer an incorrect answer on a multiple-choice question is, the person choosing anything other than the one correct answer will not get any credit despite perhaps being less wrong than others who get the question wrong. This nurse would put up my Arabic calligraphy supplications to Allah on the bulletin board which I made in art class therapy and took down other people's artwork which previously had been hung after I explained they contained polytheistic invocations and claimed they "disturbed/triggered my psychosis". Two Muslims patients were in this zone, neither prayed with me but they were technically there for mental health so inshallah they were excused. One was named Samir who was from Iraq and couldn't read Arabic nor English because he left schooling at age 6 because his father got killed by the Shiite Iraninan military during war and he had to support his family. Samir believed some Shiite people in Arizona did magic to him years ago and enjoyed talking to me and listening to my Arabic recitation of Quran and duas which he understood. The other

Muslim was named Marshall and we would talk from time to time. Once a random elderly female patient came up to me and Marshall as we were talking and asked if I was Muslim. She said she was a witch and wanted to hear me read. So I recited Surah Fatihah and she groaned with pleasure saying it felt so good and she would go to my church if she got out. I explained we don't go to church and magic was sinful disbelief. She said she just likes to trick people with it for fun so I advised her to stop and warned Marshall to be careful and explained how sometimes it seems there are crazy people or magicians but it's just a jinn inside the person and not really that person themselves. I don't know whether this lady was a legit dark magician or just doing illusionary cultural pop magic but two different people in my time in the hospital openly confessed to me in all seriousness that they did magic for real.

The problem was the American secular psychiatric world doesn't believe in the existence of magic, jinn, nor devils, nor angels, and unofficially not even

God or prophethood. So every time I admitted being crazy insisting it was magically induced they thought I was actively crazy because to them only crazy people use the word magic. I was sane by then as the pills had kicked in but you couldn't even talk about magic being a potential cause without raising eyebrows and alarm. So gradually I learned if I just stop using the word "magic" then I'll be let free.

Every Wednesday on Floor 5 zone 2 they would have a Christian come to read verses of the bible to the patients as a form of therapy. I was offended when I found out what they were going to do and doubly pissed off because the floor below said it basically was illegal to talk about religion at all in the hospital, let alone try converting and preaching. After I learned what the guy was going to do I left the area instead of voicing opposition. Afterwards the Christian preacher came to me in the lunchroom to talk about why I left. So we had a very long conversation about religion. I discovered this guy was Mormon and he got paid to teach people the bible in the hospital as "therapy". So I condemned this hypocrisy and compared him to myself who is doing it for free and not extorting people using faith to grow my finances. I explained the falsity of the Mormon polytheism of desiring to be gods and their following false prophets, which they actually believe in a democratically elected prophet alive today who when he dies their council elects another person to be prophet. I told the nurses and the hospital interns, as they listened to us speak, that this is the last guy on the planet who should be preaching to mentally ill people in fact I emphasized he should be a patient if they only knew what Mormons believed. I then publicly explained to all people within earshot the falsity of Mormonism and their extremely false claim that Thomas Monson is a prophet walking the earth today, as he was the Mormon prophet at the time; now deceased and replaced with a new false prophet. I then offered Islam to this Mormon preacher after exposing the errors of the bible composition, the lack of linguistic connections to the languages of the prophets and the polytheism and anthropomorphism of Christianity and pressed him to accept Islam more than I did any others at the hospital. Later I explained to the hospital interns who observed the conversation, how different people get treated differently based on who they are and as Prophet Jesus was harsh with hypocritical rabbis sometimes harshness is correct. In response the Mormon preacher just said he knew and heard all I had said about the bible's errors before. So I said if he knows then why do you stay upon falsehood when you know it's false, why don't you become Muslim and accept the truth? He didn't have any answer and said goodbye and that he would see me next Wednesday. The same day I got a visit from the hospital's Muslim chaplain saying he was told about me from his Christian co-worker who was concerned about me. The funny thing is not that I had been in the hospital 19 days without being told they had a Muslim chaplain that could visit me, but that I already met this guy outside of the hospital at the mosque where Ismail was imam.

So he asked me, "What are you doing here?" I told him I was doing ruqya on my family and got sent here because they think I'm crazy. The chaplain said to be careful because ruqya can be dangerous and sadly the non-Muslim doctors don't know anything about that world at all so it's almost useless talking to them about it because they disbelieve in it.

As the time came near to be discharged my new doctor in 5 zone 2, finally back from vacation, made several derogatory remarks about Islam to me. I told a nurse I think I should report him to the mental health abuse hotline just as I reported my therapist in 4 zone 3. Before I made the call regarding his illegal anti-Islamic remarks the nurse got the doctor to talk things out with me. I refuted point for point his remarks and then the doctor said that I was cured because in the past when I faced a conflict like that then I would've just reported it and fought the war on my own. Since I asked a nurse their opinion on the matter before acting and reporting him that showed true development so there was no need to report him because I was going to go home tomorrow. So I agreed to ignore his illegal comments to get out. Incidentally I was discharged hours before the Mormon preacher was set to return. As I left, the former marine who allegedly physically fought "Islamist extremist terrorists" in Afghanistan wished me well and gave me a hug. I mention such to show how I was in the hospital, diagnosed as a crazy radical extremist/terrorist by therapists and patients and doctors and ISNF alike yet the former Marine soldier who reportedly fought Islamic extremism militarily felt I was good enough to hug and wish wellness to despite me never changing my beliefs of intolerance and even openly trying to persuade him to become Muslim. In comparison this is exactly the opposite of what modernist liberalist "Muslims" say will happen if people with the Salafi or mythological "Wahhabi" creed of hatred for all things unislamic preach. They slander us saying people turn away from Islam entirely because of "you people". Yet actual non-Muslim military fighters of extremism, or crusaders if you will, turn to us in friendship attempts which we refuse. Why? Because just as the prophets were mislabeled those who truly follow the prophets are mislabeled by their enemies too because nobody wants to admit the truth to be other than what they are upon. So it is always the case of people either joining Salafiyyah Islam as proper Muslims or they deviate in one way or another and turn away by either ignoring prophetic Islamic preaching or combatting it, both of which options will result in doom. There are many examples I could give of this where I hate preach politely sticking to prophetic fundamental principles and turn enemies into people who want to be friends with me, despite me maintaining hatred the entire time until they become Muslim. This book doesn't allow me to enumerate many occurrences of enemies of Allah who I hate being in love with me despite my known enmity for their religion and person. If people become Muslim they get love and special treatment. Yet the disbelievers turn to and value the idea of friendship with a genuine Muslim because our hatred is mixed with justice, mercy and kindness according to their level of evilness and opposition to Islam. The bigger of an enemy to Islam they are, the more of an enemy we are to them. However, we are only enemies because Allah said to take his enemies, all disbelievers, as enemies. We also have to treat Allah's enemies strictly the way Allah says and non-violent combatants are not violently combatted. So as long as someone isn't a soldier fighting Muslims on the battlefield, kindness is the general rule despite our severe powerful hatred for them and their evil. The less evil they are the less we hate them and more kind we become. We always wish for goodness for every creature and we do not know if they may repent one day or not so we never shut that door. I may hate someone today and then religiously have to love them tomorrow or vice versa. For Muslim innovators there are rules as well. The Muslim hatred for disbelievers is oftentimes more pleasant than the "love" which non-Muslims express for each other. In reality it's not love, interfaith friendship or affection on the Muslims part, it's merely the justice and merciful kindness of prophetic Islam. Everyone has different treatment allotted because nobody is equal. Everyone is blessed or cursed by God differently. The problem is the doctrine of equality and unjust criminal unislamic hatred has created many false perceptions of what prophetic Islamic hate is and how it is practiced.

I was officially diagnosed by the anti-Islamic remark making doctor with Schizoaffective disorder Bipolar type. This is one of the rarest types of mental illness in the world with 75% of diagnosed cases being misdiagnosed. Many people confuse Schizophrenia or Schizoaffective or even Bipolar with Split Personality but the one who has multiple personalities is someone with an entirely different disease called Dissociative Identity Disorder. Schizophrenia is basically insanity or delusions while Bipolar is extreme mood swings. So basically I was diagnosed with insanity + extreme mood. Yet it is an inaccurate diagnosis because the mental health industry says an individual must be symptomatic for 6 months before being diagnosed with that disease. I first went insane in May 2017 for understandably extremely stressful reasons mixed with nutritional deficiency and sleep deprivation. I stopped being insane in August 2017, about 3 months later. So I was not crazy long enough to be professionally diagnosed as I was. Only because the ISNF ban letter which I shared with the hospital said "ongoing for several years" did the doctor diagnose me as they did while in a hurry to prevent a lawsuit by me. The doctor who diagnosed me actually only saw me for three days before I threatened him with legal action for making illegal anti-Islamic remarks. Plus there is no accepted diagnosis of magically induced insanity in the health insurance codebooks to be able to bill for injuries caused by magic. The doctors say the pill I started taking during my second hospitalization rebalanced the brain and after I decided my plan of only eating imported foreign food was unfeasible then my nutrition improved. Doctors told me that I have to take an anti-psychotic medicine for the rest of my life as a precaution. Essentially I was so stressed and simultaneously happy in struggling against Qadri since it was a peaceful type of Jihad that it caused mania in my brain that led to ever increasing happiness that caused insanity.

Honestly the most stress I ever had was when I made takfir of my former friend/teacher, which by itself if you are sincere and knowledgeable then making takfir should cause you to experience stress sufficient enough to cause brain damage and illness. Muhammad was told in the Quran that he had grief over people's disbelief to such an extent it could cause death, so surely if you make takfir and don't feel extreme stress over it then something is wrong. While the angriest I have ever been was when the ISNF masjid noor jamat refused to let another lead us in jamat when I publicly refused to pray behind Qadri due to heretical reasons and accusations of magic. While the happiest I had ever been was in the hospital while expecting death. The happiness I experienced within the hospital was so intense that all the suffering of previous life on earth was forgotten. If I had been confined to that hospital room for eternity without anything to enjoy but just had that same dopamine flow of pleasure in my brain I would've been satisfied and considered myself in paradise. To this day I don't even regret any of the hardships I endured in the ordeal because that happiness level was so high that all the pain prior to it and after it doesn't matter to me much. In fact, if I attain paradise and get to that level of that happiness again, as I had in the hospital while insane, that would be enough for eternity. Yet paradise is much more pleasurable than what an insane person experiences in their brain during mania. Explicitly doctors have explained that my brain was so happy that it was overloaded with bliss so much it was unhealthy. Thus the pills they prescribe actually reduce my natural God-given pleasure which I enjoy from Islam without TV, Music or the sins of Kafir culture. Following strict Salafi Islam fully as much as possible refuting Kuffar and Innovators makes me so happy that medically it's imbalanced. Doctors told me that whatever I was doing I was more happy than a normal human is supposed to be, so their "medicine" is designed to reduce my happiness. Thus it is hard to imagine why people do sins to entertain themselves, which never results in lasting happiness once the music or fantasy or drug wears off. While then many people stress to me happiness is the most important thing in life instead of practicing the Islamic religion as I propose. Truthfully Islam despite the opposition of others and my own desires made me so happy it was harmful, so clearly happiness is less important than people think and if it is important in any sense then Islam is the best way to attain it. So either way if happiness is not that important then Islam wins and if happiness is most important, whether in this life or the next, then Islam also wins that competition too. The next test in life however would be sticking to Islam even if I was medically made to feel depressed. Because it's easy to practice when life is pleasurable and easygoing. Yet when momentum shifts and things get sad and hard, this more accurately reveals one's true character. Essentially many Muslims are capable of waging Jihad peacefully or otherwise and have fun doing so, but what happens after they get injured and disabled for life and have to continue living as they were not martyred on the battlefield but only wounded? What happens when they suffer the loss of a limb or anything other than their religion, as in my case my brain faculties due to toxic unnatural medicine? Especially if the war seems to have momentarily been won by the evildoers. Most people think they will either get victory or martyrdom but many more actually get a wound and then must live with it for a long time afterwards. Whereas spiritual wounds can give you a fate worse than death without even knowing it.

The day I got out of the hospital, when getting into the car I put on an Islamic lecture to listen to as I usually did as my mom drove me home. However to my surprise the lecture got turned off and some "new rules" were laid down. As part of my conditional release from the hospital I had agreed to move in with my parents at their countryside house, far from the masjids, to be with someone to observe me as well as assist them in taking care of my grandmother. So I was now faced with a new challenge of living with non-Muslims in the same place, which I hadn't done since becoming a Muslim. Because I had gotten rid of my car before hospitalization due to my plans to study abroad then the additional rule of "no driving our car, until you get a job" was particularly bitter to swallow. Especially since I was used to driving to mosques to pray 5 times a day and had no intention of working as long as the USA military was killing Muslims. My main rule for me living in America was still to legally avoid taxation until I moved overseas or the war in Afghanistan ended. Regarding studying overseas the doctors wrongly intimidated me saying, *"How are you going to get your medicine if you are studying overseas? What if they don't have the pill and you go crazy?"* I did not know how to answer that hypothetical scenario. I did not know that my medicine was available worldwide, though they should've, and that some schools in Muslim countries even give foreign students free healthcare and stipends while they live there. So in reality had I applied to study abroad and been accepted, even with my medical needs, I would've had free education and free healthcare and free housing and a free check every month to pay for needs and wants. Essentially I would have been able to live for free in a Muslim country as long as I was passing my studies of choice, Arabic/Shariah. So what was the problem? The main problem was the non-Muslim doctors didn't think going to a Muslim country would be good for my "mental health treatment" so rather than help me achieve what I wanted to achieve they fraudulently made it seem like an unrealistic crazy plan to move abroad and avoid USA taxation. My parents didn't want me to move either and since my dad had said the Shahada to become a Muslim prior to my 2nd hospitalization I figured I could stay a little bit longer in America to teach him Islam correctly, lest I leave and he get misguided by heretics or relapse back into disbelief.

My dad hadn't learned much during my hospitalization though we would give each other the salaams and Mr. Agwa tried teaching him wudu to wash himself for prayers. So finding myself now in almost a parent role over my father having to teach him his religion, and loving him as a Muslim rather than hating him as a disbeliever, as mercifully as I could I had to teach in gradual steps so as not to overwhelm him with too much information all at once. The priority was teaching him Tawheed, Creed and how to pray. Yet I wasn't with him daily to pray all 5 times each day together because I was still living in the old house while transferring stuff to my parent's countryside residence. Since he hadn't been taught yet he didn't know how to pray and therefore didn't. However we did go to Friday prayer together at the Salafi mosque in Buffalo. I didn't have my dad publicly take his shahada in front of everyone because it is not necessary to become a Muslim and I never did it myself due to shyness so it wasn't something I felt suitable for him if I hadn't done it and it isn't necessary. On his first Friday Jumuah as a Muslim we tried to teach him how to do wudu but he struggled washing his feet as is required. I probably should have taught him this before getting to the masjid but I didn't know he didn't learn it after Mr. Agwa tried teaching him weeks earlier. Then dad begged me to let him just go inside and that he would do the wudu properly next time. So trying to be merciful as befits a Muslim son to their Muslim father, despite it invalidating the prayer, I acquiesced realizing that teaching my dad patiently will take all my might, mercy, patience and wisdom as it would be the hardest thing I have ever done. Though teaching anyone Islam, especially family, is the most rewarding activity one can do. My dad listened to the Khutbah and though I knew his prayer wouldn't count due to incomplete wudu I was so happy to have my dad pray alongside me. My dad was a little nervous though since he was the only guy using a chair while praying as he wasn't flexible enough to prostrate as everyone else did. There was nothing wrong with that though and it is common for elderly or less able people to sit in chairs instead of prostrating and it doesn't ruin their prayer at all. Afterwards my dad was approached by other Muslim brothers who tried teaching him a few things, but my dad felt overwhelmed and pressured so didn't like it. Afterwards despite my gradual attempts to slowly teach my dad Islam he got more and more distant. I began to realize he didn't really know what he signed up for when he said the shahada to become a Muslim and this was holding him back significantly. Eventually as my attempts to schedule time with him to learn religion were postponed and delayed and then cancelled and rebuffed, excuses began to be made. While in the hospital my dad observed my attempts to convert one of my doctors to Islam and he said, "That doctor doesn't deserve to be Muslim." So there wasn't any faking on my dad's part, he genuinely had become a Muslim but when it came time to practice he procrastinated and made excuses as many Muslims around the world often do. Later to my dismay my dad would say how he doesn't have to pray the 5 daily prayers because only extremists do that and the ISNF people didn't so he doesn't have to either. I tried to explain how that organization was deviantly unislamic and that the 5 daily prayers are an obligatory pillar of Islam that cannot be neglected or rejected; but my father was convinced I was unique in praying 5 times a day and other Muslims only did it on Fridays or when convenient for them, as he himself witnessed empty masjid noor at prayer times prior to my ban. Sadly this comparison methodology of "other Muslims" setting the benchmark versus and against the prophetic methodology I was teaching him led to conflicts in his understanding of Islam. My dad even took from ISNF that Jesus was more than just a prophet and confusingly thought he was other than a human, due to ISNF celebrating Christmas with their "Happy Holidays" sign which he said they told him I had vandalized. I explained I'm not an extremist as ISNF wrongly said and that Muslims correctly believe as Allah and Muhammad taught that Jesus was a 100% human prophet of God miraculously saved from the dangerous plots of his enemies who is not God incarnate nor a son of God despite his mother being a virgin when she gave birth. Rather Jesus is like Adam who was 100% human without father nor mother as a test and example of the power of God to create creatures. Yet due to the "dawah" ISNF had done my dad was convinced I was the only Muslim in the world that thought Jesus was not God or the son of God, despite this being clear in the Quran and Hadith and consensus of the Muslim world. My dad sincerely said that the other Muslims at the mosques don't believe that, he thought this because of the corrupt "preaching" leaders like Qadri and Rasul Khan and Khalid Qazi do to kuffar. My dad said how if Muslims really believed as I said then ISNF and others wouldn't preach what they preached if Islam was really that different from what Christianity teaches. So I said that is correct, they shouldn't preach that sinful stuff as they do because it causes confusion and when I tried to stop them that's why we had conflict because they wouldn't stop. Thus I got banned from the mosque because of it. Then my dad figured that since I had been diagnosed as crazy by medical doctors and the mosque had indeed banned me then I must just be crazy and Islam doesn't teach as I proved to him and that Muslims really don't have to pray five times a day and other incorrect notions. My dad then decided that if I had been truly correct as I said then I wouldn't have gotten mental illness and been prescribed a pill for the rest of my life. I explained this is destiny that we accept, which doesn't alter facts of the prophetic faith of Islam which you yourself acknowledge was true and now have to follow as it was prophetically taught despite how it is commonly taught or mispracticed in America. To which my dad then falsely claimed he was only pretending to be a Muslim while I was in the hospital because if he didn't it might have stressed me out and made me sicker. This is sadly the position my father maintains until this day. I know deep-down that he was awe-struck by the Quran and genuinely believed from the little he read that it was true divine revelation. The problem was more likely his fear of changing his lifestyle and becoming a minority, subject to face opposition from the world as I had received. Basically he feared the pressure and had difficulty understanding how sometimes believers get wounded in battles with hypocritical heretics or disbelievers. Do you know my evidence that he truly believed prior to his avoidance and eventual open apostasy from Islam? The fact that he now refuses at all costs to read anything I've written or any Islamic material. To date this is my 30th book and I've published in alternate formats aside from physical, such as ebooks and audiobooks. My shortest book is 32 pages long or 39 minutes in audiobook format. Now as a father who claims to "love his son" the only way this could be true is if he read his son's books. It is impossible to love something and then not read their books if you have the ability. For example, if you love God you will read God's book the Quran and if you love God's prophet Muhammad you will read his teachings in the Hadith, similarly for anyone loved who has disseminated their teachings in literary format. It is a contradiction of the tongue to profess love for something or someone who you simultaneously neglect and ignore. As a father especially, if he thinks Islam is wrong then it is an obligatory duty for him to refute my Islamic writings line by line correcting my mistakes. Even if he thinks Islam is right it is obligatory to refute my mistakes line by line. The same applies to all my family and anyone who claims to love me or be a friend. If they aren't Muslim it's impossible to love me, similarly if they don't read my books and correct my errors. In reality my father's false claim of "love" for me is more comparable to his affection for his pet birds and the wild animals he feeds. My father gives me food and shelter and he also gives his pet birds food and shelter. In fact, he talks to the birds nicer than he does to me most of the time. In actuality if we decide based on behaviors/actions then my father must love the birds he cares for more than his only child. Such is the case with disbelievers in that their "love" is superficial lip service rarely having any real substance. I feel confident my dad won't even find out I've written this about him because my father is terrified to read any books I've written, as are many others. Why? This is because of the standard rule of Islamic truth versus falsehood. If my dad reads any of my books he will be faced with two options. Either the information about Islam being true is correct or incorrect. Next he will have to respond accordingly. If it is correct he must accept Islam, as he did before, and act like a Muslim to ever consider himself a good person going forward after such exposure to Islamic truth. Because for Islam to be true in his personal secret opinion and then not believe it or practice it himself then he knows that would mean he is evil for having rejected the truth. Even if he doesn't say "what you wrote is correct and Islam is true" if he knows it himself after reading then he himself will know that to not be Muslim he is ignoring what is right and it will eat him up inside with guilt until he is eventually punished by Allah for such disbelief. Thus he follows the Satanic opinion that his ignorance of the truth will lead to a more blissful life than knowing the truth to be something he doesn't think he can adjust to. Now if he read my books and found errors, as a family member he is religiously obligated to correct those errors. To date not a single member of my family has reviewed a single book of mine or commented letting me know of any errors, but they don't become Muslim either. Thus proving their insincerity and lack of concern over my soul and final destination. As it is now, my family members must believe 1 of 2 things. I am either right to try to be Muslim or a mistaken fool and if they think I'm right to try then they would try to be Muslim too, and if they think I'm a fool and cared about me they would try to correct me. If they don't even have the courtesy to correct my assumed error if they think I'm in error, such a person would not be my well-wisher for not correcting my error they think is error, for true friends correct each other when in error, family even moreso; as I try my best to correct them under the circumstances. Truly what other options would good family have? I see only these two options for a sincere family member of either joining me in guidance or correcting my error. Neutrality and silence are not options for sincere or loving people. Whereas all religions agree that on Judgement Day Muslims and their non-Muslim families will separate forever. So "family unity" is illusionary or temporary when we are already planning for an eternal life of non-interaction without visitation. To avoid permanent separation a sincere family member or friend who read my books would correct any and all of my errors to protect me from sin or join me in my attempts to practice Islamic goodness and invite others to it. My dad however is not up to such a challenge so he would have to pass that job on to a more intellectual religious person. However what if that more intellectual religious person then comes back and tells my dad, *"You know what I read your son's book and he's right! Surprisingly Islam is the only true prophetic faith!"* Then my dad would be in the same boat but worse off because he would have more evidence against him as indicating evilness for not being Muslim, and not only would his son be on his case but his former religious superior would be too and he would've lost a co-religionist leader simultaneously and thus have less reason/excuse to be upon a false faith. My dad knows from his experience before that Islam is true and that my books likely prove this further with minimal errors so he doesn't pass the job of reading my books on to others who are more smart or spiritual. Instead he resorts to the standard reaction of someone who fears becoming a Muslim and changing their lifestyle to enter paradise. That reaction is to either ignore or combat Islamic preaching and it's the same reaction all disbelievers and innovators have no matter the era or culture. This is the standard rule. Non-Muslims either flee or fight. They could fight peacefully with lies or attempts at corrupt reformation of Islam via proxy innovators or hypocrites. Or they could get violent with Crusades or wars on "Islamic extremism". Yet this standard remains the factual reality of the attitude and reaction to all genuine Islamic teachings. Everyone exposed to Islam has these three options. 1. They either become Muslim no matter the difficulties they face because they know they will enter paradise and have goodness in this life as a result. Or 2. they ignore Islam as much as possible by any and all measures or ignore enough to feel vindicated in the eyes of others as not deliberately unjustifiably ignoring. Such as how my father claims he "read a few pages of some of my books and realized what they are all about" so he then says he "doesn't have time to waste getting brainwashed or scammed." Or 3. such a person will combat Islam when they realize us Muslims will not stop the preaching of Islam to them. Even if we did stop individually to them as they falsely say is all that they desire, due to circumstances we won't stop communally doing the job to others who will become Muslims and then restart the process with them or others in the community they are in. So as a result of the eventual tide of Islam sweeping their religious community, culture and values away or at least causing confrontation and religious "disunity" or "hatred" then they choose to take defensive or offensive measures against the prophetic faith they have already chosen to disbelieve in with or without researching sincerely. The noisy claims of non-Muslims to only be fighting against "radical" Islam or "extremism" are impossible to be true. This is because anything different than the prophetic truth is radical extremism. Now if you are a non-Muslim thinking Christianity or some other false religion is the prophetic truth then by default everything else aside from your denomination is extreme deviation from that truth. So from a kafir perspective all forms of Islam are wrong and the world would be better without any Islam in it at all. Such is a honest natural obligatory opinion to have of Muslims and Islam if one disbelieves in it or thinks something else is the true religion. The claim that people just don't want others to be upon an extreme version of falsehood is inaccurate and false. Examine whether it is okay to go to hell forever as long as I'm doing so peacefully without harming others? That's basically the claim the proponents of war on "radical Islam" make. They claim it's okay to be a devil and invite others to worship other than our Creator but just do it peacefully without violence or keep your devilishness private without spreading it. Yet it is impossible for people on earth to live without doing so according to their values and thereby sharing values or religiousness with others. So as long as one is alive they are sharing their inner faith outwardly even if unintentionally. Thus if upon falsehood they are corrupting the world as long as they are interacting with creatures. So theoretically only if the non-radicals are imprisoned in a monastic life closed off in solitary confinement can they be harmless to others. In reality though the people upon religious falsehood are harming themselves and others every second they are in sin or error. The idea that someone is okay with another person being upon a different religion *"as long as it's not an extreme version of a wrong religion"* is equivalent to saying *"I'm pleased with you going to eternal hell but I just don't want you take a certain route that makes me more uncomfortable."* If they were honest they would say don't be upon a false religion period whether extreme or violent or not. A violent extremist version is no less dangerous than a peaceful non-extreme version of a false faith. So everyone promoting this popular worldwide nonsense of religious tolerance of non-extremist faiths is not only incorrect but they are blatant corrupt liars and breeding a new form of religious extremism as well. The prophets of God never ever said, *"It's okay to disbelieve as long as the disbeliever isn't harmful to others."* On the contrary they told us everyone who disbelieves is to be hated and will go to hell forever whether they are peaceful or violent and that some types of disbelievers are to be harmed and some are not. It's as simple as that previous statement. We do not tolerate falsehood in any form, some people merit harm even if upon the truth but not all people of falsehood are to be harmed according to the prophetic faith of Islam. Problematically entire peoples and nations were raised for hundreds of years without such a clear policy regarding religion and violence so they still haven't come to the correct policy of how to deal with religious differences. Plus since they have false religions that would be defeated by Islam if everyone was restricted to peaceful equal preaching then world peace is not an agenda of people who stand to lose if the world allowed peaceful honest religious examination. Anyways the topical point of this paragraph was that my Muslim dad apostated primarily due to destiny and misconceptions taught to him by other alleged Muslims trying to teach Islam in non-prophetic methods that led to entire religious confusion about what Islam is because of Muslims misrepresenting it in the name of preaching Islam with wisdom.

Meanwhile I evaluated my options with my new medicine regiment.   The medical professionals kept trying to convince me that I was on the road to homelessness if I refused to fund the USA war machine via taxes because the war in Afghanistan would never be over and if it did end it certainly wouldn't be a Muslim victory. Regardless I rescheduled my appointment with the Court to legally change my name to Abdullah Bin-Kevin for September 14th, 2017. My mom took me to the Court and voiced her opposition to the Judge stressing that it would be harder for me to get a job, as she desired, if I changed my name so while she opposes it she allows it since she respects my desire/identity. I told the Judge I'd rather be treated like a Muslim in America even if persecuted as a result rather than be confused as a non-Muslim due to my name being Gregory. The Judge asked me if I believed in Shariah law, which is a question that had nothing to do with me changing my name. As imagined it is a screening question for terrorist radicalism, because similar to how my dad had misconceptions many non-Muslims incorrectly think there is such a thing as a "Shariah Muslim" and a "non-Shariah Muslim" whereas the radicals believe in Shariah law according to them and the "moderates" do not. So on the record in the Court I calmly answered by saying, *"I do believe in Shariah law but not as it is practiced today. I believe in the Shariah law as taught by prophet Muhammad."* and the Judge was pleased with my response due to her ignorance of the topic. The Judge then approved my name being legally changed from Gregory Heary to Abdullah Bin-Kevin. However there was just one more form I had to fill out, an affidavit with the newspapers announcing the change publicly. The Court office did not have any more of those forms available at the time, so I had to wait and was given 90 days to complete the name change.

Sadly within those 90 days therapists, doctors and the drug induced fatigue, reduced thought prowess and depression from the medicine slowly but surely convinced me that I was unable to work even if I wanted to and that I was permanently disabled. I still wanted to change my name legally but because I had decided to apply for disability benefits and my medical history was all in the name of Gregory, I figured it would be detrimental to my case if I changed my name. After months of therapy and pills I became depressed and thought I was destined to be homeless as soon as my parents died unless I was declared disabled and got supported by the government for life and moved into a group home for the mentally disabled after my parents died. Marriage was never going to happen since I was unable to earn due to my refusal to pay taxes to the war machine and my alleged inability to travel overseas to earn elsewhere. Plus even if I did ever go overseas to earn I'd still have to pay USA taxes unless I revoked my citizenship because America oppressively is nearly the only country that taxes its citizens everywhere they are on the planet even if in a foreign country earning foreign income. So I cancelled my plans to study Islam overseas thinking I was just meant to be homeless, since doctors said I couldn't stop the pill and falsely made it seem I needed to stay in America forever for medical treatment. My main daily concern was how future homelessness would make it harder for me to practice Islam, pray on time and fast Ramadan according to the correct moon sighting each year. Astonishingly the government authorities determined in 2018 that I was disabled and I began to receive Social Security Income. However because I hadn't worked long enough to qualify for Social Security then I was put on SSI which is for disabled people who didn't pay in enough to qualify for Social Security payments but are projected to be homeless if the government doesn't pay them. Thus to protect society from the costs homeless people put on the community the government finds it cheaper to pay such people, especially if they are medically proven to be disabled. So I gladly thought now at least I won't be homeless. However contrary to what many think, you are not allowed to keep the money you get while on SSI. There are strict limitations because you technically didn't earn it by paying into the system via previous taxation. I was only given about $500 a month and wasn't allowed to own more than $2,000 in total assets at any time, if I ever owned more than $2,000 for the rest of my life they would stop paying me and I'd be screwed. Essentially the Federal American government gives people on SSI the bare minimum necessary to buy food each month, it's not even enough to cover food and rent. Instead the government cuts deals with housing authorities to get SSI people discounts on housing so they can pay for food and rent at a discount. It's essentially a trap where they give you money but restrict it so you cannot get enough money to buy a car to get a job and have to live in poor government housing for the rest of your life. I figured at least that's better than being homeless after my parents die. As Muslims and non-Muslims are forbidden by hadith from prophet Muhammad to inherit each other then it didn't matter if my kafir parents left me with wealth because I wouldn't be religiously entitled to it. Since I wasn't going to accept any inheritance from non-Muslims and it didn't seem that my parents planned on becoming Muslim before death then as someone who was disabled according to doctors and the government then I was literally faced with homelessness. The medical professionals repeatedly said I would be homeless if I refused to fund the USA war machine against Muslims. Still I was upon truth, although I must add if it was necessary it would be Islamically permissible to pay taxes to fund the war machine as I later learned my policy of refusing to pay taxes that shed Muslim blood while not unislamic did indeed make my life potentially very difficult and was potentially incorrect if it led to homelessness as the professionals advised me it would. I figured time would tell and I was willing to risk potential homelessness for the sake of not having Muslim blood on my hands due to paying taxes that funded the kafir anti-Islamic military. And despite what I was told by everybody I had faith that eventually the Muslims would be victorious against their enemies in Afghanistan and elsewhere, as Allah promises and fulfills those promises regardless of the odds and opposition against true goodness.

In 2018, after almost a year without any communication I emailed Qadri an apology.

Email Sent Monday, Jul 23, 2018 at 3:16 PM

I apologize for reciting Quran during fajr salat.

I had psychosis hours before that and likely during it and was not in a sane state of mind. I have mental illness and was diagnosed with schizoaffective disorder last year. At the time I thought you were a magician who did sihr al junun to me and i tried killing you by reciting surah alaq. That was wrong please forgive me.

I also apologize for calling you a munafiq when you led salat even though iqama was already called for someone else. It may be you did not hear or know. That was wrong please forgive me.

I do not plan to return to masjid noor as I have moved and am not seeking the ban to be lifted.

I just seek forgiveness and personal reconciliation. I do not want to be resurrected a khariji.

I want to recant my takfir of you and would like you to clarify some points.

1. *That Jews and Christians are disbelievers/kuffar.*

2. *That shirk is kufr.*

3. *That all non-Muslims are disbelievers.*

Those 3 reasons were why I did takfir of you because you denied those 3 points in conversation to me.

Could you please affirm them so I can be at ease about you?

If you don't then just tell me why so I can understand your point of view and my own errors. If there is anything else I did wrong then I ask for your forgiveness.

As expected behavior from a Munafiq, but not from a Muslim, this public religious figure Mr. Qadri did not reply to my email; so I guessed while magic is unproveable my concern for him being heretical was still accurate. In October 2019, over two years after my ban, I emailed the newly elected ISNF representatives (the president, vice president, treasurer, secretary and imam of the other ISNF masjid taqwa in Niagara Falls) the following email and got the following reply:

Email Sent Sunday, Oct 20, 2019 at 2:45 PM

I got banned from masjid noor and want to reconcile with Imam Qadri

To: president@isnf.org

Assalaamu aleikum wa rahmatullaha wa barakatuhu

My name is Gregory Heary and/or Abdullah bin Kevin

I used to pray at masjid noor from 2012-2017 until I was banned by Imam Qadri and former isnf president Rasul Khan.

In 2014 Mr. Qadri became the imam and in 2017 Mr. Qadri debated with me that Christians and Jews being Ahl-Kitab and marriable cannot be kafirs due to their special designation and it is wrong to call them disbelievers. I said their shirk is kufr and makes them kafirs/disbelievers. He said shirk is not kufr and that Jews and Christians are not all disbelievers.

Therefore I left and prayed at masjid huda for awhile while continuing to give proofs and admonish him via email. Then I returned to masjid noor to reconcile with him in person but he wouldn't speak with me. I left him notes and called and texted but he refused to discuss our difference in aqeedah. During this time I would pray by myself in the masjid after the jamat instead of in jama because one can't pray behind one who holds heretical beliefs such as that. The reason I continued praying in masjid noor instead of another masjid was because so few people came to jamat that the prayers Qadri didn't lead(cuz he wasn't there) needed extra people so much so that sometimes nobody except me showed up for salat. Thus since masjids must have salat established and I knew if I left masjid noor there would be salat with less than 3 or even 0 then I felt I could not abandon masjid noor just because of my disagreement with Imam Qadri even though that meant I'd miss some jamat by not praying behind him.

I suggested to him that others lead us until the dispute were resolved but he refused to give up his spot or discuss the issue or just say that all non-Muslims including jews and christians are disbelievers to resolve the dispute.

On 5/3/2017 at Fajr Mr. Qadri came late after the iqamah was called for someone else and still led prayer despite the hadith of Isa pbuh and Mahdi where

Mahdi leads Isa pbuh because iqamah is called before Isa arrives. I informed him of this error and he laughed about leading even though doing so was wrong and doubly wrong because he knew I would pray separately if he led.

At that point I thought he was a Munafiq, publicly called him such thereby making takfir and I tried to inform other Imams and Masjids via email so he could get fired. In the process I had a panic attack that I thought was a jinn attack since I never had a panic attack before.

After Asr that day I overheard another person telling him I'd pray behind him if he said shirk was kufr and all non-Muslims were disbelievers but instead Mr. Qadri pretended he had no idea why I don't pray behind him though I knew he knew because he told me so before in emails and text messages that he knew why I wasn't praying behind him and he disagreed with my beliefs. Other people upon hearing why I don't pray behind him said "We can't say Christians are disbelievers because we are married to Christians and love them." Mr. Qadri did not correct them.

Then I was praying by myself after Isha on 5/3/2017 and Mr. Qadri with microphone said "Will someone please tell this brother to stop bothering us." because apparently my recitation in qiyam was too loud for them reading hadith. I found this appalling because at Masjid huda people came late to prayer their Imam remained silent the whole time waiting for their prayer to stop before starting his own lecture. Also before our dispute when I asked him in the name of allah to read hadith after fajr too he refused. So I knew he didn't care that much for hadith. And since he 100% knew how to end the dispute with me, by saying others should talk to me it was further proof for me that he persisted upon heresy.

I then came down with psychosis/insanity from the stress of trying to reconcile with Mr. Qadri plus the brain damage of the panic attack and concluded Mr. Qadri had done magic to me. Later I would be hospitalized and medically diagnosed with psychosis but did not know what that was. Thus recognizing a unexplained bout of insanity I thought it was magic from him.

Thinking it was magic on 5/6/2017 at fajr after publicly accusing Qadri of being a magician I asked Qadri and this time everyone else present to let another lead us and he and they refused. I said to Qadri "May you die before you finish the salat if you lead." and recited surah alaq during fajr hoping to kill him via recitation of Quran during the jamat over his recitation which I thought was magic. I later realized that was wrong and I apologized to him via email explaining I had psychosis at that time thinking sihr al junun was done to me by him. Yet because of that incident I got banned from masjid noor by him via text message. Regardless I returned to the masjid on 5/7/2017 to apologize and reconcile but the sunday school security guard asked me to talk outside and after I went outside he said the imam banned me and that the cops will be called if I ever came back so to this day I've not come back.

On the phone with my Christian mother when Mr. Qadri was banning me to her she asked "Why are you even talking to me about this when I'm a disbeliever?" and he reportedly laughed telling her that "I don't consider you to be one even though your son does".

On 5/26/2017 former ISNF president Rasul Khan wrote a letter to my parents and the Amherst police chief banning me from the masjid saying I was no longer welcome at masjid noor and that local law enforcement was notified and would comply in preventing me from returning.

As a result of such stress I was hospitalized for a total of 32 days due to psychosis and diagnosed with Schizoaffective disorder. But now I take medicine for it and no longer believe Qadri did magic to me but I still believe he holds the heretical beliefs for which I made takfir of him.

I understand you may not believe what I claim to be true as true about Mr. Qadri not considering him to hold such a heretical beliefs that Jews/Christians are not kuffar/disbelievers. I didn't include the evidence I have of emails and text messages from him proving my claim to make this email shorter and because such evidence could be easily dismissed if he currently changes his position.

Anyways it is unanimous that if he still believes Jews and Christians are not disbelievers then for this reason he is a disbeliever and should be fired from his position. If you need evidence of the obligation of considering Jews/Christians to be Kuffar/disbelievers then let me know and it will be provided inshallah but it is unanimously obligatory and disbelieving it is one of the 10 widely known nullifiers of Islam.

I also understand you may not be able nor willing to take action to fire him regardless of him holding the heretical beliefs I charge him with or not.

My point for this email however is not to get Qadri fired, nor to get unbanned from masjid noor. I will wait til the akhira for recompensation for getting mental illness and banned from the masjid. The purpose of this email is to learn inshallah that Imam

Qadri changed his position so I can revoke my takfir of him.

The prophet saws in sahih hadith said what means "Whoever says to his brother, 'O disbeliever,' it returns to one of them" and "Whoever accuses someone of disbelief, or of being an enemy of Allah, while he is not like that, it will return back to him." thus takfir is a very serious thing to make on Qadri as I did. According to the Prophet saws without a doubt one of us is a kafir since takfir has been made. I don't want it to be me or him. Therefore I want to revoke it just to be safe but can't till I have doubt about him having those heretical beliefs that he expressed. However despite my apologies and attempts to reconcile in email and text messages Qadri refuses to communicate with me and I've not heard from him since 2017.

So could you do 1 of the 3 following things?

Upon asking Qadri if he believes Jews/Christians are disbelievers or not then:

if he says yes could you inform me so I can revoke takfir of him?

if he says no could you direct him to the proper authorities so he can be educated and repent and if not repent then fired?

if I am wrong about anything in this issue inform me what to believe, say, do so I can repent and be correct or more correct?

Ten days later I received the following email reply from a Security Guard company called Forseti Protection Services.

Email Received Tuesday, Oct 29, 2019 at 11:01 AM

Abdullah bin Kevin,

Attached is a letter on behalf of Masjid Al-Noor regarding your expulsion. Please review the attached. This email and letter shall serve as formal notification of Cease and desist of unwanted actions. Your attention to this matter is urgent and appreciated.

A copy of the attached has been forwarded to the Board of Directors, Amherst Police Department and Masjid Al-Noor Legal Representatives.

Forseti Protection Group

Gregory Heary / Abdullah bin Kevin,

Your communication and actions are unwanted, unwelcome and infringe upon Masjid An-Noor, our members, the Qur'an and by the Sunnah of Prophet Muhammad Ibn Abdullah, the peace and the blessings of Allah be on him.

All communication, including electronic communication via phone calls, text, email, social media, and full stay away from Masjid An-Noor properties remain enforced. You are hereby notified, your actions and communication have been forwarded to Amherst Police Department, and subject to legal action including but not limited to arrest, should you fail to cease and desist.

The purpose of the Masjid An-Noor is to advance the cause of Islam and serve Muslims in Western New York. In furtherance of its purpose, Masjid An-Noor provides a focus for the coordination of local Muslim affairs in accordance with the norms of the Qur'an and the Sunnah and shall establish educational institutions for local Muslims of all ages, shall foster a positive understanding of Islam in American society, and shall promote a spirit of brotherhood, equality, and commitment to justice.

In May 2017, the Board of Directors voted on your expulsion from Masjid An-Noor. The Board determined your behavior warranted loss of rights to participate or attend any Masjid An-Noor properties for a minimum of five (5) years. After said time, you can petition for a hearing to determine future status. Based on this determination, you will be eligible to petition reinstatement in May 2022.

This decision is within the boundaries of the Holy Qur'an and the Qur'anically sound hadiths and Sunnah's of Prophet Muhammad.

Sincerely,

Forseti Protection Group

On Behalf of the Board of Directors Masjid Al-Noor

Cc: Masjid Al-Noor Board of Directors

4640 Broadway
Depew, New York 14043
855-367-7384

Although there were new ISNF leaders they were upon the same, if not more oppressive, policy as the old ones. I looked at the picture of the clean-shaven new ISNF president and realized he, Shahid Mehboob, was present in the group on May 3rd 2017 the day I broke my vow of silence and discussed with Qadri, Payraw and others how Ahl-Kitab are Kuffar. I was also surprised to learn that I was banned from the other ISNF masjid taqwa because I had never been there before and had no problems with them or their imam. In ISNF's cease and desist order from all communication they said I was going against the religion and they were right in some degree for a few minor things, but they never said what I was wrong about or why with any proofs. Wherein they also innovatively used the bida term "holy Quran" innovatively mixing an English label, that has no proof to be used as a label for the Quran, with Arabic in a copycat mode of Christian texts and never even replied to the salaams I sent in my email. It seemed ISNF had a problem with me and my creed and unislamically unethically had a vote on my expulsion, likely in private secretly amongst only board members, to ban me for 5 years minimum from all their mosques and all communication methods under threat of legal prosecution if I ever directly communicated again by any method. I was never before informed such a vote even took place and nobody ever asked for my side of the story before the vote occurred either. So I had no way to defend myself and this vote is not how Shariah law or even basic morality governs matters of Creed disputes. It is criminally unjust to convict and punish someone without even having a trial where they can defend themselves and explain the issue. Plus I was never a member of ISNF because I never signed up on their paperwork forms or paid any dues to be a group member. So they never had any authority to ban me from ISNF because I never joined. I was and am just a Muslim who used to pray at one of ISNF's masjids. So religiously they can only ban me from Allah's houses based on Shariah law and not ISNF desires. Whereas everyone of all religions knows and agrees that to ban someone from a house of worship in such a manner is irreligious no matter what the issue is or what the religion is. Thus proving my point even further that ISNF is not an Islamic Society but an ignorant innovating club. Their individual members amongst their leadership are too stupid to be considered apostates and their lower level paid members don't even know the creed of the leadership or frequent the masjid enough to know the issue of their imam. I didn't even know who the board members were myself from 2014-2017 despite praying there 5 times a day, because these board leaders are titles without substantial meaning. Sadly they hired one Munafiq to be their Imam and because he said to ban me they blindly follow with religious taqlidi conviction because of their partisan hizbiyyah and foolishness.

Imran ibn Abi Anas reported from a man of Aslam who was one of the Companions of the Prophet, that the Prophet said:

"*Snubbing a believer for a year is like spilling his blood.*"

Source: Al-Adab Al-Mufrad 405 Grade: Sahih

Hisham ibn 'Amir al-Ansari, the cousin of Anas ibn Malik whose father was killed in the Battle of Uhud, that he heard the Messenger of Allah say:

"It is not lawful for a Muslim to snub another Muslim for more than three nights. As long as they are cut off from each other, they are turning away from the Truth. The first of them to return to a proper state has his expiation for that inasmuch as he was the first to return to a proper state. If they die while they are cut off from each other, neither of them will ever enter the Garden. If one of them greets the other and he refuses to return the greeting or accept his greeting, then an angel returns the greeting to him and Shaytan answers the other."

Source: Al-Adab Al-Mufrad 402 Grade: Sahih

It goes back to big business religions following the profits, instead of the prophets. Many don't realize the situation for what it is, but then again it's not uncommon to find people buying poison, even if it's clearly labeled. Some even justify their purchase of poison by saying they like the flavor. Think twice before giving money to a religious charity. Are you doing it because it will please God or are you doing it because it's customary? Are you doing it publicly or privately? Anonymously or not? The same principle applies to any religious teacher, if money is involved eventually it will influence the content of what is being taught; it is inevitable. The teacher who gets paid money can never possibly teach their students morality effectively with 100% sincerity. I don't mean to offend anybody who is in the religious field, I'm just trying to explain why religion should not be treated as a commodity or industry. Because wherever that is the case more often than not you will discover that such a person's true object of worship is money, even if they claim otherwise. Those who worship wealth or desire worldly ranking and prestige are not guides to paradise, they are manipulating religion for their own satanically inspired purposes. The majority of people find it difficult to receive honest helpful religious advice that tells them what they are doing is wrong, or that they should do more good deeds and less evil deeds. So if it is hard to accept religious advice when they get it for free, then how could it be that people are paying someone for sincere religious advice? Yet what's even worse is that if a religious leader is paid a salary then if they ever make any mistake or misguide someone by accidental ignorance or misunderstandings, then that can make their whole income sinful because they'd be getting paid to misguide people. Sadly oftentimes the case is that a cohort committee, board, or society of people with reputation/wealth in the community end up calling the shots and exerting influence upon the community regardless of whether their decisions/policies agree with their religion or not. In practice usually such committees violate their religion in attempts to promote various community activities. Then they make membership of their pseudo-religious community a club which requires payment for you and your opinion to count. Whereas none of the prophets had a policy where you had to pay membership dues each year to be considered a member of the religious community. And they had religious communities at that time since the religious places of worship needed community leaders just as they do today. Of all the companions of prophets who went out and built places of worship not a single one of them ever instituted democratic systems where people voted for positions, had treasurers, vice presidents, boards, committees and constitutions or club charters. For thousands of years places of worship operated without elections or political circusry. No companion of any prophet of God ever instituted such a scheme for a place of worship nor it's community and they most certainly didn't have paid membership dues either. If you believed in the religion and prayed there just once, then such a person was automatically a full-fledged member with a valid opinion as long as their opinion was legitimate according to the religion. You didn't need to pay to pray the way places make you do today. It's unbelievable such organizations exist where people pay to be a "member" of a place they are supposed to pray in. You can actually be attending a place of worship to pray on a daily basis but if you don't pay the "membership fees" they'll say you aren't a member. Ironically those who do pay the price to pray tend to barely pray at the place so they don't even get their money's worth, yet because they "pay their dues" they are an honorary member with political influence over the governing body of the religious building. It's truly funny for me because I don't pay membership fees and I pray at places more than the ones who pay to pray there. You'd think they'd be praying there more than me since they are paying more than me. Sadly though it seems those who are paying from home tend to have more authority at places of worship than those who are consistently praying there. What lesson does that teach? If it's a "religious organization" why does paying give one more political points and credentials than praying? Of course actions speak louder than words but sometimes silent payments of money seem to talk louder than actions. No such organization of a place of worship with paid membership is rightly guided. If you are paying to be a member at a place of worship then you should know that club will cause problems and not follow the religion as it is supposed to be followed. That's a guarantee, if they have paid membership then they will cause problems. You are literally paying them to cause problems and that they require payment for membership is a problem in itself, thus they have caused a problem even before they got paid to cause problems with that money they pilfer. They basically hold a religion ransom claiming you have to pay to belong. In reality they take the power away from the religious and give it to the rich, thus they want membership to be paid so they can pay for power they wouldn't get otherwise if leadership and influence were determined by religious criteria. They don't want the poor to have any influence thus they exclude them with the fee and they know the religious intellectuals won't pay to join a sacrilegious organization when the very principle of paying to be a member contradicts their religion. With such "religious organizations" the best policy you can have with them is to not join even if they pay you to join. I won't even join such organizations even if they tried to pay me. But most won't ever offer to pay you instead they want you to pay them. Instead stay far away from them if you want to enter heaven. As much as they may try to trick you into thinking paying for membership will get you a better seat in paradise, it won't so don't. God does not want you to pay to belong to such shameful religious rackets. Also don't be mistaken by the false slogan of "joining in order to reform". Institutions don't get fixed by you joining them, by you joining them all that means is that they have corrupted you. Rather than you join them, they should change and join you. If any such religious organization ever asks you why you don't join them or get involved, then tell them you were wondering the same as to why they don't abolish their religious racket and hypocritical sacrilegious political tyranny to join you in practicing the religion correctly. Some of these religious rackets are so filthy that they will even rent the place out for people to have religious celebrations. For example if there is a celebration for a religious ceremony for a baby or a wedding or funeral they will actually charge people a fee to use the space owned by the religious organization in order to celebrate something the religion proscribes they celebrate. Basically the religion says you should do X as part of your religion and the organization says *"Well if you want to do X on our premises, as our religion says you should/must do, then you're going to have to pay us to reserve or use the space."* It's pathetic that people pay for the "privilege" to practice their religion and celebrate a religious event at a religious place which is supposedly created to serve the communities religious needs. Why do they even have the space if they won't let people use it without paying for it? Sadly I've seen places of worship where they charge a few hundred dollars for parents to enroll their kid in the children's weekend education program and then if you are a "registered member of the society" you enjoy a 10% discount on the price you pay them to teach your child their religion. Yet they claim to be a religious organization when they won't even teach their religion at their place worship to children without getting paid to do so. That's really religious aye? You have to pay them to preach to you and pay again for them to teach your kids. Sometimes it's hard to wonder whether you are practicing a religion or paying for a product at a store. It's truly scandalous that many places dare to charge their members who already paid for membership another fee to have their kids get taught religion. Being a paying member doesn't even entitle you or your kids to get taught religion. To me it sounds exactly like a business where you get a discount on what they are selling if you have a membership card. Except unlike the stores these places and organizations frequently require an oath of allegiance and subservience to them and all their decisions, which is sinful to make in their religion anyways because of the way the organization is designed in a sacrilegious way let alone with how it's run and what it does and/or doesn't do. One must ask if that is how God desires religious societies to operate? Did God send prophets who taught people to teach kids religion for a price? Did prophets ask people for a salary for being their prophet? Did any prophet of God ever accept a salary from his people? Yet simultaneously kids' classes for religion at places of worship occur where the nations boast about religious freedom. How is it religious freedom if a kid can't be taught their religion at their place of worship unless their parents pay money? That doesn't seem free to me. Neither a cost nor a discount for such classes should exist. While if the teachers are getting paid, they shouldn't be teaching religion since that they agree to work for such organizations indicates they don't really know their religion to begin with. Yet what's worse is that the teachers typically don't even get paid because they are volunteer teachers, it's purely a religious education racket by the religious organization and they don't even properly teach the kids. Instead the money the organizations get paid fills their pockets and is not invested in the kids' religious miseducation. Tragically one will typically discover that the most prominent and influential board/society/committee members tend to be the least religious. I honestly don't know how it happens but it does, must be proof that democracy results in stupidity. Usually these corrupt modern boards/committees have their leadership determined by elections wherein each paying member gets an equal vote for candidates, who obviously must have paid the membership fee to be eligible as a candidate in the election. Islamic organizations don't operate this way, because of Shariah but also for logistical and integrity reasons which are justification enough even if one were ignorant of the Islamic Shariah. For example typically Muslim women don't pray much in the masjid since it's more rewarding for them to pray at home, the logistics of segregated areas, and spiritually safe traveling to/fro without unnecessary temptation, etc. So imagine if in theory a hypothetical masjid were to hold elections to determine who the administrative leaders were to be. If the paying male members and paying female members get a vote then those votes cannot under any circumstances be equal. Why? Because the women don't come to the masjid much to know which guys are religious and go to the masjid, while the segregation and lack of female masjid attendance means the men don't know who the religious women are either. Therefore because the Muslim women are guaranteed to be unaware of the religious qualifications/qualities of the men and the Muslim men are guaranteed to be unaware of the religious qualifications/character of the women then the men cannot legitimately choose the best woman via election nor can the women choose the best man via election due to their lack of knowledge regarding the religiosity of the members of the opposite gender. So in any hypothetical election a man's vote for a man must necessarily be worth more than a woman's vote for a male candidate, and a woman's vote for a woman must necessarily be worth more than a man's vote for a female candidate. Hence male and female voters cannot be counted equally. That's one reason Islamic administration cannot be established democratically. The other is that even if one were to have separate administrations for men and women, voting would still be unjust because not every member's opinion on who should be the leader is equal. For example a brand new convert who doesn't know anything about the religion cannot possibly have the same amount of influence in their vote as a scholar or person who spent years practicing the religion. Similarly the guy who only comes once a week to pray cannot possibly have an equal vote as someone who comes 5 times a day 35 times a week to pray. Why? Because the one who barely comes to pray won't know who comes 5 times a day and the one who does will know and thus is better informed to cast a vote for a religious candidate due to the differences in the level of religiosity amongst the voters of the same gender. Therefore the knowledge and religiosity of male voters means no two Muslim men can possibly have an equal say in who should be the leader of an administration because no two Muslim men are equal in knowledge or religiosity or familiarity with the knowledge and religiosity of the candidates who can be elected. This is why it is utterly impossible and sheer criminality for any organization to determine the leadership/administrators via elections or voting. I swear to God every single organization who does this is getting their leader in an unjust unintelligent matter and guarantee they will not have the best possible candidate for the job, it is utterly impossible for elections where all votes are equal to be just. Every election wherein every vote counts equally is a crime guaranteed to result in illegitimate leaders. This is why never in the history of Islam has there ever been an election for Islamic leadership wherein every person got an equal vote for various qualified candidates. It has never happened and never will. Now does that mean absolutely no "Muslim organizations" determine their leadership via elections? Sadly no. Some ignorant Muslims do this because they don't know about Islamic Shariah nor can they see how democratic elections are insanely unjust and illegitimate. However every single Muslim group which operates democratically has a plethora of problems, sometimes even to the extent that some of the members are heretical and not even considered Muslims according to Islam. Most heretical organizations, within non-Muslim democratic nations, which claim to be Muslim operate according to democratic methods but no Islamic organizations do. Not a single one. Yet do understand I'm not saying any/every organization that operates democratically is inherently staffed or participated in by heretics falsely claiming or ignorantly claiming to be Muslims. Many democratic groups are, but generally speaking "democratic Muslim organizations" have membership lists composed of people who are idiots that misunderstand Islam and democracy. So while democratically organized groups may have Muslim members, those Muslim members by virtue and definition of their membership in such an organization are fools who know little about Islam. The hard part is they may not know that because of their ignorance and arrogance, while it can be extremely hard to make them understand that without them thinking you are extreme or ignorant yourself. However hypocrites know democratic methods are designed to be unjust and result in religiously lackadaisical leadership and this is why they use and promote those methods. That's because hypocrites, idiots and people who don't practice Islam too much can't become leaders via legitimate Islamic procedures for determining leadership as stipulated by the Islamic Shariah. Fortunately, Muslims have Shariah so they know explicitly how religious organizations should determine who the leaders and administrative positions should be held by, but religions other than Islam tend not to specify how to get the best most qualified people for such positions so non-Muslims tend to have even worse leaders than the rare ignorant Muslim groups that may use democratic means to get their leaders. I won't go into the lengthy explanation of how exactly Shariah selects Muslim leadership here or in this book, but an example from the Catholic Church is a useful analogy. To determine the Pope, Catholics have the theoretically most knowledgeable, pious people (alleged to be the Cardinals, who were appointed by the allegedly most knowledgeable and pious Catholic (the previous Pope)) choose the leader by voting. Of course this is unjust for the reasons stated above but the point is that not every member of the Catholic Church has an equal say in who their leader will be. Everyone can see how it would be chaotic and disastrous if the Pope were determined by a global election where every Catholic or self-proclaimed Catholic aged zero-oldest got an equal vote. Since to get a religious leader you can't just let general laypeople, have too much influence because of the very fact they are laypeople who are less knowledgeable and less practicing than the religious and clerical (who are not always more religious or knowledgeable than the laypeople). Yet although Catholics get this point to some extent when it comes to picking their Pope as leader, commonly they too have general elections for lesser leadership positions, despite all the top positions in the Church being appointed positions by the hierarchy. This is pure hypocrisy since if religious hierarchy were the best method to pick a leader then every leader at every level should be chosen via the same method, instead of just the top positions. Of course if the hierarchy were corrupt then naturally such a method wouldn't be the best, nor would any hierarchy of a false faith be anything but corrupt since a false faith cannot have anything but corrupt adherents. Yet the point is that the best method of selecting a leader should be employed at every level no matter what that method is. I believe that method is Shariah because I'm Muslim, but if there were a better method then it must be used at every level. For example if Catholics pick the Pope one way then every leader in the institution should be picked in the same manner. While if say a government chooses their President via election where every registered voter has an equal vote, then for that method to be the best method to pick the President then it must also by definition be the best method for picking every position in that government and every government employee would have to be appointed via a general election where every registered voter's vote counts equally. If this is not practical or deemed the best way for lesser positions then it cannot be deemed practical nor the best method for higher positions. By virtue of disproportionate application, without a consistent method applied at every level in every situation one cannot but be stuck using a method different than the best. Basically by definition if you don't use X method for determining who gets positions #1-infinity then you should not use X method for determining who gets any position at all. If you don't use the same method for everything then you shouldn't use that method for anything. The reason people do not have the best leaders possible nor are positions filled by the best people for the job is because the best method is not being applied or utilized. And where do you learn what the best method for determining leadership is? From God. How do you learn stuff from God? From God via God's book, or by learning it from God's prophet(s). Thus if a community really wanted to follow their prophet, they wouldn't have these committees, societies, board elections, presidents, chairpersons, membership fees, educational fees, etc. Instead of such "religious committees" following the prophetic policies when making communal decisions, these religious rackets are designed to make the popular decisions. Whereas religious leadership is supposed to make the correct unpopular decisions, but the committee members can't even get influence or power unless they attain popularity. Those who gain their position via popularity will have popularity as their priority so as to keep their position, since once they have power they don't want to lose it and thus in reality they have little power because they are afraid to use it lest using it the right way causes them to lose it. Regardless usually organized religious rackets tend to be popular within religious communities, but where do they meet when they make decisions effecting the community? Is it in the public prayer area of the place of worship itself? Of course not! They wouldn't dare concoct their sacrilegious plots in the "house of God" publicly where semi-religious and religious people pray and could observe their diabolical decision making process possibly refuting it or making them anxious due to their sacrilegious audacity. Instead it's all done behind closed doors in secret offices or "meeting rooms". Their chosen setting for their meetings proves how unreligious they are, because if they were religious they would have their religious meetings that decide the affairs of "God's house" and place of prayer at God's house itself, especially when it's known the devils avoid such locations. How in the world can "religious leaders" determine the correct decisions for the religious community, who worships at a house of God, to take when they aren't even having the meetings take place in God's house? Clearly that shows they don't want God to help them making the decisions which inevitably effect God's house and his worshippers. Muhammad would have his religious meetings with his advisors and the members of the community in the same exact spot where he led the public prayers. Literally the same spot he led the prayers in the masjid was the same exact spot where he would make decisions regarding the masjid or Muslim community or state. Which especially regarding politics is highly significant. What political leader today has their office in the "house of God" and their "political seat of power" where they make decisions is the same place they publicly go to pray? Why don't people see these leaders for the types of people they truly are? Really how can you consider a person to be religious if the biggest and more important decisions they make in their life is made at locations other than the house of God? How can God be guiding your decision-making process if you aren't making those decisions in God's house? God could still guide one's decisions outside of his house, and frequently does but logistically you are more likely to be guided if you are inside of God's house at the time rather than outside of it. Why? Because God said so, his prophets said so and nearly every religion teaches that the devil's don't enter God's houses much or in as much force as they possess outside of them. So while some may think it unusual for one to spend lots of time in a place of worship, truly it's the smart thing to do. Personally I doubt the legitimacy of a religious organization's decisions if the decisions are made in secret and/or not in the public prayer areas of places of worship. Religious clubs are supposed to make religious decisions, not make decisions about religion. Thus if they are making good religious decisions they would be meeting in a religious place, not some classroom, office, cafeteria, hall or board room. If they can't even pick the best religious place to meet in when making decisions how can they make the best decisions? Simply put they can't, don't and won't, that was obvious when they created a religious club with paid membership built on sacrilegious political doctrines with positions obtained/determined via illegitimate unjust sacrilegious methods. When you actually think about it, their secret meetings in non-religious places/rooms almost implicate them as conspirators who prefer devils to be present at their decision-making meetings rather than angels. In comparison prophets would have their meetings in public with the people in the prayer areas of the houses of worship. Although just because someone frequents a place of worship in itself doesn't mean they are good people or even religious, since hypocrites frequented Muhammad's masjid in Medinah and they were the worst of all people and least religious. Similarly if one was in a house of idolatry or one where false religions are taught and other than God is worshipped in then that would be one of the worst places to be in as those places despite being advertised as "houses of God" would literally be the houses/temples of devils and you will find the worst types of people in them. Trust me, I used to spend lots of time in churches, you find the worst types of people there; though most Christians consider those types to be the best but they think that because those people are great actors/actresses and both the thinkers and those thought of are ignorant regarding religious realities and truths. Yet if even the hypocrites in the prophet's time who didn't even believe in his religion frequented the prophetic places of worship then what does that say about modern religious leaders who come to the places of worship even less than hypocrites used to do? Hypocrites in the past were more religious than most of the modern religious leaders/organizations who "lead us" today. Truly those who faked it with the prophets were more religious than those who actually believe in those prophets and practice their religion today. Yet somehow the religious leaders today portray themselves as pious and religious. It's hard to know who is more ignorant regarding religion, our religious leaders who don't know, can't/won't preach and don't practice or us for thinking such leaders are religious or respectable. Honestly I find the religious leaders of the modern era funnier than the professional comedians and clowns. But then again I try not to look in the mirror too much, so that could be why. With the caliber of religious leaders we have today, we don't even need to have Satan and his soldiers as spiritual enemies. Then for the occasional staged events (discussions/meetings) where the public (by which I mean only members who pay) get invited to attend to roleplay and give the illusion of legitimacy to religious organizations, the events still aren't held in the "house of God" or prayer areas but some other nearby location like a banquet hall or something. Customarily such "religious societies" have annual meetings or public events at an eating area where they partake in gluttonous activity all the while thinking they are religious being "involved with religion" doing something God likes. Let's face it those people are coming for food and the opportunity to fraternize, not because of their faith. Think otherwise? See what happens when the food isn't free and it gets turned into a fundraising event, which of course the "religious organizations" hold fundraising events to get even more money out of people than they ordinarily do because "*somehow or for some important unexpected reason they need more, a lot more, and soon, from you, and remember our religion says you should give charity to us*" (perpetually). Whereas I don't mean to mock fundraisers done for legitimate reasons by sincere organizations, but it's just extremely easy for "religious organizations" to have habitual fundraisers and exploit the religion for financial sales pitches. In 2025, ISNF had a $200 per plate fundraising dinner, and for a table of 8 it was $1600 which is no discount but a huge cost because the food they serve doesn't cost $200 per plate. Instead of food if they were actually religious they would sell Salafi books at a markup if they still wanted to fundraise but they value feeding the congregation's guts at exorbitant prices more than their hearts, brains and souls. $200 could get you a big library of Islamic books but this allegedly "Islamic Society" rather than giving something of substance that will benefit people for a very long time, for $200 they give them one plate of food. Is that the prophetic methodology? For example both Jesus and the Jewish Pharisees encouraged people to give in charity to religious organizations for religious reasons, but they did so for very different reasons in slightly different ways. And keep in mind I said that Jesus and the Pharisees both did it "in slightly different ways", so that shows how easy it is to be fooled thinking a group is prophetically motivated when they are in reality profitically motivated, or sincerely motivated versus satanically motivated. Some groups are even sincerely motivated but for satanic reasons due to stupidity. Some of the religious rackets even have paid positions! I'm not joking either. Hopefully you aren't so desensitized by spiritual scam artists that you find the news of religious groups having paid positions to be normal or unshocking. If you aren't shocked by such news then you're probably familiar with a lot of bad phony religious organizations and don't know the reality about them or have a prophetic disposition yourself. So even if there are those organizations with paid positions, the way you feel about those organizations and positions can also indicate quite a few things about yourself and your religiosity. If you think it's perfectly fine and normal to get paid for having a position within a religiously motivated organization then you actually have an abnormal religious disposition at odds with the prophetic perspective. I mean that'd be comparable to thinking it's fine and normal to sell a religious book to somebody. Could you even imagine such religious insincerity? Such authors, publishers and readers don't know the value of the religious information they are buying and selling. My books end up costing me money and any royalties end up going to charity and such royalties don't even cover the cost of publishing to begin with. The only reason I list my books for sale is because if I don't then the potential readers who benefit will be limited to my own small social network. So to maximize benefit to the world I'm forced to sell but then because I don't have the personal budget to market and advertise effectively, I actually lose money when publishing costs + time spent + advertising costs are weighed against the pitiful royalties. The vast majority of authors actually lose money on their books unless they pay hundreds of thousands to get fake TV "interviews" and get advertising agencies. Anyways regarding paid religious positions, those whose position comes with a salary will usually be treated as a person bought with a price tag, that will be replaced and exchanged for someone else if they make unpopular decisions that contravene the majority, their employer or the organization. Ironically both the paid religious leader and the boards/committees tend to blame each other when people complain to them, yet sometimes they both agree and are wrong at the same time. In those instances it's really sad for members of a community who want to practice their religion correctly because those who want to practice correctly frequently tend to be the small non-influential minority, at least in the West. The prophets were rebuked for telling people about religion for free. The fact that our society today makes religious leadership a paid position implies several things. First of all it implies nobody wants the job, because it is very difficult and carries an enormous responsibility hence there is lower supply than demand. Secondly it implies that people are buying religious advice and it is not being freely given. This means that most of the religious advice given today is tainted and not entirely sincere. If it's not sincere then it's probably not sound or correct advice. Let's say a person had a large income from immoral means and then they gave a large donation to a charitable religious organization. If that religious organization was sincere in their religion they would advise the person while returning their donation by saying that they didn't want that person's illicit contaminated money and that the person should quit gaining sinful wealth. How many religious organizations would do that today? However just because a religious organization may not be sincere doesn't necessarily mean their religion is wrong, they could just be hypocritical. A hypocrite doesn't have your best interests for salvation in their heart and being around them might contaminate you with the disease of hypocrisy. Whereas the religious leader who is paid can never make the difficult unpopular right decisions because their financial interest conflicts with the interests of their religion. To illustrate this one time a religious leader told me that a reason my parents don't listen to my advice to them regarding religion is because I live in their house and get paid by them for doing work in and around their house, and that if I really wanted them to respect and listen to my religious advice then I had to move out of their house and be financially independent. Now perhaps you agree with such a sentiment. However the religious leader who told me this at the time was living in a house owned by the religious organization who paid to maintain/repair it and they also paid his salary. Thus when he criticized me saying my parents won't listen to my religious advice or instruction because I live in their house and financially get paid by them, he was in the exact same boat except the religious organization he is supposedly the leader of had the role with him which my parents had with me. So if he is correct in his analysis of my situation, as most would agree, then he must also be in a position without influence over the religious organization even though he is publicly portrayed as the community's leader. And that is why many religious communities pay their leaders, because the organizations know that if they pay the leader then they will watch what they say and be flexible due to the financial risk. But the religious leader who isn't getting a single penny from the people, he will fearlessly tell them exactly what they need to hear even if they don't want to hear it and apply pressure to stop his preaching the religion as the prophets taught it. That's why most places won't accept some religiously qualified person who offers to lead the community for free because they know that the free preachers plan on making them into good religious people who don't live the sinful lifestyles they currently enjoy and want to maintain. Some religious organizations go so far to maintain the status quo of their power over people that they will reject a free offer by a qualified leader in order to pay someone else who is less qualified to lead the community in religious worship. Regarding religious leadership you get what you pay for. If you want someone cheap in morals, knowledge and religiosity then pay them money and if you want someone who is religiously knowledgeable, upright and beneficial then the only payment they will accept is sincere attention and religious actions when they advise people to practice their religion in the correct prophetic way completely. As some say there should be separation between church and state, I say religious leadership must be financially independent of the people they are leading. Religious leaders don't get paid by those they lead, followers get paid by those they follow. A good religious leader can't be hired because their services aren't for sale. The services of a good religious leader are given for free because their advice is priceless. The more they are paid monetarily then the less their advice is worth.

Instead of religious leaders, most places of worship have religious employees wearing the uniform and title of a leader without the authority or influence. While you are more likely to find the leaders sinful than sincere. Although frequently people don't even get what they pay for because these "religious leaders" take days off. Can you believe it? Their job is getting paid to help people do what God wants and they take days off? Did God tell them to not guide the people on X day of the week? Did prophets take a day off from preaching and teaching? True religious leaders don't take days off because their religion is too important and being a religious leader is a 24/7 job where the boss is God. There is no "day off" when God gives you a job. God's definition of a religious leader's workweek means you work all week, every week, even when you're weak. When they take a "day off" it's not a day off, it's just a day that they aren't doing their job that's what it is. Oh but these "leaders" don't just take days off, they take vacations to exotic places leaving the sinners who paid them to guide them behind. Could there be a worse example? I don't care what somebody preaches, if they are a religious leader and take days off or vacations then by taking days off they are teaching people it's okay to take a vacation from their religion. Of course they may not intend to teach that but that is what they are teaching. They are what I call "sacrilegious religious folk". Some who are explicitly paid to lead others in prayer don't even show up to the prayers. What does that teach people when the religious leader who literally is getting paid to pray doesn't show up? Why would anybody else come to the place of worship to pray? Why even have a religious leader if they aren't going to come and lead you daily in religious prayers? If they aren't there then they clearly aren't a religious leader because if they were they'd be there leading all of the prayers. These are just some of the lessons these allegedly religious pseudo-leaders teach via their actions, but what they preach via their speech is sometimes even worse. Seriously as much as I detest religious leaders who take "days off", sometimes when you hear what they say you pray that they take more days off. The problem is that originally our religious leaders were the prophets but today our leaders are profiteers. Many see religion as a business and this is not what the true religion is. Religion is a way of life, the true religion is the way of life our Creator wants us to live by. Religion involves both belief and actions, but religious businesses would have us neglect one or the other, or both. I'm not advocating you shouldn't give charity, but consider who your religious teacher(s) is and why. Why would they require your money if the Creator was paying them and their main focus was teaching you to get rewarded in the afterlife? Of course some may say that payment of preachers is necessary so they have time to study to preach, but if that is a true necessity then they should get the minimum that is actually necessary unless the Islamic government is cultivating them and wants to pay them more to prevent others corrupting them with bribes, such as is done with Shariah Court Judges who are paid well to prevent bribes. Yet if it's the case that a religious position is paid then spiritually how can they get paid vacation days then? If they really want a vacation they can have it but it should be unpaid because the whole reason for paying them in the first place is to save time so they can pray, teach and preach not so they can play.

Unfortunately today many "religious people" are really business people and they cannot sell you the ticket to paradise as they claim. Whenever you talk to a religious person, listen to them, or read their materials, always consider the following: Are they advising you or are they advertising to you? Sadly, myself included, many can seem to be sincerely sharing religious advice when they are simply arrogant promoting a righteous knowledgeable self-image. Sometimes people may not preach for money, fame, or power but neither is it for God's sake, they can be addicted to preaching. Though Satan can and does make sincere people think they are addicted to get them to stop, some people preach because doing so makes them feel superior and better than others or it just helps them improve their self-esteem and ego. So even if someone is preaching the truth 100% there can always be underlying motives within that makes them insincere, arrogant and corrupt. Fame will ruin your faith. A sound preacher is like finding a pure freshwater raindrop in a saltwater ocean and finding a sincere sound preacher is like finding a microscopic molecule inside the atom of that fresh raindrop that's in the ocean of saltwater. And then what happens if God blesses you with coming across such a preacher or their message? Most us fail to implement the good they teach us to do. Who is worse, corrupt preachers or those who are too corrupt to be affected and change when exposed to prophetic teachings?

In 2019, a kind doctor, I got a new one every year due to the clinic changing residents, told me that I wasn't doomed to be homeless or live in a group home as others had informed me. This doctor told me that since I was on SSI then it was possible for me to get an apartment within walking distance of a mosque at a discount and move out of my parents and even get married and have kids all without paying taxes to the war machine. This gave me much hope of a better life. As excited as I was about the possibility of marriage and praying in the mosque regularly again I feared having kids while being "disabled" and having minimum poverty level funds would limit their ability to eventually migrate. While researching online, since my parents got internet at their house in 2020, and I was mostly offline the last two years, I learned that some Muslim countries now offered citizenship by investment and others offered permanent residency though both options were expensive. Despite the cost and what most Muslims in America get incorrectly told, it is now feasible that if you have enough money you could move to a Muslim country without a job or schooling and live there amongst Muslims and even buy citizenship in Muslim countries. I figured it was potentially possible that if I got a job and got married and had kids I could eventually save up enough money to migrate and move my future family overseas so we could practice Islam completely as the religion obligates. After moving and paying for a Muslim nation's citizenship I could revoke my American citizenship and finally be free from funding the war machine. The only questions were what kind of job would I be able to get that didn't involve compromising my religion too much and how would I get it and when. It wasn't as though I wanted to be disabled living off the government, I just didn't want to fund war against Muslims and doctors told me I was disabled and couldn't get out by going to school overseas and that the wars against Muslims by America would never end. Since the proposed laws allowing Americans to opt out of having their personal tax dollars fund the military if they objected on religious or humanitarian grounds were defeated in Congress, I figured eventually I would have to compromise on my rule of non-payment of taxes if I was to ever get out of America according to the doctor's plans. But for the time-being at least the Federal Government was paying me rather than me paying them, so in essence my disability was decreasing the funds the Federal government had to spend on guns.

Surprisingly the anti-Islamic Trump administration negotiated a ceasefire agreement with the Taliban and signed the Doha agreement on February 29th, 2020. While the deal was unfair to the Taliban it was still a promise by the USA military to withdraw troops and stop fighting Muslims in Afghanistan with taxpayer dollars. The Taliban kept their part of the deal to not harm American soldiers in their country despite Americans continuing to bomb them contrary to what the USA agreed to do in the treaty. I dreamed the seeds of Shariah would grow and the puppet democratic Afghani regime would be defeated, repent or surrender; since they didn't sign the ceasefire agreement. I hoped Islam could become the law of Afghanistan once again. I was comforted in the fact that if I paid taxes in the future then at least they wouldn't be spent on sinfully killing Muslims in Afghanistan. I was more loyal to the Muslims overseas than American kuffar because religious faith is a stronger bond than nationalism, family and everything. I preferred homelessness despite the hardship rather than the guilt of earning and paying non-Muslims taxes because of loyalty to Muslims who I never met, entirely due to them being Muslims and following Islam as far as I knew. With the ceasefire signed I started applying to halal jobs wherever I could and scheduled some interviews. Then the Covid-19 pandemic occurred and the job search was halted as quarantine took place on a global level.

In early 2021, I mentioned my dispute with Qadri once more to imam Ismail of Masjid Eiman in Buffalo via text, email and on the phone asking if I was wrong to make takfir. Ismail said I could not be banned from the mosque. I just asked Ismail if anything I did was wrong and what I should do to get Qadri to repent from heresy under the circumstances. Ismail said he would talk to Qadri to set up a possible three-way reconciliation meeting. I said Qadri would never agree to that and I don't think it is a good idea anyways due to

ISNF's cease and desist order from all of my communication. Ismail thought otherwise and told me he will just talk to Qadri and everything will be fixed. Later in March 2021 when I called Ismail, he said to me on the phone that he had spoken with Qadri "many times" and Qadri said to Ismail he forgives me for anything and everything I did, BUT Qadri doesn't ever want to have a meeting with me or discuss our different religious beliefs. Ismail told me Qadri wants it to be that I have my beliefs and Qadri has his and we never discuss anything and leave each other alone. However, this is not an Islamic position when accusations of takfir get made due to different creeds. Someone is clearly wrong in a major way and people are upon different religious denominations if not religion itself. Also Ismail said Qadri told him if I want to return to the ISNF mosque again then Qadri has no problem with that BUT I have to contact the ISNF board to get permission because it is not up to him. Whereas since I contacted ISNF in October 2019 and they issued a cease and desist from all contact with threat of arrest if I do ever contact them, as included previously, and which I think Qadri would know about, I figured this was Qadri trying to insincerely entrap me. Realistically how can it be okay with Qadri for me to go back to the mosque where he is imam if simultaneously he never wants to talk to me again about our difference in creed which prevents me from praying behind him and causes me to pursue his employment termination? It is a contradiction since Qadri knows I won't pray behind him until he repents or teaches me of my error in creed so I recant my takfir of him. So after lengthy contemplation on what to do next, since I have to be very cautious due to legal threats of arrest if I communicate with ISNF members by any means, I texted Ismail on June 12th, 2021 three months later that ISNF gave me a cease and desist order etc. and Qadri seems like a Munafiq. Ismail texted me back saying to forget about Qadri and ISNF, just focus on worship and to stop backbiting. This was incorrect and not sincere Islamic advice. Prophetically one of the two parties is guilty of crimes that amount to potential eternal hellfire and Ismail is saying to just ignore what happened, not because that's what Islam says but because that's what his friend Qadri wants me to do. So, after letting my anger at such cowardly possibly hypocritical advice cool down for nearly a month, on July 8th, 2021 I texted Ismail back as follows,

> "Quran 4:148 and hasan al basri said there is no backbiting regarding an innovator. Did the man who urinated in masjid Nabawi get banned and boycotted? No. As per hadith the insane are unaccountable, I was insane when I got banned 4 reading quran during salat and I apologized. It is illegal 4 muslims 2 boycott another muslim for more than 3 days as per hadith as isnf and Qadri do. While ban from mosque is unprecedented. I see 2 logical options 4 u. If Jews/Christians are kuffar u must correct Qadri and isnf error cuz I cant and they wont accept from me. If Jew/Christian not kuffar u must correct me cuz I believe they r and make takfir of Qadri who don't. And hadith say to help ur brother whether oppressed or oppressor by stopping the oppression. Quran says fitna is worse than killing and hadith says deen is naseehah. And on qiyamah this case and all litigants, intermediaries + judges will answer to Allah."

Ismail replied to me saying *"jazakallahu kheirun"* in one text meaning may Allah reward you with that which is good, followed by another text message that said *"I will try my best"*. Yet I haven't gotten any update from him on his efforts in trying to persuade ISNF and Qadri and don't think it wise to seek updates on the matter either. Ismail texted he will try his best by which I hope he meant to fulfill my mission to get Qadri and ISNF to see the truth of the kufr/disbelief of Christians and Jews. Although when I left a voicemail and texted Ismail in 2022 asking if he could help me find a spouse he didn't reply at all so I doubt I will get any results on this issue from him either way. Later I horrifically seen videos online with Ismail lecturing in the ISNF masjid and treating Qadri respectfully as if they were close friends, despite Ismail privately telling me Qadri was in error regarding his creed and Ismail would try fixing him. While writing this book I almost considered reaching out to Ismail to see if progress was made, only to learn he had undergone heart surgery. So now I don't want to cause him any heart stress by bringing up the topic again to him. Yet Ismail's tone seemed to indicate he misunderstands how to deal with heretics of such a degree as Qadri displayed himself to be. Regarding the etiquette of dealing with innovators or Ahl-Bida I wrote the book "Beware of Ahl-Bida" which details the legal restrictions on interacting with people of innovated religious creeds according to the Quran, Sunnah and Salaf. Basically Qadri and ISNF treated me the way Ahl-Bida are supposed to be treated, when Muslims are in power, despite me being as sincere as possible in claiming to be Ahl-Sunnah and Qadri being in truth from Ahl-Bida though he claimed the opposite.

On Ramadan 1st 2021 my grandmother Florence died. I had spent many hours with her since her husband Joseph died in 2017 and she lived in the same house as me for several years before getting her wish to live in her own house with 24/7 nurses to care for her. She never repented from her blasphemous wailing upon Joseph's death saying "God is no good" and I witnessed her live a painful scary accursed miserable life, which I believe was a punishment from Allah for her religious crimes. Being a Christian alone is enough to face such hardship and ultimate hellfire but my grandmother was not even a Christian according to Christianity. She suffered immense pain from various diseases like arthritis and had hearing loss to such an extent that communication was near impossible. Her final years daily schedule consisted of sleeping and watching TV that she barely heard and eating sparingly if she was awake while begging others around her to tell her what she should do with her life. Such is how it is when someone doesn't know the reason Allah created them or the prophetic truth. Florence would repetitively ask, "What should I do? What should I do? What should I do?" in desperate misery and when she prayed at night her prayers were curses against herself. Being deaf she didn't know everyone could hear her prayers, or she didn't care, but when she was in pain she would tearfully pray that God kills her repeatedly. That's what she wanted from God. She didn't beg for paradise or mercy or forgiveness or safety from hellfire or even worldly comfort from her distress. Florence's number one desire from God was that she be destroyed and her supplications to God match word for word what Islam teaches that people in hell will say when they will ask for permanent destruction in hell prior to God forbidding them to speak for eternity. But it wasn't all doom and gloom regarding her religion. When Florence wanted someone to get anything she would ask for "Mary". Not God, or Jesus or a Ghost as the trinitarian Christians propose we should ask for things. Florence asked for "Mary" every time she wanted something good. The problem was there was nobody named Mary around so everyone thought she was senile. But when lucid she would clarify on occasion that she was asking Jesus' mother Mary. This is shirk polytheism that dooms one to eternal hellfire if not repented from, but it was done so much by this former Catholic who was falsely taught to worship Mary instead of God that it became comical. She would ask "Mary" for everything and everyone became Mary to her, even her own relatives. When she wanted water she'd ask for Mary, when she had to get help to go to the bathroom she'd ask for Mary and then when people would come help her she would be further embarrassed because she didn't know if it was Mary or not Mary that was helping her. Sadly she didn't even know she was approaching the death she desired when she died and was deprived of a chance to repent correctly or sincerely. Thus my grandmother's only hope of Salvation is if she was too senile to accept Islam when it came to her and if so then she will be given a special difficult test when raised from the dead on Judgement day to determine if she would've became Muslim had she not been so senile. Yet even if she were that senile what excuse will she have for saying publicly that "God is no good!"? So despite my personal familial bias, based on the facts I know of her I don't think my Grandmother Florence has any shot at paradise even if one claimed without certainty that she qualified to be one of the few who get a special test on Judgement day due to legit inability to embrace Islam in their life. Because one who slanders God in any way is an enemy of God, not someone who is confused about the certain Islamic prophetic truth but desiring to be good. From what I know she died as a polytheist who hated God even according to polytheistic Christian standards. I don't mean to mock my grandmother but her story teaches a valuable lesson for those who utter statements of blasphemy against Allah, whether knowingly or unknowingly. Just the single statement I heard her say after her husband died in that "God is no good" alone could have earned her such an evil end and an eternity in Hell, aside from all the other sins in her life. So the lesson is watch your words carefully. You make one error regarding religion and you might doom yourself so much that it becomes irreparable and you might even damn yourself further in ignorantly seeking relief from your self-imposed curses as my grandmother did in her prayers which I witnessed. After her slander of

God she would be heard asking for evil to be brought down upon herself because God did not facilitate her to ask for goodness from God.

Narrated Abu Huraira:

The Prophet; said, "A slave (of Allah) may utter a word which pleases Allah without giving it much importance, and because of that Allah will raise him to degrees (of reward): a slave (of Allah) may utter a word (carelessly) which displeases Allah without thinking of its gravity and because of that he will be thrown into the Hell-Fire."

Source: Sahih al-Bukhari 6478

Likewise my atheist Paternal Grandfather Ken made similar stupid errors that seem to have doomed him. Currently Ken is still alive at the time I write this, so I don't know what his end result will be. Last I spoke to Ken in 2022 he hadn't eaten solid food for months and he was nervous about going in for yet another potentially life-ending surgery to have his throat reopened so he could eat food again. Ken was/is a business minded individual who is of the opinion that since his forefather faith of

Catholicism is a scam then all religions are money-making scams. I knew this wicked attitude of his already so I didn't bother talking about religion to him but Grandpa Ken of his own accord, just days before having a life-threatening surgery, proudly said, "*I'm done with religion in my life.*" And such a statement is even dumber than what Florence had said in her wailing. Literally the guy can't eat food and is likely to die in surgery in a few days and instead of asking any type of deity there is for blessing or paradise he boasts that he proudly has no place for religion in his life. Can you guess what happened to him? Allah kept him alive and the surgery went on as planned and he survived and Allah hasn't allowed him to eat solid food ever since three years and counting, while he probably lives in a similar condition if not worse condition than Florence did. These people who think Allah will not punish them are already in the process of punishment and don't even know it because Allah doesn't want them to know it until it is too late or they change themselves and deserve the blessing of insight into their true condition and the reality of life/religion.

In August 2021, the longest American war in history ended in retreat as the Afghan withdrawal scheduled by the Trump administration was eventually completed by the Biden administration due to the Taliban's liberation of Afghanistan from foreign and unislamic occupation. Weeks earlier on August 3rd 2021, the puppet president Ghani claimed on TV that within 6 months there would be no more Taliban insurgency and they would be crushed never to rise again. Whereas just 12 days later 100% of the territory of Afghanistan was popularly under Taliban control and the hundreds of thousands of military members who Ghani said were going to fight and defeat the Taliban, peacefully surrendered and joined the Taliban to the consternation of the unislamic international community. The conquest of the capitol city Kabul itself was only a formality to prevent looting due to lack of security. Factually more people were harmed in the famous January 6th 2021, riots at the

White House in the USA when the Trump to Biden presidency transition took place than when the Taliban conquered the capitol city of Afghanistan after 20 years of war from an international coalition fighting against Shariah. Such are Islamic conquests via Jihad. They are as bloodless as possible and as peaceful as possible. Similarly, was the recent conquest of Syria in 2024 by the Sunni Mujahideen over the Shiite and Russian self-declared Crusaders which occurred after 13 and a half years. The Muslims in Syria were confronted with enemies on all sides, even extremist Khawarij like ISIS and Secularist Kurds funded by Euromerica, making the unislamic rebellion turned civil war a multi-party battle royal. Muslims were reduced to a single province in Idlib and clung to patience, prayer and the Sunnah of Muhammad while the world largely sadly abandoned them. Then after an 11-day Jihadi campaign the entire Assad regime territory from Aleppo to Damascus was conquered with less than 2,000 casualties despite the Shiite Alawi Tyrant Bashar Assad having killed more than 600,000 Muslims and disappearing countless others during the previous 13 years when trying to stay in power. The point is when Muslims properly practice Islam, then situations improve despite the forecast and expectations. This book is not about the fiqh of Jihad or a history of recent wars so I cannot elaborate much on these. Yet suffice it to say that when I was told in 2017 that I was crazy to abstain from paying taxes to the USA military until the war in Afghanistan ended or I moved overseas, hoping Muslims would win in Afghanistan, it turned out Allah's promises are true and the expert opinions and plots of non-Muslims vanish when the command of Allah is established. Despite being told I must compromise my religious principles or else be homeless, it turns out being patient upon the prophetic faith is much easier and enjoyable than sacrificing the Sunnah as understood by the Salaf. With the war finally over in Afghanistan, surprisingly to some, with a total Muslim victory it was now time to put my plans to move overseas into action and get a job; before the next American tax-payer funded war on a Muslim nation starts.

During the Covid-19 Quarantine pandemic I took many courses online related to Islam and job training. I obtained a Diploma in Islamic Studies. Yet during my job search, despite having the name of Gregory Heary still, I faced a lot of job discrimination. I would go to interviews, get offered jobs and then after informing the employer I'm Muslim and have to pray at certain times during the day some would explicitly and illegally tell me that I cannot do so. At the time I did not know Muslims were guaranteed the right to pray on-time in the USA workplace since the 1964 Civil Rights Act and that it is illegal to prevent them from taking prayer breaks including preventing Friday prayer at mosques. Whereas since I was still on SSI, without a personal vehicle and forced to keep my total asset count under $2,000 I didn't have much money to spend on a lawyer and my parents didn't want to help me sue any discriminatory employers. They told me I was extreme and to just get any job I could even if it meant not praying on-time. Yet this is the same country where many ignorant Muslims insist they are better able to practice Islam than in Muslim countries which legally guarantee all Muslims get to pray their 5 daily prayers in Masjids and announce the athan 5 times a day throughout the nation. Had I missed a prayer without a Shariah excuse, such as insanity, sleep or menstruation/post-natal bleeding the correct Scholastic opinion is that it is equivalent to apostasy based upon the Quran and Hadith and the opinions of the Sahabah and Salaf. All praises be to Allah that I stuck to prayers instead of payments and didn't compromise my Salat punctuality for the sake of a salary.

After awhile, I decided to use the resources available to me as a SSI job-seeker to have governmental people work with me to help me get a job. I later realized though that these work promoters did not have my best interests in mind. For example, I had an interview where the company offered me a job to create laundry detergent on an assembly line. I wanted this job a lot because it seemed very compatible with my religious values and was free of many workplace sins. The shift was at night and I only would have to do the nighttime and dawn prayers at work. They gave me a contract to sign but said I could only perform the nighttime prayer and not the dawn prayer because everyone has to take breaks at the same time. So I said I would think about it, left deciding not to compromise and told my government helper about what happened. He said he would get me that job and call the interviewer informing them that what they said was illegal discrimination. I waited and never learned what happened and would reapply to the company without ever getting another interview. This advocate later told me months later that he indeed called the interviewer that same week and they denied my claims and said that prayer was no issue. So naturally I wondered why the advocate the government was paying to help me get a job didn't get me the job then as they had offered since I had wanted the job and had a standing offer on the table. Had he told me they said prayer was no issue, contrary to what they said in person, I would've called back and signed the contract. Evidently had that happened though I would have a job and then my governmentally paid advocate would be out of a job very soon and be unable to "help me" any further. So despite the job and interview skills honed by such help, it was not philanthropic aid designed from humanitarian motives. There are entire industries designed like this where people are paid to help others and then don't do their job as best as possible because they want to remain on the payroll "helping others". Eventually after over 2 years of job searching and over 3 years after being declared disabled by the American Federal Government I acquired a job as a Laundry worker at a Hotel in Buffalo, New York. The Department Manager Karen seemingly had no issue with me not shaking her hand after I explained the Islamic prohibitions between cross-gender contact and she said she would allow me to pray whenever I needed. Then the female General

Manager Danielle extended a hand to shake welcoming me to the team. I again had to explain how I don't shake hands with women due to Islam because Karen just stood there smiling and didn't explain on my behalf. As I signed the contract the HR person baited and switched me paying $1.50 less than the advertised rate because when HR asked if the pay rate was discussed during my interview I honestly said the rate was not discussed during the interview. I didn't complain though because I was desperate to work. Yet rather than let the company get a tax credit for hiring a "disabled" person on SSI I decided not to fill out that detail in my paperwork thereby depriving them of the tax credit just as I got deprived $1.50 per hour. Within the department my refusal to touch women was not an issue because Karen only hires men because in her experience women can't and won't do as good of a job in that role. However, my very first day at my very first full-time job while exciting was not without religious tension. When I asked where I could pray I was accommodated, and then my coworker/Supervisor Ace surprisingly said he was going to pray with me too. Yet Ace was just joking at the time due to his friendly humorous demeanor and class-clown personality. I later learned there was another Muslim that worked there in another department who was oddly named Abdul though we never prayed together due to working in different departments. On my second day at work, I was trained by a teenager named Danny whose mother named Pattie also worked at the hotel as a housekeeper. While going about our work, Danny's mom Pattie told him in front of me not to talk to me because *"He's like Abdul."*, who I had not even met at that time. Soon afterwards a different female housekeeper who I had already witnessed cussing out the Laundry department several times the day before said as Danny and I walked by to another lady housekeeper, *"You better move cuz he won't say excuse me, or sorry, he won't talk or say nothing to nobody cuz that's how he is! Don't talk to him and don't even brush up against him cuz that's his religion..."* This character was named Zulaika, a name of Muslim Arabic origin, despite her being an openly lesbian Christian from Spanish Caribbean roots. Zulaika would routinely harass and discriminate against me and speak vulgarly to others in the workplace making a very hostile environment so much so that many would quit their jobs due to having to work with her. I figured out everyone knew I was a Muslim who didn't touch women, because of workplace gossip. So despite illegal discrimination, I just would work my best and be kind and well-mannered as Islam requires while picking my moments to share the prophetic truth if possible or through example via my superior manners obtained from Islam. Another character Bob, who professing to be a devout Christian, witnessed some of Zulaika's discrimination also made discriminatory remarks of his own. But Bob was of higher moral fiber than Zulaika despite both sharing hard to hide enmity for Islam/Muslims. Bob told me something like, *"You have to throw away that Quran in the garbage if you want to come closer to God. Pick up that Bible."*

Now what do you think someone like myself who openly wholeheartedly hates all non-Muslims, believes 100% in Shariah law and has been accused publicly in mosques of being affiliated with violent radical terrorist organizations and banned from mosques with FBI case files on him did upon hearing such a remark? Do you think I chopped his head off on the spot, as the media portrays people with my hate-filled beliefs do? No. Before I share my reaction reflect on the situation. Would this type of comment ever be said to a Muslim living in a Muslim country where the national religion is officially Islam? No. So why would Muslims from overseas want to expose themselves to such a work environment for the sake of alleged worldly gains which don't even add up when you factor in the excessive sinful American taxes? These types of discrimination and derogatory comments don't exist in Muslim lands, even if they aren't fully practicing Islamic laws there and have issues. Furthermore every single Muslim in America has at one time or another felt the hatred and persecution of the non-Muslims with pressure to be ashamed or insulted for being upon prophetic truth. I don't know any Muslim in non-Muslim countries who considers themselves as free from being dehumanized at some time or another. So the question isn't really what I did, it's why would honorable Muslims expose themselves to such an environment when there are many countries where such hostility is prevented by law and enforced to such an extent that it is unthinkable of occurring? Islam is a treasured value in other countries, in America it is combatted harshly with enthusiasm. The only reason I started working is so I can move myself and my family away from America so my kids never have to face such devilishness inshallah. Not everyone is capable of standing up to such mass bullying and religious pressure to conform to kufr. Case in point ISNF bends over backwards to please these types of people in the hopes of being considered equals which is treatment Muslims will never attain from non-Muslims no matter how well-mannered they are. As Allah has promised in the

Quran. Upon hearing the blasphemous put-down advising me to commit an act of disbelief in Islam at work, I had five options according to Shariah law. Out of the 5 options 3 are good options, 1 is sinful in the vast majority of cases except in rare instances and 1 is always sinful and usually a type of minor or major disbelief. The 5 options are as follows: 1. If you witness an evil/error you forbid/prevent it via your hand/force. (This is ideal but not always possible, practical, wise or the best option.) 2. If you witness an evil/error you forbid/prevent it by using your tongue or communication abilities. (This is more common, and frequently more practical, wise or best.) 3. If you witness an evil/error then based on 4:140 of the Quran you hate it in your heart but instead of using force or communication to forbid/prevent it, instead of denouncing it you simply leave the place of sin (preferably with social dignity if possible, although the one who flees sin is always honorable with God) so you are no longer witness to it. (This type of forbidding is sometimes socially difficult but very effective since the forbidding via the movement of the feet and lack of presence imply and convey a sense of denouncing that typically provides less risk of social backlash.) Basically if you can't forbid something then just walk away so you are away from the evil. 4. You hate it in your heart but do nothing at all to stop the evil/error either by the hand or tongue nor do you flee the scene of the crime (evil/deviance/sin). In most cases this is sinful and amounts to conveying implicit acceptance of and silent promotion of the evil. Very rarely does one have a valid excuse to do this instead of options #1-3, but Satan always makes us think we should. 5. People witness evil/error and join in, praise, enjoy or promote it. (This is nearly always sinful except in cases of military espionage and sometimes doing this can be minor or major disbelief.) Of these 5 possible options for every scenario one must have knowledge of the nature of the evil, as well as how to choose the best option of 1-3 (rarely ever 4) and how to best enjoin good/forbid evil after deciding which type of 1-3 steps to take. Every scenario and circumstance is different and frequently little time is afforded to one before they must make a decision. Hence one must prepare for such situations in advance by gaining the knowledge of what is right/wrong and how to correctly enjoin good/forbid evil in the most effective prophetic manner in every possible scenario. Much of it though is based on trial and error where unfortunately you end up upsetting a lot of people before experience teaches you how to wisely and most effectively enjoin good and forbid evil as an individual. Scholars are the ones who disseminate that type of knowledge. So basically in my case I could refute Bob which might've inflamed the situation leading to more sinful remarks, I could leave the environment which might have resulted in me being fired since I was on the job, or I could change the topic. Those were the only three Islamically legal options which I felt I had to forbid the evil in such a scenario. So I ignored the comment, smiled at Bob politely and pretended I didn't hear him changing the topic. I didn't go into a lengthy refutation or explain how it is rather difficult to throw away the Quran that is partially memorized within the heart and mind. Basically I changed the topic without comment and later utilized a similar phrase to encourage giving up difficult sins though the Quran is a blessing rather than a vice. This is how the Quran teaches to repel evil with what is better. Even though with my extensive biblical knowledge I could have gone tit-for-tat I played the slow game and remembered how I once was when I was a Crusader Christian who hated all Muslims and Islam. My coworker Jeff twisted his head and looked at me in stunning disbelief at my tolerance not believing how a super religious Muslim who even stops working to pray could withstand such a direct offensive insulting religious remark in their face and not even display any anger. Yet this is what Islam teaches Muslims to do in the face of opposition, our polite hatred has manners that is exercised even when our enemies combat us illegally and oppressively. I could've had Bob fired or at least critically condemned for that remark but in the long-term how is that going to help him realize the truth of Islam so he can become Muslim and enter paradise? At the end of our time working together Bob would grow to consider me as a friend despite my hateful position towards him and all of the other non-Muslims remaining the same. I even asked Bob on one of our last days working together how he would rank me as coworkers go, as he had over 10 years at that job, and Bob said I was all the way up at the top among the best. I did leave a gift for Bob behind when I eventually got another job. To respond to his remark and hopefully educate him I left him a copy of my book "A Muslim Analysis of the Bible" thereby answering his derogatory anti-Quranic comment scholastically at length in comparative religion fashion after having formed a relationship so perhaps his ignorance regarding religion will be removed. Similarly, Zulaika also warmed up to me despite her enmity and by the time she departed the hotel she was on relatively good terms with me too. Other characters would come and go at the hotel.

Ace got fired for too much goofery, replaced by his relative Jason. Jason expressed that while he was in prison he was about to become a Muslim himself but then he got released and never ended up converting because religion is harder to practice outside of prison than inside. Jason was seemingly convinced about Islam but he seemed entrapped by the temptations of freedom and the easiness of sin in America. Such a case was similar to Joel in that Joel was convinced of Islam but Satan tricks them with the allure of sin and the difficulty with practicing Islam as a minority in a non-Muslim or unislamic environment. Simply put, if in prison or a Muslim country such people would happily be Muslim but if tested with freedoms and societal pressures they can find excuses to delay doing what they know is right. Jason ironically thought for several months that I was a foreigner despite my name being Gregory because he had trouble imagining how in the world a local Caucasian Buffalonian non-Muslim would join Islam, he was even more surprised when I shared my Christian rap history with him. Alas Jason soon departed as well and surprisingly I was put into a supervisor role against my wishes only 5 months after hire. I hated supervising because of the extra responsibilities and authority with additional religious judgement from God upon supervisors for any mistreatment being too risky for me to enjoy. Supervising others is like doing your job and also having to make sure everyone else is doing their job too and it takes all the fun out of the workplace because it's your butt on the line if someone else disobeys or does wrong. Personally I prefer to lead by example and rather than order another to do something I'd rather do it myself, but professionally such a personality is not very compatible with a supervisory position because good supervisors have to delegate rather than take the whole burden of the workforce upon their back, even though they will be judged by God for everything their delegates do. Basically supervising is a type of rulership and rulership is a very risky religious role. Only a fool desires leadership and authority because they don't understand the spiritual consequences. I served a total of 5 non-consecutive days being Supervisor of the Laundry Department and I insisted a promising new hire Derek, who was Danny's brother, or anyone else be made supervisor instead of me. Derek despite being another former Marine, albeit without combat experience, didn't have issues with my religion or religiosity and we'd actually have conversations about religion at length. Despite Derek having a huge red cross tattooed on his back he actually espoused some Hindu beliefs such as reincarnation and Karma due to his dad being Hindu. Then the hotel started getting actively incarcerated prisoners to work for them in order to get tax credits from the government. One of these prisoners nicknamed Tank had a Muslim mother and was raised Muslim but fell into crime as a youngster selling drugs etc. He said he knew I was Muslim just by looking at me due to my beard and pants above the ankles. One day Tank decided to test me in front of Supervisor Derek and asked what I believe about people like him, Derek, Karen and people who don't practice Islam but try to be good. So I replied similarly to how I explained in my book "The Sunnah of Sacred Hatred" gently politely explaining on the spot how God hates all people who don't worship God correctly whether that's by not praying their five obligatory daily prayers or by being upon false religions. I shared how I hate all such people personally but because I hate them only because God hates them then I treat them case by case how God taught us to treat them. Plus since anyone can change at any time my love and hate for people is not constant and is subject to change if I see apparent signs that indicate God loving or hating them. Whereas I further explained how seemingly "good people" can be enemies of God and despite being charitable or "good to people" treating co-creatures nicely is not enough to be a good person in the sight of God. Good treatment to others is just one aspect of worshipping God correctly, if you commit heresies but are the best mannered person you are much eviler than the rude person who worships God correctly. Ideally the prophetic faith is practiced 100% with all your relationships but your relationship with God is more important than the one with other creatures and God is not going to reward a disbeliever who is good to other creatures or consider them as good because they are disobeying and in major violation of God's laws regarding monotheism. I further added that just because someone is an enemy of God spiritually that doesn't mean you get violent treating them like a military combatant in a warzone because that's not how prophets taught us. Additionally any "goodness" a disbeliever in God does is rewarded by God for them in this life but they get nothing in the afterlife for it except for a better spot in Hell, since by busying themselves with goodness they were less evil and less sinful than other enemies of God who busied themselves with badness. Lastly I stressed the important thing is how you finish your life, because someone could be loved by God today and hated by God tomorrow if they change for the worse or they could be hated by God now and loved by God by the time they die upon goodness and I cited the hadith which prove this fact thereby preventing any misunderstandings thinking my love/hate was non-flexible. So Tank then told me he knew that's what I believed already about them all and that he just wanted to see if I would say it out loud in front of everybody; then we laughed. I taught this hatred publicly at work as politely and calmly as possible and there was no blowback or outrage because it is prophetic truth that the prophets taught people to hate those who disbelieve in prophets and their religion. That's why God puts them in Hell after they die, because God hates some and loves others since nobody is equal to each other contrary to what philosophers incorrectly postulate. The problem is people get confused due to misinterpretations and misapplications of hate by disbelievers and extremists alike. So I told all my non-Muslim coworkers who were present in detail how and why I hated them for religious reasons with a smile on my face and they had no issue with it. Yet the ignorant Muslims then cave and say this cannot and should never be done to such an extent they deny it as part of the religion and change the prophetic creed to suit their own inabilities at understanding and reacting under pressure. So they sell their souls to the devil in their cowardly fear of the enemies of Allah knowing they consider them hated enemies of Allah. Sometime later another character appeared at the hotel named Marcus. This guy had a twisted sense of humor and he threatened to fight me after work just for fun but I didn't think he was serious. However others took his threats seriously and I heard he even got written up by management for his intimidating threats to me though I never complained myself. By this time though I didn't even have to defend myself in the workplace because through my Islamic manners and work ethic the non-Muslims, whom I had openly expressed hatred for, would defend me in my presence and absence to get Marcus to act professionally. In fact, Derek's mom, Pattie, who herself told her son Danny on day two that he shouldn't talk to me, rushed to my defense against the threats of Marcus and publicly said, *"Why would you want to fight Greg? He's the nicest one out of anyone here."* I mention this to show how despite the heretic Qadri of ISNF insisting I was an evil Khariji terrorist, the non-Muslims defended me from their own co-religionists by labeling me as the nicest person in the building despite my enmity of them which was publicly preached by that time. Thus by uncompromisingly sticking to the truth Allah gave me the protection and respect the liberal Muslims crave to achieve from disbelievers for which they sell-out the faith in the hopes of smelling. Eventually my charm worked on Marcus too. Two other prisoners entered the Laundry department as well during my tenure but to my surprise they were claimants to Islam. Though currently incarcerated on work-release these Muslim prisoners would pray with me sometimes. That's when things took a difficult turn. For these Muslims were imprisoned for unislamic crimes and a little less knowledgeable about Islam and rough around the edges manner-wise. Prior to them working with me everyone else knew I would pray at the earliest minute possible on-time during the workday, sometimes three times a day during winter. The problem was I couldn't compel or force the other Muslims to pray with me and had to walk a delicate balance of choosing whether I'm going to pray on-time alone at the earliest possible valid time or wait until they were also ready to pray at work so we could get the multiplied reward of praying together. Sadly despite me fighting hard for the right and ability to pray on-time at work they didn't value our blessing as much and feared praying at work lest that cause them to get sent back to prison for not working. Since it was Summertime, most days there was a valid way for them to pray their 5 daily prayers outside of the work shift, especially days we got out of work early. So technically we didn't have to pray together if they didn't want to and I wasn't going to force anyone to pray with me because it is unislamic to do even to Muslims let alone non-Muslims. Yet I knew this type of arrangement wouldn't work in the wintertime when multiple prayers might come in during one shift. In winter we would be faced with a situation of either we pray at work or we miss an obligatory prayer, and I wasn't going to miss a prayer. So the question was are these Muslim prisoners going to pray with me daily in Winter when they are sometimes lazy to do so in Summer, or is it going to turn into a situation where I'm telling non-Muslims it's time for me to pray and other Muslims are not doing so nor praying? Personally I follow the strong correct position that if a Muslim man misses a prayer without insanity, accidental sleep or accidental forgetfulness then that is an act of apostasy that takes one outside the faith of Islam which must be repented from as soon as possible. So fearing another case of possible religious conflict and takfir while also realizing my migratory goals would be sped up if I increased my income then I decided to start looking for another job. Despite all my efforts to practice Islam in America and get a job it turned out having other "Muslims" work with me was the reason that made me take steps to quit.

This is because unislamic Muslims can have negative influences on one's character due to lowering the natural guard that one has up against non-Muslims due to the hatred for them. Since one loves all Muslims as long as they are Muslim despite their major or minor sins and hates all of the non-Muslims despite their major or minor "good deeds" which aren't even considered good in God's sight due to incorrect intentions and unprophetic methods, then Muslims naturally influence Muslims more. Despite non-Muslims telling me when I was off the other Muslims didn't pray at work like I did, such testimony was not accepted by me since they are known as gossipy back-biting liars. However, I feared a scenario where I prayed alone and then witnessed the other "Muslims" miss a prayer time window because then we would have a problem with them calling themselves Muslim if they weren't practicing. This is because there is no such thing as a non-practicing Muslim. You can be an extremely sinful Muslim but even still if you practice you practice, if you don't' you aren't one of us even if you say you are. Likewise, even if you practice your creed can nullify your practices. But if you aren't' even practicing then by default it is known you are fraudulent. But how do you tenderly walk this tightrope act with non-Muslims surrounding you in the workplace while realizing these Muslims are fresh out of prison life and criminal culture knowing very little about Islam? If I publicly kick them out of the faith they might just leave altogether and not even try to be Muslim ever again. Whereas if I patiently taught and motivated by example then maybe even if they were religiously technically non-Muslims due to not praying sometimes then perhaps by them thinking they are Muslims they will stick to it despite the pressures to apostate and eventually they will grow to practice properly 100%. Thus it was a delicate situation to be in and avoidance was my reaction since I had little experience with such a scenario. Eventually all praises be to Allah the Muslim prisoners would often pray with me on-time when necessary and I personally did not witness them miss a single prayer time-window. If I had seen them miss a single prayer time-window we would have had big problems but I never witnessed them miss a prayer and didn't take offense that they occasionally choose to pray outside of work instead of with me. I gave them the benefit of the doubt and even if they weren't praying it would be better for them to be treated as ignorant fools who didn't know that missing one salat was kufr than give them a frightening admonition or ultimatum that if they missed a prayer it would lead to boycotting or takfir. The general rule is you always make every excuse you can to keep an apparent Muslim within the fold of Islam and only as a last resort is an apostate or heretic label ever used in an deeply analyzed emergency that is 100% certain based on hard facts. All praises be to Allah that when Winter came they ended up praying with me every day I worked at the hotel without any prayer time-windows expiring. Surprisingly I also learned that Marcus, who had previously wanted to fight me, had once converted to Islam in the 1990s and used to go to the same Salafi masjid in Buffalo that I attended for Friday Prayers. Marcus had fallen out of practice though as he relapsed into his previous lifestyle. Marcus was like Tank in that regard in that they knew Islam was true but they just couldn't practice themselves in a non-Muslim environment because of the traps of the devilish society. Yet despite Marcus initially publicly wanting to fight me, we developed a relationship too. After finding out he was once Muslim I asked Marcus if he wanted to pray with me and the other Muslims at work when the time came. Marcus admitted he forgot how to make ablution and pray because it had been so long since he prayed but it seemed to me that he was willing. Later that very same day before it was time for prayer, Marcus got fired on the spot; so we never ended up praying together. Yet in hindsight his past enmity towards me was likely a test by him to see just how Islamic I was and how I would react if threatened physically by an apparent non-Muslim, similar to how Tank tested my creed publicly regarding love/hate despite knowing what Islam teaches in such regards. Such is Islam and the peculiarity of people, there is no room for half-heartedness in belief or practice of Islam. If you claim Islam then you have to commit wholeheartedly every second. Once you utter the shahada to become a Muslim that is a lifelong contract/covenant with Allah that is going to be tested by devils until you die and get resurrected and finally enter paradise if Allah wills.

Later I'd end up getting five other jobs, some blue collar and some white collar. Sometimes I was the only Muslim and other times I'd find other Muslims in the workplace. Sadly sometimes those Muslims I worked with at later jobs who were not prisoners on work-release had less pride in their faith and adherence to praying together than the prisoner Muslims did. It's almost understandable for actively incarcerated Muslims fearing prison to fear taking a break to pray together if it wasn't absolutely necessary, but when you are then with non-prisoners on a white collar job where you can take breaks anytime you please and they neglect praying together for no good reason at all shows the state of the Muslims and Islam in America. Once I even had a job processing USA passports. Clearly passing the background check to gain access to government databases despite ISNF's claim of ISIS affiliation in the past must have meant their terrorist case against me was totally baseless according to the USA government itself. Yes, an alleged terrorist such as myself was allowed by the USA government to process passport applications because the government knew I was innocent from the slanders of the Muslim community. Now I work remotely in the legal industry while working towards getting a higher paying remote job that will qualify me to get a remote work visa to move to the Arabian Peninsula in a few years inshallah, where I then plan to buy citizenship from one of the Muslim countries currently offering it and ultimately revoke my American citizenship so I never again have to pay USA taxes funding their anti-Islamic military.

Since becoming employed in 2021, I started the search for a spouse by asking religious members in the community for them to aide me in setting up supervised pre-marital meetings with suitable candidates. Eventually I had to turn to online resources and Salafi matrimonial websites as the American Muslim community resources were sparse, at least for me. As a disclaimer most of the so-called Muslim matrimonial websites operate in forbidden means and are dating sites in disguises or scams. At the time I was only able to find three platforms that actually followed Islamic rules for such sites wherein the female's guardian would be the point of contact. During my courtship process I would send every potential candidate a 40-page PDF summary of how I got banned from the ISNF masjids and thus was diagnosed with mental illness. Within this PDF my religious positions regarding disbelieving Christians and Jews as well as Hatred were explained well therein and I wanted to ensure my future wife and I were on the same page. Plus you cannot hide illnesses from marital matches either. Now I didn't put on my profile that I got mental illness but every person that I got into contact with I let them know my traumatic story. There were about 5 different potential candidates I sent my story to before I ended up getting engaged. Every single family I sent my story to had no issue with me making takfir of Mr. Qadri due to him uttering heretical blasphemy and everyone agreed that Christians and Jews are disbelievers. Some of the potential matches even consoled me saying how they felt sorry I had to endure such abuse from a cruel individual. Not a single person to this day in any context has ever said as Qadri said that Christians and Jews are other than disbelievers or that we aren't to hate non-Muslims. Ultimately Allah blessed me with a suitable match and I got married in a Shariah court in Dubai, UAE in 2023. Since according to Islam a Muslim woman can only marry a Muslim man and I was getting married in a Shariah court then because my legal name was Gregory Heary I needed a document proving I was indeed a legit Muslim. I ended up getting a basic Muslim conversion certificate from the Niagara Wheatfield masjid from Mr. Agwa. He was the imam who diagnosed me in 2017 as having magic done to me by Qadri. So out of all of WNY the guy who knew I made takfir of Qadri and himself once said Qadri did magic to me was the guy who certified my Islam so I could get married overseas. There was just one issue on the wedding day. My document was not up to diplomatic standards because it didn't have a date on it. So graciously the Shariah Court verified my Islam verbally and scheduled an extra appointment so I could get a diplomatically graded Muslim certificate proving I was officially Muslim according to Shariah law according to government standards of Muslim countries worldwide. Following, I have included the images of this original Arabic Shahada certificate and the certified translation to prove the Muslim UAE government says I'm Muslim according to Shariah law despite the American organization of ISNF banning me from two mosques and issuing a cease and desist order from all communication with ISNF members.

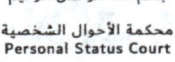

بسم الله الرحمن الرحيم

محكمة الأحوال الشخصية
Personal Status Court

الإشهاد رقم : 2023/4195

إثبات اسلام

طالب الإشهاد : جريجوري هيري
الجنسية : امريكا

بيانات الشاهدين :

	الشاهد الأول	الشاهد الثاني
الإسم	عبدالحميد عبدالرحيم	محمد اكرم خان
الجنسية	الهند	الهند

الحمد لله وحده و الصلاة و السلام على من لا نبي بعده، فإنه فى الاثنين 24 من شهر شوال سنة 1444 هـ الموافق 15 من شهر مايو سنة 2023 م لدى أنا د. أزهري الحاج محمد الشيخ القاضي بمحاكم دبي الإبتدائية - محكمة الأحوال الشخصية حضر المذكور أعلاه وهو بحالته المعتبرة شرعا وقرر قائلا :

أنني كنت (نصراني الديانة) وقد هداني الله وشرح صدري للإسلام منذ 11-12-2011 في امريكا بنطق الشهادتين وأني أشهد أن لا إله إلا الله وأشهد أن محمداً رسول الله وقد برئت من كل دين ومعتقد سواه وقد أخترت لنفسي اسم (عبدالله)

و بناء على الطلب و بحضور الشاهدين عبدالحميد عبدالرحيم و محمد اكرم خان أصدرنا هذا الإشهاد للعمل بموجبه

التوقيع
القاضى /د. أزهري الحاج محمد الشيخ

صفحة 1 من 1

هذا المستند موقع و معتمد الكترونياً و يمكنكم التحقق من صحته بالدخول على موقع محاكم دبي (خدماتنا الالكترونية العامة - الاستفسارات)

TRANSLATION CENTER
Legal Translation
In the Name of Allah, the Most Gracious, the Most Merciful

DUBAI COURTS   **GOVERNMENT OF DUBAI**

(BARCODE)   (QR CODE)
3/1/2023/5151

PERSONAL STATUS COURT
Certificate No. 4195/2023
Declaration of Embracing Islam

Applicant:	Gregory Heary	
Nationality:	USA	
Witnesses' Details:		
	First Witness	**Second Witness**
Name:	Abdul Hamid Abdul Rahim	Mohammad Akram Khan
Nationality:	Indian	Indian

Praise be to Allah the One, May Allah's peace and blessings be upon the last prophet, thereafter, on Monday, 24th of Shawwal 1444 A.H, corresponding to 15th of May 2023, before me, I, **Azhari Al Haj Mohammad Al Sheikh**, the Judge at Dubai Court of First Instance– Personal Status Court, the above mentioned person appeared in his legal capacity and stated as follows:

"I was (a Christian) and now Allah has guided me and opened my heart to Islam by uttering the two declarations of faith, I witness that there is no God but Allah and that Muhammad is His slave and His messenger, on 11/12/2011 at the United States of America. I hereby declare that I am released from any other religion and faith but Islam. Furthermore, I have chosen a new name for myself, i.e. (Abdullah)."

Upon the applicant's request and in the presence of the witnesses **Abdul Hamid Abdul Rahim** and **Mohammad Akram Khan**, we issued this certificate to act accordingly.

Signature
Judge/Dr. Azhari Al Haj Mohammad Al Sheikh
(Barcode Affixed)
3/1/2023/5151/JD1787

Page 1 of 1

This document is signed and authenticated electronically, you may verify its validity by visiting Dubai Courts website (our public E-Services – inquires)

As you can see the Shariah Court itself made it a declarative stipulation of my Islam that I be *"released from any other religion and faith but Islam"* and it had included details that I used to be Christian before. This is because Christians are disbelievers according to Islam and to become a believer/Muslim one must renounce all religions including Judaism and Christianity. So there is no leeway room for someone to say Jews and Christians are anything other than disbelievers in Islam, as Qadri heretically teaches in America or as ISNF blasphemously teaches in their interfaith events that "no faith has a monopoly on salvation". Additionally as a bonus my name was technically finally officially or unofficially changed to Abdullah according to the UAE Muslim certificate. My mom and I enjoyed our three-week trip to the UAE very much and it was a very eye-opening experience regarding the blessings of Muslim government. My non-Muslim mom openly says to this day that she didn't want to come back to America because it was so much better there than in America. So when you have non-Muslims saying they'd prefer to live in Muslim lands and they aren't even Muslim then how can Muslims in non-Muslim lands possibly justify their migration to dar ul kufr and remaining there falsely claiming it's better for them? Even if there are some flaws there is no comparison to the blessings of being in a Muslim majority nation where Islam is the official national religion when compared to a secular or non-Muslim majority country. To those Muslims who have never been to a Muslim majority land, you have truly lost out and foolishly don't know what you are missing. Don't believe the lies told by those in the non-Muslim lands. Go yourself and explore and experience. Just hearing the Athan alone five times a day where there are so many masjids that you can hear the qiyam in one masjid while you are in the other is a blessing kafir countries cannot provide. To even miss a single salat in jamat at all in a Muslim country requires one to do so purposely despite the whole society structure facilitating and promoting community worship. Whereas in America you not only can't realistically pray 5 times a day in the masjids 35 times a week, as laws in Muslim countries allow and promote, but American "Muslims" might not even have enough people to form a jamat in the masjids or have genuine Muslim leaders to pray. Qadri being a case in point where he's not even a Muslim but he's in charge of a mosque to an extent that he kicks Muslims out, boycotts them and reports them to the kafir police in the name of Islam and the Muslim community. It's hard not to practice Islam in a Muslim country as a Muslim. Whereas in a non-Muslim country they make it hard to practice Islam and the innovators there will further punish you if you try too much because your pitiful islamicness according to Western standards is too flavorful for the dilutors' tastebuds.

Another incident that happened in a mosque in America, I witnessed in 2022, was when a guy called Yakub claimed he was a prophet after the Friday Jumuah. Yes, I saw and heard with my own ears an individual heretically claim they were a prophet in a mosque. I thought they were either insane or afflicted with a heretical 5-percenter false understanding. Yet that person claiming prophethood in a mosque was treated with kinder manners than Qadri and ISNF treated me. I don't fully know what happened to the self-proclaimed prophet Yakub, because I left to go to a medical appointment before seeing how his dialog turned out and never saw him in that mosque again afterwards. Though still I know he wasn't reported to the police, or given a ban or cease and desist order by the mosque leaders despite preaching heresy of epic proportions to Muslims. The point is that heretical innovators or Ahl-Bida treat the true Muslims upon Salafiyyah worse than they would someone falsely claiming to be a modern prophet.

In October 2023, Khalid Qazi's deviant MPAC-WNY group had another interfaith event at the ISNF masjid noor where Mr. Qadri serves. It was announced as follows:

In Co-Sponsorship with Buffalo Stake of the Church of Jesus Christ of Latter-Day Saints, Congregation

Havurah, The Islamic Society of Niagara Frontier, Jaffarya Center, Masjid Nu'Man, Network of Religious Communities, North Presbyterian Church, and Westminster Presbyterian Church of Buffalo

THE WALK OF ABRAHAM

THE FOURTEENTH ANNUAL

Wednesday, October 11, 2023

During this event the Mormons, Jews, Shia members of Jaffarya Center, the heretical black supremacist "Nation of Islam" of Masjid Numan, and Presbyterian Christians all gathered together in a interfaith banquet at masjid noor. It's entirely impossible for someone like Mr. Qadri or even a genuine Scholar to preach to these 8 different religious groups simultaneously converting them all to Islam or even trying to connect them together when they have such diverse contradicting creeds. So this meeting is further indication for me that if Mr. Qadri as leader of masjid noor tolerates such diverse religious interfaith cooperation in his masjid after all that happened between us and the advice I gave to him directly and through Ismail, Anwar and others then Mr. Qadri to this day must still be upon the kufr that Jews and Christians are not kuffar and has even evolved further to include the Shiites and NOI sects as non-disbelievers.

In further attempts to resolve my ordeal, I reported the spiritual abuse of Mr. Qadri to the website insideshaykhsclothing.com which is for victims of abuse by Imams in the USA and they said they don't resolve differences in aqeedah/creed. I also reported this situation to facetogether.org which is another organization devoted to Muslims who abuse positions of authority in the USA and Canada but they said my problem is beyond their scope to handle. I also emailed the Shariah Board of NY in May 2021 explaining the matter and asking them if they could arbitrate between me and Qadri/ISNF but got no response from them. Yet then later the same Shariah Board of NY gave a lecture at the ISNF masjid noor on "Halal Food" despite my case I submitted for Arbitration according to Shariah law against Mr. Qadri due to him being heretical.

Again, similarly with my matrimonial quest, all the organizations I contacted agreed Jews and Christians are disbelievers according to Islam but they just have no capacity to bring action against ISNF or Qadri despite their blasphemies due to the political, religious and legal structure of America. Other individuals say Qadri and ISNF aren't even worth the time/effort to correct and to let them go to hell upon their foolishness. Or they don't comment at all on my case thinking I'm a mental illness patient with crazy claims or that it is too much information for them to be bothered with.

Based on my experiences with Mr. Qadri I label him a Munafiq afflicted with a Neo-Murjiah type of fear of takfir of known kuffar but I'd be willing to conditionally revoke takfir if he makes his repentance known based on condition that it's not a lipservice false repentance. Yet so far Mr. Qadri makes no efforts to repent or reconcile. So, despite the stress/risk I make takfir of Mr. Qadri for the time being until Allah provides an alternative that I deem lawful. Which would be either Mr. Qadri's repentance, Qadri's termination/resignation or someone correcting me and my beliefs if they are erroneous/wrong so I can repent. Yet since everywhere and everyone I go to ask about the matter agrees with me, even if they are publicly upon other than Islam, then it is overwhelming to consider Mr. Qadri as wrong as I had concluded. I'll be the first to admit I was wrong and insane in some things I did during our dispute. I've even apologized to Mr. Qadri and ISNF via email and would do so again if necessary but cannot currently do so due to the cease and desist order from all communication. Mr. Qadri clearly expressed unislamic beliefs of kufr to me and then oppressively boycotted and banned me and basically got away with the crime so far, as it would appear to many.

Regarding my main mistakes of innovatively speaking only Arabic that compounded the problem or publicly not praying behind Mr. Qadri these are both errors that are less than disbelief in Islam. The errors Mr. Qadri made are much more severe and my errors are a result of the extreme circumstances that hypothetically should never exist. You truly have to search very extensively to find any relevant information on what should be done in the situation I found myself in. So naturally being put in an extreme scenario where as a 6-year non-Arab Muslim in a non-Muslim majority land which is hostile to prophetic Islam where the local masjid prayer leader expresses clear-cut kufr and stubbornly refuses to change caused extremism. I didn't know what to do and few would be expected to know what to do if they found themselves in my situation. The mistake of only speaking Arabic limiting my speech is easily identified as an innovative method I used ignorantly. Regarding me publicly refusing to pray behind Mr. Qadri this is something Scholars have disagreed and debated on, and it is not automatically a clear-cut error or innovation as many may unwisely presume. Many incorrectly use the rulings pertaining to obeying or praying behind "the Imam" in authority which are for the political government leader of the Muslim nation and misapply them to the local "imam" at a basic masjid building. Regarding the political Imam then I agree one prays behind the political "Imam" even if it is known he is an innovator IF there is no alternative. Such a prayer itself though is still differed upon as to whether one should repeat it or not depending on the innovation and the circumstances. Yet when you have alternatives everyone agrees you don't pray behind someone who you know is an innovator particularly if their innovation equals disbelief in the religion, as Qadri's did. Now I was wrong to miss congregational prayers by not praying behind Qadri publicly because I should have went to another mosque even though it was farther away. Yet I tried all I could to get Qadri to change his heresy and even offered to set a schedule with him multiple times where if he refused to change his beliefs so they agreed with Islam then I would just go to the ISNF masjid when he wasn't there. Yet Qadri refused to accommodate me in any manner and totally refused all diplomatic efforts. As I explained to ISNF themselves, it was a situation where if I didn't go to the masjid and Qadri missed a salat as he occasionally did, then the masjid may have zero prayers performed in it and thus cease to be a masjid at all and be transformed into a Musallah where only some of the 5 daily prayers are offered there. Thus without Qadri cooperating with me I found myself forced to go to preserve the status of the masjid being a masjid and thereby risk a confrontation. When together with Qadri, had I just prayed behind him even if I repeated it then people would be mistaken regarding his reality. Likewise the pressure of me not praying publicly should have caused a conversation to take place that resolved the dilemma but ignorance and arrogance dominated the arena and such dialog never took place at all. Therefore my mistakes while still mistakes were only made possible if many other extreme mistakes took place. Whereas the ignorance of American Muslims was vastly underestimated by me. So mistakes were made by all involved, may Allah forgive those who repent or don't know better.

Sheikh al-Islam' Ibn Taymiyyah said: "*As for the case of prayer behind one from the people of desires whose innovation falls under the category of kufr, it is here that they disagree over praying the Friday prayer behind him. So they say that such kufr requires it to be repeated, because he prayed behind a disbeliever. But this issue deals with takfir of the people of desires, over which people have become confused. They report two narrations from Malik about it, two opinions from ash-Shafi, as well as two narrations from Ahmad. The same with Ahl Kalam, they mention two opinions from Ashari. The madhhabs of the Imams are full of details about it. The reality of the matter is that with a saying of disbelief, then takfir is generally applied to its practitioner. Therefore one of them would say, "Whoever says this, then he is a disbeliever." But the individual who says this is not judged to be a disbeliever, until evidences are established for him that avoiding this makes one a disbeliever...*

So one cannot testify that a particular individual among the people of the qiblah is going to the Fire because of the possibility that one of the conditions of the threat may be absent, or one of the preventive factors may exist in his case. For example; it may be that the prohibition has not reached him, or maybe he repented from doing what was unlawful, or he did tremendous good deeds that would remove the threat of punishment for that unlawful act, or he may have suffered afflictions in this life that atone for it, or he may be among those who are interceded for.

So this is the same with the statements that amount to disbelief on behalf of the speaker, he could be someone whom the texts required to be aware of the truth have not reached, or he could be aware of them, yet not certain of the authenticity, or he could be unable to understand them, or he could have some misunderstandings about it which Allah would forgive him for. So any person among the believers who is mistaken while struggling to seek the truth, then Allah will forgive him for his mistake no matter the case. This is so whether that is an issue of creed or an issue of action. This is the view of the companions of the Prophet and the majority of the Imams of Islam.

Issues are not divided into fundamentals – which one is a disbeliever for rejecting, and branches – which he is not a disbeliever for rejecting. Distinguishing between types of issues in this regard – calling some fundamental issues, and others secondary issues – is baseless, it is not from the companions, nor those who followed them in truth, nor even the Imams of Islam...

It is also contradictory, for if it is said to one who differentiates between these two types of issues, 'What is one fundamental issue for which kufr is applied to the person who makes a mistake in it, and what is the difference between that and secondary issues?' Then he answers, 'A fundamental issue is an issue of creed, and a secondary issue is an issue over correct action.' Then it is said to him, 'But the people have divided over whether Muhammad saw his Lord or not. And whether Uthman was better than Ali or was Ali better? As well, over many a meaning in the Quran and the authenticity of some hadiths. These are some issues related to knowledge of creed, but kufr is not levied for them, by consensus.

Yet the obligation of prayer, zakah, fasting, hajj, and the prohibition of fornication and wine are issues of action, and the one who rejects this is considered a kafir by consensus.'

If he says, 'The fundamentals are unquestionable.' Then the response is, 'Many issues related to acts are unquestionable, while many of the issues related to knowing are not certain. A matter is unquestionable or uncertain to someone depending upon circumstances. It may be that a matter is unquestionable to a person due to the clarity of the decisive evidence to him, like if a person heard a text from the Messenger and was certain that it came from him. But someone else may not be so sure, by virtue of the lack of certainty that comes with the absence of a text reaching him, or it not being confirmed to him or his inability to understand the proofs…

The point here is that the Madhhabs of the Imams are filled with distinctions between the general category and the individualized case. It is for this reason that a party have mentioned disagreement over that, they did not understand the scope of their sayings."

Following is a collection of the 4 main Sunni Madhhabs rulings on prayer behind an innovator whose innovation is known and confirmed.

Hanafi School:

- "As for the innovator, Abu Hanifa did not allow prayer behind an innovator. Abu Yusuf said: 'I dislike that the imam of the people be a person of innovation or desire.'" [Al-Ikhtiyar Li-Ta'leel Al-Mukhtar (1/58)]

- Al-Badr Al-Ayni said: "Muhammad narrated from Abu Hanifa and Abu Yusuf that prayer behind people of desires is not permissible." [Al-Binayah Sharh Al-Hidayah (2/333)]

- "According to Al-Hulwani, prayer is prohibited behind those who delve into speculative theology." [Tabeen Al-Haqa'iq Sharh Kanz Al-Daqa'iq wa Hashiyat Al-Shalabi (1/135)]

- "In 'Al-Mujtaba' and 'Al-Mabsut': it is disliked to follow an innovator in prayer." [Al-Binayah Sharh Al-Hidayah (2/333)]

Maliki School:

- "Malik said: Innovators should not be married, nor should one marry into their families, nor greet them, nor pray behind them, nor attend their funerals." [Al-Mudawwanah (1/177)]

- Al-Abhari stated: "As for his dislike of praying behind the people of innovation, it is because they are not on the right path, and thus they should not be made imams to be followed. Don't you see that it is disliked to pray behind a sinner? Similarly, the innovator is the same." [Sharh Al-Mukhtasar Al-Kabeer by Al-Abhari (4/633)]

- Abu Al-Asbagh Al-Jiyani reported: "Whoever is known for some sectarian views contrary to the community, like the Ibadis, Murji'ah, Qadariyyah, or the like, one should not pray behind them or behind a deviant imam. Whoever does pray behind them should repeat the prayer, whether in time or afterward, for the prayer is the head of the religion, and it deserves the utmost caution." [Al-I'lam Bi Nawazil Al-Ahkam (p. 729)]

- Al-Qarafi said: "As for the people of innovation and desires, there is no distinction among their various ranks. Even if we permitted the leadership of sinners, we would prevent it for them, as it would proliferate innovation by making it prominent." [Al-Dhakhirah by Al-Qarafi (2/240)]

Shafi'i School:

- Judge Husayn said: "The testimony of those who are not considered disbelievers from among the people of the Qibla, including those displaying innovation, is accepted, but prayer behind them is disliked." [Al-Ta'liqa by Judge Husayn (2/1031)]

- Al-Ruyani stated: "As for those openly promoting religious innovations, especially by criticizing the righteous predecessors, it is disliked to pray behind them, but if one does, the prayer is valid since this does not expel them from Islam." [Bahr Al-Madhhab by Al-Ruyani (2/263)]

- Al-Baghawi said: "It is permissible to pray behind people of innovations and desires, but prayer behind an innovator is more disliked than behind a sinner." [Al-Tahdhib in Shafi'i Jurisprudence (2/269)]

- "Abu Ishaq said: Praying alone is better than praying behind a Hanafi, and this is based on the validity of prayer behind a Hanafi." [Rawdat Al-Talibin by Al-Nawawi (1/341)]

- Al-Nawawi stated: "It is disliked to pray behind a sinner and also behind an innovator whose innovation does not reach the level of disbelief. As for one whose innovation amounts to disbelief, it is not permissible to follow him." [Rawdat Al-Talibin wa 'Umdat Al-Muftin (1/355)]

Hanbali School:

- Imam Ahmad said: "One may pray behind a sinful person but not behind an innovator or a flagrant sinner, except if one fears them, in which case one should pray and then repeat the prayer." [Al-Riwayatayn wa Al-Wajhayan – Fiqh Issues (1/172)]

- Harb Al-Karmani said: "The position of Abu Abdullah [Ahmad ibn Hanbal] is that prayer should not be performed behind innovators." [Masail Harb Al-Karmani, Book of Purity and Prayer – Ed. Al-Sarie' (p. 525)]

- Harb Al-Karmani also mentioned: "I do not like prayer behind the people of innovation, nor the funeral prayer over their deceased." [Masail Harb Al-Karmani from the Book of Marriage to the End – Ed. Fayez Habis (3/971)]

- Ibn Qudamah said: "Whoever follows in prayer an imam who openly displays his innovation, speaks of it, calls to it, or debates on its behalf, must repeat the prayer … because the one who publicly displays his innovation leaves no excuse for the person praying behind him." [Al-Mughni by Ibn Qudamah (3/17)]

The Islamic Shariah ruling unanimously agrees an innovator is not to ever have a leadership position where they are leading people in prayers. However sadly sometimes it happens where innovators get such a position despite being disqualified due to their disbelief. Sometimes people don't know about them and sometimes they know and still innovators acquire such a position. In such a case a blanket ruling cannot be applied because there are too many factors and variables. So cases like mine are extremely unique and require emergency Scholastic intervention to resolve. There is no one fatwa for all. I ignorantly didn't follow the advice of Sheikh Jalal Abul-Rub who advised me to just avoid that masjid and innovator by praying elsewhere, and as a result I suffered. Such was my destiny. You live and you learn and I share the story so others may benefit from the lessons. Ideally a simple conversation could have prevented much traumatic drama for the whole community. However when Satan inflames emotions, the easy solutions become difficult as anger is dangerous. Yet when you are face to face with someone who is a genuine Munafiq and dealing with someone pretending to be Muslim who has a leadership position then crazy things happen that ordinarily would never be imaginable to any Muslim or hypothetical scenario.

I never ever plan on going back to ISNF's masjid noor no matter what. I feel ISNF is an insincere and ignorant organization of American Muslims who unknowingly teach unislamic beliefs and since 2014 had a prayer leader in Qadri who has kufr creeds. To me I feel the Quranic ayat forbidding praying in masjid dirar apply, especially since the ISNF expansion of their mosque was done by the very same people who banned me from the masjid.

Therefore the masjid there is not a mosque built upon piety. I could extensively argue with evidences they were wrong/unislamic to ban me in the first place, or without investigation into my actions/reasons/sanity, or for five years minimum, or to issue a cease and desist from all types of communication with all ISNF members but it's not worth it because I decided I will never return there regardless of the circumstances; even if they fix themselves and beggingly invite me back. On the contrary I actually expect reward for every salat that passes while I'm alive and could've theoretically been in the ISNF mosque(s). So you do the math. I was unofficially banned on May 6th 2017 and officially banned on May 26th, 2017. Therefore multiply 5 times a day, times 27 for the reward of praying in congregation and that amounts to 135 times the reward I am entitled to per obligatory prayer. That doesn't include any of the Tahiyyatul masjid salat which Muslims perform every time they enter a masjid before sitting down nor Sunnah prayers, so that's possibly many more prayers, or more or less depending on the day and number of times one breaks wudu. We'll just say 140 to be generous only counting the obligatory prayers. Then multiply that by 2 because ISNF didn't do justice by banning me from just 1 mosque where the heretical imam is, but they banned me from 2 mosques total, maybe even more if they build more. So that's 280 prayer rewards per day I seem entitled to from the criminals since May 26th, 2017 up to the present time. Oh and since deeds are multiplied in Ramadan by 700 fold or more this 280 a day isn't even realistic, the truth is it's much more than the reward of 280 prayers per day, especially when you factor in other damages like insanity and "emotional distress" and reputational harm and the side-effects of hospitalization and taking a pill daily due to the real physiological harm caused by Mr. Qadri and ISNF. We'll be generous though and calculate 280 per day. If we multiply 280 times 365 per Gregorian year we get 102,200 prayer rewards. Since it has been 8 years I've been banned, at the time of this writing, then that's 817,600 prayer rewards the people in power at ISNF, particularly Mr. Qadri are liable to pay me back on the Day of Judgment since they have taken those rewards from me due to their unislamic actions done in the name of Islam. In reality that 817,600 is a generous undershot of the real number because we are not accounting for the Ramadan bonuses nor any others, such as Duha prayers or Tahajjud or Itikhaff, or Sunnah, or Tahiyyatul masjid, or the Ribat by staying in the masjid between prayers, or the super reward for each step taken to the masjid. Safe to say they easily owe me over a million in prayer rewards, possibly billions or trillions if we really want to do the math; which I don't. And that's the reward of my prayer in the masjid that I could've earned, not their prayers rewards which might be worth less than one of my prayers especially due to invalid creeds, or insincerity, incorrect methods or other things. I don't mention this statistic to brag or be complacent, or give false understandings that I am able to give up striving on the path to paradise. I mention this to terrorize the oppressors if they should ever read this and to discourage others from crimes lest they fall into such an enormous debt themselves through sinful transgression of another person by any means at all. Furthermore, since taking a pill in 2017 it forces me to sleep about 10 hours a day as compared to my pre-pill healthy normal of 6 hours a day. So that's four hours a day every day that have been robbed from me due to brain damage induced by Mr. Qadri and ISNF even if no magic were involved. Legal experts in America even told me I could easily sue them for financial compensation from damages, but I don't because they wouldn't pay it out of their own pockets but take the money from the Muslims who give charity to them and such a tactic is against Shariah law because it is not a valid blood money case to be entitled to financial litigation in my view. Still though 4 hours a day lost is 1,460 hours a year which I don't have due to health issues as a result of psychological warfare and oppression. Allah may reward me anyways for what I intended to do with such time but still the time lost in my life is worth adding to the list of debts Mr. Qadri and ISNF owe.

Yet despite my debt theory, if I am wrong to make takfir then I wish to repent but I think even if I'm unqualified to make takfir then Mr. Qadri is still more wrong for having the beliefs he expressed to me and stubbornly refused to change and then spiritually abusing me via boycotting prior to the ban from the masjid. The ban doesn't bother me much anymore, but if I'm making takfir of someone and I know they are miles away leading an entire masjid of people astray then it makes me feel angry and that I must expose him so people are aware of the reality. Simultaneously I never know if Mr. Qadri changes their mind since I'm banned from communication so they might have repented and then I'm still in takfir mode against outdated ancient critical errors. Islamically in an ideal scenario an investigation and intervention or something should be done revealing Mr. Qadri's beliefs on this matter and he should sincerely repent or I should be corrected as to what to do Islamically in this matter. But we live in America, land of the free for all and home of religious Bida. So the Islamic solution is sadly not available in this land.

Truly if you examine American history and culture or their religion/values, they possess some of the worst known to planet earth. Religiously America is like the Wild West Settler era where every gunslinger fends for themselves because there is no government religious authority to enforce religious criminal law. For example, the Christian denominations themselves have no legal authority to stop other heretical Christian groups from springing up and promoting heresy. So with that being the case in an allegedly predominantly Christian nation, what hope do Muslims have of getting the non-Muslim government to shut down Muslim heretical activity? Factually the heretics will just play the takfir card and equate the orthodox or even the non-orthodox Muslims as Khariji Takfiris linked to radical violent militant groups. Whereas the US government not knowing any better and not caring to study Islam to determine which minority Muslim person/group is correct will just take the side of the public establishment over the individual or pick a side via one of the unjust democratic numbers game of people power or money might. Heretics are given the benefit of the doubt from Secular governments. Similar to how non-Muslims lie about Islam, Ahl-Bida lie about Salafiyyah or Orthodox Islam or Fundamentalism equating it with extremism and heresy because they fear being exposed as ignorant innovating heretics themselves by true Muslims. Simply even going to a non-Muslim government to rule in a Muslim sectarian religious dispute itself is unprecedented and has no real basis legally in Shariah. To live in the land of the free means to live in a land of religious innovation and heresy. When America declared it to be a fundamental principle that they would make no law establishing or respecting religion, then that is equivalent to making a law allowing and establishing all satanic blasphemy and heresies. And anyone who comes with claims of takfir against another group has no credibility in the secular courts to make their case. It's almost comparable to a Jew coming to a Muslim Shariah court and declaring certain Christian denominations are heretical. Just as the Catholic Church cannot launch an inquisition in America against heretical Christians due to being without power or authority, the Muslims cannot combat heresy effectively in America either. All we can do is peacefully say X is wrong and walk away letting the criminals accept or reject our sincere advice as they will or won't. There is no relevance in America regarding whether there is a Muslim upon the truth or an alleged Muslim upon falsehood, the State simply doesn't care and thinks Islam is wrong to begin with and if they meddle in it they will only compound the problem further due to ignorant arrogance and characteristic injustice. The people of falsehood know this and utilize it for their advantage. This is why nearly every single heretical group that exists in any religion can be found in America. In the "United States" there is no religious unity, it's a free for all and all are free to do anything they damn well please. Secular countries are breeding grounds for bida and heresy because by nationally and legally taking a hands-off approach to any and every non-violent religious group inside its borders, then it amounts to patting heretics on the back promoting deviance. Forget giving heretics a slap on the wrist, in America they will give the heretics a parade. Afterall when everyone is incorrectly deemed equal then truth and falsehood lose importance. The hadith where prophet Muhammad informed his followers about the 73 different sects or denominations that will arise claiming to belong to Islam is most likely to occur due to Secular and Non-Muslim lands allowing "Muslims" in their lands. It's far less likely a Muslim nation would allow 73 different denominations within its borders. Classically the Muslims who knew Arabic but lived outside the cities where Shariah was implemented were considered "Bedouins". Usually Bedouins were more ignorant regarding Islam and likely to be less well-mannered than urban and suburban Muslims living within society ruled by Shariah. But keep in mind those "Bedouins" knew Arabic well and were devoid of most kafir influences and social pressures. Today the Muslim living in non-Muslim majority territory is worse off than the Bedouin was. Especially since the Muslim in non-Muslim lands is even less likely to know Arabic and is constantly influenced with immense pressure to conform to unislamic culture and religion. Bedouins were well-known to be the lowest rung and weakest link of the Muslim nation due to many reasons. So what then of non-Arabic Muslims in a Kafir country? Even if they know Arabic, still by being in a non-Muslim land they are worse off than Bedouins were in the prophetic era. So the best a Muslim can be in the non-Muslim land is likely to be worse than what the worst Bedouin was upon in the Muslim lands. Therefore the strategy for true Muslims in America is an uphill battle. Ideally you get out as fast as possible and never come back. If you can't leave then while here you try to practice Islam as best as you can and try recruiting others to join the true faith while stemming the continuous tidal waves of bida that continue to grow and clash against those upon truth and falsehood alike. Basically it's big mess where Muslims aren't supposed to be in America to start with, but most of us are here due to circumstances out of our control. Historically the first Muslims in America were the black African slaves that were imported by force. So if all the black slaves had kept their faith safe from the heresies of non-Muslim American pressure then all the black African-Americans would be Muslims today. Obviously many are not because generations living in a non-Muslim religious melting pot dilutes attachment to Islam and principles of love/hate and loyalty/allegiance/disavowal. That example of the majority of African-Americans ultimately discarding Islam in one form or another paints an accurate picture of the future for those Muslim immigrants from other nations/continents that come to America. Within five generations extreme dilution of the deen if not apostasy is expected.

Nearly nobody is coming to America saying, "*I am better able to practice Islam in America.*" There are a plethora of Muslim countries to go to for that. And for those who flee persecution that have a valid excuse to emigrate from their homeland, that doesn't give them an excuse to come to America. They have many other Muslim and non-Muslim countries to choose from. They could go to the continent of South America which is much more religious and conveniently never waged any military wars against Muslims for hundreds of years. The 3rd American president Thomas Jefferson intentionally created the "Marines" military branch exclusively to fight Muslims overseas in Africa. Thomas Jefferson possessed an English translation of the Quran and as an influential founding father of America, he thoroughly designed America to be an environment hostile to Islam just as Christopher Columbus and the Spanish always intended it to be ever since they first set sail in 1492; the same year Spain gave Muslims an ultimatum to convert to Catholicism, move out of Spain or die. The idea non-Muslim American hatred of Islam is just a post 9/11 phenomena has no basis, it's been there since before the Christians even came to America to colonize. So know that just because a Muslim immigrant may be temporarily excused to leave their homeland that doesn't mean you can enter anywhere you choose. It is only allowed for Muslims to go to non-Muslim countries generally if they are a Scholar or advanced Student of Knowledge preaching Islam, a diplomat, a merchant doing business temporarily, or for dire specialized emergency medical treatment that is unavailable elsewhere. There is no such thing in Islam as moving to America for economic prosperity, education or "freedoms". The problem is that fundamentally the majority of Muslim people who move to America from overseas are those who are ignorant of Islam and less religious than average Muslims in Muslim lands. You don't have to be a genius to know Muslims are better off amongst co-religionists than in a non-Muslim majority nation of any type. You don't see

Christians moving en masse to live in the Muslim middle east because they have more religious sense in that regard. They send their preachers, soldiers, celebrities and business people. Not their commoners who are barely Christian to begin with. Sadly Muslim migrants are often the worst of our global community but then they come to America and pool their money together to build a mosque and then think they are the best of the best because they are establishing houses of Allah where there never was one before. Then non-Muslim people surprisingly convert to Islam despite the Muslims efforts to sugarcoat and transform it into something else. But when we go to practice at the mosque others have built, the foreign Muslims and descendants of ignorant foreign Muslims have problems with people wanting the real deal genuine prophetic Islam as compared to the diluted innovative cultural Islam mixed with heresies or foolishness. Then a conflict occurs similar to how my conflict turned out, or radicalization and extremism of various varieties occur, or apostasy or at the very least community disunity.

The ultimate solution is similar to the solution taken by the founders of the Sokoto Caliphate. Uthman dan Fodio preached in Africa amongst Muslims steeped in Bida in the 1700s CE. He was a Scholar, not a layman. Uthman preached Islam as best as possible teaching students how to teach others. The Muslim rulers allowed him for a time until eventually the rulership changed and became hostile to his orthodoxy and condemnation of bida. Peacefully Muslims preach the truth as long as possible until violently prevented. Then what? Then we move elsewhere to more Muslim-friendly countries. That is what Uthman dan Fodio did. He preached as much as he could spreading genuine Islam as best as possible until he was threatened by the ruler. Then he didn't revolt, he moved and the Muslims left to go with him to spread Islam elsewhere. Then the adherents of bida attacked them and they waged Jihad. After the dust settled an entirely new nation was formed, known to history as the Sokoto Caliphate. It was not a Kingdom but a Caliphate in Africa and historically one of the best Muslim nations that has ever ruled on earth. Then gradually it declined and was colonized by Britain in the 1900s. Likewise the founding of Saudi Arabia after the efforts of Muhammad ibn Abdul Wahhab show a similar path to statecraft and national reform upon the prophetic methodology. Yet such national transformative projects are to be led by the genuine Scholars of Islam. Not students of knowledge even. Genuine scholars change nations for the better. The problem is everyone wants to do something big not realizing they are small pieces of a small puzzle piece. So people act without knowledge or instructions due to extreme circumstances, such as I did. Basically people have neglected Islam a long time and the centuries worth of problems are going to take a long time to fix completely if such a thing is even possible on a worldwide level. The good news is that victory belongs to Allah and the believers in the dunya and akhirah.

Just looking at the situation today as compared to one thousand years ago. Islam has spread globally faster and further than any other faith. Sure many forms of heresy have spread, even on national scales such as with the rise of Shiite states. But so has Salafiyyah spread to areas worldwide despite all attempts to stop the true prophetic creed and manhaj. Sure, many areas of bida exist but considering how Muhammad started as one individual man with an entire planet of disbelief then we are certainly doing much better today. Nobody today would say there is only 1 Muslim alive yet that is what we started with. Yes dilution happened and quality dipped as quantity grew but overall the future is optimistic. Much work remains but the global trend towards Islamic dominance is overwhelming. There will be battles back and forth but even if innovation takes an upperhand, the descendants of innovators may reform because this religion is perfectly preserved and accessible. Just considering translations alone, current generations have so much more access to genuine Scholastic

Islamic knowledge than past generations. Even in just the last few years the translated Islamic literature has multiplied. So even without Arabic, which is crucial to Islam, the Muslims globally are best able to access the prophetic data than ever before in history. The revival of the prophetic manhaj may not be as fast as overnight but it is continuing to spread with or without aide from me or you. May Allah bless the correct dawah.

As bad as Secularism is, it is has defeated Christianity in the Christian lands and Christianity is now a dying religion waiting for Jesus to come and deliver the final death blow as Muhammad prophesied. Prior to that Saul/Paul's invention of Christianity opposing the Islam of Jesus ended most forms of Western paganism. This way of Saul/Paul uniting pagans upon the polytheism of Christianity was allowed by Allah in my opinion because it paved the way for those pagans to come closer to Islam so that future generations would be more inclined to accept prophets and the prophetic faith. Imagine if Paul's Christian heresy was crushed immediately and everyone in the west was instead upon ancient paganism. Would not the world be worse off and less Islamic? Sure the Christians are disbelievers on the road to hell, but the sincere ones research and repent, as I did, and then embrace Islam because of the inclination towards following prophets of God. Whereas a pagan would be less likely to have done research into Islam or repent. Thus the heresy of Saul/Paul actually made mass conversion to Islam more likely in the future than it would have been had Pagans just remained Pagans. So you then see how Allah allows heresies and bida to spread because while it is hated by him legislatively it is a bridge towards eventual guidance for future generations. The whole world doesn't change overnight. Some will never change. Yet step by step the world is improving religiously from an Islamic perspective. For instance, during the papal crusades there were smaller numbers of Muslims in non-Muslim lands. And yes there were thousands of Muslims living in Europe while the medieval Crusades were ongoing, and those

Muslims were funding the Crusaders just as they do today making excuses to avoid Hijra. Yet one thousand years ago the non-Muslim political leaders hated Islam and Muslims so much they would travel to the middle east themselves to engage in hand to hand military combat. Since then despite the enmity still expressed and hidden within, the Kafir political tone and zeal has diminished dramatically. Another point about Muslims citing the emigration to Christian Abyssinia as proof they can live in dar al-kufr (most of which are dar al-harb) is that the Muslims did that when there was no such thing as a Muslim city in the world, let alone a Muslim nation. Therefore the evidence used to justify Muslims living in a non-Muslim land is extremely flimsy because when the Sahabah did that in the past there literally was no Muslim lands they could go to, but today that's just not the case. If Muslim lands existed during the time of the Muslim emigration to Christian Abyssinia Muhammad would have ordered the Muslims to move there, but there weren't any

Muslim lands so that is why some Muslims went to Abyssinia. When Muslim lands exist, no matter how poor or corrupt they are, the ruling for living in non-Muslim lands is different than it was during the time when there were no Muslim lands at all. So just because someone can confidently and eloquently cite Muhammad or Muslims as having done something or not done something in the past, doesn't mean that's the Islamic thing to do in similar situations today. Similarly for the anti-hijra or reverse-hijra crowd who cites the precedent of Muslim minorities living in Abyssinia, if you suggested Muslims today go to Abyssinia/Ethiopia they will ridicule the notion as ridiculous despite there being more sense in Muslims moving to Abyssinia/Ethiopia than to America. Hijra is still obligatory until today but it is also known that not everyone will follow the Islamic law and move or be able to move to Muslim lands. So since many of the Muslims will still for whatever reason live in non-Muslim lands despite the laws prohibiting that, Allah facilitates such due to the eventual changes that will occur due to it. Yes, Allah may punish the pioneers of Islam in the Western world for their errors despite entire nations being guided to Islam hundreds of years later. Allah uses hypocrites to do his will and guides many people through the words and deeds of wicked hypocrites. Sometimes Allah will use a sinful insincere hypocrite whom he will punish eternally in hellfire as a sign for someone else to believe in and practice Islam whom he will reward forever. Muhammad said Allah will spread Islam to many via the efforts of wicked hypocritical Muslim preachers who will burn in the hellfire forever while those they preach to will go to paradise forever if they follow the advice. I may or may not be the former but Godwilling you will be the latter. Whoever Allah guides no one can lead astray and whoever Allah allows to go astray then no one can guide. Truly only Allah can guide someone, not even Noah, Abraham, Moses, Jesus or Muhammad could guide people they cared about and they were prophets with miracles and revelation. Guidance is not constant, you may be sincere one second and an arrogant hypocrite the next. Sincere deeds can become insincere deeds long after they are done. Those who can be consistently sincere upon guidance are those who are truly blessed beyond measure. Being guided yesterday doesn't mean you will be upon guidance tomorrow, and being sincere one minute doesn't mean your sincerity will last for even a full 60 seconds. Thus sincerity in life is one of the best gifts Allah can give you and without having it one can not enter paradise. Thus always ask Allah for sincerity, knowledge to go with it and distinguish right from wrong and the ability to do what is right and avoid all that is wrong. But overall isn't it better to have heretics go overseas get punished and then through their diluted preaching of heterodox Islam it results in the non-Muslim nation embracing genuine Islam hundreds of years later either directly or over time after years of experiencing Bida? Ideally we start with the truth from the beginning and unite upon Salafiyyah. That's the pure prophetic way and works best most speedily.

But does that mean we stop all the innovators by force from preaching heretical Islam in the West? It's impossible. We have to accept Allah's destiny and make the best of a bad situation. We can't abandon the non-Muslim world to the practitioners of Bida without comment or concern, but even though we are unable to prevent it eventually the tide will turn and Bida will vanish or evolve. Surely every Muslim would agree if the non-Muslim Kuffar turned into nominal Muslims or even heretical Muslims it may be a better global picture. That's not to say we want toxic heresy to conquer anyone. But overall considering the long-term picture every step towards genuine Islam is an improvement. Demographic wise the innovators will typically outnumber the true Muslims anyways. What I'm saying is that though a current generation may be upon falsehood and be punished by Allah when they die, they may be taking the steps today that lead to their descendants embracing prophetic truth down the road. Looking at the situation now where Muslims are allowed to publicly preach in Christian lands due to secular law while Christians cannot preach in Muslim lands due to Islamic or Muslim laws then who has truly won the war? It's a foregone conclusion that if only one religion can legally publicly preach in both lands then a clear advantage is had. Thus Muslims have the edge and with the truth of Islam victory is guaranteed no matter how many lies or wars are waged to stem the tide. Christianity in effect broke the barriers of Paganism to the prophetic faith. Then Secularism broke the Christian barriers to the prophetic faith. Other barriers may arise but overall the trend is that there are less and less barriers to people learning the truth of Islam and practicing it than ever before. Therefore in that regard it is sometimes better when masses of non-Muslims get exposure to bida than having zero exposure to Islam at all. Allah will guide who he blesses and many notable true Muslims upon Salafiyyah were guided initially due to the efforts of heretics or innovators or fools. Then Allah increased their guidance even more. So sometimes Allah uses people who are in error to take others out of error into guidance despite later punishing those original people who were in error. For this reason as severe as Mr. Qadri and ISNF's crimes against Allah and Muslims are, they are still a benefit to some degree to Islam despite profoundly contradicting it on core fundamental levels. Our goal though is not to get good results globally but individually. I'd much rather go to paradise without changing the world than be a catalyst for improving the world while going to Hellfire. But other people feel differently and would rather influence the world for the better and go to Hell for doing so in unislamic methods without correct intentions. Anyway you look at it the game is in the favor of the prophetic faith. If the Innovators win in the West, eventually they will lose in the future. The goal for us should be to save yourself and your families from the Hellfire prior to even considering anything else. Trust that Allah knew what he was doing when he sent Muhammad to the world. Everything has been planned for and accounted. Muslims might go through some tough times but historically the long-term trend is leveraged in favor of the truth. Just as the people of Bida cannot be harmed much by the people of Salafiyyah legally in non-Muslim countries the people of Salafiyyah cannot be harmed much by the people of Bida either. In a fair game the truth always wins. Even in lopsided unbalanced affairs the truth always wins. Even if in theory Ahl-Bida gain an upper hand and persecute the true Muslims the victory still belongs to the Muttaqun because when one suffers for Allah's cause they are rewarded and when the opponent gains in the cause of the devil they are losers under all circumstances though they may not perceive it. In all end-game scenarios the true Muslims will win, so don't worry about it. Instead worry about your personal salvation most importantly and act accordingly. Realistically there are so many Muslims today that there are too many to be physically capable of performing the obligatory Hajj pilgrimage ritual. Individually every Muslim must make Hajj in Mecca if they are able to, but we have so many today that if all the billions of Muslims tried to do Hajj there isn't enough room for them to do it. And that's another miracle of Islam in that Allah and his prophet taught us Hajj is a conditional obligation upon those able to do it, and if you aren't truly able then the obligation is lifted. Logistically Hajj can no longer be performed by 100% of the Muslims because there are so many. But despite this fact that there are too many Muslims for us to even perform communal pillars of our faith, you have doom and gloom fortunetellers bewailing the condition of Islam and Muslims when in reality we are growing at a faster than manageable rate. The plethora of anti-Islamic kafir and heretical propaganda serves to increase Islamic awareness despite its evil intentions to distort the truth. The negative publicity is raising Islamic Awareness positively. Sadly the low quality of Muslims is the main reason that hinders the quantity from increasing. Which is why the Muslims who aren't devout and knowledgeable about Islam shouldn't be in any of the non-Muslim societies because they are misrepresenting Islam making it harder to spread the message. Honestly there are many Muslims in America who in their attempt to spread Islam they make it harder for Islam to spread. This is because they don't have knowledge about Islam and lack sincerity. In reality they are just spreading an idea about Muslims and Islam in order to make their own lives in America more comfortable. Muslims can't "go with the flow" in unislamic non-Muslim societies. The "flow" of unislamic ideologies, cultures and systems are toxic, oppressive, immoral, lead towards the hellfire and are inferior to Islam as anyone who compares them objectively will realize. The trouble is that if all the practicing Muslims leave the West then the West will be left with nothing but deviant people claiming to be Muslims who will give them an incorrect view of Islam. Then just as Paul's doctrine which developed in Rome and Greece went back to replace the religion of Jesus in the holy land, the deviant Westernized self-proclaimed "Muslims" may try to conquer the

Islamic lands and impose their falsehood thinking the proper Muslims are deviant. Honestly the greatest obstacle for me preaching Islam to people in America has come from Muslims themselves. These broadcasts where people say how all these foreign Muslims coming from overseas are trying to spread Islam, seem mainly false to me. From my perspective, generally it's native disbelievers who become Muslim who try to spread Islam while the foreign Muslims come to the West in order to get money, "educations" or safety and many of them thwart the spread of Islam in the West because of their own ignorance, fears, self-interests, habits, indifference, lack of confidence and misconceptions. Then the foreign Muslims, or born and raised western Muslims descended from foreign Muslims, chastise and ignorantly tell us reverts that there are no Islamic Shariah compliant Muslim countries in the world today, so we just have to deal with it, accept it and adapt to unislamic standards and preach how they preach because the confrontational style of preaching is "too harsh/insulting" and won't work; even though it's the only way that does work and turn males into men and females into women. The problem is the foreign Muslims really don't want to see the West implement Shariah. Honestly do you really think the Muslims who came to the Western world for business and school would be pleased if Shariah were implemented here and all the sinful stuff became illegal? Or would they move to escape Islam like they did when they came to the West because their Muslim countries were too Islamic for them? For Muslim reverts we're either going to implement Shariah in our native lands or we will leave, so they should either find us a country to move to or let us refute the kafir system and reform our own people. The big issue is that the Muslim reverts want to change their countries and/or move; but the other Muslims just want to fit in with the unislamic Western system and live comfortably. The reverts want to fit in with Islam and change their countries just like they changed themselves, but the other group wants to fit in with kufr and kafirs and are changing Islam to do so. As a message to all Muslims, if you are ever residing in a non-Muslim land then you are there to change it and guide it to Islam, you are not there to improve the Muslim image; every person is created to spread Islam throughout the land even though the disbelievers hate it and yes the disbelievers hate it because Allah said so. Thus if they don't hate the Islam you are presenting either they are on the road towards Islam or you aren't teaching the truth of Islam but a distorted version which they like but God hates. I'm not saying Muslims can't live with disbelievers peacefully but what I am saying is that the goal of a Muslim is to live under Islamic laws amongst Muslims and not under kafir laws or kufr systems or with any non-Muslim majority. Scholars have even stated that Muslims cannot ever have all non-Muslim neighbors, and if they don't have Muslim neighbors then they should either move so they have at least 1 Muslim neighbor, or actively preach Islam until their neighbors become Muslim or move. Rather than Western Muslims wondering about how the non-Muslims view them, they should worry about conveying the message of Islam to them, so they stop being disbelievers and can become believers in Allah. The non-Muslims should be adjusting themselves in order to live with us not the other way around. Just imagine how much faster Islam would spread if every Muslim got on the same page of the Kitab and Sunnah according to the correct Salafi understanding? If that were to happen then global overnight success would be much more realistic. Yet alas humans will never cease to disagree, as Allah says, so just make sure you personally agree with the full undiluted fundamental prophetic faith. Islam cannot be stopped, the only important thing for you is which type of Islam will you follow and die upon?

To this day I still don't want to make takfir because it's very stressful and risky but feel I have to make takfir of Mr. Qadri based on his verbal expression to me in February 2017 that Christians and Jews aren't disbelievers, and that non-Muslims aren't all disbelievers, and that shirk isn't kufr. Nobody else has to make takfir of Qadri because they don't have the proof I have encountered. Admittedly the cease and desist order, bans and Qadri's refusal to discuss even at the behest of third-parties intermediating complicates matters. Yet this book itself is a victory and tool to give victory against Satan and his allies.

Therefore, Godwilling after I move in a few years time to a Muslim country I plan to take my case to the Shariah court specialist who deals with Takfir to determine my mistakes and possibly have them write Mr. Qadri an email or send ISNF a statement detailing their errors. Also I or someone else could send copies of my relevant books to Qadri's home address, which I plan to do after I migrate. The goal is victory over Satan who has deceived Qadri or so it would seem. I probably would not even give this book to Qadri himself until after I revoke my USA citizenship thereby being protected from extradition. If he ever gets a copy of this from me indirectly then he should know I don't even live in America and am not American by the time he reads this. Thus ISNF's legal team will be hard pressed to charge any crimes against me. Plus all I've written is verifiable truth. They could only say as Ismail mistakenly said that it is considered backbiting or gossip however that is a misapplication of the term. For the prohibition of backbiting does not apply regarding heretics nor non-governmental oppressors. In fact, concealing Munafiqs and Ahl-Bida from the people when having the proof I have could be criminal in itself. That doesn't mean everyone is fit to know because not everyone is fit to fix the problem. In America it almost seems nobody can fix the issue as long as Qadri and ISNF are arrogantly ignorantly stubborn in their unislamic creeds and methodologies. That doesn't mean we don't try to correct them and this is me trying to correct them and warn the leaders while sharing lessons learned so similar copycat cases don't occur throughout the land. I'm sure Qadri is not the only deviant to fall into such a fundamental Aqeedah error and be appointed Imam of a mosque in America. In fact, you have many heretical leaders of mosques in America but many go undetected. Others are well-known to belong to deviant sects or ideologies and little can be done to advise and correct them either. The difference is they don't hide their deviance as Qadri and ISNF do under the name of Sunnism. So the most dangerous Muslims spiritually are these types who pretend and mislabel themselves while teaching, preaching and practicing other than Islam. The crisis ideally would be resolved with Qadri's personal sincere repentance and reentry into Islam. Thus as gently as possible I will do my duty in stages while working on myself and my situation. Qadri made himself clear for years that he refuses to communicate with me and made it difficult. Yet this factual report could be shared with Muslim community leaders so they are aware at the minimum despite potential inability to act as Islam requires. Therefore the heresy will not be hidden from all and will be exposed on the Day of Judgement to all. If Qadri repents then it is better for him and Muslims. Yet since he committed such a grievous error in my opinion it is very difficult for him to repent from this, especially as Ahl-Bida rarely repent. Qadri's repentance to Allah is one thing but his righting the wrongs committed on other Muslims such as myself is another. For me to personally forgive him for his crimes against me would require an extreme effort. Just as he lied about me to the community and my family and friends he would have to tell the truth to all those and right the wrong. Just as he banned me and fought against me he'd have to unite and support me and I don't see how that's possible anymore since for him to even communicate he'd have to do serious efforts since all my contact information changed and will change again. It seems to me we won't ever be able to directly communicate again because of the actions that have been taken by his party and the chain-reaction it caused. Plus since Qadri's crime involved abuse of Imamship then it only seems fit that he never ever serve as an Imam of a mosque because the Shariah is clear that apostates even if they repent are not allowed to ever again assume authority positions over Muslims. So basically if Qadri wanted my personal forgiveness he would have to quit being an Imam for the rest of his life and that's very hard for someone like him to do and Satan will give him excuses saying he's qualified and won't abuse authority again, like he has for years continuously, but if he were sincere Qadri would repent and quit of his own accord then migrate to a Muslim country since Hijra erases the sins before it and Qadri is not strong enough faithwise to live amongst non-Muslims without diluting and compromising his religion in my analysis and experience with him. Allah could forgive him without doing all of that but I'm just saying if he wanted me to feel at ease regarding him and accept his repentance those would be my conditions. At the minimum since he banned me from two masjids with a minimum 5 year ban from each, totaling 10 years minimum, then Qadri if he were fair would quit being an imam for at least 10 years before ever considering it as a possibility again. Plus since Qadri had heretical beliefs and was disqualified from being an Imam since 2017, possibly even longer, then he should return all the money he got paid from his salary from 2017 until present and reimburse the Muslim community for the free housing he got while defrauding the Muslims by believing in kufr. However since he probably is unable and unwilling to do that and ISNF would just pocket the funds and spend it on further deviance, I don't insist on his financial repayment even though that is what justice dictates. The safest position would be for Qadri to shun leadership for the rest of his life since he has transgressed in extreme manner and done crimes he knows are crimes to maintain it. Qadri has proven he does not have what it takes to be a Muslim leader and is easily corrupted by corrupters. That's if he repents he would listen to my sincere advice on how to rectify his calamitous errors. On the pessimistic hand if Qadri were a Munafiq as I diagnosed him, he would likely throw any book of mine he saw away and try pressing charges or something for even sending him a book even if it wasn't this one. But I'm not going to share my whole playbook in this book, there are ways to still take actions against Qadri should he stubbornly cling to falsehood and leadership. I'll keep some surprises up my sleeve. Yet at the very least I would hate to be in Mr. Qadri's position when the angel of death eventually comes to collect his soul when he himself has put up barriers to his own repentance to Allah and forgiveness from those he has mistakenly wronged. I'm much happier I got banned and injured than to be the "healthy" Imam whose deeds are invalid according to Islam as long as he is upon heresy. Truly can anyone be more wretched and accursed than someone who does all the work of a Muslim Imam at a mosque and is actually hated by Allah and gets no credit for any goodness because of heretical beliefs nullifying all their actions? If he were Muslim and wronged me then we would just meet in the afterlife and settle the score with his deeds, but if he dies upon the last known belief he expressed to me he won't have a single good deed to trade with despite doing the speech and actions of goodness in most of his life. So then he'd get my sins as recompense unless I forgive him then but the only way I'd forgive him then if I hadn't before is if he had sincerely repented as advised and Allah promised me extra reward for doing so. Truly if Qadri doesn't repent he's screwed and he knows it, or at least he should, it is possible he fooled himself but if so then that's an even more pitiful position to be in. Thus I don't bother wasting time cursing him anymore because he already is cursed as far as I know. Occasionally since I try supplicating daily for Allah to bless all Muslims and guide all humans and jinn to Islam I recognize this supplication includes Qadri as a human. So technically I ask Allah for Qadri's guidance daily indirectly thus I refrain from cursing anyone anymore because it's not as beneficial to me. Instead I leave the decision to Allah, one of my duas will definitely be granted regarding Qadri. Either Qadri will be cursed or blessed, and Allah alone knows best which. But I'm eager to meet Qadri on the Day of Judgement and finally be able to ask him if he repented from his kufr statements and beliefs which he banned me from the mosque for disagreeing with. He can and has run and hid in this worldly life. But on the Day of Judgement there will be nowhere for Qadri to hide and I will ask Allah to judge between us in justice as to whether non-Muslims are kuffar or not and what the divine judgement in our dispute is to be. For my part I tried all I could to resolve the situation before then but Qadri has decided to postpone it until then. Truly oppression is not something to fear for it makes the oppressed love to die and meet Allah. Anger though can have a bitter taste thus we ask Allah to protect us from his anger and getting angry because as Muhammad taught his companions anger is the root of all sins. Anger is why I seemingly lost the battle with Qadri, since it clouded my judgement. Thus whenever battling the forces of Satan know that your anger is more of an enemy to you than anything else. Anger for the sake of Allah is a virtue but getting angry for Allah's sake is different than being angry and acting upon it or having anger overpower you. Likewise Anger is what caused Qadri to deviate and transgress. So typically anger only destroys and hinders civilized progress because it is difficult to manage correctly with controlled precision.

Tragically many people follow positions rather than proof and consider someone's position as a proof over someone in a lesser position. Basically they weigh the truth based on titles rather than facts even if the non-positioned less titled has the truth on their side, many are totally blinded by the societal statuses and labels. I was not error free in this ordeal, yet still Mr. Qadri made far bigger errors than me in our interactions especially in regards to his creed and manners. The Muslim community in America does not seem equipped to deal with issues of heresy or takfir. Takfir itself is complex and a legal verdict that comes with strings attached, such as automatic divorce from Muslim spouses and other serious losses potentially even including one's life if one were to merit execution by the State. So understandably a local imam at one masjid has little power to do anything to a deviant imam at another masjid in America. Know that one can technically commit major disbelief while still being a Muslim due to the presence of a preventative factor, such as compulsion, insanity, ignorance or misunderstandings due to language or something. Even a mistake in interpretation can prevent takfir (declaring one to be a disbeliever). Again it is very risky to label one claiming to be a Muslim a disbeliever, because whenever labeling someone a disbeliever either the one labeled is a disbeliever or the labeler is for wrongfully labeling. Though unknown to many, wrongly labelling a disbeliever itself does not necessarily expel one from Islam, it would mean the label of disbelief would apply to that person due to their mistaken labelling but there may be preventative factors that prevent labeling a mistaken Muslim takfiri(labeler) as a disbeliever. It could be minor disbelief or major disbelief or if major there may be excusable reasons for the mistaken labelling. But just because the prophet said the label of kafir will apply to one of the two when takfir of a Muslim occurs it doesn't automatically mean if one mistakenly labels another, especially due to anger or a valid mistake, that you are defacto disbeliever just because you incorrectly label a Muslim person a disbeliever. This is a popular problem where some label takfiris as disbelievers thereby falling into the very same error they themselves are condemning causing a domino effect. People will say you can't make takfir of anybody, but those very same people then make takfir of takfiris for having made takfir. Or worse instead of educating takfiris their first solution is to boycott, imprison or fight them with the stigma and isolation causing the ignorant Muslim takfiri to become even more misguided, extreme and dangerous. Someone can be kafir by action of kufr, in this case mistaken takfir, without necessarily being a major disbeliever non-Muslim, just as those who don't rule by the law of Allah are linguistically kafirs though not necessarily major non-Muslim disbelievers by virtue of such speech or action though it is kufr/disbelief. There is such a thing as a linguistically labeled kafir who is not a non-Muslim disbeliever though kafir is a label usually used for non-Muslims. Similarly the Sahabah fought military battles against each other though the prophet said fighting a believer is kufr and fighting a Muslim is kufr, still no Sahabi made takfir of another Sahabi even though they knew fighting each other was an act of kufr because the Quran says when <u>two groups of believers fight</u> to reconcile between them or unitedly fight the one that transgresses. This indicates that the kufr of fighting a believer or Muslim is not a defacto expulsion from Islam. Or else the Quranic verse would not label both parties of fighters as believers. The level of kufr, intentions and circumstances factor in when determining one to be believer, Muslim or disbeliever. The circumstances must always be factored in when branding someone a disbeliever, even regarding something as grievous and seemingly apparent as physically fighting or killing a believer. You really have to know what you are talking/writing about and some even say only a Scholar is capable of making takfir of a self-proclaimed Muslim or else it is automatically sinful even if you do it correctly because such takfir is a legal verdict that involves the loss of their rights. Allah knows best. Ultimately since I would share this story with my children so they learn the lessons they need to learn, then it is natural to share publicly so perhaps the reader may benefit as well.

Regarding my "mental health" experience. In 2023 I finally got a Muslim psychiatrist who told me that after 5 years without psychotic episodes then the brain can potentially heal and I could stop taking medicine eventually. Since I have been well over 5 years without insanity, my brain could've healed since 2017 and the chemical balance could be restored. Currently the psychiatric world has no biological tests to tell whether someone is crazy or not or has chemical imbalance in their brain or not to determine what medicine dosage is the least necessary dosage. The islamophobic doctor who diagnosed me with the Schizoaffective disease was unprofessional making derogatory remarks about Islam to me while in the hospital and only saw me less than 3 hours during 3 days out of 26 because he was on vacation. So I never believed his diagnosis much because he didn't really fulfill the criteria to match me with that diagnosis and he was openly anti-islamic to an illegal extent. But when you get overmedicated it effects the brain and the brain thoughts and mood so one starts to fall for the lies later doctors tell based on your file and self-admitted crazy episode and low standard of life they set for you. Basically it is in the psychiatric industries interest to have you be disabled in a vegetative state over-medicated supported by the government for life dependent on a drug allegedly to stay sane. Then when you add Islamic preachiness to the mix they definitely have an interest in downgrading your lifestyle doping you up. Essentially many people lose money if people get healed from illness. People take drugs, go insane and then get out of the hospital and never take pills and walk around sane. But because my psychotic episode was not drug induced and in the USA the medical world doesn't believe magic exists or that a devil could cause insanity symptoms as the

Quran says can happen, as consumers of riba/usury/interest will stand on the Day of Judgement by one beaten to insanity by shaitan, they just say, "*Well it's possible that DNA genes predisposed you to have a mental illness and it was triggered by stress. So it is now activated and is a genetic irreversible condition as far as we know so far. Take this pill for life and X dosage seems right to my guesstimate.*" Basically in plain terms saying "Its destiny you went crazy." Which is not a medically scientific explanation. Destiny is not disputed but destiny is not a description of the medical issue that occurred or is ongoing. Medically psychiatry is very far behind other fields of medicine and much of it is guesswork on how symptoms of insanity or mental health problems can be treated. Personally I had started taking 15 mg worth of medicine daily in 2018 after switching from a different medicine that was prescribed in 2017. I later requested to go from 15 mg to 10 mg in 2021 and I was warned I could go crazy if I did so. I didn't go crazy. Then in 2024 I went from 10mg to 5 mg despite the doctor in 2021 telling me they would never ever go lower than 10 mg for me. So, I have already proven myself sane at lower doses than medically thought possible. New medicines can come out too that reduce the side effects which are worse than the disease of insanity. Currently doctors don't do tests for what genetic makeup causes insanity or mental illness or if you even have the "crazy gene" in your DNA. No tests were done on me aside from an initial CT scan in 2017 to discount other brain conditions and annual bloodwork to check for drugs and nutrition levels. They don't have an unbiased nonmanipulable objective test for mental illness of the brain, nor do they do it on a routine basis to see if the brain is still damaged. They just say if you are ever crazy take a drug until you behave and then keep taking it forever just in case. Bones break and then heal. The brain is even more active in repair abilities with neuroplasticity but they ignore this, except when in therapy, because they don't know what actually causes non-drug craziness to begin with and entire industries exist to treat it that cannot be honest in saying we don't really know how it happens or how long it lasts for. Plus nutrition can actually change your DNA gene activation. Essentially nutritional therapy can change genetic destiny to some extent. All they really know regarding my case is I went crazy twice in 2017 for reasons unknown and that taking a pill and talking to me about mental hygiene and healthy thinking reduced symptoms to the extent I can live outside of the hospital apparently sane according to the legal medical definitions since 2017 until present. But has the brain healed to an extent that I no longer need medicine at all? The Muslim doctor said it only takes 5 years for some to potentially completely heal. As a disclaimer everyone is different and don't make any medical decisions yourself based on my analysis or case. In short mental illnesses are possible to recover from to an extent that no medicine is needed and people do recover from it. Some need meds forever and some don't, and some need them for temporary timeframes and never get told how long that is for because doctors don't know themselves because mental illness is a imprecise little known science without much proven or confirmed about it.

As I write my plan is to test the theories and see if I go crazy on zero medicine or not. This plan may change and I might go crazy and go back on medicine or I might have healed from magic or any brain damage and be able to live without medicine again. Such a plan must be done medically responsibly in gradual stages though to limit the chance of rebound psychosis and personally while I recognize that it would make for a much happier ending if I could write that "I stopped taking medicine and lived happily sanely ever after." That might not happen. And if it does I don't need to boast of it and if it doesn't I don't need your pity. My health could get worse or better but Qadri need not know and that's why instead of waiting to publish until it is known whether I fully recovered from my alleged "mental illness" or not is not the reader's business. If I recover and say so then Qadri may think he is less sinful. If I don't Qadri may be glad his damage is long-lasting. By me not letting him know through this book whether I fully recovered from the brain damage his stress and/or magic caused it keeps him in a more repentful position and my private life has more privacy. Plus I don't want to add unnecessary pages to the length of this already lengthy book.

Another point on the topic of magic is that if I believed at one time magic was done to me by Qadri then why risk him repeating the magic by such an expose or instigation through future indirect communication? Firstly magic is nothing serious. Realistically a magician's magic is just the devil humiliating them through empty rituals they make up. A magical ritual does nothing itself, it's just a disgrace for the magician that persuades the devils to put in extra effort to harm someone they already planned to harm anyways. It's not as though you or anyone else is under the radar of the invisible devils and Iblis has no ability to harm you unless a magician says or does some magic. Iblis is trying 100% of the time maximum effort to hurt every human and believer as much as possible. It's not as though magic increases the power of anything. It's essentially just an order from one criminal to another and the crimes devils commit for magicians will not have any effect on a believer unless Allah is pleased for that to occur. Yes sometimes magic has effects since Allah allowed it out of wisdom for the end results. But you don't stop goodness for fear of magic. In fact, if someone takes the caution to purify their creed, speech, deeds and lifestyle according to Salafiyyah then most magic will have zero effect on them at all. And even if it does then it's destiny we are to be satisfied with. The point is never fear a magician and think they have any power to do anything even though magic is real and has effects. Muhammad taught us the antidotes to magic and all forms of disbelief and religious error. So if you stick to the truth it won't even matter to you. If you do get hurt then know that a wound Allah allows to afflict a believer is best for them because Allah always grants the believers the best for them until he meets them one on one. Therefore never fear magic or magicians or even Iblis or his armies of devils amongst humans and jinn. Only fear Allah and disobeying Allah in any way. For Allah is the most powerful friend and most powerful enemy and everyone is always either amongst the friends of Allah or the enemies of Allah. There is no tolerant neutrality. And the enemies of Allah will never have success in comparison to the friends of Allah.

In conclusion despite his past oppression of me, as I perceive it, I still don't want Qadri to burn in Hell forever without having done all I could to correct his creedal errors. If it were up to me, he could burn in Hell forever, but I don't want to go to Hell myself for giving up on him or the Islamic duty I have to enjoin good and forbid evil and personally promised Qadri I'd do my duty towards him. My silence regarding my ordeal is not an eternal solution nor beneficial so I share this experience so lessons can be learned by the reader when navigating the tumultuous religious landscape of Islam in America or elsewhere. Not every story of truth versus falsehood has a 100% happy ending in this world for every person involved. Sometimes members of the right party seemingly get defeated on earth before ultimate victory is achieved by the party of Allah. And that is one key verse of the Quran in that "the party of Allah" is successful. That doesn't mean every single individual member of the party of Allah will win every battle they ever fight because even Prophets suffered some losses. Yet ultimately the victory belongs to the party of Allah even if after a long time and the unjust seemingly escape immediate justice for a time. The battle against bida in America will likely intensify over time before the end of time. Even if Ahl-Bida win more territory and numbers it is known how things will turn out in the long-term as Allah has informed us through the teachings of Muhammad which have been preserved and spread exclusively in full through the Salafis ever since.

It is narrated on the authority 'Abdullah bin Mas'ud that the Messenger of Allah observed:

Never a Prophet had been sent before me by Allah towards his nation who had not among his people (his) disciples and companions who followed his ways and obeyed his command. Then there came after them their successors who said whatever they did not practice, and practiced whatever they were not commanded to do. He who strove against them with his hand was a believer: he who strove against them with his tongue was a believer, and he who strove against them with his heart was a believer and beyond that there is no faith even to the extent of a mustard seed.

Source: Sahih Muslim 50

Narrated Mu'adh ibn Anas:

The Prophet (ﷺ) said: If anyone guards a believer from a hypocrite, Allah will send an angel who will guard his flesh on the Day of Resurrection from the fire of Jahannam; but if anyone attacks a Muslim saying something by which he wishes to disgrace him, he will be restrained by Allah on the bridge over Hellfire till he is acquitted of what he said.

Source: Sunan Abi Dawud 4883 Grade: Hasan

Narrated Jabir ibn Abdullah:

The Prophet (ﷺ) said: If any man is among a people in whose midst he does acts of disobedience, and, though they are able to make him change (his acts), they do not change, Allah will smite them with punishment before they die.

Source: Sunan Abi Dawud 4339 Grade: Hasan

It is reported that Sufyān Al-Thawrī said:

"If you loved a man for Allāh and then he innovates in Islām and you don't hate him for it, you never [truly] loved him for Allāh."

Source: Abū Nu'aym, Ḥilyatu Al-Awliyā

Fudayl Ibn Iyaad said:

"If Allah knows about a man that he hates an innovator, then I am hoping that Allah will forgive him. Even if his (good) deed is little. A follower of Sunnah will not support a follower of innovation except out of hypocrisy and whoever turns his face against a follower of innovation Allah will fill his heart with Faith. And whoever rebukes a follower of innovation, Allah will make him safe on the Day of Greatest Terror. And whoever humiliates a follower of innovation Allah will raise him hundred ranks in

Paradise. So never be a follower of innovation for the sake of Allah forever."

Source: Sharus Sunnah by Imam Barbaharee

Al Shatibi said:

"The masters of practical religious innovations for the most part, do not like to debate anyone, nor argue with any Scholar about what they seek to achieve, for fear of scandal that they would find no Shariah support for their opinions. It is always their habit that whenever they find a strong Scholar, they would adulate and flatter him, and whenever they find an ignorant layman they would baffle him with problems in Shariah to shake his beliefs and put him to confusion as regard the religion. Once the signs of confusion appear on him, they would soon throw on him their religious innovations by degrees, one by one, and accuse the men endued with knowledge of being devotees of this world, who dedicate themselves to it, versus those (religious innovators) who are the devotees of Allah selected by Him apart from others. Furthermore they may present to him some statements belonging to the extremist Sufis as witnesses to what they claim, until they lead him to the fire of Hell. But by no means would they come to the matter in the right way, and debate with the Scholars endued with knowledge over it."

Source: Kitab Itisam

Ata al Khurasani said:

"Allah barely allows for the innovator to repent."

Source: Dhamm Al kalam 794

Imaam Ibn Qayyim said:

"From the conditions of repentance (tawbah) of the caller to bid'ah is that he makes clear that which he used to call to from innovation and misguidance, and that guidance is its opposite, just as Allaah has laid down the conditions of repentance for the People of the Book who's sin was concealing that which Allaah had revealed of clarification and guidance so as to misguide the people with that. So they had to rectify the deeds in themselves, and to clarify to the people that which they concealed from them, so Allaah said:

"Indeed, those who conceal what We sent down of clear proofs and guidance after We made it clear for the people in the Scripture – those are cursed by Allah and cursed by those who curse – except for those who repent and correct themselves and make evident [what they concealed]. Those, I will accept their repentance, and I am the Accepting of repentance, the Merciful." [al-Baqarah: 159-160]"

"Just as Allaah laid down the conditions of the repentance of the hypocrites whose sin was that they [tried] corrupting the hearts of the weak believers whilst they showed bias in favor and adherence to the Jews and the polytheists who had enmity to the Messenger– and with that they made themselves seem apparently as Muslims, only as a show, to be seen and heard. So upon them was to rectify in replacement of their corruption, and to hold fast to Allaah in replacement of holding fast to the unbelievers from the People of the Book and the polytheists, and to make their Religion sincerely for Allaah rather than just to show and be heard by the people – so this is how the conditions of repentance and its reality is understood, and Allaah's Aid is sought."

Source: Uddatus Sabireen

It was mentioned to Ahmad Ibn Hanbal that a man from the people of knowledge made a mistake and erred, and that he had repented from his mistake. So Imām Ahmad said:

"Allāh will not accept that from him until repentance and recantation from his [erroneous] saying is made apparent — and he announces that he said such-and-such, and that he has repented to Allāh, the most High, *for his saying and has recanted from it. If he makes that apparent, then his repentance is accepted."*

Then Ahmad Ibn Hanbal recited:

"Except for those who repent and make right their mistake and openly declare [the truth which they concealed]." Quran 2 verse 160

Source: Ibn Rajab in Dhayl 'Alā Tabaqāt Al-Hanābilah

Ibn Muflih said:

"As for innovation, then repentance from it is by affirming it, and to recant from it, and to believe in the opposite of what he believed previously…" Then he said: *"It has been narrated from Al-Marrūdhī that Ahmad Ibn Hanbal said: "When a innovator repents, then leave him in that state for a year until his repentance is verified to be correct."*

He used as a proof the narration of Ibrāhīm At-Taymī when the people differed with him concerning Sabīgh Ibn 'Asal (the innovator) when he warned from sitting with him. So after a year had passed, he said:

"Now you may sit with him but be cautious of him."

Source: Al-Ādāb Ash-Sharī'ah

Hasan ibn Shaqiq said:

"We were with Ibn Mubarak when a man came to him. So he (Ibn Mubarak) said to him: 'Are you that Jahmi?' He said: Yes.

He (Ibn Mubarak) said: When you go out from here, then never come back to me.

The man said: But I am repenting. He (Ibn Mubarak) said: No. Not until you show from your repentance the same as what you showed from your innovation."

Source: Ibanah As Sughra by Ibn Battah

Quran 58:20-22

إِنَّ ٱلَّذِينَ يُحَادُّونَ ٱللَّهَ وَرَسُولَهُۥٓ أُوْلَٰٓئِكَ فِى ٱلْأَذَلِّينَ (٢٠) كَتَبَ ٱللَّهُ لَأَغْلِبَنَّ أَنَا۠ وَرُسُلِىٓ إِنَّ ٱللَّهَ قَوِىٌّ عَزِيزٌ (٢١) لَّا تَجِدُ قَوْمًا يُؤْمِنُونَ بِٱللَّهِ وَٱلْيَوْمِ ٱلْءَاخِرِ يُوَآدُّونَ مَنْ حَآدَّ ٱللَّهَ وَرَسُولَهُۥ وَلَوْ كَانُوٓاْ ءَابَآءَهُمْ أَوْ أَبْنَآءَهُمْ أَوْ إِخْوَٰنَهُمْ أَوْ عَشِيرَتَهُمْ أُوْلَٰٓئِكَ كَتَبَ فِى قُلُوبِهِمُ ٱلْإِيمَٰنَ وَأَيَّدَهُم بِرُوحٍ مِّنْهُ وَيُدْخِلُهُمْ جَنَّٰتٍ تَجْرِى مِن تَحْتِهَا ٱلْأَنْهَٰرُ خَٰلِدِينَ فِيهَا رَضِىَ ٱللَّهُ عَنْهُمْ وَرَضُواْ عَنْهُ أُوْلَٰٓئِكَ حِزْبُ ٱللَّهِ أَلَآ إِنَّ حِزْبَ ٱللَّهِ هُمُ ٱلْمُفْلِحُونَ (٢٢)

Indeed, the ones who oppose Allah and His Messenger - those will be among the most humbled. (20) Allah has written, "I will surely overcome, I and My messengers." Indeed, Allah is Powerful and Exalted in Might.

(21) You will not find a people who believe in Allah and the Last Day having affection for those who oppose Allah and His Messenger, even if they were their fathers or their sons or their brothers or their kindred. Those - He has decreed within their hearts faith and supported them with spirit from Him. And We will admit them to gardens beneath which rivers flow, wherein they abide eternally. Allah is pleased with them, and they are pleased with Him - those are the party of Allah. Unquestionably, the party of Allah - they are the successful. (22)

Quran 5:51-56

۞ يَـٰٓأَيُّهَا ٱلَّذِينَ ءَامَنُوا۟ لَا تَتَّخِذُوا۟ ٱلْيَهُودَ وَٱلنَّصَـٰرَىٰٓ أَوْلِيَآءَ ۘ بَعْضُهُمْ أَوْلِيَآءُ بَعْضٍ ۚ وَمَن يَتَوَلَّهُم مِّنكُمْ فَإِنَّهُۥ مِنْهُمْ ۗ إِنَّ ٱللَّهَ لَا يَهْدِى ٱلْقَوْمَ ٱلظَّـٰلِمِينَ (٥١) فَتَرَى ٱلَّذِينَ فِى قُلُوبِهِم مَّرَضٌ يُسَـٰرِعُونَ فِيهِمْ يَقُولُونَ نَخْشَىٰٓ أَن تُصِيبَنَا دَآئِرَةٌ ۚ فَعَسَى ٱللَّهُ أَن يَأْتِىَ بِٱلْفَتْحِ أَوْ أَمْرٍ مِّنْ عِندِهِۦ فَيُصْبِحُوا۟ عَلَىٰ مَآ أَسَرُّوا۟ فِىٓ أَنفُسِهِمْ نَـٰدِمِينَ (٥٢) وَيَقُولُ ٱلَّذِينَ ءَامَنُوٓا۟ أَهَـٰٓؤُلَآءِ ٱلَّذِينَ أَقْسَمُوا۟ بِٱللَّهِ جَهْدَ أَيْمَـٰنِهِمْ ۙ إِنَّهُمْ لَمَعَكُمْ ۚ حَبِطَتْ أَعْمَـٰلُهُمْ فَأَصْبَحُوا۟ خَـٰسِرِينَ (٥٣) يَـٰٓأَيُّهَا ٱلَّذِينَ ءَامَنُوا۟ مَن يَرْتَدَّ مِنكُمْ عَن دِينِهِۦ فَسَوْفَ يَأْتِى ٱللَّهُ بِقَوْمٍ يُحِبُّهُمْ وَيُحِبُّونَهُۥٓ أَذِلَّةٍ عَلَى ٱلْمُؤْمِنِينَ أَعِزَّةٍ عَلَى ٱلْكَـٰفِرِينَ يُجَـٰهِدُونَ فِى سَبِيلِ ٱللَّهِ وَلَا يَخَافُونَ لَوْمَةَ لَآئِمٍ ۚ ذَٰلِكَ فَضْلُ ٱللَّهِ يُؤْتِيهِ مَن يَشَآءُ ۚ وَٱللَّهُ وَٰسِعٌ عَلِيمٌ (٥٤) إِنَّمَا وَلِيُّكُمُ ٱللَّهُ وَرَسُولُهُۥ وَٱلَّذِينَ ءَامَنُوا۟ ٱلَّذِينَ يُقِيمُونَ ٱلصَّلَوٰةَ وَيُؤْتُونَ ٱلزَّكَوٰةَ وَهُمْ رَٰكِعُونَ (٥٥) وَمَن يَتَوَلَّ ٱللَّهَ وَرَسُولَهُۥ وَٱلَّذِينَ ءَامَنُوا۟ فَإِنَّ حِزْبَ ٱللَّهِ هُمُ ٱلْغَـٰلِبُونَ (٥٦)

O you who have believed, do not take the Jews and the Christians as allies. They are [in fact] allies of one another. And whoever is an ally to them among you - then indeed, he is [one] of them. Indeed, Allah guides not the wrongdoing people. (51) So you see those in whose hearts is disease hastening into [association with] them, saying, "We are afraid a misfortune may strike us." But perhaps Allah will bring conquest or a decision from Him, and they will become, over what they have been concealing within themselves, regretful. (52) And those who believe will say, "Are these the ones who swore by Allah their strongest oaths that indeed they were with you?" Their deeds have become worthless, and they have become losers. (53) O you who have believed, whoever of you should revert from his religion - Allah will bring forth [in place of them] a people He will love and who will love Him [who are] humble toward the believers, powerful against the disbelievers; they strive in the cause of Allah and do not fear the blame of a critic. That is the favor of Allah; He bestows it upon whom He wills. And Allah is all-Encompassing and Knowing. (54) Your ally is none but Allah and [therefore] His Messenger and those who have believed - those who establish prayer and give zakah, and they bow [in worship]. (55) And whoever is an ally of Allah and His Messenger and those who have believed - indeed, the party of Allah - they will be the victorious. (56)

Quran 9:105-107

وَقُلِ ٱعْمَلُواْ فَسَيَرَى ٱللَّهُ عَمَلَكُمْ وَرَسُولُهُۥ وَٱلْمُؤْمِنُونَ ۖ وَسَتُرَدُّونَ إِلَىٰ عَٰلِمِ ٱلْغَيْبِ وَٱلشَّهَٰدَةِ فَيُنَبِّئُكُم بِمَا كُنتُمْ تَعْمَلُونَ (١٠٥) وَءَاخَرُونَ مُرْجَوْنَ لِأَمْرِ ٱللَّهِ إِمَّا يُعَذِّبُهُمْ وَإِمَّا يَتُوبُ عَلَيْهِمْ ۗ وَٱللَّهُ عَلِيمٌ حَكِيمٌ (١٠٦) وَٱلَّذِينَ ٱتَّخَذُواْ مَسْجِدًا ضِرَارًا وَكُفْرًا وَتَفْرِيقًۢا بَيْنَ ٱلْمُؤْمِنِينَ وَإِرْصَادًا لِّمَنْ حَارَبَ ٱللَّهَ وَرَسُولَهُۥ مِن قَبْلُ ۚ وَلَيَحْلِفُنَّ إِنْ أَرَدْنَآ إِلَّا ٱلْحُسْنَىٰ ۖ وَٱللَّهُ يَشْهَدُ إِنَّهُمْ لَكَٰذِبُونَ (١٠٧)

And say, "Do [as you will], for Allah will see your deeds, and [so, will] His Messenger and the believers. And you will be returned to the Knower of the unseen and the witnessed, and He will inform you of what you used to do." (105) And [there are] others deferred until the command of Allah - whether He will punish them or whether He will forgive them. And Allah is Knowing and Wise. (106) And [there are] those [hypocrites] who took for themselves a mosque for causing harm and disbelief and division among the believers and as a station for whoever had warred against Allah and His Messenger before. And they will surely swear, "We intended only the best." And Allah testifies that indeed they are liars. (107)

Quran 2:9-16

يُخَٰدِعُونَ ٱللَّهَ وَٱلَّذِينَ ءَامَنُواْ وَمَا يَخْدَعُونَ إِلَّآ أَنفُسَهُمْ وَمَا يَشْعُرُونَ (٩) فِى قُلُوبِهِم مَّرَضٌ فَزَادَهُمُ ٱللَّهُ مَرَضًا ۖ وَلَهُمْ عَذَابٌ أَلِيمٌ بِمَا كَانُواْ يَكْذِبُونَ (١٠) وَإِذَا قِيلَ لَهُمْ لَا تُفْسِدُواْ فِى ٱلْأَرْضِ قَالُوٓاْ إِنَّمَا نَحْنُ مُصْلِحُونَ (١١) أَلَآ إِنَّهُمْ هُمُ ٱلْمُفْسِدُونَ وَلَٰكِن لَّا يَشْعُرُونَ (١٢) وَإِذَا قِيلَ لَهُمْ ءَامِنُواْ كَمَآ ءَامَنَ ٱلنَّاسُ قَالُوٓاْ أَنُؤْمِنُ كَمَآ ءَامَنَ ٱلسُّفَهَآءُ ۗ أَلَآ إِنَّهُمْ هُمُ ٱلسُّفَهَآءُ وَلَٰكِن لَّا يَعْلَمُونَ (١٣) وَإِذَا لَقُواْ ٱلَّذِينَ ءَامَنُواْ قَالُوٓاْ ءَامَنَّا وَإِذَا خَلَوْاْ إِلَىٰ شَيَٰطِينِهِمْ قَالُوٓاْ إِنَّا مَعَكُمْ إِنَّمَا نَحْنُ مُسْتَهْزِءُونَ (١٤) ٱللَّهُ يَسْتَهْزِئُ بِهِمْ وَيَمُدُّهُمْ فِى طُغْيَٰنِهِمْ يَعْمَهُونَ (١٥) أُوْلَٰٓئِكَ ٱلَّذِينَ ٱشْتَرَوُاْ ٱلضَّلَٰلَةَ بِٱلْهُدَىٰ فَمَا رَبِحَت تِّجَٰرَتُهُمْ وَمَا كَانُواْ مُهْتَدِينَ (١٦)

They (think to) deceive Allâh and those who believe, while they only deceive themselves, and perceive (it) not! (9) In their hearts is a disease (of doubt and hypocrisy) and Allâh has increased their disease. A painful torment is theirs because they used to tell lies. (10) And when it is said to them: "Make not mischief on the earth," they say: "We are only peacemakers." (11) Verily! They are the ones who make mischief, but they perceive not. (12) And when it is said to them (hypocrites): "Believe as the people (followers of Muhammad , Al-Ansâr and Al-Muhajirûn) have believed," they say: "Shall we believe as the fools have believed?" Verily, they are the fools, but they know not (13) And when they meet those who believe, they say: "We believe," but when they are alone with their Shayâtin (devils - polytheists, hypocrites), they say: "Truly, we are with you; verily, we were but mocking." (14) Allâh mocks at them and gives them increase in their wrong-doings to wander blindly. (15) These are they who have purchased error for guidance, so their commerce was profitless. And they were not guided. (16)

Quran 18:103-104

قُلْ هَلْ نُنَبِّئُكُم بِٱلْأَخْسَرِينَ أَعْمَٰلًا (١٠٣) ٱلَّذِينَ ضَلَّ سَعْيُهُمْ فِى ٱلْحَيَوٰةِ ٱلدُّنْيَا وَهُمْ يَحْسَبُونَ أَنَّهُمْ يُحْسِنُونَ صُنْعًا (١٠٤)

Say: "Shall We tell you the greatest losers in respect of deeds? (103) "Those whose efforts have been wasted in this life while they thought that they were acquiring good by their deeds! (104)

Quran 4:59-63

يَٰٓأَيُّهَا ٱلَّذِينَ ءَامَنُوٓا۟ أَطِيعُوا۟ ٱللَّهَ وَأَطِيعُوا۟ ٱلرَّسُولَ وَأُو۟لِى ٱلْأَمْرِ مِنكُمْ ۖ فَإِن تَنَٰزَعْتُمْ فِى شَىْءٍ فَرُدُّوهُ إِلَى ٱللَّهِ وَٱلرَّسُولِ إِن كُنتُمْ تُؤْمِنُونَ بِٱللَّهِ وَٱلْيَوْمِ ٱلْءَاخِرِ ۚ ذَٰلِكَ خَيْرٌ وَأَحْسَنُ تَأْوِيلًا (٥٩) أَلَمْ تَرَ إِلَى ٱلَّذِينَ يَزْعُمُونَ أَنَّهُمْ ءَامَنُوا۟ بِمَآ أُنزِلَ إِلَيْكَ وَمَآ أُنزِلَ مِن قَبْلِكَ يُرِيدُونَ أَن يَتَحَاكَمُوٓا۟ إِلَى ٱلطَّٰغُوتِ وَقَدْ أُمِرُوٓا۟ أَن يَكْفُرُوا۟ بِهِۦ وَيُرِيدُ ٱلشَّيْطَٰنُ أَن يُضِلَّهُمْ ضَلَٰلًۢا بَعِيدًا (٦٠) وَإِذَا قِيلَ لَهُمْ تَعَالَوْا۟ إِلَىٰ مَآ أَنزَلَ ٱللَّهُ وَإِلَى ٱلرَّسُولِ رَأَيْتَ ٱلْمُنَٰفِقِينَ يَصُدُّونَ عَنكَ صُدُودًا (٦١) فَكَيْفَ إِذَآ أَصَٰبَتْهُم مُّصِيبَةٌۢ بِمَا قَدَّمَتْ أَيْدِيهِمْ ثُمَّ جَآءُوكَ يَحْلِفُونَ بِٱللَّهِ إِنْ أَرَدْنَآ إِلَّآ إِحْسَٰنًا وَتَوْفِيقًا (٦٢) أُو۟لَٰٓئِكَ ٱلَّذِينَ يَعْلَمُ ٱللَّهُ مَا فِى قُلُوبِهِمْ فَأَعْرِضْ عَنْهُمْ وَعِظْهُمْ وَقُل لَّهُمْ فِىٓ أَنفُسِهِمْ قَوْلًۢا بَلِيغًا (٦٣)

O you who have believed, obey Allah and obey the Messenger and those in authority among you. And if you disagree over anything, refer it to Allah and the Messenger, if you should believe in Allah and the Last Day. That is the best [way] and best in result. (59) Have you not seen those who claim to have believed in what was revealed to you, [O Muhammad], and what was revealed before you? They wish to refer legislation to Taghut, while they were commanded to reject it; and Satan wishes to lead them far astray. (60) And when it is said to them, "Come to what Allah has revealed and to the Messenger," you see the hypocrites turning away from you in aversion. (61) So how [will it be] when disaster strikes them because of what their hands have put forth and then they come to you swearing by Allah, "We intended nothing but good conduct and accommodation." (62) Those are the ones of whom Allah knows what is in their hearts, so turn away from them but admonish them and speak to them a far-reaching word. (63)

Quran 49:9-10

وَإِن طَآئِفَتَانِ مِنَ ٱلْمُؤْمِنِينَ ٱقْتَتَلُوا۟ فَأَصْلِحُوا۟ بَيْنَهُمَا ۖ فَإِنۢ بَغَتْ إِحْدَىٰهُمَا عَلَى ٱلْأُخْرَىٰ فَقَٰتِلُوا۟ ٱلَّتِى تَبْغِى حَتَّىٰ تَفِىٓءَ إِلَىٰٓ أَمْرِ ٱللَّهِ ۚ فَإِن فَآءَتْ فَأَصْلِحُوا۟ بَيْنَهُمَا بِٱلْعَدْلِ وَأَقْسِطُوٓا۟ ۖ إِنَّ ٱللَّهَ يُحِبُّ ٱلْمُقْسِطِينَ (٩) إِنَّمَا ٱلْمُؤْمِنُونَ إِخْوَةٌ فَأَصْلِحُوا۟ بَيْنَ أَخَوَيْكُمْ ۚ وَٱتَّقُوا۟ ٱللَّهَ لَعَلَّكُمْ تُرْحَمُونَ (١٠)

And if two factions among the believers should fight, then make settlement between the two. But if one of them oppresses the other, then fight against the one that oppresses until it returns to the ordinance of Allah. And if it returns, then make settlement between them in justice and act justly. Indeed, Allah loves those who act justly. (9) The believers are but brothers, so make settlement between your brothers. And fear Allah that you may receive mercy. (10)

Quran 41:33-36

وَمَنْ أَحْسَنُ قَوْلًا مِّمَّن دَعَا إِلَى ٱللَّهِ وَعَمِلَ صَـٰلِحًا وَقَالَ إِنَّنِى مِنَ ٱلْمُسْلِمِينَ (٣٣) وَلَا تَسْتَوِى ٱلْحَسَنَةُ وَلَا ٱلسَّيِّئَةُ ٱدْفَعْ بِٱلَّتِى هِىَ أَحْسَنُ فَإِذَا ٱلَّذِى بَيْنَكَ وَبَيْنَهُۥ عَدَٰوَةٌ كَأَنَّهُۥ وَلِىٌّ حَمِيمٌ (٣٤) وَمَا يُلَقَّىٰهَآ إِلَّا ٱلَّذِينَ صَبَرُواْ وَمَا يُلَقَّىٰهَآ إِلَّا ذُو حَظٍّ عَظِيمٍ (٣٥) وَإِمَّا يَنزَغَنَّكَ مِنَ ٱلشَّيْطَـٰنِ نَزْغٌ فَٱسْتَعِذْ بِٱللَّهِ إِنَّهُۥ هُوَ ٱلسَّمِيعُ ٱلْعَلِيمُ (٣٦)

And who is better in speech than one who invites to Allah and does righteousness and says, "Indeed, I am of the Muslims." (33) And not equal are the good deed and the bad. Repel [evil] by that [deed] which is better; and thereupon the one whom between you and him is enmity [will become] as though he was a devoted friend. (34) But none is granted it except those who are patient, and none is granted it except one having a great portion [of good]. (35) And if there comes to you from Satan an evil suggestion, then seek refuge in Allah. Indeed, He is the Hearing, the Knowing. (36)

Quran 4:132-139

وَلِلَّهِ مَا فِى ٱلسَّمَٰوَٰتِ وَمَا فِى ٱلْأَرْضِ ۚ وَكَفَىٰ بِٱللَّهِ وَكِيلًا (١٣٢) إِن يَشَأْ يُذْهِبْكُمْ أَيُّهَا ٱلنَّاسُ وَيَأْتِ بِـَٔاخَرِينَ ۚ وَكَانَ ٱللَّهُ عَلَىٰ ذَٰلِكَ قَدِيرًا (١٣٣) مَّن كَانَ يُرِيدُ ثَوَابَ ٱلدُّنْيَا فَعِندَ ٱللَّهِ ثَوَابُ ٱلدُّنْيَا وَٱلْـَٔاخِرَةِ ۚ وَكَانَ ٱللَّهُ سَمِيعًۢا بَصِيرًا (١٣٤) ۞ يَـٰٓأَيُّهَا ٱلَّذِينَ ءَامَنُوا۟ كُونُوا۟ قَوَّٰمِينَ بِٱلْقِسْطِ شُهَدَآءَ لِلَّهِ وَلَوْ عَلَىٰٓ أَنفُسِكُمْ أَوِ ٱلْوَٰلِدَيْنِ وَٱلْأَقْرَبِينَ ۚ إِن يَكُنْ غَنِيًّا أَوْ فَقِيرًا فَٱللَّهُ أَوْلَىٰ بِهِمَا ۖ فَلَا تَتَّبِعُوا۟ ٱلْهَوَىٰٓ أَن تَعْدِلُوا۟ ۚ وَإِن تَلْوُۥٓا۟ أَوْ تُعْرِضُوا۟ فَإِنَّ ٱللَّهَ كَانَ بِمَا تَعْمَلُونَ خَبِيرًا (١٣٥) يَـٰٓأَيُّهَا ٱلَّذِينَ ءَامَنُوٓا۟ ءَامِنُوا۟ بِٱللَّهِ وَرَسُولِهِۦ وَٱلْكِتَٰبِ ٱلَّذِى نَزَّلَ عَلَىٰ رَسُولِهِۦ وَٱلْكِتَٰبِ ٱلَّذِىٓ أَنزَلَ مِن قَبْلُ ۚ وَمَن يَكْفُرْ بِٱللَّهِ وَمَلَـٰٓئِكَتِهِۦ وَكُتُبِهِۦ وَرُسُلِهِۦ وَٱلْيَوْمِ ٱلْـَٔاخِرِ فَقَدْ ضَلَّ ضَلَٰلًۢا بَعِيدًا (١٣٦) إِنَّ ٱلَّذِينَ ءَامَنُوا۟ ثُمَّ كَفَرُوا۟ ثُمَّ ءَامَنُوا۟ ثُمَّ كَفَرُوا۟ ثُمَّ ٱزْدَادُوا۟ كُفْرًا لَّمْ يَكُنِ ٱللَّهُ لِيَغْفِرَ لَهُمْ وَلَا لِيَهْدِيَهُمْ سَبِيلًۢا (١٣٧) بَشِّرِ ٱلْمُنَٰفِقِينَ بِأَنَّ لَهُمْ عَذَابًا أَلِيمًا (١٣٨) ٱلَّذِينَ يَتَّخِذُونَ ٱلْكَٰفِرِينَ أَوْلِيَآءَ مِن دُونِ ٱلْمُؤْمِنِينَ ۚ أَيَبْتَغُونَ عِندَهُمُ ٱلْعِزَّةَ فَإِنَّ ٱلْعِزَّةَ لِلَّهِ جَمِيعًا (١٣٩)

And to Allah belongs whatever is in the heavens and whatever is on the earth. And sufficient is Allah as Disposer of affairs. (132) If He wills, He can do away with you, O people, and bring others [in your place]. And ever is Allah competent to do that. (133) Whoever desires the reward of this world - then with Allah is the reward of this world and the Hereafter. And ever is Allah Hearing and Seeing. (134) O you who have believed, be persistently standing firm in justice, witnesses for Allah, even if it be against yourselves or parents and relatives. Whether one is rich or poor, Allah is more worthy of both. So follow not [personal] inclination, lest you not be just. And if you distort [your testimony] or refuse [to give it], then indeed Allah is ever, with what you do, Acquainted. (135) O you who have believed, believe in Allah and His Messenger and the Book that He sent down upon His Messenger and the Scripture which He sent down before. And whoever disbelieves in Allah, His angels, His books, His messengers, and the Last Day has certainly gone far astray. (136) Indeed, those who have believed then disbelieved, then believed, then disbelieved, and then increased in disbelief - never will Allah forgive them, nor will He guide them to a way. (137) Give tidings to the hypocrites that there is for them a painful punishment - (138) Those who take disbelievers as allies instead of the believers. Do they seek with them honor [through power]? But indeed, honor belongs to Allah entirely. (139)

Quran 103

وَٱلْعَصْرِ (١) إِنَّ ٱلْإِنسَٰنَ لَفِى خُسْرٍ (٢) إِلَّا ٱلَّذِينَ ءَامَنُوا۟ وَعَمِلُوا۟ ٱلصَّٰلِحَٰتِ وَتَوَاصَوْا۟ بِٱلْحَقِّ وَتَوَاصَوْا۟ بِٱلصَّبْرِ (٣)

By Al-'Asr (the time). (1) Verily, man is in loss, (2) Except those who believe (in Islâmic Monotheism) *and do righteous good deeds, and recommend one another to the truth (i.e. order one another to perform all kinds of good deeds (Al-Ma'ruf) which Allâh has ordained, and abstain from all kinds of sins and evil deeds (Al-Munkar) which Allâh has forbidden), and recommend one another to patience (for the sufferings, harms, and injuries which one may encounter in Allâh's Cause during preaching His religion of Islâmic Monotheism or Jihâd). (3)*

At this point I was ready to end the book here during Ramadan 2025 despite the rather unhappy ending of my apparent defeat which led me to write this book as a desperate last-ditch effort to try to get Qadri fired or repent. So, I began to edit my book hoping somehow it would make a difference against all odds. I would routinely check the ISNF website from time to time since 2017 hoping one day to see they had gotten a new Imam replacing Qadri but horrifically I saw Qadri was imam and the president who banned me, Rasul Khan, had been promoted further to the top position as Chairperson of ISNF Council of Trustees. I felt hopeless regarding my dream of a change in leadership. In November 2024, I emailed a friend my frustration with the lack of options to right the extremely wrong situation.

In America we don't have the resources available to adequately deal with the situation and it is especially controversial because I went medically insane half-way through the dispute and got diagnosed with mental illness. So many people just dismiss me as crazy, despite email and text message evidence, most people don't want anything to do with it, because they lack understanding of how insanity is caused and how its cured and how it works, and those who bother to listen say that they can't help because there is no way to persuade ISNF to fire Qadri no matter what evidence I bring even though he is guilty as charged though I am not entirely innocent of wrongdoing myself.

So I figure the best answer will come from a legitimate judge versed in cases of takfir and maybe they could even write a recommendation to ISNF or a letter of admonishment to Qadri because despite my belief that Qadri is unqualified to be imam of a masjid even if he repents from his heretical beliefs, in the end one wants everyone to believe in islam correctly.

I am willing to go to a proper shariah court in a Muslim country for a solution. So far ISNF and Qadri aren't' even willing to talk to me in any mode of communication, even when other local WNY imams request them to. I wasn't 100% correct in everything I did, especially after insanity kicked in due to stress or magic but I want us all to go to paradise eventually or so I claim. I just figure if Qadri can't be fired regardless of his error then the next best thing is to fix that error so despite justice not being done perhaps the harm of satanic forces and doctrines will be reduced.

I don't have any strong support in this country to help in this matter or I'm too shy and pessimistic to get such support due to the socialization required to obtain it and the risks of the extremist label while in America. I may share more details on how this turns out in future but I figure it is not effective seeking help from Americans anymore because they won't be able to help and I may get harm if I try to get help from them.

The people in this country cannot implement the rulings of takfir so they are not qualified to say if it is done correctly because they cannot do anything about it so they don't specialize in it. If I go to someone who actually has handled cases of takfir in a legal setting before then they are better able to handle the matter even if from afar than anyone in America would be despite being near geographically.

Yet I was completely surprised when I checked ISNF's website in March/Ramadan 2025 to ensure I was spelling names correctly for this book. To my utter astonishment they had a new Imam listed and Qadri's name was nowhere to be seen. I also found out ISNF had a job posting for a "Resident Imam" for masjid noor paying $70K that had closed months before I finished this book. In February 2025 ISNF had announced on their Instagram channel the hiring of their new Imam for masjid noor. So just like that without explanation Qadri was gone! I did further inquiry and learned he was "let go" but due to my restrictive cease and desist order that was as far as I dare to dig into the details. Yet to me "let go" is a polite way of saying fired and there was no indication Qadri voluntarily relinquished the position he had so unislamically fought me to maintain. It was known to many in the community that Qadri intended to stay as the imam permanently as long as possible. After further research I found out ISNF had a new President and Rasul Khan oddly was no longer listed as the Chairperson for the Council of Trustees despite both Qadri and Rasul Khan being the top two leaders of ISNF according to their website in

November 2024. Naturally I was overjoyed at such a miraculous turn of events that led to a seemingly hopeless cause being accomplished without me even realizing it. Such is the power of supplication to Allah by the oppressed. It might take a longer time than desired but the oppressed who pray to Allah sincerely are guaranteed to be answered according to Islam and that even applies if they were non-Muslims, so surely a proper Muslim's dua against a Munafiq oppressor would be answered even if the whole community united against it; and they did. Everyone without exception told me that there was nothing that could be done about Qadri to get him fired or removed from his position no matter how much evidence I had he was heretical. So I desperately resorted to Allah and even began to doubt myself in the possibility of such a prayer becoming reality. That's why I initially wrote this book out of desperation with the circumstances. I was hoping best case scenario Qadri repents and quits himself, or repents and unislamically kept the job or got fired if he didn't repent. But all that was many years down the road potentially best-case long-shot scenarios. Surprisingly I learned Allah has removed Qadri less than 8 years after I tried getting him fired from his position as Imam. The allegedly impossible task of having a Munafiq removed from his position as Imam for heresy was accomplished by Allah.

Despite the apparent reality and odds, Allah overturned reality and expectations to have ISNF themselves end up firing a heretic in Qadri who they previously sinfully supported despite breaking and abusing the laws of their own religion to do so. You would think if ISNF were going to fire Qadri they would have done so at my behest in 2017 when I tried getting him fired for heresy, or perhaps in 2019 when I tried again, or in 2021 when I advised other imams to try. Yet in 2024 despite staunchly supporting Qadri the past 10 years with Qadri living rent-free at the ISNF house next to masjid noor with known plans of dying there many years in the future while in office, Qadri lost his job and his residence despite fighting me so hard to keep it dooming his soul in the process. Such is the power of Allah against his enemies even if such enemies pretend convincingly to be Muslims fooling the masses. Everybody has plots but the plot of Allah cannot be overcome and the disbelievers will never achieve a lasting victory over the believers. Every sinner should fear such a powerful deity who has prepared the hellfire for additional punishment.

Therefore we surprisingly are able to include the semi-happy ending. I say semi-happy because the true happy ending would be victory over Satan by having Qadri fully repent for his errors and crimes. This might or might not occur because it depends a lot upon Qadri. Even though I plan to email Qadri in the future, since the cease and desist order from contact with ISNF members no longer applies to Qadri, asking him to repent after I get advised from Shariah Court judges on how best to invite him to repentance it is my opinion that this book can share valuable lessons. Of course due to the length and colored pages the admittedly high printing cost will discourage most readers limiting its impact. However that may be better for me because while there are valuable lessons that can be learned from such a factual story of spiritual warfare I also fear sins for mentioning sins of non-heretics who are not exempt from the prohibition of backbiting. I therefore doubted since Qadri was no longer in authority whether I should scrap this book project entirely because of mentioning fitnah. Yet then I remembered the fitnah that took place amongst the best generation of the Salaf and how important the reputation of the Sahabah is yet their errors during the fitnah civil war that occurred are still explained as such to this day despite our love and respect for them. Additionally the fitnahs prophet Yusuf (Joseph) experienced with his family and the women who had him unjustly imprisoned were explained publicly during his lifetime so lessons could be learned. While all sinners regret their mistakes and errors, sometimes while it is sinful to mentions sins and mistakes which should be hidden it can be necessary to prevent others from being ignorant of lessons they could and should learn so as to be safe from repeating the errors others made before them. In summary, though some characters in this book may dislike being mentioned as I have done, there is real attainable benefit in mentioning their mistakes as mistakes and my own mistakes as mistakes. I am trying to fight the intention of anger or arrogance when writing this book and perhaps publishing this entire saga is just one more mistake of mine along with the rest I've discussed in this book and have committed outside of this book. The day we get our book of deeds is a scary day indeed. So, I ask forgiveness from those who feel wronged by me sharing this story in such detail. It is a gray area mentioning non-heretical criminals by name especially when they may have corrected their errors. For example, regarding Joel, the monk in training turned Muslim turned apostate, I learned Joel moved to Saudi Arabia as an English teacher in 2022. So most likely Joel repented from apostasy and is Muslim today though since I lost contact with him I could only confirm Joel moved and lives in KSA today without being able to verify his Islam myself. Thus I could be saying stuff about people's past that while factual is no longer the case by the time you read this story. Inshallah Joel is Muslim once again and if so it's another example of me despairing at something occurring only to have Allah make it happen. May Allah guide all the characters we meet and those we don't throughout life to Islam and the Sunnah, and that is partially why I mention the names too so you the reader can supplicate for guidance for them by name perhaps and perhaps that may get me a credit that may offset the harm I did by mentioning them negatively. I felt if I changed character names to protect identification it would be a form of fiction and fiction aka lying is forbidden. Silence may be better though bitter. However bida is important to be wary of and the damages it can do especially if/when the opponent of bida is fighting it with bida themselves as I ignorantly did to the best of my ability. Again I was not 100% correct in what I did during this fitnah, very few ever are 100% correct during fitnah. Yet that is the whole point of fitnah being a trial and ordeal in that nobody escapes it entirely correct and safe. Regret is inevitable when fitnah takes place. Due to it being easy to imagine a similar scenario as mine occurring to others in America or elsewhere I feel my story is better to share than to conceal. Likewise since some of my errors were public then I feel I must repent publicly and as such I am setting the record straight explaining my mistakes in full context. Whether I concealed it or not I would be brought to account so perhaps by sharing it someone could better point out my errors to me so I'd better be able to repent. Yet such repentance must be made known similarly to how the sins were made known. So I'd gladly write extra editions making edits of this if I discover my takfir of Qadri was wrong as it may have been or if Qadri notifies me of his genuine repentance someday. Suffice it to say Bida is the greatest poison to religion in the world and fighting it to the best of one's ability is the most difficult Jihad there is. Many mistakes are often made and become beloved to those who make them. Sometimes Allah may forgive the errors made in the course of such battles and sometimes not. But the Battling of Bida must go on for the prophetic faith itself is at stake. So if you don't fight bida then you already lost your soul and surrendered to Satan. Neutrality is not an option and safety is hard to attain. By accepting the fact of fitnah harming communities it should motivate people to strive to find solutions through genuine study of the Sunnah according to the way of the Salaf so that as many of us as possible can attain the precious salvation which all members of free-willed species seek. May Allah forgive us, bless the Muslims, guide humans and jinn to the correct path of Islam, and speedily support the believers against the disbelievers of every kind for all of time.

Abdullah ibn Amr reported:

"The Messenger of Allah, said, "We are in such a time when the strangers are blessed." It was said, "O Messenger of Allah, who are the strangers?" The Prophet said, "Righteous people among many evil people. Those who disobey them are more numerous than those who obey them."

Source: Musnad Aḥmad 6650 Grade: Sahih

Amr ibn 'Awf reported:

"The Messenger of Allah said, "Verily, the religion began as something strange and it will return to being strange, so blessed are the strangers who restore my Sunnah which the people after me had distorted."

Source: Sunan al-Tirmidhī 2630 Grade: Hasan

Ibn al-Qayyim said:

The people of Islām are strangers amongst mankind. And the believers are strangers amongst the people of Islām. And the people of knowledge are strangers amongst the believers. And the people of the Sunnah who separate it from the desires and innovations, they are strangers. And those who call to it and have patience upon the harm of the opposers, they are the severest of them (all) in strangeness. However, they are the people of Allāh in truth. There is no strangeness for them (in reality), (rather) their strangeness is only in relation to the majority about whom Allāh, the Mighty and Majestic, said, "**If you were to obey most of those upon the Earth they would misguide you from the path of Allāh**" (6:116). So the ones (mentioned in the verse) are (the real) strangers to Allāh and His Messenger and their strangeness is the deserting (type of) strangeness.

Source: Madārij al-Sālikīn (3/195).

Abu Umamah reported:

The Messenger of Allah said, "A group of my nation will continue to be victorious upon the religion, overpowering their enemies. None who oppose them will harm them, except what afflicts them of difficult circumstances, until Allah brings his command while they are like so."

Source: Musnad Aḥmad 22320 Grade: Sahih

Imam Ahmad Bin Hanbal (d. 241 AH) said:

"if the Victorious Group are not the" **Ashaabul Hadeeth"** then I don't know who are they "

Source: Ma'rifatu Uloom Ul Hadeeth Lil Haakim

Ibn Muflih (d. 763 AH) said: *"Ahul Hadeeth, they are the Victorious Group, established upon the Haqq (Absolute truth)"*

Source: Al Adaab Ul Shar'rah 1/211

Imam Sufyaan Thawri (d. 161 AH) about Ahlul Hadith said, *"Angels are the guardians of the heavens and "Ashabul Hadith" are the guardians of the earth"*. Source: Sharaf As-habul Hadith

Quran 17:71

يَوْمَ نَدْعُوا كُلَّ أُنَاسٍ بِإِمَامِهِمْ ۖ فَمَنْ أُوتِيَ كِتَٰبَهُ بِيَمِينِهِ فَأُولَٰٓئِكَ يَقْرَءُونَ كِتَٰبَهُمْ وَلَا يُظْلَمُونَ فَتِيلًا

"(And remember) the Day when We shall call together all human beings with their (respective) Imam [their Prophets, or their records of good and bad deeds, or their Books like the Quran, the Taurat (Torah), the Injeel etc.]. So whosoever is given his record in his right hand, such will read their records, and they will not be dealt with unjustly in the least."

Ibn Katheer (d. 774 AH) said in Tafsir of this verse:

*"And Some Salafs said: This (verse) is the Greatest honour for the **Ashaabul Hadeeth** because their Imaam is the Prophet Muhammad"*

Jalal Ud Deen Suyuti (d. 911 AH) wrote similarly:

*"There is not a Greater honour than that (verse) for the **Ashaabul Hadeeth** because they Do Not Have an Imaam other than Him (Sal Allahu Alaihi Wasallam)".*

Abdullah ibn Mas'ud reported:

The Messenger of Allah, gave us the combination of all good things and their endings, for he taught us the statements of prayer and the statements of need. The statements of prayer are, "All greetings, prayers, and good things are for Allah. Peace be upon you, O Prophet, and the mercy of Allah and His blessings. Peace be upon us and upon the righteous servants of Allah. I testify there is no God but Allah, and I testify Muhammad is His servant and His Messenger." The statements of need are, "All praise is due to Allah. We praise him, we seek His help, we seek His forgiveness, and we seek refuge in Allah from the evil within ourselves and our evil deeds. Whomever Allah guides, there is none to misguide him. Whomever Allah leads astray, there is none to guide him. I testify there is no God but Allah alone, without any partners, and that Muhammad is His servant and His Messenger." Then, he would add to his statement with three verses from the Book of Allah, "O believers! Fear Allah in the way He deserves, and do not die except in as Muslims,"(3:102) and, "Fear Allah, in Whose Name you appeal to one another, and honor family ties. Surely, Allah is ever Watchful over you,"(4:1) and, "Fear Allah and say what is right. He will bless your deeds for you, and forgive your sins. Whoever obeys Allah and His Messenger has truly achieved a great triumph." (33:70-71)

Source: Sunan Ibn Majah 1892 Grade: Sahih

Jabir ibn 'Abdillah reported:

The Messenger of Allah, would praise Allah in his sermon, as He deserves to be praised, and then say, "Whomever Allah guides, no one can lead him astray. Whomever Allah sends astray, no one can guide him. The truest word is the Book of Allah, and the best guidance is the guidance of Muhammad. The most evil matters in religion are those that are newly invented, for every newly invented matter is an innovation, every innovation is misguidance, and every misguidance is in the Hellfire."

Source: Sunan al-Nasa'i 1578 Grade: Sahih

Quran "Surah Fatihah" aka Chapter 1

ٱلْحَمْدُ لِلَّهِ رَبِّ ٱلْعَٰلَمِينَ (٢) ٱلرَّحْمَٰنِ ٱلرَّحِيمِ (٣) مَٰلِكِ يَوْمِ ٱلدِّينِ (٤) إِيَّاكَ نَعْبُدُ وَإِيَّاكَ نَسْتَعِينُ (٥) ٱهْدِنَا ٱلصِّرَٰطَ ٱلْمُسْتَقِيمَ (٦) صِرَٰطَ ٱلَّذِينَ أَنْعَمْتَ عَلَيْهِمْ غَيْرِ ٱلْمَغْضُوبِ عَلَيْهِمْ وَلَا ٱلضَّآلِّينَ (٧)

[All] praise is [due] to Allah, Lord of the worlds - (2) The Entirely Merciful, the Especially Merciful, (3) Sovereign of the Day of Recompense. (4) It is You alone we worship and You alone we ask for help. (5) Guide us to the straight path - (6) The path of those upon whom You have bestowed blessings, not of those who have evoked [Your] anger or of those who are astray. (7)

www.ingramcontent.com/pod-product-compliance
Lightning Source LLC
Chambersburg PA
CBHW071146060526
44107CB00132B/243